Out of Steam

Out of Steam

Dieselization and American Railroads, 1920–1960

Jeffrey W. Schramm

Lehigh
University
Press

Bethlehem: Lehigh University Press

Associated University Press
2010 Eastpark Boulevard
Cranbury, NJ 08512

The paper used in this publication meets the requirements of the American National Standard for Permanence of Paper for Printed Library Materials
Z39.48-1984.

Library of Congress Cataloging-in-Publication Data
Schramm, Jeffrey W., 1969–
   Out of Steam: dieselization and American railroads, 1920–1960 / Jeffrey W. Schramm
      p. cm.
   Includes bibliographical references and index.
   ISBN 978-0-9821313-7-4 (alk. paper)
   1. Diesel locomotives—United States.   2 Railroads—Diselization—United States.   I. Title.
   TJ619.2.S374 2010
   385'.3660973—dc22   2010003730

PRINTED IN THE UNITED STATES OF AMERICA

Contents

Acknowledgments

I WOULD LIKE TO THANK THE FOLLOWING PEOPLE AND ORGANIZA-tions for their help and support. This book began a long time ago as an MA thesis and then a PhD dissertation at Lehigh University. It would not have been written if not for the support of the history department at Lehigh and especially; Dr. Gail Cooper, Dr. Steve Cutcliffe, Dr. Roger Simon and Dr. Patricia Turner, now at University of Wisconsin, Eau Claire. All provided valuable help and insight into the writing process. A special thanks goes to Dr. John K. Smith for his dedicated work as my primary dissertation advisor, a thankless task if there ever was one. I would also like to thank my current department chair, Dr. Larry Gragg of the Missouri University of Science and Technology for his help and support. Dr. H. Roger Grant of Clemson read a much earlier version of this manuscript and provided helpful comments that greatly improved the quality of the work. Other referees, some anonymous, also provided a wealth of helpful comments that greatly enhanced the text. The following institutions allowed me access to archival materials without which this work would have been impossible; the Railroad Museum of Pennsylvania, the California State Railroad Museum, the Colorado Railroad Museum, the University of Southern Mississippi, the Hagley Museum and Library, the Pennsylvania State Archives, Syracuse University, Pennsylvania State University, the Southern Museum of Civil War and Locomotive History, The Mercantile Library at the University of Missouri–St. Louis, and the Union Pacific Museum and Durham Western Heritage Museum. I would also like to thank the innumerable railfan authors and photographers without whose work this endeavor would have been impossible. Finally, I would like to thank my wife, Mara Witynski, and my parents, Robert and Carol Schramm, for their constant support and encouragement.

Out of Steam

Introduction

THE PENNSYLVANIA RAILROAD, ONE OF THE LARGEST AND MOST powerful railroads in the United States and one of the largest corporations in the world, introduced a new steam passenger locomotive in 1942. It was a massive machine and in many ways the ultimate steam locomotive. It was over one hundred feet long and when fully loaded with forty one tons of coal and 19,500 gallons of water weighed over one million pounds. It was designed to haul a full length express passenger train of 880 tons at speeds of over one hundred miles per hour. To publicize the introduction of this new locomotive the Pennsylvania Railroad drafted a short press release. The proposed headline was, "'Pennsy' Launches Streamline Land Dreadnaughts."[1] Just as the events of Pearl Harbor a few months prior had proved that the days of dreadnaught battleship dominance of the seas were over, events of the past few years had also proved that the days of the steam locomotive were as numbered as the days of the large battleship.

The technological history of American railroads in the twentieth century is dominated by the appearance and adoption of the diesel-electric locomotive. It was the single largest technological change since the beginnings of steam powered railroading in the early nineteenth century. From the first tentative experiments with diesel power in the 1920s to complete dieselization in the late 1950s, the American railroad scene was transformed. The diesel locomotive was more than a new form of motive power; it was an entirely new system of moving freight and passengers that had profound and far-reaching implications for all aspects of railroading. Diesels could move passengers and freight faster and more efficiently with much less maintenance and with much lower costs. Diesel locomotives made huge shop complexes, coal and water towers, and tens of thousands of skilled workers obsolete. Railroad operations no longer were constrained by the need to coal, water, operate, and service labor intensive steam locomotives. The diesel could do whatever the steam locomotive could do and could do it faster, cheaper, and better.

Such a monumental change to such a large and important industry raises many questions. Did the diesel win out

11

over the steam locomotive simply because it was more cost effective, or did other factors come into play? What about the rate of adoption of the diesel? If it was clearly a superior way to move trains why was there a great variety in its initial usage and adoption by different railroads? Some railroads purchased diesels in the mid-1920s, but others waited until the mid-1950s. Some were fully dieselized while others were at the same time still purchasing new steam locomotives. Were diesels worth the investment? What effects did dieselization have on railroad operations and organization? It would take some time to realize fully the potential of the new motive power to reshape operations. At the time did railroads realize the changes, inherent in the technology, that diesels would bring? Did the coal industry, a major shipper and supplier for many railroads, have any effect on the pace of dieselization? Were there any alternatives to dieselization? When considering technological change within a system, the effects of change on each aspect of the organization becomes an internal political issue. Did management merely opt for immediate short-term savings and ignore the revolutionary implications of diesel locomotives for restructuring the entire railroad industry? Was management nostalgically clinging to the steam age railroad that had dominated their careers? On the other hand, was the diesel locomotive a Trojan Horse, quietly introduced by upper management to avoid overt conflict with workers and managers? These questions are complex and must be answered to understand the process of dieselization. Various social, political, economic, and cultural influences all played a part in how, when, and why railroads dieselized.

The dieselization of North American railroads had profound social and cultural ramifications in addition to business and economic ones. That is, the decisions made by railroad management affected workers and the surrounding communities as well as the operations of the railroad itself. Likewise, decisions by government, customers, communities and workers impacted railroad operations and the decisions to dieselize. The overriding concern for railroads in motive power decisions was costs. Labor costs, fuel costs, operational costs, and maintenance costs were all analyzed and the resulting conclusions had the largest impact on the dieselization process. While costs may have been the primary factor in the dieselization story, the decision to purchase a diesel locomotive, a steam one, or none at all was seldom if ever simply a matter of cost-benefit economics. Many other variables came to play including government regulation, competitive pressures, both between railroads and with other modes like motor trucks, marketing, corporate culture and personality of management officials.

Early diesel efforts were set in motion by local municipal legislation regulating smoke, especially in New York City. Competition with other railroads, especially in the passenger market led some railroads to embrace diesel power for its speed as well as for the image that a modern streamlined diesel would bring, especially in the dark days of the Great Depression. Speed of service in time sensitive freight movement also played a role in the dieselization of some railroads. The coal industry, or loyalty to it was a major influence in the decision making process of some railroads but played a negligible role on others. The corporate culture and personalities of upper management played a surprising role in the dieselization of some of the largest and most powerful of railroads. Executives that had almost literally been raised with the steam locomotive looked upon it as an old friend and were reluctant to abandon it. The age and condition of the steam locomotive fleet, condition of bridges, rails and the rest of the physical infrastructure, traffic patterns, environmental conditions, and other variables complete the list of influences on dieselization.

Most railroads dieselized to cut costs immediately but in their overall operations did not fully realize the potential of the diesel until well after the process was complete. In some ways the full potential is still unrealized to this day. Initially, most railroads simply substituted the diesels into the place of the steam locomotives and did not fully utilize the potential of the new motive power to revolutionize operations. On many railroads there was often no true test phase in which the diesels were compared with comparable power steam locomotives, a strange course of action for such a rational and cost-accounting dominated industry. Some roads did conduct extensive, detailed tests of different forms of motive power, but this was the exception rather than the rule.[2] Even when tests were performed, the diesels were simply plugged in to the spot vacated by the steam locomotives. Railroads generally tried to integrate diesels into the existing system instead of building a new system around their different capabilities. The railroads generally did not change their corporate culture or operating philosophy to take full advantage of the new technology. This said, there were many variations among the railroad companies and even on different divisions of the same railroad. One railroad can not serve as a model for all railroads as each dieselized in its own way depending on its own particular characteristics. For instance, in 1950 the Gulf Mobile & Ohio Railroad (GM&O), stretching from Chicago and Kansas City to Mobile and New Orleans was completely dieselized. Every train that moved over the 2898 miles of road was diesel powered. Yet at the same time, the similarly sized Norfolk & Western Railroad (N&W) was completely steam powered. In addition, the N&W was still building brand new steam locomotives in its own shops. With such a difference in corporate attitudes toward adoption of the diesel, something more than simple economic cost-benefit analysis must have been at work. If diesels could work on the GM&O, why not on the N&W? The reverse is also true, if steam was still in use on the N&W, why not on the GM&O? Were the advantages of the diesel somehow dependent on the operating conditions of the various railroads? Practical main line diesels were available from the mid-1930s onward; however, steam remained in use on some railroads as late as 1959. This may not seem like a long time period, but it would be akin to going to the airport in the early 1980s and boarding a well kept and possibly only a few years old piston engine-powered super constellation or DC-6, rather than a 727 or DC-9. In the broader historical context, this is a study of how large, traditionally conservative and highly regulated organizations built around a certain technological system, dealt with the introduction of a radically new one.

During the period of dieselization the railroads were a huge, interconnected system designed to move freight and passengers. They were similar to many other systems in terms of their hierarchical organization and management structure. However, railroads differed from other systems in their geographic spread and in that they were not offering a product for sale such as steel ingots or sewing machines but instead offered a service, transportation. Railroads were also different from many other systems, such as the electric power generation and transmission system, in that they were made up of many hundreds of individual companies with differing corporate philosophies, operational constraints, and geographic spread. These companies had different responses to changing economic conditions as well as to the diesel locomotive. The railroads may have constituted a system, but it was a heterogeneous system. It can be envisioned as not a single picture, but an assembled jigsaw puzzle with greatly differing piece sizes. Once assembled, the resulting image appears whole, but in fact the underlying structure is a vastly different mosaic, each piece of which responded quite differently to challenges.[3]

At midcentury there were literally hundreds of different railroads ranging in size from small shortlines with a few miles of track and one or two locomotives to major systems with tens of thousands of miles of track and thousands of locomotives. These railroads were operating in all parts of the country hauling both passengers and freight with different operating rules and philosophies.[4] Each railroad was run by its own management team, and each motive power department had different ideas on locomotives. Even different divisions on the same railroad may have had distinctive operating rules and regulations based in part upon local environmental and historical circumstances. While broad industry wide trends can help place dieselization into the larger picture, individual railroads must be analyzed rather than relying on large scale statistical portraits. Because of the variety of companies in the railroad system during the period of dieselization, it is not possible to analyze one or even two railroads and attempt to draw conclusions that would apply to the entire railroad industry. While one-road studies are important and can contribute much to our knowledge of railroad history, comparative studies hold the promise of greater, and broader, understanding. The North American rail network was a system, although a heterogeneous one, and it can be best understood by looking at the multitude of parts as well as the whole. Dieselization affected the entire system, although at different times and in different ways depending upon local circumstances, and led to a restructuring that continues to the present. While diesels may not have been the sole variable in the restructuring of the American rail system, it is impossible to imagine the current system without diesel locomotives and the changes that they brought.

Because of regulation, rail rates and labor agreements during the period of dieselization, the railroad system was divided by the Interstate Commerce Commission into three geographic regions: eastern, western, and southern.[5] These geographic determinations also reasonably correlate with operational differences between railroads in each region. Therefore, several railroads from each region have been chosen to explore responses to dieselization under varying conditions. Railroads also ranged in size from mighty behemoths such as the Pennsylvania, Southern Pacific, and Santa Fe, to one-locomotive short lines and terminal or switching roads. Therefore, it is also essential that a variety of different sized roads be analyzed to provide a full picture of the changes wrought by dieselization upon the rail system as a whole. Thus, reflecting both geographic and size distinctions, I look at the following railroads in varying levels of detail.

Eastern Region:
Pennsylvania
New York Central
Lehigh Valley
New York, Ontario & Western
New York, Susquehanna & Western
Delaware, Lackawanna & Western
New York, Chicago & St. Louis (a.k.a. Nickel Plate Road)
Reading
Western Maryland
Baltimore & Ohio
Chicago & Eastern Illinois

Southern Region:
Southern
Atlantic Coast Line
Seaboard Air Line
Louisville & Nashville
Illinois Central
Gulf Mobile & Ohio
Richmond Fredericksburg & Potomac
Chesapeake & Ohio (Pocahontas district)
Norfolk & Western (Pocahontas district)
Virginian (Pocahontas district)[6]

Western Region:
St. Louis–San Francisco (a.k.a. Frisco Lines)
Union Pacific
Western Pacific
Southern Pacific

Atchison Topeka & Santa Fe
Chicago, Rock Island & Pacific
Chicago & North Western
Chicago, Burlington & Quincy
Denver & Rio Grande Western
Missouri Pacific

Terminal Roads and Shortlines:
Mississippi Central
Terminal Railroad Association of St. Louis
Alton & Southern

These railroads are geographically, physically, and operationally diverse enough to present a fairly complete picture of the changes dieselization brought about over the entire railroad industry. The differences between roads can be quite dramatic. Some purchased diesels in the 1920s and were fully dieselized in 1946–1947 while others were still purchasing or building new steam locomotives during the late 1940s and early 1950s.

By the period of dieselization, the vast majority of railroads were mature industries facing static growth prospects. Passenger traffic began to shift away from the rails by the mid-1920s, while motor trucks and water transportation competed for an increasingly noticeable share of freight revenue as well.[7] This trend was greatly accelerated with the growth of federal aid highways and the interstate highway system and various water navigation projects after World War II. Railroad management, both individually and collectively, saw the diesel as a way to reinvigorate their industry in the face of an uncertain future. Despite a high initial cost, the diesel-electric locomotive was much more efficient and cost effective than its steam counterpart, especially in labor and maintenance costs. There were alternatives to diesel locomotive power such as electrification, coal powered steam turbines, and steam turbine-electrics as well as gas turbines and even nuclear-powered locomotives. All of these, except nuclear power, were tried and some, especially electrification, could have been a viable alternative to dieselization with changes in regulation and policy.

The effects of dieselization on the workers of the railroad and the communities along it are much harder to deduce than the efficiencies of the locomotive powerplants. However, there are some effects that can be observed. For example, the loss of locomotive shops in one community in favor of consolidation in another could be seen as a double-edged sword, cutting in one's favor or to one's detriment depending upon location. Many skills that were unique to servicing steam locomotives were lost, and only partially replaced with those necessary for servicing the diesels. Thus, the trade-off was far from even. Steam locomotives were maintenance intensive and required specialized skills such as boilermakers, pipefitters, water treatment engineers, foundrymen, and the like. The maintenance of standardized diesels required far fewer workers, predominately general mechanics and electricians.

The dieselization of American railroads has until recently not been a topic of great scholarly historical interest. I hope to begin to rectify this situation by performing a marriage of the best elements from the "railfan" and academic areas, together with critical analysis, to provide a balanced, informed, and analytical look at dieselization from an operational perspective. The diesel transformed the American (and global) railroad industry but it could not stave off further decline. Many railroads that happily embraced diesels in the immediate post war period were still facing evaporating traffic and bankruptcy a scant ten years later. This shows us the limits of what new technology can do when it is not accompanied by wholesale labor, management, social, and governmental policy restructuring to take full advantage of the new technology. Perhaps most importantly, dieselization shows that individual attitudes toward technological change can have a major impact on the course of technological development.

1
Shiny New Things

IN JANUARY 1945, IN COXTON, A TOWN NEAR THE HEADWATERS of the Lackawanna River in the mountains of northeast Pennsylvania, a steam locomotive-powered freight train is waiting in the snow and fog for helper locomotives to help push it over the summit of the Pocono mountains to the Lehigh River valley. The Lehigh Valley Railroad is shipping huge amounts of freight for the war effort, including supplies and munitions destined for the east coast and shipment to Europe. The locomotive the crew is operating is a war baby, built only two years before in 1943 to help handle the wartime traffic. The 4–8–4 type locomotive, named Wyoming type on the Lehigh Valley, incorporates the latest advances in locomotive technology, and is one of the most efficient and technologically advanced steam locomotives in service in the country. Helper locomotives have been required on this grade for almost as long as the railroad has been in operation. Locomotives would couple on to either the front or back of the train and help pull or push it up the long grade and over the summit.[1] However, this time something is different. Instead of the usual one or two coal burning, smoke-belching steam locomotives that have performed this job for years, on this day a bright red, streamlined, diesel-electric locomotive emerged out of the snow and fog. This diesel locomotive consisted of four separate units, all operating in unison and controlled by one crew from one cab.[2] The crew of the freight train had seen diesels before in switching service in yards and on the docks in and around New York City. But this was different; these diesels were no small "yard goats." They were out on the main line and judging by the speed at which they were ascending the grade, were doing a good job, better in fact than the old steam locomotives. At the top of the grade the diesels uncoupled. As the steam locomotive and its freight train accelerated downgrade into the Lehigh River valley, the crew speculated on what would become of these new-fangled diesels. They had heard about other railroads' experiments with diesel-powered freight and were well aware of the inroads that

19

diesels had made into the passenger business. However, none of them could have foreseen that within three years their train would have diesel power, and in six years the steam locomotive, symbol of railroading itself, would be gone forever from the Lehigh Valley Railroad. Similar scenes were happening on railroads all across the continent from Los Angeles to Boston, and from the swamps of Florida to the shores of Puget Sound. Massive and powerful steam locomotives were being shunted aside by shiny new streamlined diesels. By the end of the 1950s steam locomotives would be gone from the rails that they had traveled for over 130 years. The passing of the steam locomotive would transform the railroad industry and have far reaching effects throughout American society.

Railroads and the United States literally came of age together. Perhaps no other single technology has had as much of an effect upon the growth and development of the continent as the railroad. Railroads have been a key component of America's transportation network for over a century and a half. Although first introduced in England, they experienced their greatest growth and development in the United States. From the early experiments in the 1830s, to the completion of the transcontinental link in 1869, to the golden-age of the turn of the century, the railroad not only provided transportation for people and goods but also provided a market for goods and services, controlled and absorbed vast amounts of capital and employed millions of workers, directly and indirectly. The large scale industrialization of the American economy and continent would not have been possible without the railroad. The steam locomotive is perhaps the best symbol for the transformation of the United States from a coastal agrarian country to a continental industrial powerhouse. Steel rails and steam locomotives tied the country together into a single economic and social entity.[3]

By the turn of the century American railroads were nearing their peak of power and influence. They totally dominated both the movement of passengers and freight. Without much exaggeration, railroads hauled everyone and everything everywhere. Railroads like the Burlington and New York Central were household words and as familiar to the general public as United Airlines or Ford Motor Company are today. There was scarcely a community in the country where the whistle of a steam locomotive could not be heard. From prosaic commodities like coal and grain to high value mail and express, railroads hauled it all. Railroads were mature but innovative industrial corporations and increasingly began to embrace new technologies like electrification. The economic power of the railroads was almost total, only great lakes and coastal shipping could claim to also be a partner in transportation of people and goods.

The incredible economic, and by extension political and social power of the railroads generated resentment. Shippers continually pushed for lower rates while many members of the general public felt, with some good reason, that railroads were predatory and monopolistic corporations. This distrust of railroads manifested itself in ever increasing government regulation. While the Interstate Commerce Commission was formed in 1887, it had little power to enforce regulations until after the turn of the century. The first two decades of the twentieth century were in many ways the golden years for railroads, however they experienced increasing pressure from organized labor and the government. The growth era from 1865 to the 1890s with its financial chicanery was over and railroads began to refocus their business strategies. The Interstate Commerce Commission or ICC was playing an ever increasing role in regulating railroads. Progressive era legislation enacted in 1906, 1910, and 1912 all gave the government and especially the ICC more power over the railroads and their business practices.[4] Federal intervention was needed in 1916 over a threatened nationwide strike for an eight hour day. Despite this increasing regulation, most railroads remained strong and profitable but there were some troubling signs. Some areas had multiple railroads offering similar service between cities. For instance, four major railroads offered direct service between Chicago and New York. Two were prosperous, the Pennsylvania and New York Central while two were more troubled, the Baltimore & Ohio and especially the Erie. The question of what to do with weaker roads like these was a source of much debate and analysis.

During World War I the railroads suffered huge problems moving the crush of military traffic to east coast ports and were nationalized under the United States Railroad Administration or USRA. The USRA was successful in eliminating the traffic bottlenecks and produced several well designed standardized types of locomotives but also increased wages, which, together with increasing fuel and material costs and static freight rates further cut into railroads profits. Because of the gridlock on the rails motor trucking saw its first real opportunity to take traffic away from the rails. While the actual tonnage hauled by trucks was small, the precedent was set and many would remember how trucks came to the rescue while the railroads were paralyzed. After the experience of the USRA most observers, be they government or railroad management, agreed that outright nationalization was not the best course of action for the nation's railroads, although some in government and organized labor argued that nationalization, as had happened in many European countries, was the best option.

With the challenges of World War I over, 1920 marked a shift in the way that American railroads operated both their business practices and their trains. Costs had increased greatly during the period of government control, especially labor costs. The USRA was disbanded and railroads returned to private control, although under even heavier regulation due to the 1920 Transportation Act. This act allowed the ICC to set maximum and minimum rates with the goal of ensuring that railroads would earn 6 percent returns on investment. The act gave the ICC unprecedented control over financial matters such as the issuance of railroad stock and bonds and over construction of new lines or abandonment of superfluous track. It also directed the ICC to study the consolidation of railroads into several large competing systems rather than the hundreds of strong and weak companies then extant.[5] Similar consolidations had happened in Canada, with the creation in 1918 of the government owned, Crown Corporation, Canadian National Railways and in Britain with the 1921 ordered consolidation into four large systems.[6] The ICC was never known for its speed and it took the better part of a decade to come up with a consolidation plan, by which time it was already made obsolete by ensuing events.[7]

While some in management were preoccupied by the consolidation schemes of the ICC and the opportunities to be had on Wall Street in the 1920s, operations officials had to come up with ways to efficiently and cost effectively move freight and passengers, all without the option of increasing rates and fares without ICC approval. With this increasing ICC control, railroads decided to consolidate and solidify their existing business and to look at other ways to increase their profits that were not heavily regulated. Expansion into new geographic areas was no longer an option as the country was covered with a web of lines. Maximum rail mileage was reached in 1916 with over 250,000 miles of track. Large mergers and corporate consolidations were not widely pursued due to the necessity to have ICC approval which could take many years. The prospect of forced consolidation also kept most railroads from merging or otherwise acquiring new lines as they could be forced to divest them when the final ICC plan was revealed. With the new regulatory environment after 1920 especially, railroads had to find new ways to do business and enact savings that were not regulated by the ICC. In the face of this new business environment, the railroads changed their emphasis from physical expansion and price competition to economic efficiency in operations. Railroads would have to find other ways to grow their business rather than laying new track or cutthroat competition on price and rates. This in turn led to greater competition between railroads in areas of speed, service, and efficiency. Further exacerbating the competition between railroads themselves was the additional threat of growing numbers of unregulated trucks and automobiles. On the far horizon was the possibility of commercial air transport. The search for efficiency dominated the history of American railroads in the twentieth century. With their halcyon growth days behind them, the railroads turned to many areas in search of greater cost-effectiveness and efficiency. They had to find appropriate and profitable business segments instead of moving everyone and everything everywhere, all the time.

This search for efficiency meant different things to different people, both within and outside railroad management. For low and midlevel operations officials, efficiency meant moving freight and passengers as smoothly as possible for the lowest overall costs as possible. Minimizing costs was not the only consideration. Freight and passengers had to be transported, ideally on time and on schedule. Locomotive designers and motive power officials, many with engineering degrees, treated efficiency in a more theoretical manner and were interested in thermodynamic efficiency of locomotives and in squeezing as much work out of each pound of coal for the lowest overall costs. The desires of operations and motive power officials were not always compatible. A locomotive that saved fuel at the cost of increased maintenance might delight locomotive designers but frustrate operations officials by being out of service for repairs too much of the time. Upper management was less concerned with things like pounds of coal burned per ton mile and more concerned with controlling costs, especially the rapidly increasing labor costs. Many in government including the ICC were concerned with efficiency in regard to competition. It was believed that unfettered competition bred inefficiency and would need to be regulated or possibly even eliminated with forced consolidation.

A statistical snapshot of the railroads in 1920 after the end of USRA control provides a good baseline from which to make further analysis and to compare the later introduction of the diesel locomotive. (See table 1 in appendix) 1920 stands as the peak year for railroad power and influence. In that year direct railroad employment peaked at over 2 million. It was also the peak year for railroad passengers carried, over 1.2 billion. This number has never been surpassed, not even in the war years of 1942 to 1945.[8] After 1920 the railroads began to lose market share to other forms of transportation, especially passenger automobiles.

As business boomed in the 1920s, railroads sought to increase their efficiency and control their costs in new ways. With labor as the largest single cost, railroads tried to eliminate or at least make more efficient use of labor. Employment slowly declined from its high in 1920, but by 1929 there were still almost 1.7 million workers employed directly by the nation's railroads. These employees were taking a large chunk of the total operating revenue, over 61 percent in 1923 and over 64 percent in 1929. One way to control these labor costs was to use larger and more powerful locomotives. These larger locomotives would enable longer trains, which would enable more ton miles to be hauled with the same crew expenses, generating gains in productivity. While these locomotives would still need a crew, it would no longer be necessary to use two or more locomotives, each with its own crew, on a train or to use multiple smaller trains. New locomotives would also require less maintenance and fuel than older, less efficient and worn out locomotives. New locomotives also promised higher speeds, which were becoming more important as railroads increasingly were competing on speed and service rather than price. The railroads as a whole invested heavily in locomotives and other new equipment as well as upgrading right of way and structures in the 1920s. Much of this upgrading of track was done to enable more efficient operations. For example, tight curves and short steep grades were smoothed out to eliminate bottlenecks and enable faster train speeds. In the banner year of 1923, 4360 new locomotives were purchased. The vast majority of these locomotives were steam and were much larger and more efficient than locomotives produced before World War I. (See table 3 in appendix) A few of these locomotives were electrics for the increasing electrification programs of the 1920s, all undertaken with greater efficiency in mind. The late 1920s saw the first successful experiments with diesel motive power. Small diesel switchers appeared in yards, industries, and especially on the docks in and around New York City in response to municipal antismoke ordinances. They quickly impressed officials with their cost effectiveness.

The Great Depression hit the railroads hard. Total operating revenue in 1932 was about half of what it was in 1929. Net operating revenue was even lower. Many railroads were bankrupt and operating under receivership. The railroads did what businesses were supposed to do, compete aggressively for the remaining business. They did so by speeding up freight schedules and instituting fast, streamlined passenger service. In many cases these faster schedules and new trains required new locomotives. However, with money especially tight, the railroads as a whole could not invest in a large amount of new motive power. Nonetheless, some railroads with the capital to do so did significantly invest in both new steam power and new diesel passenger power. Especially interesting were the years 1936 and 1937. With business beginning to trickle back after the nadir of 1932 and 1933, some railroads invested substantially in new motive power. Steam was the still the clear winner, although diesels were making a good showing. Diesels had benefitted from several years of intense, high speed passenger service on such trains as the Burlington Zephyr, Santa Fe Super Chief, and Union Pacific City of San Francisco. With the "Roosevelt Recession" of 1937 and 1938 the railroads did not repeat their large purchases in 1938 but seemed to adopt a wait and see approach. With war clouds gathering in 1939 and 1940, traffic began to climb. Railroads were finally approaching the levels of revenue that they earned before the Depression. They now finally had additional capital to spend. While substantial portions went to new facilities and upkeep of lines that had not received adequate maintenance during the Depression, some was left over for new locomotive and other equipment purchases. By 1940 the capital spent on new equipment was roughly equivalent to what railroads had been spending in the late 1920s. A significant chunk of this spending was for new, more efficient locomotives, including new main line diesel freight locomotives, introduced in 1939.

The war years were a mixed blessing for the railroads. The wartime traffic in freight and passengers finally put an end to the Depression and many companies were able to once again operate in the black. Outright nationalization on the USRA WWI pattern was avoided but the huge increase in traffic, while bringing much needed revenue, did take its toll. Maintenance on track, cars, and locomotives was deferred to enable as many trains to move freight and passengers as possible. The flood of traffic was almost too much for the railroads to handle. They also had to compete with other war industries as well as the armed forces for available labor. Some railroads responded to this labor shortage by hiring women, although not in as great numbers as manufacturing industries. The wartime traffic led to record revenues of over $9.5 billion in 1944. However, costs also climbed; total operating expenses in 1944 were over $6.3 billion. Net operating income peaked at almost $1.5 billion in 1942 and remained above $1 billion for 1943 and 1944.[9] While revenues were climbing, net income did not keep pace after 1944. Costs were taking up more and more of this record revenue. With a shortage of labor and with increasing labor costs, railroads emphasized labor savings as they had in the 1920s. To handle this crush of wartime traffic as quickly and efficiently as possible, the railroads invested heavily in new locomotives. Both diesel and steam were purchased and immediately put to work. While there were many steam locomotives idled in the Depression years, many of these older and smaller locomotives were simply worn out and more useful as scrap. To move the maximum of war material with the minimum of costs and effort, new modern locomotives were needed, not old obsolete types brought out of retirement.

With the war won, most railroads spent 1946 catching their collective breath. New locomotive orders were down and many railroads seemed to be awaiting the final verdict on the diesel and its usefulness. Would the many diesels purchased during the war continue to impress not only operating crews but the accountants back at the home office? What about the economy? Would the Depression, vanquished by war, return now that the war was over? By the end of 1947 the verdict was in on all counts. Diesels, which had proved themselves in the cauldron of war, were the overwhelming although not the only choice for new motive power. The economy was beginning its postwar boom and the Depression appeared to be gone for good. However, for the railroads there were some disturbing signs: revenue per ton-mile and per passenger-mile were lower than in 1920 even though overall revenue was higher.

Most alarming for the railroads were greatly increasing costs. While costs increased during the war, revenue and traffic growth were at least almost keeping pace; however, with the war over and traffic back to manageable levels, costs kept increasing at an accelerated rate. Postwar inflation increased material prices more in the few years since the war than from 1933 to 1945. Fuel costs were especially important as they were almost three times what they were at the beginning of the war. Wages also increased. From 1939 to 1948 wage rates increased 86.5 percent. Hourly wages and salaries together took up roughly half of total operating revenue.

Table 1. Railroad Material Price Indexes

(May 1933 = 100)			
Date	Material and Supplies	Fuel (coal & oil)	All Material
December, 1939	130.7	134.3	131.9
December, 1941	146.4	148.4	147.0
December, 1943	159.5	180.5	166.2
December, 1945	170.0	195.9	178.2
December, 1946	199.2	228.5	208.5
December, 1947	228.4	295.4	249.8
June, 1948	242.2	321.4	267.4
October 1, 1948	264.1	335.3	287.5

Source: J. H. Parmelee, "A Review of Railway Operations in 1948," Railway Age (January 8, 1949), 94. Mr. Parmelee was Vice-President and Director of the Bureau of Railway Economics of the Association of American Railroads.

The increase in material and labor costs, even if driven primarily by inflation, was not offset by a corresponding increase in rates and fares. Again, from 1939 to 1948 freight rates increased 44.2 percent, while passenger fares increased only 25.4 percent. Railroads had to go though the ICC to have any rates changed. This was a time consuming process, and there was always the possibility that the commissioners would turn them down. As if this was not enough, taxes were taking an ever larger chunk out of revenues. From a total of less than 500 million dollars in 1946, taxes, including payroll taxes, more than doubled to over 1 billion by 1948 and over 1.2 billion by 1950.

This environment, in which railroads were doing well but costs were increasing much faster than rates and fares, is the background for the full scale dieselization efforts from 1946 to 1960. Flush with profits from the war and facing skyrocketing costs the railroads did what any good business is supposed to do, invest in new equipment that holds the potential to control those costs. With a similar regulatory environment as the 1920s but with new more efficient motive power available, railroads chose the diesel to control costs and to operate more efficiently. Railroads purchased thousands of diesels from 1947 to 1960 to replace steam locomotives. The peak years were 1950 to 1953 with over 3000 units purchased each year. These new locomotives enabled the retirement of many thousands of steam locomotives that were for the most part beginning to show their age and require more and more maintenance. The diesels gave a healthy return on investment, in some cases over 25 percent per year in cost savings. Most of the savings came from decreased labor costs, especially maintenance, but savings were also achieved in fuel costs and in greater availability and efficiency. Many times diesels were able to move trains over the road faster than steam power. However, these results varied greatly from railroad to railroad. Some railroads tried out diesels and found that the expected savings did not justify the high purchase price.

It is easy in hindsight to look back and say that the fast embrace of the diesel made sense for the railroads and that the diesel was superior to steam in almost all aspects. However it was much less clear at the time. The response to diesels in the trade press, specifically *Railway Age* is especially illuminating. The magazine published highly detailed articles describing new diesels in the 1930s and 1940s. For example, the record breaking 39 hour, 34 minute run of diesels from Los Angeles to Chicago was extensively documented in an article from November 1935.[10] The magazine also recounted the operational cost savings that diesel locomotives were able to generate. For example, another 1935 article, written by a representative of the Alco Locomotive Works, a steam and diesel locomotive manufacturer, asserted that, "So far the Diesel-electric locomotive has proved to be economical in the switching field."[11] Other articles detailed cost savings in streamlined diesel passenger service. While the press was positive, it was not overly so. A third article from the same year illustrated this point. Written by a representative of Westinghouse, a diesel and electric locomotive manufacturer, the article stated, "It is not claimed by anyone familiar with railroading and also with Diesel equipment that the steam locomotive is doomed to extinction."[12] If a diesel locomotive manufacturer took such a conservative view, one can only imagine what the rest of the industry felt. In many of the articles and especially in essays there is a strong tone of conservatism and resistance to change. Railroaders and equipment manufacturers were reluctant to embrace the diesel partly because of an emotional attachment with the steam locomotive. As the Westinghouse article goes on to state, costs, both purchase and operating, were the overriding issue in further use of diesels. The article ignored potential cost savings from operational changes.

While diesels were the topic of many articles, steam power too was well represented. For example, a prominent article from July 1940 detailed the many ways that existing steam power could be modernized for faster and more sustained service.[13] New and highly advanced steam locomotives were also covered in detail.[14] Editorials in the 1930s focused on conflict with labor and New Deal legislation rather than embracing either form of motive power. Wartime editorials repeated similar themes of free enterprise and the dangers of socialism and totalitarianism. A continual topic of the editorial pages were government subsidies of competing forms of transportation, especially water and road improvements. The editorials focused on the perceived unfair advantages being given to competitors rather than attempting to ward off competitors by improving railroad operations or by seeking government largesse themselves.

The advertisements in the magazines are also illuminating. Steam locomotive manufacturers and parts suppliers made up a majority of all advertisements even after the diesel had proven itself on streamliners during the mid- and late 1930s. Only during the war did a large number of diesel locomotive ads appear, especially from the Electro-Motive Division of General Motors (EMD). These ads were generally conservative in nature and consciously tried to tie the new diesel locomotives to the traditions of railroading. Many would show a steam locomotive from the 1840s along with a new diesel. The text would emphasize that the diesel was another in a long line of technical improvements dating back to the beginnings of railroading. Diesels would not be a threatening revolutionary new technology but would simply continue the traditions of railroading. Steam locomotive builders Baldwin and Lima continued to advertise modern steam locomotives until 1947, although steam and diesel builder American Locomotive (Alco) was emphasizing its diesel offerings by then. While most ads concentrated on performance and cost issues, some tried a more emotional approach. For example, a full page ad for Lima Locomotive Works in December 1940 contained a photo of a locomotive engineer speaking with a small boy. The text read, "They'll still be using steam locomotives when you grow up, Sonny. Maybe, when you grow up, you'll be at the throttle of a faster and more powerful Lima built 'Daylight' than this one."[15] While this may have been wishful thinking on Lima's part, clearly in 1940 the verdict was still out on the diesel for some in the railroad industry.

Despite large scale dieselization, the 1950s saw a continual erosion of traffic from the railroads. Passengers fled the rails first, going into tail-finned automobiles driven on the growing interstate highway system and by the end of the decade onto Boeing 707 and other jet aircraft. From 1946 to 1960, the railroad share of commercial intercity passenger traffic in the United States declined from about 65 percent to less than 30 percent. Freight also declined but not quite as severely. Freight traffic share declined from near 66 percent to about 45 percent.[16] The one bright spot in the 1950s was truck trailer on flatcar traffic, which almost tripled from 1955 to 1960.[17] With the introduction of the interstate highway system in 1956, people and freight now had a high speed, long distance, federally subsidized option to the railroads. Not surprisingly many chose to utilize that option. The railroads recognized the threat

to their business from subsidized competitors and tried
to reform the system. A 1960 report from the Association
of American Railroads stated, "Our entire transportation system would be economically stronger, not weaker,
if fully compensatory user charges were established for
all commercial carriers."[18] The railroads were pushing for
less federal funding for roads, airlines and shipping, not
more federal funding for themselves. With memories of the
nationalization of 1918 to 1920 and the attempted forced
consolidation plans of the 1920s still in the heads of senior
executives and in a politically charged cold war environment, the railroads simply could not ask for government
support but instead triumphed the free enterprise system,
even though their competitors were benefitting from bil-
lions of dollars of government capital. The railroads, both
individually and collectively, tried to promote a more level
playing field, but the efforts came to naught.

De-industrialization, especially in the Northeast and
the increasing shift to a service economy also affected
railroads. Many railroads, especially those in the East,
chose mergers as one way to cut costs further and streamline operations. While railroads resisted outside consolidation in the 1920s and 1930s, in the 1960s and beyond
they chose to consolidate themselves. While some mergers were successful, many were not, and by the late 1960s
most railroads operating in the Northeast were facing
bankruptcy. Railroads in the South and West fared better but many were also in bad shape by the 1970s. The
bankruptcy of the Penn Central and the creation of Conrail was the largest and most public but by no means the
only manifestation of the difficulties faced by railroads in
the 1960s and 1970s. Other railroads like the Rock Island
and the Milwaukee Road also went bankrupt. Ultimately
it would take substantial labor concessions, the creation
of Amtrak and regional commuter authorities and deregulation of freight rates with the Staggers Act of 1980 to
enable the railroads to achieve a somewhat more advan-
tageous business climate.

Whether plowing capital into new locomotives from
1947 to 1960 was a worthwhile investment in the short and
long term is debatable. In the short term diesels did as a
whole save money for railroads and allowed them to control some of their skyrocketing costs. In the longer term
the answer is less clear. Many of the railroads that were
the last to fully dieselize have survived the subsequent

fifty years in relatively good shape, while most of the earliest dieselizers no longer exist. In fact, much of their track has been pulled up. Some of the early dieselizers were only marginally profitable to begin with, and diesels simply prolonged the inevitable. Some of the late dieselizers have been successful because they had relatively stable and strong traffic bases such as coal or served growing areas like the west and southwest. Thus, in some cases diesels were a good investment, while for other railroads they clearly were not. This illustrates that the entire industry must be broken apart into railroad-sized pieces to answer these complex questions. The large scale statistical portrait above provides the context and the necessary information on which more detailed analysis of the dieselization of individual railroads can take place.

Railroads have been the subject of innumerable popular, historical, economic and policy studies over the past century. Surprisingly few have a direct bearing on the dieselization experience however. In wider historical scholarship there are several studies that add insight into the dieselization process and help to make sense of the many variables and the complex influences in the decision making process of various railroads. In historical scholarship some have treated dieselization as a natural progression, something that had to happen eventually.[19] These deterministic studies dealt with some of the economic incentives for dieselization, but they did not consider all variables. For example, they analyzed fuel and labor savings, but not operational differences in servicing, train size, and scheduling. To date, scholars generally have not fully explained the complex social and technical effects of dieselization. Although some studies have examined a broader range of issues, most of them have not performed in-depth analysis on multiple individual railroads.[20] The importance of changes in railroad company upper management is vital to the dieselization story and is addressed somewhat in these histories but not specifically in the context of dieselization. Fewer historians, if any, have looked at the introduction of diesel locomotives from a systems perspective. Diesels were more than a new way to move trains; they embodied, within the technology, a fundamental shift in the way that the rail system could operate. Their impact was far-reaching and could be felt many years after they vanquished the steam locomotive from American rails.

A wealth of secondary sources have illuminated aspects of this work. Much of the contemporary scholarship in the history of technology may be glimpsed in this work, but a select few deserve further mention. The characteristics of large integrated technological systems have been investigated by Thomas P. Hughes who asserts that over time systems attain momentum which discourages "radical" innovation. Those who run and manage a system develop a vested interest in it and accept only those innovations that do not alter its configuration significantly.[21] They control the technology and discourage radical innovation. Inherent in Hughes's analysis is the assumption that the revolutionary aspects of a new technology are apparent to those who want to protect existing systems. This is certainly true with dieselization. The capabilities of diesel power had been amply demonstrated by the mid-1930s, yet there were those in the industry that still did not realize or simply denied the potential. Incremental improvements to steam locomotives were pursued because they would bring small improvements while maintaining the existing system. Diesels would upset the existing rail system including the delicate balance with rail labor and were not pursued widely until rapidly escalating costs forced railroads as a whole to take a close look at the advantages of the diesel.

Steven Usselman has done much work on railroads and their response to technological changes. Although he analyzed the railroads of the late nineteenth century, many of his observations hold true for dieselization. Railroads adopted technological innovations for many differing reasons depending on local corporate and other conditions including government regulation and issues of public safety. He states that "widely different factors could influence the decision to adopt a new device."[22] This statement is applicable for diesel locomotives. The innovation patterns he describes that were established during the 1870s and 1880s were still evident during the 1930s. He asserts that railroads channeled innovation into "pipelines" that focused effort on some areas while neglecting others.[23] This is evident in the early stages of the dieselization story. Railroads, long accustomed to incremental innovations in steam locomotive technology, continued to seek these small innovations while ignoring the potential of the diesel. They only fully embraced the diesel after they were forced to by rapidly changing economic conditions.

Usselman, like Hughes, goes on to state that the innovation pipelines were chosen to minimize possible disruptions.[24] This again is the case in the dieselization story. Railroads sought to minimize disruptions to operations and existing labor relations while enjoying some of the benefits of the new technology.

Usselman's insights do not stop there. He also recognizes the intense emotional link that Americans had with the railroads. He states that this emotion, "together with the obvious significance that railroads held for social and economic relations and the uncertainties inherent in innovation, insured that the disputes through which railroading took shape went well beyond the matter of how best to provide efficient transport."[25] While he was referring to the late nineteenth century, his conclusions were also applicable to the early and middle twentieth. This emotional link to railroads is seen in the incredible public attraction to the modern streamliners of the 1930s as well as in the nostalgia for steam exhibited by some railroad managers and the public in the decade and a half after the end of World War II.

While American railroads have been the subject of much research, dieselization specifically has not been a topic of great historical interest. The railfan community has produced a wealth of magazine articles and books on aspects of dieselization, but most do not look at it from a critical perspective.[26] Many of the railfan publications contain vast amounts of useful data. Listings of locomotives, while providing little if any analysis, provide a wealth of data on the number, type, manufacturer, and service dates of all the locomotives owned by a particular railroad.[27] Other publications such as the popular *Trains* magazine and the publications of the various individual railroad historical societies provide much useful information.[28] These railfan sources can provide information that is lacking from other sources, and, when put into context, can illuminate larger issues.

The scholarly work done specifically on dieselization is limited and mostly confined to economic studies that do not adequately address the multiplicity of influences on the dieselization process. Fred Cottrell, in a short article from 1951, details the response by workers, families, and town leaders to dieselization in a small western town that was dependent upon steam locomotive servicing facilities.[29] It is a useful but limited article that concisely and

succinctly summarizes the problems such as loss of jobs
and tax revenue faced by many communities during dieselization. He asserts that often those who have the most
vested interest in a community lose the most when the
railroad decides to cut back or close facilities.

In his economics dissertation, Richard Hydell looks
at the dieselization of the Erie Railroad. He asserts that
because of the age of the steam locomotives of the Erie,
the railroad followed a rational path in acquiring new
capital equipment, diesel locomotives.[30] While his conclusions are essentially correct for the Erie, he made two
oversights. First, he extended conclusions drawn from the
experience of the Erie to all railroads. Second, he assumed
that steam and diesel locomotive types were nearly equivalent in their three specific service classes—branch-line,
freight, and high-speed service. He assumed that steam
and diesel locomotives could perform the same work in
the same way. This was not the case. Diesels were more
flexible than steam locomotives. They also had much less
down time for repairs or greater availability for usage as
well as greater low-speed performance and less need for
on-line servicing.[31] These characteristics, unique to the
diesel locomotive, enabled large numbers of steam locomotives of different types to be replaced by but a few types
of diesels. Hydell also asserted that other effects, such as
management resistance to diesels and wartime production constraints, had little effect upon railroads' adoption of diesel locomotives.[32] While this may have been the
case for the Erie (but even there it is highly debatable) it
almost assuredly did not hold true for the rail industry
as a whole. The general weakness of his work, and most
economic studies is that he looks only at the locomotives
themselves rather than seeing them as an integral part of
a larger system. There are a few other dissertations that
deal specifically with dieselization, but none of them look
at it from an operational or a systems perspective. They
look at the manufacturing and production side rather than
how railroads purchased and used the new locomotives.
They also fail to examine broader social and cultural
trends. Indeed, most of them are economics dissertations
that, while useful data sources, do not provide adequate
analysis and show a lack of historical understanding.[33]

John K. Brown looks at the premier steam locomotive
producer of the nineteenth century, Baldwin. He asserts
that Baldwin, and by extrapolation all steam locomotive

production, while flexible, was labor intensive and subject to the cyclical nature of the capital equipment market.[34] Steam locomotive manufacturers offered custom made products, tailored to the exact specifications of the buyer, in contrast to the later manufacturer-imposed standardization of diesel locomotives. Brown does briefly look at the decline of Baldwin and the rise of the Electro-Motive Division of General Motors (EMD), and more specifically how Baldwin's preoccupation with incremental improvements in steam locomotive technology blinded the company's management to the revolutionary aspects of the diesel.[35] He also states that the standardization of the diesel, while contrary to over eighty years of locomotive building tradition, aided the diesel locomotive manufacturers in the battle to replace the steam locomotive.[36]

The response of locomotive builders such as Baldwin, Alco, and the Electro-Motive Division of General Motors to dieselization was the subject of a dissertation and a later book by Albert Churella. His findings are essentially that the established steam locomotive builders did not fully realize the potential of the diesel and did not enact the necessary changes in manufacturing, management, and marketing to enable them to compete in the diesel arena.[37] On this note Brown would concur. Churella realized the distinctive nature of the diesel locomotive and its potential to reshape railroad operations, but the actual use of locomotives on the railroads themselves was not the emphasis of his work; instead he chose to focus on the business practices and corporate culture of the locomotive builders and their response to technological change. The final sentence of his book concisely sums up his argument and is also applicable to dieselization from the point of view of the railroad companies themselves in addition to the locomotive manufacturers. "The ultimate lesson of the locomotive industry is that technology often changes more rapidly than the people whose careers depend on it and that, to be exploited effectively, technological change must be accompanied by more than plant modernization, by more than research and development, by more than government action; it must be accompanied by fundamental changes in the hearts and minds of those who attempt to control it."[38]

The most recent scholarly work on dieselization is a dissertation by Mark Mapes.[39] In his work he examines in depth the dieselization of the Pennsylvania Railroad. He identifies many differing motives in the dieselization of the PRR including loyalty to the coal industry, early anti-smoke legislation, and competition with other railroads.[40] These and other motives would appear in other railroads' decisions as well. However, as mentioned previously, the experiences of the large and powerful Pennsylvania railroad (PRR) can not be extrapolated to the entire railroad system. In many ways the PRR was unlike the vast majority of other north American railroads, not the least of which was because of its sheer size.[41] The PRR was also the leader in gross revenue during the period of dieselization and had much more available capital than most other railroads which meant that they were more readily able to pay for diesels.

The railroad industry, because of its unique characteristics, long history, government regulation, labor relationship and economic power dealt with technological change in a unique way. The regulation of the industry, especially after 1920, forced the railroads to look to new technologies to control costs rather than rate increases. The heavily unionized labor forces of railroads from 1920 to 1960 ensured that any operational or business change with a large impact on labor would be contentious. Management generally preferred to direct resources to and benefit from incremental improvements in steam locomotive technology unless forced to look toward the diesel by other influences. The diesel, although adopted by different railroads at different times and in different ways depending on local characteristics, was a revolutionary technology that held the potential to dramatically reshape the railroad industry. It had a huge impact on labor and did, as intended, save money and control costs for the railroads. The diesel was not a panacea though. The growth of highway transportation in the postwar era combined with deindustrialization and a stifling regulatory environment all conspired to have many railroads in dire straits by the late 1960s. Further restructuring of the financial, regulatory, labor and policy environment was necessary before railroads began to look like healthy businesses again.

2

The Care and Feeding of
Steam and Diesel Locomotives

AMERICAN RAILROADS FACED MANY CHALLENGES AFTER 1920. THE regulatory and business environment had changed and the labor environment was changing rapidly. The way that railroads operated had to change in response. With rates and other financial and business options regulated or outright controlled by the ICC, the railroads explored other options to streamline their businesses and operate more efficiently. One way that railroads responded was by adopting new technologies that held the potential to lower their costs and effect other operating efficiencies. However, not all technologies were the same or held the same potential. The adoption of new technologies was dependent not simply on the potential cost savings or operating efficiencies that they would produce but on a multitude of complex factors. To understand dieselization we must understand much more than simply what a diesel locomotive is or even how it works. We need to get inside the "black box" of the technology and not simply treat it as a monolithic entity. This is also true of the steam locomotives that the diesels replaced. Locomotives embodied the hopes and desires of the railroad in much the same way that an automobile embodies the hopes and wants of its owner. While locomotives themselves are important and indeed vital to our understanding, we must also look at how and why they were designed, built, operated, and serviced. The decisions of the locomotive designers, maintenance forces, and upper management must be addressed. All locomotives, be they steam or diesel, were not created equal. There were many variations and types depending on manufacturer, railroad, and service performed. Like all technologies, locomotives were shaped by a multitude of forces. These forces and the actors involved need to be addressed to better understand dieselization. To fully understand dieselization, the basics of railroad operations including the operating efficiencies and procedures of steam locomotives must be analyzed.

Steam locomotives and railroads literally came of age together. They were inseparable. The entire railroad system was constructed around the operational needs of the steam locomotive. From the Baltimore & Ohio "Tom Thumb" of the 1830s to the huge Union Pacific "Big Boy" over one hundred years later, steam locomotives were the heart and soul of the railroad. The steam locomotive was the physical manifestation of the railroad and in many ways of the rapidly expanding and industrializing country itself. The cultural and emotional attachment of the railroad industry and even the nation itself to the steam locomotive was huge and not surpassed by any major technology arguably until the advent of the automobile. Steam locomotives were ruggedly built machines that required much personal care in the form of frequent fuel, water and maintenance. The railroad system and in many ways the expanding nation was designed and constructed to meet the needs of the steam locomotive.

Steam locomotives were first developed in Britain and were strange looking machines with a great many gears, pistons, rods, and other moving parts protruding from seemingly everywhere. These early experimental machines set the groundwork for further development. Due to the diverse operating conditions in the United States different locomotive designs were needed and quickly developed. By far the most successful of these uniquely American designs was the 4–4–0 type called the American Standard type or simply the American. The four wheel leading truck helped to keep the locomotive on the rails through curves and over poor track, while the four driving wheels provided enough tractive effort or pulling power for most passenger and freight applications.[1] The American type was the forerunner for most other steam locomotives in the United States. While the American itself was a fairly radical innovation from prior locomotive types, most further innovations based on the American type would be incremental and evolutionary in nature.

While the American type was a good locomotive suitable for most jobs, by the Civil War it was becoming inadequate for jobs that required more tractive effort, such as climbing mountain grades or pulling long, heavy trains. The answer was to add more driving wheels, creating the 2–6–0 Mogul type and the 4–6–0 Ten-wheeler. The Mogul offered 50 percent greater tractive effort than the American and was quickly put to use in heavy freight service.[2]

The Ten-wheeler, with its four wheel leading truck and six drivers was adopted by many railroads as the standard heavy passenger engine of the late nineteenth century. While the Mogul was successful, it quickly became outmoded by ever larger and heavier trains. As before, the railroads added another set of drivers to create the 2–8–0 Consolidation type. First built in 1866 for the Pennsylvania coal hauling Lehigh Valley Railroad, the Consolidation became the standard freight locomotive for most railroads by about 1900. It offered more pulling power than the Mogul and Ten-wheeler but still had a leading truck for stability at speed. The Consolidation was the most popular steam locomotive type with over 21,000 built for North American railroads.[3] After more modern locomotives entered service, older locomotives like the Consolidation were shifted to secondary jobs, but many remained in service until the end of steam.

As freight trains grew longer and heavier and as passengers demanded ever more speed, locomotive development split into two paths. Locomotive development progressed from the general service locomotives such as the 4–4–0 to more specialized types that were optimized for particular services such as the passenger 4–6–0 and the freight 2–8–0. Freight needed simply raw pulling power or high tractive effort while passengers increasingly needed high speed and therefore higher horsepower. This change in mindset by railroad managers and motive power officials from a general purpose locomotive to specialized designs for different types of service was complete by about 1900 and would shape the future of steam locomotive development. It would have a profound effect upon later diesel locomotive development.

Locomotives of this era were sources of pride for their crews and owners and were decorated in a manner that illustrated this. Prussian blue boiler jackets, bright paint schemes with gold pinstripes, and even deer antlers above the headlight were all commonplace. Many early locomotives were named rather than numbered, the most famous being the General and the Texas from the Civil War "great locomotive chase" and the Jupiter present at the golden spike ceremony in 1869. The social and cultural attachment to the steam locomotive developed along with the technology. The steam locomotive, and by extension the railroad itself, was more than simply a way to move goods and passengers but was intimately tied up with the history and culture of the expanding and industrializing nation. The steam locomotive in a real way symbolized the strength of the nation.

Early steam locomotives may have been extensively decorated but were inefficient from an engineering and thermodynamic perspective. This was not a large concern during the expansion era of railroading since they operated on cheap and plentiful fuels such as coal or wood. Indeed, as with automobiles in the 1950s and 1960s, efficiency and fuel economy were clearly secondary considerations to performance.[4] During the later nineteenth century, coal won out as a fuel because it was more compact and economical and wood was becoming increasingly scarce, especially on the western plains. Steam locomotives became an important consumer of coal with a large proportion of national coal output going into the fireboxes of locomotives. In the twentieth century some locomotives began burning low-grade oil, especially in the Southwest and Far West where oil was more widely available than coal. The oil used in these steam locomotives was heavy, industrial grade heating oil, just above asphalt in consistency.

With increasing emphasis on costs and a large number of college trained engineers and managers entering the industry, in the 1890s the relative thermal inefficiency of locomotives began to be a source of concern for railroads and locomotive builders.[5] With the new science of industrial thermodynamics, they gradually researched developments such as compounding cylinders, higher boiler pressures, superheaters, and feed water heaters. These incremental innovations were able to raise the efficiency at times to near 10 percent from the standard 4 percent. Many of these developments were first used in marine and stationary steam engine applications. Locomotives with compound cylinders were able to extract more energy from each ounce of steam by using the steam exhausted from one cylinder (the high pressure cylinder) as feed for a second one (the low pressure cylinder). Thus, the steam exerts pressure and does work in two cylinders or sometimes more before being exhausted out the stack. Many compound locomotives were produced in the early decades of the century. Compounding did have drawbacks including the cost, weight, and complexity of the additional cylinders and valve gear. This lead to increased servicing costs. Most compound locomotives were also limited to relatively slow speeds. Other incremental and evolutionary developments all served to wring more work from each ounce of steam. Superheaters took the steam and heated it an additional 200 to 400 degrees Fahrenheit. At this temperature the steam would not cool enough to condense in the cylinders, a major source of inefficiency.[6] Superheaters made compounding less necessary and many later steam locomotive designs abandoned compounding due to its complexity and higher service costs.

Higher boiler pressures and, therefore, temperatures made possible greater force of expansion in the cylinders and, therefore, more power and greater efficiency. By the period of dieselization, from 1920 onward, most modern steam locomotives were operating with pressures from 200 to 250 pounds per square inch with some as high as 300, the practical limit for conventional fire tube locomotive type boilers.[7] Feed water heaters preheated the incoming boiler water by heat exchange with the exhaust steam from the cylinders, still at 250–300 degrees. The less heat exhausted up the stack, the more efficient the engine. Another major development of the 1920s was the introduction and widespread use of the automatic coal stoker. With a stoker the fireman no longer had to shovel coal into the firebox. The stoker could provide coal at a rate surpassing that of even the most brawny fireman and enabled larger fireboxes and hence, larger locomotives. The stoker did not make the fireman obsolete, however, for he still directed the placement of coal by the stoker, monitored the boiler, tended the fire and made sure that it was burning properly.

After many experiments with compounds and other innovations to steam locomotives, railroads discovered that pure thermal efficiency, in engineering terms, was not as important as the costs of maintenance and servicing. It was cheaper to use a bit more coal in an inefficient locomotive than to pay for the increased maintenance and time out of service that compounding would bring. It did not matter how efficient a locomotive was, if it was in the shop and not able to pull a train it was a poor investment. While railroads learned this lesson in the early years of the century, some would repeat their mistakes a generation later with an emphasis on theoretically efficient but overly complex steam locomotives in the late 1930s and 1940s. This tension between theoretical efficiency and power and the everyday concerns of serviceability and maintainability is a central theme of the dieselization experience of American railroads. Motive power officials and locomotive designers were continually enamored with theoretical gains in power and efficiency while operating officials and crews were much more concerned with reliability and servicing issues. The increased locomotive weight that developments such as compounding brought was not initially a large concern. Locomotives had to be heavy to utilize their power fully and many large noncompound locomotives weighed just as much as compound ones. Weight did become an increasing concern in the 1920s, however. With ever larger locomotives railroads found that rails and bridges needed to be strengthened. Often larger roundhouses and other servicing facilities were needed as well.

Whether it burned coal, wood or oil, a steam locomotive consumed much more than just fuel.[8] The steam in the cylinders was generally used only once and then exhausted up the stack. To generate steam, locomotives had to carry their own water to replenish the supply in the boiler as well as fuel. Therefore, railroads had to build and maintain both coal and water stations along the right of way at correctly spaced intervals, roughly twenty miles for water and one hundred miles for coal.[9] Water use was especially heavy in mountainous areas where locomotives struggled up heavy grades. Boiler water had to be treated. Extraordinarily hard water could foam when boiled and was a hazard to the inner workings of the boilers and had to be softened.[10] While water was not a large cost, it was a cost for railroads, generally water and water treatment cost roughly 10 percent of fuel costs. Availability of water was not generally an issue in the east but was problematic in areas of the arid west. Locomotives also needed sand. Sand was used to increase the friction between the wheel and the rail. It was used when starting heavy trains and when ascending grades. Sand was stored in a dome on top of the boiler and directed beneath the wheels by small tubes. Coaling, watering and sanding took a fair amount of time and caused additional maintenance and scheduling problems that had to be addressed. Coaling and watering a locomotive could take twenty to thirty minutes or more, while watering alone consumed five to fifteen minutes. In addition more time would be lost slowing for the service stop and then getting the train back up to speed when finished.

Steam locomotives were maintenance-intensive machines. The myriad moving parts, from the pistons and rods to the brake equipment, all had to be serviced at regular intervals. Much basic servicing had to occur on a daily basis. The problems of converting the reciprocating motion of the pistons to the rotary motion of the drivers made en route lubrication of the pistons, bearings, and connecting rods critical. Almost all locomotives built before the 1940s had simple brass friction bearings on the wheels and rods. These bearings had to be oiled and greased often, usually while taking on water and coal. At most stops the engineer and fireman would descend from the locomotive cab and "oil around" the locomotive to ensure proper lubrication. These bearings also required constant care from shop mechanics to ensure that they were working properly and not overheating, which could cause fires or a broken axle.[11] The expansion and contraction of the boiler tubes caused by heating and cooling, as well as the corrosive effect of coal smoke and cinders, took its toll on equipment. After each trip the ashes and clinkers had to be emptied out of the firebox. This required ash pits at every terminal. Periodically cinders also had to be cleaned out of the front of the smokebox, which required workers to unbolt the front plates of the engine and climb in with a shovel. All this maintenance took a lot of time and employed a large number of workers. Whenever a locomotive was in the shop or roundhouse, it was not out earning its keep by pulling trains. The expected useful life of an early twentieth century steam locomotive in its primary job and without extensive rebuilding was roughly thirty years. After this time necessary repairs became too expensive to keep the locomotive in service.[12]

Steam locomotive maintenance required large shop complexes and smaller maintenance facilities at many locations along the railroad. Major cities would almost always have locomotive servicing facilities for each railroad as would many smaller towns and division points.[13] For example, the Lehigh Valley, a medium-sized railroad that ran from Newark, NJ (opposite New York City) through New Jersey, Pennsylvania, and western New York State to Buffalo, had some sort of locomotive servicing facility in almost every sizable town and larger shop complexes in Easton, Lehighton, and Coxton (Wilkes-Barre), Pennsylvania; Oak Island, New Jersey; and Manchester, Niagara Falls, and Buffalo, New York. They also had smaller shops on branchlines at places like Delano and Hazleton, Pennsylvania and Perth Amboy, New Jersey. All the heavy repairs were done at the main shop located at Sayre, Pennsylvania. This shop even built main line steam locomotives up until 1929.[14] The Lehigh Valley was typical in this regard.

Many railroads built their own locomotives in their own shop complexes. The Illinois Central built and heavily rebuilt locomotives in its Paducah, Kentucky, shops until the end of steam. The Pennsylvania railroad built thousands of locomotives in its expansive Juniata shops complex in Altoona, Pennsylvania. The St. Louis—Southwestern or Cotton Belt built locomotives in their Pine Bluff, Arkansas, shops. These were not small switching locomotives but large powerful machines that were easily the equal of the offerings from the commercial builders Alco, Baldwin, and Lima.[15] This illustrates that steam locomotives, while large and powerful machines, did not need extensive, custom built machinery to build and maintain them. Almost any heavy shop complex with a foundry could have built a locomotive from steel and other raw materials. The extensive roundhouses, shops and other facilities required a sizable skilled workforce. Boilermakers, machinists, pipefitters, and many general laborers were required. Even the smallest roundhouses would employ dozens of workers while large shop complexes could employ thousands.

Steam locomotives were maintenance intensive but did not require highly specialized equipment or machining to exact tolerances. A steam locomotive would require tolerances of .01 inch while a diesel engine would require tolerances of .0001, two orders of magnitude difference. Diesels also required more specialized knowledge, especially of electrical systems, while steam locomotives required more general mechanical aptitude. To draw a parallel, the steam locomotive would be akin to a Model T that could be repaired by a shade tree mechanic or out in the barn with general tools. The diesel locomotive would be more like a current, computer-controlled automobile that has to be taken to specialized service facilities for all but the most basic maintenance. The old adage of the shop forces was that on a steam locomotive it took a worker five minutes to find a problem and five hours to fix it while the on a diesel it took five hours to find a problem and five minutes to fix. Steam locomotives had much of the machinery out in plain view where it could be relatively easily accessed. Even such a large repair as replacing boiler tubes could be performed at many facilities.

To appreciate more fully the dieselization process, specific steam locomotives should be compared and contrasted with their diesel counterparts. Steam locomotives were classified in different ways by various railroads and builders. Many times, railroads changed the classification systems with new management. Although there was no universal system, the Whyte system was the most common and, while far from complete, at least offered a relatively simple means of classifying steam locomotives. This system, established in 1900, designated locomotives by their wheel arrangement. The first number is the number of wheels in the leading truck, the second (and third if applicable) the number of drivers, and the last the number of trailing wheels (see table 2). While this system has many shortcomings, it is universal and can be used to describe locomotives of any era and from any manufacturer. Many locomotive types were also named. The most common names are included in the table. In the text locomotives are referred to by either name, Whyte designation, or both.

By the early 1900s, many factors went into determining what type of locomotive should be built for what type of service. The wheel arrangement, weight on drivers, driver diameter, number and size of cylinders, simple or compound, and other elements were all determined by the intended service of the locomotive. Locomotive design was based on empirical experience and varied greatly from railroad to railroad. Each railroad determined the characteristics that it required individually. A 2–8–0 type on the Pennsylvania railroad would not be the same as one built for the Illinois Central or Union Pacific. Each railroad contracted with the steam locomotive builders for locomotives custom built for its own unique operational parameters. These included size and weight, fuel, power, and many others. Steam locomotives were not mass produced machines but were batch produced to individual requirements for each order. The mechanical and motive power officials on each railroad had the ultimate authority in designing the motive power for their railroad. When standardized, mass produced diesels entered the scene, these officials lost much of their power and prestige.

Table 2   Steam Locomotive Classifications

Representation	Whyte System Designation	Name
OO	0–4–0	Switcher
OOO	0–6–0	"
OOOO	0–8–0	"
oOOO	2–6–0	Mogul
oOOOo	2–6–2	Prairie
oOOOO	2–8–0	Consolidation
oOOOOo	2–8–2	Mikado
oOOOOoo	2–8–4	Berkshire
oOOOOO	2–10–0	Decapod
oOOOOOo	2–10–2	Santa Fe
oOOOOOoo	2–10–4	Texas
ooOO	4–4–0	American
ooOOo	4–4–2	Atlantic
ooOOO	4–6–0	Ten Wheeler
ooOOOo	4–6–2	Pacific
ooOOOoo	4–6–4	Hudson
ooOOOO	4–8–0	Twelve Wheeler
ooOOOOo	4–8–2	Mountain
ooOOOOoo	4–8–4	Northern
ooOOOOOo	4–10–2	Southern Pacific
ooOOOOOOo	4–12–2	Union Pacific

Duplex and Articulated Locomotives		
ooOO=OOoo	4–4–4–4	(Duplex)
oooOO=OOooo	6–4–4–6	"
ooOO=OOOoo	4–4–6–4	"
OOO=OOO	0–6–6–0	(Articulated)
oOOO=OOOo	2–6–6–2	"
oOOOO=OOOOo	2–8–8–2	"
oOOOOO=OOOOOo	2–10–10–2	"
oOOO=OOOoo	2–6–6–4	"
oOOO=OOOooo	2–6–6–6	Allegheny
ooOOO=OOOoo	4–6–6–4	Challenger
ooOOOO=OOOOoo	4–8–8–4	Big Boy

This is not a complete list but covers most twentieth-century locomotives.

Because switching locomotives operated at low speed and needed to have a high tractive effort, they needed a small driver diameter, relatively high weight on drivers, and usually a large number of drivers. Typical custom switching locomotives of the 1920s and 1930s were 0–6–0 or 0–8–0 type with small diameter drivers, usually around 50 inches. Many railroads also used older road locomotives for switching. Smaller 2–6–0 and 2–8–0 types that had been displaced from road freight trains were put to work in yards and industrial areas where their small size and lower power were not a disadvantage.

Road-freight locomotives needed to have high tractive effort for moving tonnage but also the capability to attain a good speed. Higher speeds required locomotives to have leading trucks to help them track effectively through curves and switches. While the 2–8–0 Consolidation was adopted almost universally for road-freight power in the first decade of the twentieth century, it began to be again outclassed by ever longer and heavier trains. Cars were increasingly made of steel instead of wood and not only weighed more but were able to carry much more. Speed also became an increasing concern after 1920. To make a locomotive faster and more powerful, its steam producing capacity must be increased. To do this a larger boiler as well as a larger firebox with more area for burning coal is necessary. To support this larger firebox a trailing truck is also necessary. Therefore the 2–8–0 was turned into the 2–8–2 Mikado type, which quickly became the preferred freight engine of the 1920s.[16] If more tractive effort was needed, the Mikado could be stretched into a 2–10–2 Santa Fe type, so named for the Santa Fe railroad, the first to use the new locomotive type in heavy, western mountain service. Typical driver diameters for these locomotives were fifty to sixty five inches.

As the 1920s continued and competition heated up, speed became ever more important for freight train operations. It was no longer good enough to simply couple as many cars to a locomotive as it could take and send it out on the main line at ten to twenty miles per hour. Freight, especially perishables such as meat, fruit and vegetables, and time sensitive freight like mail and express, now had to move at forty, fifty, or even sixty miles per hour. For roads that needed to move freight at speed, a new type of locomotive was in order.[17] Just as increasing the steaming capacity and hence the speed of the 2–8–0 Consolidation led to the 2–8–2 Mikado, increasing the steaming capacity of the 2–8–2 led to the 2–8–4 Berkshire. First built by Lima Locomotive Works in 1924, the Berkshire was a thoroughly modern steam locomotive that remained in production until well into the diesel age in 1949.[18] As with the Mikado before, the Berkshire was stretched. This stretched version became the 2–10–4 Texas type, so named for first customer, Texas and Pacific, and was widely adopted for heavy duty freight service by railroads such as the Pennsylvania, Chicago Great Western, Chesapeake & Ohio, Kansas City Southern, and Santa Fe. The Berkshire and Texas types embodied the superpower concept promulgated by the Lima Locomotive Works.[19] In essence this philosophy was that to move a heavy train at speed a locomotive had to have not only relatively large drivers but a large firebox with a large grate area entirely behind the drivers. Steam locomotives require much more steam to move at high speed than they do at low speed, which could be provided by the large firebox, but because of the added weight an extra axle was needed for the trailing truck.

Built for speed rather than just pulling capacity, passenger locomotives generally had large drivers and four wheel leading trucks. The typical large passenger locomotive of the 1890s, the 4–6–0 Ten-wheeler, was enhanced with a trailing truck to create the 4–6–2 Pacific type with large sixty to eighty inch drivers. The Pacific was first built in 1901 and was a successful design. It quickly became the standard passenger locomotive and remained in production and in service until the end of steam.[20] For most railroads the Pacific was adequate for all but the longest and heaviest express passenger trains. The long and heavy trains of a few roads necessitated something more powerful. Some railroads, most notably the New York Central and Canadian Pacific, further developed the Pacific into the 4–6-4 Hudson with added power and pulling ability. It performed well on such notable passenger trains as the 20th Century Limited. The Hudson can be considered the penultimate development of the passenger steam locomotive. For passenger service in mountainous territory or for trains that were too long and heavy for the Pacific, the 4–8–2 Mountain was developed. The Mountain was widely used for heavy passenger service but also found a use in hauling time-sensitive freight, such as perishables.[21]

There were a limited number of locomotives that were designed for both fast freight and heavy passenger service and were classified as dual use. These locomotives were heavy 4–8–2 or 4–8–4 types and had many names depending upon the railroad. The most common name for the 4–8–4 was Northern.[22] The Northern combined most of the incremental improvements and good features of previous locomotives such as four wheel leading and trailing trucks and was the ultimate development of nonarticulated steam locomotive power in North America.[23] Most of the latest developments in locomotive technology were incorporated into the 4–8–4 type. Large 4–8–4 locomotives could generate up to six thousand horsepower and could achieve speeds of one hundred miles per hour and were equally at home hauling premier passenger trains or fast freight.

While the Northern, Berkshire and other examples of modern steam power were adequate for most jobs, again some roads demanded more power and tractive effort for their unique operating conditions. This led to the development of articulated and duplex drive locomotives. Articulated locomotives consist of two or more separate engines underneath one large boiler. Each engine tracks independently to help ease the locomotive around curves. Articulated locomotives may be either simple, with all four cylinders receiving steam direct from the boiler, or compound with a pair of high pressure and low pressure cylinders. Duplex drive locomotives are similar to the articulated type in that they contain two engines under one boiler, but they are contained in the same rigid frame and do not track separately. Both types were developed to put more power under the control of one crew to reduce or eliminate the use of multiple locomotives on the same train and therefore to save labor costs.

During the early years of the century, articulateds quickly progressed from the first 0–6–6–0 of the Baltimore & Ohio through 2–6–6–2 and 2–8–8–0 types to monstrous 2–8–8–2 types. These early articulateds were good at moving long strings of coal and other commodities but did so at slow speeds. Most of these early articulateds were also compound locomotives or Mallet types named after the French inventor of the type. A few notable articulated locomotives deserve mention. In a desire to place as much tractive effort as possible under the control of one crew, Baldwin built the triplex locomotives, three 2–8–8–8–2 types and one 2–8–8–8–4 in the mid-1910s. The 2–8–8–8–2 types were built for the Erie railroad, which for a time used the locomotives as helpers, a task where sustained performance is not required, but found that the locomotives could use steam much faster than they could generate it and sidelined them in 1927. The 2–8–8–8–4 was built for the Virginian railroad and never made a successful trip as it was too large to fit through the tunnels on the line.[24] While these unique locomotives were incredibly powerful they could not sustain that power long enough to do much of anything useful. The desire for ever greater tractive effort had reached a practical limit. Much more successful for the Virginian, which had many mountain grades to conquer in West Virginia as well as its name sake state, was the 2–10–10–2 type. They were ponderously slow (ten—fifteen miles per hour) but moved countless tons of coal out of the mountains and to the docks in Norfolk, Virginia.[25]

In the 1930s, with the success of the Berkshire, Hudson, and Northern types some railroads tried a similar idea with their articulateds. If adding a larger firebox and a four wheel trailing truck to the Mikado created such a successful locomotive in the Berkshire what would it do for an articulated? The answer came in the form of the 2–6–6–4, 4–6–6–4, 2–6–6–6 and 4–8–8–4 types. All were huge and powerful machines. All could likewise move heavy tonnage at high speed and over steep grades. The 4–6–6–4 Challenger was the most popular of the high speed simple articulateds and was used by railroads from the Western Pacific to the Delaware & Hudson. The last two locomotives, the 2–6–6–6 Allegheny and the 4–8–8–4 Big Boy share the titles of largest, heaviest, and most powerful reciprocating steam locomotives.[26] Each weighed in excess of a million pounds. However, they were only utilized by a couple railroads and then only in specific duties and regions. The monstrous Big Boys operated only on the Union Pacific almost exclusively between Ogden, Utah and North Platte, Nebraska while the Alleghenys were confined to their namesake mountains in Virginia and West Virginia on only two railroads.

Articulated locomotives were not without problems however. The front engine did not carry as much weight as the rear and was therefore prone to slip, especially when accelerating a heavy train. The front engine also experienced tracking problems on some locomotives at high speed and led to a rough ride for the crews. They also had twice the moving parts of a conventional locomotive and therefore almost twice the maintenance needs. Especially troublesome were the flexible steam connections to the front engine. Partly because of these reasons and partly to offset perceived developmental problems (that never manifested themselves) with large 4–8–4 and

2–10–4 locomotives, the duplex drive locomotives were developed in the United States. Eighty-one duplex drive locomotives were built, all but one for the Pennsylvania Railroad, which, together with locomotive builder Baldwin, advocated the concept. Duplex locomotives were similar to the articulateds in that they had two engines with four cylinders total under one long boiler. These engines were mounted together in a rigid frame, unlike the articulateds. The Duplex promised even greater power and speed than the best of the conventional 4–8–4 and 2–10–4 types, at least on paper.

The first duplex drive locomotive on the continent was an experimental Baltimore & Ohio machine with not only duplex drive but a high pressure, water tube boiler. Championed by George Emerson, the B&O chief of motive power, it was built by the B&O's own shops in 1937 and remained in service until 1943. It is doubtful that the locomotive saw much true operation as opposed to experimental and test runs. While the B&O learned its lesson and did not repeat the duplex drive experiment, the Pennsylvania bought into the concept wholeheartedly. Between 1939 and 1946, the Pennsylvania built eighty duplex drive locomotives of four distinct types. They looked powerful and impressive with streamline styling by noted designer Raymond Loewy, and indeed they were, at least in theory. The two most prolific locomotive models were the Q2, 4–4–6–4 freight locomotive and the T-1, 4–4–4–4 passenger locomotive. The T-1 especially was an impressive machine. These machines pulled full length passenger trains on flat track at over one hundred miles per hour across Ohio and Indiana. Since both types were so powerful, they were slippery machines and had trouble starting trains.

The Pennsylvania duplex drive locomotives were incredibly huge and powerful, but they had a dismal service record. In addition to the slipperiness of the T-1's noted above, they were plagued by valve problems and other ailments that kept them out of service and confined to the shop. As Pennsylvania Railroad historian Eric Hirsimaki stated, "Maybe the T-1's could run like the wind, but they were standing still too much of the time."[27] The modern 4–8–4 Niagara class locomotives of the New York Central, the Pennsylvania's primary competitor in long distance passenger service, were achieving almost triple the monthly mileage of the T-1s.[28] The Pennsylvania stored most of both the T-1 and Q-2 models by the end of

1949, and replaced them with cheaper to operate and easier to maintain diesels. The duplex locomotives were the ultimate limit of steam locomotive development in power, speed, and overall performance and proved that the traditional reciprocating steam locomotive had reached its zenith. While large, powerful, fast and complex, they simply required too much maintenance.

Large Northerns, Challengers, Alleghenies, and Texas locomotives could move tonnage at speed, but they too entailed certain disadvantages. The ever increasing size and weight placed stress on railroads' physical plants and also necessitated larger roundhouses, turntables, and other servicing facilities. Fully loaded Big Boys and Alleghenies could weigh well over one million pounds. To even operate these huge locomotives the track had to be made of the heaviest rail available and had to be properly constructed with a solid roadbed. Bridges had to be able to withstand not only the weight of the locomotives but also the dynamic stresses involved when, for instance, an Allegheny and a six thousand ton train passed over at fifty miles per hour. Tight curves had to be straightened out or otherwise bypassed if these large locomotives were to traverse said lines. Special facilities were needed to service these behemoths. Roundhouses and shops needed to not only be large enough to fit the locomotives in the door but also had to have the tools, lifts, and cranes necessary for servicing them. The large locomotives also had an insatiable appetite for fuel and water, and in some cases special larger facilities were built to accommodate them.

The rapid development in the 1920s and 1930s of new and larger steam locomotives is a clear manifestation of the desire of railroads to operate more efficiently. Larger locomotives with all the modern appliances on board could pull more freight or passengers than older types and could do so faster and more efficiently. More powerful locomotives would also eliminate the necessity to use multiple locomotives on some trains, thus eliminating labor expenses. The newer locomotives, while requiring the same sort of maintenance as older types, would require less heavy maintenance since they were new. The modern steam of the 1920s and 1930s was also designed to put ever greater power under the control of one crew to eliminate costly double heading and to enable consolidation of trains. While cutting labor costs in operation was already a prime objective of the railroads in the 1920s, cutting maintenance costs was secondary. One new and powerful locomotive would require less maintenance than two older and less powerful ones but the type of servicing and maintenance required would not differ. The railroads could then slowly and gradually eliminate maintenance labor and hope to avoid overt conflict, either by eliminating a large amount of jobs or by introducing radically new technology. New more powerful steam locomotives were clearly operating within the comfort zone of railroad management and operating officials.

With all the emphasis on modern steam development, the majority of locomotives in service during the time period of dieselization were not considered modern power. For example, the Santa Fe Railroad, home of 4–6–4 Hudsons, 4–8–4 Northerns, 2–10–4 Texas and 2–8–4 Berkshires, had numerous 2–8–0 Consolidations built in 1900 on its roster and active until 1954.[29] The Pennsylvania Railroad likewise had several 2–8–0 Consolidations built as early as 1907 in service as late as 1957.[30] Other roads were similar. According to an internal 1944 EMD market study, of the 41,755 steam locomotives owned by the railroads of the United States at the end of 1942, 26,485 or over 63 percent were twenty-five years or older, with an astonishing 9,814 or almost 24 percent built before 1910.[31] The Moguls, Ten Wheelers, and Consolidations that had been technologically eclipsed by more modern locomotives almost fifty years before were still performing daily service for most railroads, although in less demanding areas. While many roads bought new power in the 1920s few could afford to buy large numbers of the most modern steam power during the Depression of the 1930s. When diesels became widely available in the late 1940s, most steam locomotives were twenty or more years old. This is a vital element in the dieselization story.

In the preceding paragraphs I have referred to locomotives by not just the wheel arrangement or name but also by the railroad that operated them. This is essential as each railroad operated locomotives that were custom designed for that particular road. In many cases the motive power department from the railroad would actually design the locomotive and then contract with a builder to build their locomotive.[32] While many roads operated 4–8–4 types, a Northern built for the Union Pacific differed significantly from one built for the New York Central or the Rock Island. Steam locomotives were not mass produced but were batch produced to custom requirements negotiated between the railroad and the builder. Parts were not interchangeable between locomotives of the same type unless they were from the exact same order to the same builder and had the same specifications. Even then interchangeability was not guaranteed.

By 1939 the traditional reciprocating steam locomotive had reached the limit of its development in the United States. The most modern and powerful steam locomotives on the rails had become so large and heavy that they were only able to operate on tracks and territories that were specially configured for their needs. They were also increasingly complex with many added devices designed to wring more work out of each ounce of steam. These modern locomotives were efficient and capable, especially compared to locomotives a generation earlier but were still direct descendants of the Rocket and Tom Thumb of the early days of railroading over one hundred years before. While their performance was adequate for most purposes, they required daily servicing and maintenance and needed armies of skilled craftsmen to maintain them in top form.

DIESEL DEVELOPMENT

North American railroads were literally constructed around the steam locomotive. However, things would change and change drastically during the middle decades of the twentieth century. To understand these changes and to understand why they affected different railroads at different times and in different ways a brief but thorough study of the history and development of the diesel locomotive in North America is necessary. The diesel locomotive, like the steam locomotive, embodied not only the engineering skill of its builders, but the hopes and aspirations of its builders and operators. This must be understood in order to understand the story of dieselization. What follows is not a comprehensive accounting of the diesel locomotive industry but is rather designed to give suitable background so that the actions of individual railroads as well as larger, industry-wide trends can be analyzed.

During the heyday of steam locomotives, the 1890s, the diesel engine was developed in Germany by Rudolph

Diesel.[33] The diesel engine is an internal combustion engine that uses the heat of compression instead of a spark plug to ignite the fuel. Diesels operate at much higher compression ratios than spark ignition engines and consequently achieve much higher thermodynamic efficiencies from 30 to 35 percent.[34] Diesels, like all internal combustion engines, come in either two or four cycle varieties.[35] Diesels achieved notable successes in the marine and stationary environments in the early decades of the century. Factories and industrial plants that required power often converted from stationary steam engines to diesel engines. Marine diesels especially achieved notable successes, most spectacularly in World War I submarines.

Early diesel engines had several disadvantages compared to steam locomotives for use in railroad service. They were heavy for their power output although they were capable of running at low speeds for long periods of time. They were difficult to start and stop and were better suited to constant speed operation, not a characteristic of most railroad service. Diesels had to be machined to exact tolerances, up to one ten-thousandth of an inch, and were susceptible to dirt and grime, much more so than the more simply and ruggedly constructed steam engine. There was also the problem of transmitting the power from the engine to the rails. Because of these limitations, diesels were not initially judged fit for the rigors of railroad service and were first used in the cleaner and more controlled environments of stationary and marine applications.

Almost all diesel locomotives that operated on the North American continent were actually diesel-electric locomotives. In these locomotives, the diesel engine drove a generator or alternator that produced electricity, which powered electric traction motors on the axles. The advantages of this system over other systems such as mechanical power transmission are numerous. In the diesel-electric system each axle can be powered thus producing more tractive effort than other systems. In contrast to steam locomotives where significant portions of the total weight were carried by the leading and trailing trucks, as well as the tender, the diesel-electric allowed all of the weight of the locomotive to be put to use over the driving wheels if it was so designed. At low speeds the diesel-electric was able to exert tremendous force. The reasons are complex but are inherent in the operation of electric motors. The limiting factor at low speeds was not the output of the engine in horsepower or the output of the generator, but the adhesion between the wheel and the rail. The diesel-electric system adds weight when compared to a mechanical linkage, but railroad locomotives have to be heavy to utilize fully their power. A locomotive with an abundance of power but little weight would just sit and spin its wheels.

Other transmission methods such as diesel-mechanical and diesel-hydraulic were tried. Small locomotives with mechanical transmissions were successful but they were typically so small that they were only of limited use. Some of these locomotives still exist and can be seen shuffling a car or two around at grain elevators and gravel pits or pulling carloads of tourists at the local zoo. There were a few attempts at diesel-hydraulic locomotives with transmissions similar to an automatic on an automobile, but they were not generally successful in the operating environment of the United States.[36]

Another unique technical characteristic of the diesel electric locomotive is its capability for dynamic braking. Since the late nineteenth century, railroads had relied on the automatic airbrake developed by George Westinghouse. Braking was a simple mechanical affair where brake shoes would press directly on the wheel of rolling stock, slowing the train. Air was used as the actuating mechanism for this system, much like how hydraulic fluid is used to actuate mechanical brakes in an automobile. Dynamic braking did not replace the air brake but acted in concert with it to provide better control of trains. Dynamic braking turns the electric motors on the locomotive axles into electrical generators through the flip of a switch; no mechanical transformation is necessary. These new generators exhibit resistive force that helps slow the train. The generated electricity is sent to resistor grids, usually located in the roof of the locomotive, where it is dissipated as heat.[37] Electric locomotives had originated the practice of dynamic braking and were able to go one step further by pumping the regenerated electricity back into the overhead wires or third rail. Dynamic braking reduces wear and tear on wheels and brake shoes. It is especially important in mountainous territory where prolonged conventional mechanical friction air braking would generate high brake wear and could cause potential overheating of wheels and axles, as well as possible depletion of the air reservoirs which could lead to a runaway train.

The first application of the diesel to railroad motive power was the direct result of Diesel himself. In November of 1905 Diesel teamed up with Sulzer-Imhoof of Switzerland and began to design a diesel locomotive. Sulzer did not begin to construct the locomotive until 1907, and even then it would be five years before it took to the rails.[38] It resembled a regular passenger car, complete with windows, over a 4–4–4 wheel arrangement. Internally it contained a large four cylinder, transverse mounted, V-type engine that drove a crankshaft that was directly connected to the drive wheels via side rods. This was not only a carry over from steam locomotive practice but was also common in electric locomotives of the time. Compressed air started the engine and therefore the train. At a predetermined speed the air was cut off and fuel admitted to the cylinders. This procedure was repeated every time the locomotive stopped. In trials the locomotive performed adequately, but once it entered actual service around Berlin its performance was dismal. After three trips the crankshaft broke, and after its repair a cylinder cracked six trips later.[39] The locomotive was removed from service after the last failure and scrapped in 1920. The problems were traced to the shocks that the engine endured due in part to the mechanical transmission. Every bump in the rail was directly transmitted to the precise inner workings of the diesel engine. However, this locomotive did prove that a diesel engine could at least operate in a railroad environment.

The weaknesses of the mechanical transmission quickly became apparent in the Sulzer locomotive. Other manufacturers had much better luck with an electrical transmission. Several manufacturers in different locations seemed to have the idea at the same time, but the honor of the first diesel electric drive for railroad service probably belongs to the United Swedish Electric Company. Around 1910 engineers coupled a small, seventy-five horsepower engine to a generator that, in turn, drove two traction motors that, in turn, drove wheels. This was contained in a carbody or structure that also housed limited passenger accommodations, making it a railcar rather than a true locomotive. First tests in 1912 were promising, and the car entered service in 1913 in Sweden with several others following it.[40] The Russians also achieved some measure of success with a diesel electric locomotive designed for service in Southern Russia and Central Asia, arid lands where both coal and water were scarce, while oil, from the Caspian sea region, was plentiful.[41] The locomotive itself contained two five hundred horespower engines each driving a generator connected to two traction motors. This is the first example of a diesel locomotive being used because of these external environmental factors rather than simply to save money or increase efficiency. Because of the disruptions of World War I and the Russian revolution, this pioneering effort was not repeated in the Soviet Union. Sulzer did not ignore these efforts and quickly came to the conclusion that the electrical transmission was the way to go. Beginning in 1912 they began producing diesel-electric railcars for German railways. These cars were much more successful than the earlier mechanical transmission locomotive, and some remained in service until 1939.[42]

The first effort at a diesel locomotive in the United States was undertaken not by the established steam locomotive builders Alco, Baldwin, or Lima but by General Electric. GE, a longtime builder not only of electric locomotives but also of gasoline-electric railcars, decided to try its hand at a diesel electric locomotive. They had previously built the first successful commercial internal combustion locomotive in the United States in 1913.[43] They built four diesel-electric locomotives in 1917 and 1918, but all were failures due to problems with the diesel engine.

As these examples illustrate, the weak link in diesel electric locomotive design by the 1920s was not in the transmission of power to the rails but in the diesel engine itself. The transmission problem had been effectively solved with the use of the electric generator—motor combination. A relatively lightweight, robust, high-output diesel engine with adequate control systems was needed, if the diesel-electric was to challenge the steam locomotive for dominance.

With the growth of all-weather highways and the popularization of the automobile, passenger traffic had started to shift away from the rails by the 1920s.[44] Passenger traffic in this period never amounted to more than 10 to 15 percent of the total operating revenue of most railroads except commuter dependent roads like the Central of New Jersey and Long Island.[45] In the 1920s and continuing into the lean years of the Depression, many railroads discontinued marginal or unprofitable local and branch line passenger runs while attempting to revitalize the long-distance and express runs with new, often streamlined equipment. Since passenger service was highly regulated by the ICC, the railroads were forced to keep money losing passenger service on many lines that they would have rather abandoned.

Rail motorcars replaced steam locomotives and passenger coaches on many surviving local and branch line runs. These motorcars were a diverse group. About the only thing that can be said of them collectively is that they utilized internal combustion engines housed in carbodies that also contained passenger accommodations or provision to carry baggage and express. Some of these motorcars were true diesels, but most were gasoline-electric; some were gasoline-mechanical with geared or even chain-link power transmissions. Some motorcars could pull a trailer that housed additional passenger accommodations or even a freight car or two. Others were entirely self-contained and did not have the power to pull additional cars.[46]

The motor railcar has had a long and varied history.[47] Early experiments in internal combustion for railroad use were carried out by the McKeen company in the first decade of the twentieth century. W. R. McKeen was the superintendent of motive power and machinery for the Union Pacific and built a self-propelled gasoline mechanical railcar in the UP's Omaha Shops in 1905.[48] The Union Pacific then formed the McKeen company to build and market the self-propelled railcars. The Union Pacific and Southern Pacific were large users of these early McKeen cars but many other railroads tried them out before the McKeen company was dissolved in 1920. These early railcars had mechanical transmissions similar to those found on highway trucks and busses. Some of them were literally busses with railroad wheels. Mack, most famous for its trucks, dabbled in the railcar market for a time and built many small gasoline-mechanical motorcars. Brill, more famous for its electric trolleys and streetcars also built gas electric and gas mechanical railcars.[49]

In the early 1920s, the newly formed Electro-Motive Corporation (EMC) had the idea to replace the mechanical transmission, the weakest link in the design, with an electrical generator and motor. While this was an important development it clearly followed developments in Europe and other experiments in the United States such

Photo 1. McKeen Motor Car. Courtesy of the Union Pacific Museum.

as those conducted at General Electric. EMC also realized that service and support were as important as the
manufacturing and sought to excel in this area. The first
production vehicle in 1924 included electric transmission.
The sales statistics of EMC's gas-electric motorcars illustrates that railroads were aware of their benefits. In 1924
EMC sold 2 gas-electric motorcars; in 1925, 36, in 1926,
45 and by 1928 sales reached 105.[50] It seems a bit strange
that the most advanced technology as far as motive power
was concerned was used in local, branch-line passenger
service that many railroads would just the soon abandon.
This is the opposite of where one would expect innovative
new technology to be used. The motor cars were the first
internal combustion vehicles on most railroads and gave
years of satisfactory service on their oft overlooked, local
passenger runs.

Motorcars did save money for the railroads. On some
runs the motorcars would be as much as 50 percent less
expensive to operate than comparable steam powered
equipment. In 1925 the Lehigh Valley estimated that the
use of motorcars on five local and branch line runs would
save $122,820. The cost of five motorcars and one trailer
purchased from the newly formed Electro-Motive Corporation was $183,700.[51] These new motorcars would there-
fore pay for themselves in approximately a year and a
half. Many other railroads bought and used motorcars for
the same reason. For example, the Santa Fe Railroad had
a great number of branch lines in Kansas, Oklahoma, and
Texas that served sparsely populated areas but where
passenger, mail and express service was still needed.

These motorcars gave the railroads critical experience
with internal combustion motive power and electrical
transmission. They also introduced many railroads to the
Electro-Motive Corporation which would later become
the Electro-Motive Division of General Motors and the
leading diesel locomotive producer. The motorcars were
not looked upon with much respect by the crews. They
were nicknamed "doodlebugs" and were referred to as
busses on rails, a description that was not wholly inac-
curate. Most motorcars were not streamlined and were
generally not deemed to be aesthetically pleasing. They
ambled along at twenty five—forty mph and stopped at
every hamlet on the route. They were not high speed,
high power machines. They were not even officially listed
as locomotives. The reasons are multiple. Existing labor

agreements would have necessitated employment of additional workers and a higher pay rate for locomotives as opposed to self-propelled vehicles like the gas-electrics. This would negate much of the cost savings associated with the railcars. There were also cultural reasons. The small, slow and lightly constructed gasoline powered doodlebugs were not considered the equal of the large, heavy and powerful steam locomotives by railroad officials and train and engine crews alike.

While the railroads were turning increasingly to motorcars for their branchline passenger service needs, some were also beginning to experiment with diesel-electric power. The railroads that operated in New York City faced a problem. They had to deliver goods and passengers to the city, but their smoky steam locomotives raised the ire of the residents and, eventually, the city government. Various antismoke laws were passed that sought to reduce or even eliminate the pall of coal smoke that hung over Gotham. One solution was electrification. This was implemented by the New York Central when they built Grand Central Terminal and also by the Pennsylvania when they built Pennsylvania Station in the first decade after the turn of the century. The other railroads that operated in the city operated small waterside terminals served by car floats, barges that delivered rail cars. It was not practical or economical to electrify these small switching operations, so an alternative had to be found. The alternative was to employ gasoline and diesel electric locomotives not all that different from the motorcars operating at the time. While New York may have been one of the first cities to pass legislation regulating smoke from railroad locomotives, it was not the only one. Cleveland, Chicago, and even smaller cities like Akron, Ohio encouraged the use of new forms of motive power due to antismoke ordinances in the 1920s and 1930s.

The first truly successful diesel-electric locomotive was built by a consortium of Alco, General Electric, and Ingersoll-Rand for smoke abatement reasons. Since no one company possessed the necessary expertise to build, market, and support a complete locomotive, each corporation produced part of it. Ingersoll-Rand supplied the diesel engine, GE the electrical equipment, and Alco built the car body that housed it all and undertook final assembly. It was sold to the Central of New Jersey in 1925 for operation in the small yards and terminals in and around

New York City. Dubbed CNJ 1000, it was widely acknowledged as the first commercially successful diesel-electric
locomotive and served a long and useful life not being
retired until after World War II.[52]

With the success of CNJ 1000 many other diesel switchers were put in service by railroads and heavy industries such as steel mills. These users quickly found that
the diesels had a higher availability for work as well as a
higher initial tractive effort than the small steam switchers that they replaced. Diesel switchers could work
almost twenty-four hours a day, while steam switchers
spent many hours getting needed service done. One study
from the 1920s held that for every eight hours in service
a steam locomotive needed 11.5 hours of maintenance
and servicing.[53] They had to be regularly watered and
fueled and had to have daily maintenance consisting of
shaking the grates and removing the ashes and clinkers.
Consequently one diesel switcher could do the work of
one and a half or even two steam switchers. In the tight
confines of urban switching yards, one diesel switcher
with minimal fueling facilities took up much less space
than two or three steam locomotives and the necessary
coaling and servicing facilities. This obviously saved on
labor and other costs. The switchers saved money on fuel
and did not need water. While some railroads may have
been forced into purchasing diesels initially because of
smoke abatement legislation, they quickly found out the
capabilities and cost effectiveness of the new form of
motive power.

Slightly after the introduction of diesel switchers in
and around New York City and the motorcar into local
passenger service, the long-haul, express passenger service of many railroads was revitalized with streamlined
equipment, new trains, and faster schedules. The most
famous of these streamlined trains was undoubtedly the
Chicago Burlington & Quincy "Zephyr" which entered
service in 1934.[54] Built by the Budd company, a long time
passenger car manufacturer in Philadelphia, the Zephyr
was at first glance unlike anything seen before. It was
constructed of stainless steel with a distinctive shovel
nose. It consisted of three cars including the power car
and all were articulated which meant that they shared
wheel assemblies. This made for a smoother ride as
well as saving weight. At the time and ever since many
have hailed the Zephyr as a revolutionary train. While it

clearly looked different than almost anything else on the rails and did have a revolutionary impact, it was the culmination of trends that had been long in development. It was not altogether unlike the gasoline-electric motorcars that had been operating on the rails for over ten years. The Zephyr simply was the conglomeration of many individual technological developments. For instance, the electric transmission was taken directly from earlier motorcar practice. The streamlining was borrowed from aviation practice and also simulated developments in Europe. The articulation was forecast in the M-190 motorcar of the Santa Fe Railroad.

The most revolutionary thing actually on board the Zephyr was the diesel engine itself. It contained a new design that was better engineered and more powerful for its weight than previous engines. This six hundred horespower EMC engine, designed and built by the Winton company and based on earlier US Navy submarine engines, was developed expressly with railroad service in mind. General Motors had bankrolled the development of this engine and was beginning to take an interest in dieselization of railroad passenger and freight services. With the development of this engine, all the pieces were in place to permit large scale dieselization efforts.

The effect that the early streamliners, and the Zephyr in particular, had upon the nation was striking. To officially introduce its new streamliner to the public, the Chicago Burlington & Quincy conceived a spectacular public relations demonstration. On May 26, 1934, the Zephyr ran from Denver to Chicago, a distance of over one thousand miles, in a special, thirteen hour and five minute, dawn to dusk run. Upon arrival in Chicago the Zephyr was escorted onto the main lakeside stage of the Century of Progress Exposition to officially inaugurate the festival. The effect upon the public was more than the Burlington management, especially president Ralph Budd could have ever hoped. Almost overnight the words streamliner and Zephyr entered public discourse. Thousands of people turned out track side to watch the Zephyr on its record breaking run. In the depths of the Depression the thoroughly modern, gleaming stainless steel Zephyr seemed to evoke a sense of hope. The little train settled down on a Kansas City–Omaha–Lincoln, Nebraska daily round trip. It not only cost about half as much to operate as the steam train it replaced, but hauled twice as many passengers.

While there was much more to the Zephyr than simple economics, at least on the most basic economic level the new technologies embodied in the streamlined train were paying a dividend.

The Union Pacific streamlined train M-10000 also illustrates how the streamliner developed out of the motorcar. It was an articulated 3-car train built by Pullman-Standard that drew upon many of the same developments as the Zephyr. It was streamlined inside and out and drew on contemporary aviation practice and industrial design in construction. However, under the riveted aluminum skin it was not dissimilar to a souped up motorcar. It contained an EMC (Winton) six hundred horsepower distillate engine attached to an electric transmission just like many motorcars.[55] It used the same fuel as many earlier motorcars. In its designation we also see that it was considered an outgrowth of the motorcar. The Union Pacific designated all of its motorcars with the letter M before their number. In the eyes of the motive power department the M-10000 was simply a glorified motorcar. It too called Kansas City home and ran from there west to the city of Salina, Kansas. It offered similar cost savings and increases in passenger traffic as the Zephyr.

After the success, both technological and economic, of the Zephyr and M-10000, other railroads and manufacturers decided to look into the streamliner phenomenon. This resulted in streamlined trains on the rails from Boston to Mobile to San Francisco by the late 1930s. Alco, alone among the steam locomotive builders entered the diesel streamliner business by manufacturing the engine for the Rebel streamliner of the Gulf Mobile & Northern (GM&N). The train itself was constructed by long time railroad car manufacturer, American Car and Foundry. The Rebel was also the first streamliner not to be articulated. This offered additional flexibility in operations. The GM&N and later the Gulf Mobile & Ohio capitalized on this flexibility by switching cars in and out and splitting and combining trains to allow through, streamlined service between St. Louis and Mobile and between St. Louis and New Orleans. This flexibility was also useful in case there were a mechanical problem. Instead of the whole trainset being pulled out of service just the bad coach or power car could be removed while the others could be left in service, generating revenue.

Photo 2 This publicity photo taken at Kansas City Union Station shows the Union Pacific M-10000 on the left and the Burlington Zephyr on the right. The M-10000 contained a spark ignition distillate fueled engine while the Zephyr contained a true diesel. Both were lightweight articulated trains. Courtesy of the Union Pacific Museum.

Photo 3   The Gulf Mobile & Northern Rebel diesel streamliner is seen here in December 1935 at New Orleans. While a lightweight streamlined train it did away with the articulation of the earlier Zephyr and M-10000. Courtesy of the Museum of the Rockies, Ron V. Nixon Railroad Photography Collection.

Some railroads also operated long distance, luxury streamliners quite different, at least in amenities, from their small, short distance contemporaries. The two most famous of these pioneering long distance streamliners were the Santa Fe Super Chief and the City of San Francisco. The City of San Francisco was designed from the outset as a long distance, luxury train, quite unlike the short sprints of the Zephyr and M-10000. To compete it had to have diesel power, not only for performance reasons but also for marketing reasons. What train could be advertised as modern luxury with an old fashioned steam locomotive on the front? The City of San Francisco operated from Chicago to its namesake over the rails of the Chicago & North Western, Union Pacific, and Southern Pacific and cut almost a full day off the travel time of the previous steam powered trains.

The Super Chief was undoubtedly one of the most famous passenger trains of all time. It was the fastest and most luxurious way to travel between Los Angeles and Chicago and points in between. To power this new streamlined train, the Santa Fe chose diesel power. EMC delivered two custom built long-distance passenger locomotives in August, 1935. These locomotives, the 1 and 1A, were essentially boxcars with engines inside and were not streamlined to the extent of the earlier Zephyr and M-10000.[56] Beneath the rather humble exterior were two nine hundred horsepower diesel engines in each locomotive. When operating together, the locomotive could generate three thousand six hundred horsepower, more than enough to wisk a streamlined passenger train across the Kansas high plains at ninety miles an hour. Climbing the 3 percent grade of Raton Pass on the Colorado–New Mexico border was more than the diesels could handle, however, so steam helpers were used. The 1 and 1A, along with their sister unit, the B&O 50, set the pattern for subsequent EMC and later EMD passenger locomotive production.

Streamlined trains were powered, not only by diesel-electric locomotives but also by modern streamlined steam locomotives. Many railroads decided to jump on the streamlining bandwagon by taking older passenger locomotives and giving them a sheet metal outer covering to make them appear streamlined.[57] Even in the late 1930s, with the proven efficiency of diesels for high speed passenger operation, many railroads opted for steam locomotives. The capability of the diesel-electric for high-speed passenger service had been demonstrated convincingly by the record breaking run of the Burlington Zephyr in 1934 and the subsequent streamliners such as the Super Chief and City of San Francisco. On railroads like the Erie, Lehigh Valley, Lackawanna, and even the mighty Pennsylvania and New York Central, the internal combustion engines in motor cars would be relegated to the branch lines and local runs, while the big name trains would continue to be steam powered. In contrast, other railroads such as the Baltimore & Ohio, Santa Fe, Seaboard Air Line, Gulf, Mobile & Ohio, and Chicago, Rock Island & Pacific were dieselizing their passenger services. Cost was likely a key factor. Slapping some sheet metal on an old 4–6–2 and painting it bright colors was a cheap way to cash in on the streamlining craze for the fraction of the cost of a diesel powered train.

Why did some railroads choose steam while others embraced the diesel? There are several points to consider. Diesels were still seen to be experimental. Many thought they were good for publicity stunts like the Zephyr but not for real, day in day out heavy railroading. The Zephyr and other streamliners were relatively light weight and were judged by some as not rugged enough for the day to day service that they would encounter. This conclusion was not without merit. There were other efforts at small lightweight railcars, some even with rubber tires, that were failures due in part to their less robust construction. The large coal hauling roads also had a vested interest in staying with coal powered locomotives so they would not alienate their largest shipper, supplier, and customer. Institutional inertia also played a large role. Many railroads adopted a conservative, wait and see approach. Even the Santa Fe, Union Pacific, and Burlington, roads in the forefront of the diesel revolution, operated streamlined, high-speed, steam passenger locomotives. Perhaps they were hedging their bets so that if the new diesels did not pan out over the long haul, as many thought they would, the railroads could still rely on their modern steam passenger power. Lastly, being in the depths of the Depression, many railroads simply did not have the capital to go out and purchase expensive new streamlined locomotives and cars.

While many railroads did not purchase streamliners or diesel passenger locomotives, many of the same roads did experiment with diesel switchers. Throughout the 1930s, while the streamliners were the high profile application of the diesel engine to railroad service, the lowly switcher, hidden away from the public in freight yards, steel mills, and on the docks, began to transform the industry. While the streamliners captured most of the attention with their flashy paint and custom styled exteriors, the diesel locomotive began to transform how switching, and railroading was done.

As discussed above, the first diesel switchers had been developed in the early 1920s for use in and around New York City in response to antismoke legislation. While municipal legislation may have forced the railroads into purchasing these locomotives, they soon discovered that the diesel had advantages of its own that made it an efficient and worthy performer. For slow speed switching service it was especially well suited. Railroads and heavy industries such as steel mills and iron and copper mines across the country began to experiment with diesel switchers. The production statistics reveal the success of these early switchers. Between 1924 and 1928 the Alco-GE-Ingersol Rand consortium produced thirty-three boxcab switchers similar to CNJ 1000 for customers ranging from the Great Northern to Utah Copper to Red River Lumber.[58] In the early and mid-1930s diesel switchers continued to be purchased, despite the severe decline in railroad business due to the Depression. Alco was the leading producer of diesel switching locomotives during the early 1930s but was joined by EMC in 1935 and Baldwin in 1937.[59] By the end of the decade, there were several hundred diesel switchers scattered across the country in freight yards, passenger terminals, on docks and in industrial plants.

While the switchers did their work hidden away from the public eye, some railroads in the late 1930s continued to purchase flashy streamlined locomotives. However, these locomotives were different from the custom built streamliners. As with the switchers with which they shared many components including diesel engines, these new passenger locomotives were standardized and mass produced, although with many customizing options available. The most successful of these units were the EMC and EMD E-units. EMC and some railroads recognized that despite the successes of Zephyr type streamliners they were limited in application and flexibility. More potential and a larger market existed in dieselizing existing heavyweight passenger trains or new streamlined services consisting of larger trains. The E-units were true locomotives, not just power cars that had to be mated to a specific train set like those of the Zephyr, Rebel, and City of San Francisco streamliners. An E-unit could pull everything from a small branch-line local to the most luxurious, all-Pullman Limited. This flexibility is what made the E-unit so popular and successful.[60] EMC abandoned previous box like designs, some of which were used by the Santa Fe and B&O, for streamlined locomotives and produced a rakish nose and highly styled body that seemed to be moving even while it was standing still. All internal systems were similar but appearance was highly customized by the railroads that used them in accordance with traditional steam locomotive practice. For example, the E-2 units had round porthole type windows instead of the square windows of the E-1 and oval windows of the EA and EB.[61]

In operations the new units were quite successful. The B&O, long the underdog in competing for New York–Washington–Chicago passenger service, was better able to compete with the mighty Pennsylvania Railroad by using the new locomotives. The diesels were able to maintain competitive schedules with the newly electrified Pennsylvania railroad main line between New York, Philadelphia, Baltimore, and Washington, D.C. The Santa Fe, already the leading passenger railroad between Chicago and Texas and California, put the new locomotives at the head of such trains as the Chief and the Super Chief. The E unit allowed roads to remain competitive or to enhance their existing lead in passenger service depending on the particular circumstances of the operating railroad.

Already producing a variety of switcher designs, Alco entered the diesel passenger locomotive field in 1940 with their DL-109 type.[62] It was also a streamlined dual engine locomotive of two thousand horsepower similar to the EMC E-unit but fewer were sold. The largest user by far was the New York, New Haven and Hartford Railroad which rostered sixty of the seventy-eight units built. Had War Production Board controls not limited production, the DL-109 may have been used more widely. The New Haven was noted for using the locomotives on passenger trains during the day and on fast freights overnight. While being generally comparable in performance, it was generally inferior to the EMC E-units in maintenance and servicing concerns.

Despite the successes of the passenger locomotives the manufacturers, especially EMC, realized that to truly transform the railroad industry the main line freight trains had to be dieselized. Alco and Baldwin, being steam locomotive producers did not have the impetus or desire to completely dieselize the industry and were apparently satisfied to play second fiddle to EMC and later EMD. To dieselize main line freight service would require a locomotive that was more powerful than a single 1800 hp E-unit and that was customized for freight operation. It would have to outperform the best of the steam locomotives then available such as the 4–6–6–4 Challenger and 2–10–4 Texas types but be more flexible than either. The answer was the EMC FT, the single most important locomotive in the history of dieselization and one of the most historically significant locomotives in railroad history.

The FT was, "The Diesel that did it" according to long time *Trains* magazine publisher David P. Morgan.[63] Although it may have been revolutionary in its effects, the FT clearly embodied many of the characteristics of the earlier E-units. It had a similar streamlined shape, but the nose was not as rakishly slanted as on the early E-units. The FT can in many ways be thought of as a stretched E-unit contained in two separate units. The E-unit housed two engines of 900 hp each in one unit. To get the extra horsepower needed for freight applications, EMC used a 1350 hp engine. Two 1350 hp engines would not fit into one unit without making the unit overly long so it was simply divided into two separate units. These were not initially numbered individually but were numbered per A-B unit set. The A unit had the cab with crew facilities and controls while the B unit did not. Also, initially the A and B unit were semipermanently connected with a rigid drawbar, not a normal coupler. This indicated that the units were not designed to be separated except for heavy maintenance.

The first four unit demonstrator, numbered 103A and 103B, rolled out of EMC's new manufacturing plant in LaGrange, Illinois, in November 1939. It went on a 83,764 mile demonstration tour through thirty-five states on twenty railroads from November 1939 to October 1940.[64] It demonstrated on freight and passenger trains and in all classes of service. From the Boston & Maine and New York Central to the Western Pacific and Santa Fe, the FT proved that it could handle almost any job that it was given.

The Santa Fe was so impressed with the FT that it almost immediately ordered two, four unit locomotives for use in the desert southwest, where water for steam locomotives was scarce. Orders quickly followed from the Southern, Great Northern, and Baltimore & Ohio railroads. Even the coal dependent anthracite roads Lehigh Valley, Reading, and Lackawanna ordered FTs. Diesel freight locomotives had indeed arrived, but their success was limited by the outbreak of World War II.

During the war, dieselization was put on hold. In fact, many railroads bought or built new steam locomotives to handle wartime traffic. Some of these roads wanted diesel power but had to settle for steam locomotives because of production controls. The War Production Board exercised strict control over locomotive manufacturers and all orders for locomotives had to be approved by it. The heavy use of copper in locomotive electrical gear as well as the diesel engines themselves were tightly regulated by the WPB. Steam locomotives, with their simpler and more robust construction and less use of strategic materials were not as tightly controlled. Because of the success of the FT in its demonstration tour and of the first few locomotives delivered to the Santa Fe, the WPB determined that EMC (soon to become EMD) would produce only road locomotives (the FT) while other diesel manufacturers such as Alco and Baldwin would produce only diesel switchers.[65] Alco and Baldwin still produced steam locomotives during the war including some of the largest and most powerful locomotives ever built such as the 4–8–8–4 Big Boy. These manufacturers were also responsible for production of military equipment, with EMD producing diesel engines for landing craft and other uses and Alco producing tanks among other products. Baldwin concentrated on steam locomotive manufacture including locomotives for the US Army as well as other defense-related needs such as ship propellers.

The war, while generating huge amounts of traffic, and therefore profit for railroads, was nevertheless a taxing time. Maintenance on track and facilities was deferred to enable as many trains as possible to get over the rails. Maintenance of the complex shop facilities was also put off to allow every available man and woman to work on keeping the locomotives in service and moving freight and passengers. The labor shortage added to these concerns. At the end of hostilities, the locomotives and physical plant of the railroads were tired and suffering from the effects of delayed and deferred maintenance. The real impact of the war upon the railroads was complex. Freight and passenger traffic soared to all time highs, and every available locomotive was pressed into service. The business enabled many railroads that were hit hard by the Depression to regain solvency. However, by the end of 1945 even the most modern steam locomotives built in the late 1930s had been worked hard and, while not yet obsolete, were incurring heavy maintenance costs. While the steam locomotives were tired from their exemplary service, the war effort showed that modern steam could indeed operate on passenger schedules that matched those of diesels. On some high-speed passenger runs modern steam was the equal, at least in performance, to streamlined diesels. In freight service the opposite was true. The FTs proved without a doubt that they were fully capable of moving tremendous amounts of freight day in and day out without the special attention that the earlier streamliners received. The Santa Fe especially, with their main line through the desert southwest, proved that the diesel freight locomotive was here to stay. While the FT was the diesel that first was able to challenge modern steam in freight service, it was not the diesel that totally vanquished steam from the rails. With many tens of thousands of steam locomotives operating from Fairbanks, Alaska to Miami, Florida, it would take quite some time for diesels to eliminate steam from the rails.

After the war was over and War Production Board controls no longer applied, the three large diesel locomotive builders, EMD, Alco and Baldwin were joined by a fourth, Fairbanks-Morse. All of them began to add to their designs using research and experience gained during the war years. EMD improved on the FT with the F-2 and F-3 locomotives introduced in late 1945. The F-3 was phenomenally successful with 1807 units sold to United States and Canadian railroads.[66] EMD further refined their designs with the subsequent F-7 and F-9 locomotives introduced in early 1949. The F-7 was even more successful than the earlier F-units with 3849 units constructed for railroads in the United States, Canada, and Mexico.[67] While the F-units were a huge success, they were optimized for over-the-road through freights and passenger service. They did not have good visibility to the rear and were difficult to use for switching.

What was needed was a jack of all trades locomotive that could perform passenger, through freight, local freight, and switching jobs. This type of locomotive was named the road-switcher type. Recognizing that there was a large market for such a locomotive EMD tried to develop one. Their first unsuccessful effort, produced in 1947 and 1948 was the BL-2 type. The BL-2 was a uniquely styled locomotive that was a cross between a functional road-switcher and a streamlined F-unit. It was essentially an F-unit in a different shell with somewhat improved visibility, especially to the rear. It was a stop gap measure designed to get something out while engineers finished work on a clean sheet of paper road-switcher design. The BL-2 was not successful with only fifty-nine sales.[68] After this experience and perhaps drawing upon experience of the other builders, EMD got the road-switcher idea right with the GP-7 and GP-9 series of locomotives. While the BL-2 was a failure, the GP or General Purpose line was a huge success spelling doom for the steam locomotive. The GP-7 and GP-9 could perform almost any task on the railroad equally well. They were quickly nicknamed "jeeps," a comment not only on the GP abbreviation but on their usefulness for almost any task. Their design incorporated greater visibility to the rear, necessary in local and switching operation. The hood design was also better for maintenance than the carbody design of the F-unit. The new GP units were equally at home hauling fast freight across the prairie, lugging coal across the Blue Ridge, or hauling commuters in New Jersey. EMD had found the formula for success: capitalize on the diesel's ability to perform multiple roles. While EMD still offered streamlined carbody type E and F units for a few more years, they quickly shifted production to the GP road-switcher type of locomotive.

Alco, while not being able to produce road units during the war, quickly retooled from defense work and introduced the FA and FB model of one thousand five hundred horsepower freight units in 1946.[69] These units were Alco's answer to the F-3 series of EMD and were roughly equivalent in performance. Alco also introduced the PA for passenger service in 1946.[70] They actually realized the market for a road-switcher earlier than EMD and came out with the RS-1 and later the RS-2 and RS-3 locomotives. The RS-1 was widely used by the United States Army during World War II, most notably on the Trans-Iranian Railroad and at points in the Soviet Union. The RS-1 was quite successful with over five hundred built between 1940 and 1960.[71] This long production run, longer than most other locomotives, attests to its usefulness. The RS-2 and 3 locomotives, evolutionary developments of the RS-1, were even more successful with over two thousand of both models produced from 1946 to 1956.[72] The RS series was truly multipurpose and could be found in jobs ranging from New York City commuter service to heavy coal drags in the southern Appalachians to lumber and industrial shortlines.

Baldwin considered itself a steam locomotive builder and had problems converting to diesel production. Despite some initial stumbles they did produce a number of diesel locomotives. However the road-freight and passenger offerings were notoriously unreliable and in many cases were quickly replaced or shuffled to less intense jobs. Baldwin despite, or perhaps because of its long history with steam locomotives, did not pursue diesel locomotives as aggressively as they could have. Baldwin was most successful with switching locomotives. Beginning in 1937 and continuing to the end of locomotive production for the combined Baldwin-Lima-Hamilton Company in 1956, Baldwin and its successor produced 1901 switchers for US, Canadian, and Mexican customers.[73] They were reasonably successful in operation, and a few remain in operation in industrial plants and on isolated shortlines.

Despite the success of Baldwin with switching locomotives, they could not compete with larger road power built by EMD and Alco. Baldwin's first effort was an unsuccessful experimental passenger locomotive from 1943.[74] The next Baldwin passenger locomotive, the DR-12–8-1500/2, was popularly known as the centipede. It was a large, three thousand horsepower locomotive with two one thousand five hundred horsepower diesel engines in one unit. The unique feature about the centipede was its wheels and running gear. It consisted of a 4–8–8–4 arrangement with articulated cast steel trucks. This was a clear carry over from steam locomotive manufacture, from the wheel arrangement and cast steel trucks to the effort to cram as much horsepower as possible into one big locomotive. From 1945 to 1948, forty units were produced for domestic customers and fourteen for Mexico. The units were notoriously unreliable and maintenance intensive and were quickly demoted to less intensive and critical tasks.[75] Baldwin tried to manufacture other, less powerful passenger units during the same time period but met with few sales, less than forty units over the four years from 1945 to 1948.

Baldwin's lack of success with passenger locomotives would be mirrored with freight cab units. While EMD and Alco were selling hundreds and even thousands of F-units and FAs, Baldwin managed roughly 250 total sales of their various freight cab units.[76] Baldwin was somewhat more successful with the road-switcher type of locomotive, probably because EMD did not have a good road-switcher design until the GP-7 was introduced in late 1949. Baldwin produced several road-switchers beginning in 1946. The locomotives were capable machines but were outclassed by the Alco RS-1, 2, 3 locomotives and later the EMD GP-7 and GP-9. Crews did not generally care for the rough riding Baldwins and in at least one case they earned the nickname "mules" for their stubborn and unpredictable performance.[77] As with most other Baldwins, the road-switchers were retired when major repairs were due. A handful of units remained in service on industrial railroads and shortlines, however, into the 1990s. This is most likely due to the less demanding environment and the more specialized maintenance that a smaller road could provide.

A postwar newcomer to the locomotive industry, although a long time manufacturer of heavy machinery including diesel engines, was Fairbanks Morse (FM). It produced a number of diesel locomotive designs and, while never a major builder, did add some variety and choice to the locomotive industry. The claim to fame of the FM designs was the engine itself, originally designed for a US Navy specification for a submarine engine. FM engineers thought that it was equally well suited for locomotive service. The engine was a unique opposed piston design containing two pistons in one cylinder, each driving a crankshaft. It was compact but tall, which necessitated tall hoods on the FM diesels. When properly adjusted it was a smooth running and powerful engine, but if service was needed it often required the entire upper crankshaft to be removed, a time consuming process.

FM first produced a switcher type locomotive in 1944, although they had produced engines for railcars in the 1930s. The switcher was reasonably successful with over five hundred produced from 1944 to 1961.[78] Like the other builders FM entered the freight and passenger cab unit market. The locomotives were not completely successful with only a couple hundred built. They were plagued with problems with the engines and electrical equipment. Most were scrapped or traded in for new locomotives as soon as practicable.[79] FM was more successful with the road-switcher design, building a number of road-switchers from one thousand five hundred horsepower on up, including the massive two thousand four hundred horsepower Trainmaster locomotive. During its production run from 1953 to 1957, the Trainmaster was the most powerful single engine diesel locomotive available. The 127 that were built could be found hauling commuters along the San Francisco Bay on the Southern Pacific or moving freight across the Midwest on the Wabash Railroad. After complete dieselization was almost achieved, FM left the domestic locomotive market in 1958. The intricacies of the opposed piston engine ensured that the FM locomotives would be retired relatively early in their lives. No FM locomotives were left in operation on any railroad in the United States or Canada by the late 1990s. While the opposed piston engine may have been well suited for ships and stationary applications, it did not transfer well to railroads. Also FM at its Beloit, WI plant did not have adequate facilities necessary for true large-scale mass production of locomotives like Alco or EMD.

Last and least, in terms of number of locomotives produced, was Lima. A small but progressive steam locomotive builder, it was the last to change to diesel production and the first to succumb to the diesel revolution. After the drop in new steam locomotive orders following World War II, Lima merged with diesel engine maker Hamilton in 1947 to create Lima-Hamilton corporation. Lima-Hamilton produced a total of 174 diesel locomotives from 1949 to 1951 when they merged with Baldwin.[80] The locomotives apparently performed well but suffered the fate of most nonstandard locomotives and were quickly retired once they began to show their age.

There were other builders of diesel locomotives.[81] Most of these locomotives were small mechanical transmission industrial switchers and were not employed in large numbers by the major railroads. A long time supplier of railway equipment including electric locomotives, Westinghouse entered the diesel locomotive market early with small switchers built in the late 1920s. A few locomotives were produced in the 1930s, but after the war Westinghouse did not produce any diesel locomotives although their electrical equipment was used on many Baldwin built locomotives. General Electric supplied electrical equipment to most Alco diesel locomotives and produced small locomotives themselves, especially the forty-four ton type which was just under the ninety thousand pound cut off for using firemen on locomotives. A forty-four ton locomotive therefore would only have an engineer, saving money that would normally be spent on the salary of an additional crew member. Most railroads found the forty-four ton type to be too light to adequately move many cars and they were therefore confined mostly to industrial plants and other similar locations.

The locomotive industry continued to evolve in the 1960s and 1970s with GE entering the large locomotive field in 1960 replacing Alco as the number two builder. Alco finally gave up and left the locomotive manufacturing business in 1969, although their Canadian subsidiary, Montreal Locomotive Works, remained in business for a few years longer. EMD was the number one producer until the late 1980s when they were overtaken by GE.

Although they were both designed to do essentially the same job, steam and diesel locomotives were quite different not only in construction but in their capabilities and especially in the maintenance required. Diesel locomotives had several operating advantages over steam. First was high starting and low speed tractive effort or pulling power. Steam locomotives were limited in this regard due to the size of the cylinders as well as the diameter of the driving wheels. If a steam locomotive could start a train from a dead stop, it could move it at any speed up to the optimum speed of the locomotive. Diesels were the exact opposite. Even a small low powered diesel locomotive could move a train but did not have the power to accelerate the train to speed. Diesels had a decisive advantage in servicing. Diesel locomotives were not tied to trackside coal and water facilities like steam locomotives. This was a huge advantage and could drastically reduce travel times of freight and passenger trains alike. Diesels also did not require the same amount of manual en route lubrication since they did not have the large reciprocating rods and linkages of steam locomotives. Lubrication of the diesel engine itself was completely automatic. Diesel locomotives also had maintenance advantages over steam locomotives. Steam required daily care, from starting the fire and raising the boiler pressure to banking the fire at night and cleaning out the ashes and cinders. Diesels could simply be started and stopped nearly instantaneously, like an automobile. Longer term maintenance, however, was less clearly in favor of the diesel. Diesels were complicated machines with large engines as well as electrical equipment. All this machinery would require periodic repair in heavy maintenance facilities. Diesels had more parts and therefore more potential things to break or wear out and need replacement. Diesels were mass produced machines with all the advantages thereof. Parts were interchangeable between locomotives of the same model. Steam locomotives were essentially custom built for each application. Parts generally were not interchangeable even between locomotives built by the same builder for the same railroad. Steam locomotives during much of the period of dieselization did have a couple of important advantages. The first notable advantage was a lower initial cost. A steam locomotive could be half as expensive as a diesel of similar power and capability. Steam was also a bit more rugged and forgiving of poor maintenance.

Steam locomotives were custom built machines and differed greatly between manufacturer and railroad. Diesels were mass produced and differed only between manufacturer. Steam locomotives became much more powerful and efficient in the 1920s and 1930s but this came at the cost of added complexity and greatly increased size and weight. All steam locomotives, regardless of type, power or size, required extensive daily servicing and maintenance. This servicing and maintenance required extensive facilities and thousands of skilled workers. Diesels, while still in development in the 1920s and 1930s, did not require extensive daily maintenance and servicing. Diesels were complex machines with not only diesel engines but with complex electrical gear. The longer term maintenance and repair needs of this complex machinery were less clear than the short term lack of daily servicing. In terms of pure performance, steam and diesel were similar. Modern 1930s steam locomotives could move heavy trains at high speed as easily as diesels. With the exception of things like dynamic braking which was diesel specific, performance between early diesels and their modern steam counterparts was roughly equivalent. Now that the capabilities and requirements of operating both forms of motive power are known, the dieselization experience of individual railroads will be much easier to understand.

3
Dieselization Deciphered

THERE WAS NO ONE SINGLE MODEL FOR THE DIESELIZATION OF THE North American railroad system. Some railroads experimented early and often with diesels, while others actively resisted the tide of dieselization. Still others initially embraced diesels for some uses and not for others. There were many roads that maintained a dual motive power strategy utilizing both steam and diesel locomotives for many years. The reasons for these differing strategies are many and include government involvement, geography, size, operational characteristics, and business and corporate differences. The diversity of the North American railroad system at midcentury precludes a single model during the period of dieselization. There were literally hundreds of different railroads operating in all parts of the continent hauling both passengers and freight with different operating rules and philosophies.[1] In 1950 for instance, there were 127 class 1 railroads alone. Each railroad was its own corporate entity and had its own management and corporate structure and culture. Even different divisions on the same railroad may have had distinctive operating rules and regulations based in part upon local environmental and historical circumstances. Therefore, it is not possible to analyze one or even two railroads and draw conclusions that would apply to the entire railroad industry. The rail network was a system, and it can be best understood by looking at the entire system rather than at one specific part. However, the railroad system was a heterogeneous one composed of many small parts that operated semi-independently. To simply look at the overall picture while overlooking the individual details would be to miss much of the story of dieselization. Likewise, to only analyze one railroad would also miss the diversity and depth of experiences that American railroads had with the diesel. Dieselization affected the entire system, although at different times and in different ways depending upon local circumstances, and led to the restructuring of the American rail system in the face of a dramatically changing external business environment.

Even these broad economic trends effected different railroads in different ways. Roads with stable sources of revenue or operating in areas where industry was expanding
in the postwar era had a much different experience than
roads with a heavy passenger base and declining on line
industrial traffic. This restructuring continues to the
present. The diesel locomotive was the single most important technological change in railroading during the last
one hundred years but diesels were not the only agent of
change. While diesels may not have been the sole, or even
the leading, variable in the restructuring of the American rail system, it is impossible to imagine the current
system without diesel locomotives and the changes that
they brought.

The traditional story of dieselization emphasizes the
timing of diesel purchases and the builder of the locomotives. Doing so can shed some light on the process but this
approach has its limitations. Following this approach,
railroads are usually divided into three categories (early,
middle and late) based on their initial diesel purchases.
Early dieselizing railroads were characterized in the following ways. They were among the first to experiment
with diesel power, usually in the form of a significant
number of prewar switchers but also perhaps including
early streamliners and passenger locomotives. Many of
these early dieselizers also bought significant numbers of
EMD's FT model freight locomotives. While none of these
roads were fully dieselized before the war, they did dieselize or at least embarked upon a full scale dieselization
program during or immediately after the war as soon as
they were able to purchase enough locomotives to satisfy
their needs.

The bulk of the railroads generally did not experiment
much, if at all, with diesel power before the war. This may
have been due to financial difficulties or simply to a lack
of interest in diesel motive power. During the war they
saw the advantages gained by the early dieselizing roads
and decided to embark upon dieselization programs in the
late 1940s. Having missed the production of the EMD FT
and other units like the Alco DL-109, these roads bought
postwar units like the EMD E-7 passenger locomotive and
F-3 and F-7 freight locomotives and the Alco FA and PA
locomotives.

Some railroads were characterized by their active
resistance to dieselization. These roads remained almost

entirely steam powered even after the war and many explored new forms of coal burning steam power such as turbines, both direct drive and electric drive. These roads also bought new steam locomotives or heavily modernized their existing fleet during and after the war instead of purchasing diesels. When they did dieselize in the 1950s many of these roads missed the cab units like the EMD F unit and the Alco PA and FA. Instead these roads purchased the first of the large road-switcher offerings such as the GP-7 and GP-9 from EMD and various RS models from Alco.

There are several problems with this tripartite classification scheme. Forcing over one hundred individual railroads into three broad categories is problematic. A few railroads did conduct early experiments with diesel power but at the same time continued to invest in and search for improvement in their steam fleet. During the 1930s and early and mid-1940s some of these roads actively pursued a dual motive power strategy. Perhaps they did not want to put all their eggs in one basket until the clear winner was revealed. For instance railroads such as the Burlington, Union Pacific, and Illinois Central experimented early on with diesel power including streamliners but still continued to develop and purchase modern steam power. This dual motive power strategy does not easily fit into the above classification scheme. The early-middle-late classification scheme also assumes that the advantages of the diesel were obvious to everyone and it discounts the capabilities of modern steam and downplays geographic and corporate diversity. This periodic classification, while useful, fails to get beneath the surface and look at the many complex decisions to dieselize of the individual railroads.

In spite of the great diversity of the American railroad industry and its experience during dieselization, there are patterns of change that can be identified. The overwhelming consideration in dieselization was cost. In the highly regulated competitive environment of the 1920s, efficiency became the new goal of the railroads. In the Great Depression maximizing revenue from what little business existed was paramount. As stated earlier, railroads were facing rapidly increasing costs in the WWII and postwar period, which were not being met with corresponding increases in rates and fares. The desire to control costs, not the desire to increase performance or operational efficiency was the leading factor in dieselization. However, even this desire to control rapidly escalating costs manifested itself differently on different railroads. While the primary factor in dieselization was cost, other factors, namely, government regulation, competition, geography and environment, publicity and passengers, management philosophy and culture, traffic patterns and the coal industry all played a part in the decision to dieselize. Each of these factors will be analyzed with examples from the railroad industry. The rest of this chapter is organized as follows. Following the three ICC geographic regions, a series of railroads are analyzed to see what factors played a part in their decisions to dieselize. Emphasis is not placed strictly on the timing of locomotive purchases but on the complex interplay between various factors such as costs, competition, and operational characteristics that led to the embrace of the diesel.

During the middle decades of the century, the ICC divided railroads into three distinct geographic districts. The eastern district was roughly everything east of Chicago, Peoria, Illinois, and the Mississippi river and north of the Ohio and Potomac rivers. This district included the major trunk lines such as the Pennsylvania, New York Central, Baltimore & Ohio, and Erie, as well as smaller regional roads like the Boston & Maine and Western Maryland. The southern district was everything south of the Ohio and Potomac and east of the Mississippi. This district included roads like the Atlantic Coast Line, Southern, and Norfolk & Western. The western district was everything west of Chicago and the Mississippi.[2] This district included all the western transcontinentals like the Union Pacific, Southern Pacific, and Santa Fe, as well as other roads like the Chicago Rock Island & Pacific and Denver & Rio Grande Western. Within each district there were further divisions. For instance the western district was divided into a northwestern region, a central western region, and a southwestern region. For this study the only subdistrict or region that is important is the Pocahontas region of the southern district which was the states of Virginia and most of West Virginia. For the purposes of this study, shortlines and terminal roads are separated and placed at the end of chapter 4. Because of their size and operating conditions these roads cannot be analyzed with the rest of the railroads. We begin in the east, continue west then south.

EASTERN DISTRICT

We begin our survey of dieselization in the east. The eastern district was the heart and soul of industrial America in the middle decades of the twentieth century. From the coal mines and steel mills of Pennsylvania to the auto plants of Michigan and Indiana to the manufacturing and port cities of Baltimore, Cleveland, Chicago, and New York, all were connected by a web of railroads. Some of the largest and most powerful railroads in the world operated in this district as well as dozens of smaller roads. The variety in geography and railroad size was mirrored in the way that the companies responded to dieselization.

Lehigh Valley Railroad

Our journey begins with the eastern region Lehigh Valley Railroad. The Lehigh Valley was a midsized road of 1,229 miles of line operating from Newark, NJ, opposite New York City, westward through New Jersey to the Lehigh Valley of Pennsylvania.[3] There it turned north and ran through the anthracite coal region to Scranton and Wilkes-Barre. It continued north into New York State and ended its main line at Buffalo. It had an extensive network of branch lines in Central and Western New York State as well as in the anthracite coal region of Pennsylvania. For the first eighty years of its existence, the Lehigh Valley was primarily a coal hauler. It was initially built to transport anthracite coal to Philadelphia via transhipment on the Delaware Canal or similar shipment to New York via the Raritan Canal or the Central of New Jersey Railroad.[4] Lines were built northward to Lake Ontario and westward to Rochester, Buffalo, and Niagara Falls. Anthracite would be shipped to these cities for local use, transferred to other railroads such as the Erie for shipment further west, or loaded upon lake boats for distribution via the Great Lakes.[5]

The Lehigh Valley joined other railroads like the Delaware, Lackawanna & Western, Central of New Jersey, Lehigh & New England, and Reading in serving the anthracite coal fields. It also competed with other nonanthracite dependent railroads such as the Pennsylvania, New York Central, Erie, New York, Ontario & Western, and New York, Susquehanna & Western. The northeast was an extremely competitive area for railroads with five major roads offering New York to Buffalo service alone. Buffalo was not only an important industrial city but also a transportation gateway to the Great Lakes and the Midwest. Since freight rates were heavily regulated by the ICC by the 1920s and throughout the period of dieselization, the northeastern railroads had to compete in terms of speed, handling, and other forms of customer service.

By the 1920s the Lehigh Valley was a mature railroad with limited growth prospects. The decline of the anthracite coal industry and the shift away from its use for home heating was beginning to be felt as early as the 1920s. While anthracite haulage still accounted for a high proportion of total operating revenue, tonnage was beginning to decline. Merchandise freight steadily rose as a percentage of total operating revenue throughout the period. By the 1930s the Lehigh Valley made an active effort to diversify its traffic base. It concluded agreements with the New York, Chicago and St. Louis Railroad, commonly called the Nickel Plate Road, and the Michigan Central Railroad, a division of the New York Central System, to interchange traffic at Buffalo that was bound for New York and other northeastern cities. The Lehigh Valley was evolving from a coal hauler, generating most of its traffic online or within its own system, to a bridge route, with less on-line traffic and more interchange traffic from other railroads, particularly at Buffalo. This traffic consisted of everything from perishables to consumer goods destined for eastern markets, to paper, auto parts, and other semifinished goods destined for eastern factories or distribution centers. The statistics bear this out. In 1921 anthracite made up 37 percent of total operating revenue, while merchandise traffic accounted for 44 percent. By 1929 it was 27 percent for coal and 53 percent for merchandise, and by 1945 the numbers were 17 percent and 60 percent respectively.[6]

With this new, time sensitive and highly competitive bridge traffic, the Lehigh Valley needed locomotives that would be able to perform more efficiently than its older locomotives then in service. These older locomotives were primarily designed for hauling coal out of the mountains. It did not really matter how fast the coal was moved, so long as it got there. Therefore, these coal haulers were optimized for slow, heavy service with a large number of small diameter drivers. These locomotives, the bulk of the Lehigh Valley freight fleet, were typically 2–8–2 or 2–10–2

types and were built in the 1910s and early 1920s. The new
locomotives had to be faster and more efficient to handle
the time-sensitive merchandise traffic cost effectively but
without sacrificing horsepower or tractive effort.

One of the Lehigh Valley's prime competitors in the Buffalo to New York corridor was the Delaware, Lackawanna
& Western, popularly referred to as the Lackawanna. The
Lackawanna was one of the first railroads in the nation
and the first in the northeast to operate the fast, powerful and efficient 4–8–4 type of steam locomotive, ordering
some in 1927.[7] The Lackawanna was having such good luck
with their locomotives that the Lehigh Valley decided to
look into purchasing some as well. Here we see a theme
that will reemerge continually throughout the dieselization story. A neighboring railroad and competitor invests
in new motive power and, to remain competitive, other
railroads in the area also modernize their power. While
the new locomotives would have increased speeds for fast
freight trains, there were reasons for investing in new
power that had little to do with actual operational performance or efficiency. Corporate pride becomes a factor.
In the fiercely competitive railroad environment of the
northeast, any perceived advantage had to be matched.
Long established railroads with a rich tradition felt that
they must remain at the cutting edge of motive power
development.

The Lehigh Valley ordered single prototypes of modern
4–8–4 type locomotives from the American Locomotive
Company (Alco) and Baldwin Locomotive Works in 1931.[8]
The tests on these prototype locomotives showed that they
would be useful, so the Lehigh Valley ordered ten from
each builder. Further orders in 1935 and 1943 swelled the
number of this type of locomotive to thirty-seven. These
locomotives could power a scheduled fast-freight train
from one end of the railroad to the other, Buffalo to Oak
Island (Newark, NJ) at speeds of sixty miles per hour
with only one refueling stop.[9] While one coaling stop was
needed several water stops and crew change stops were
needed. They were the state of the art in steam locomotive power at the time, equipped with feed water heaters,
superheaters, and mechanical stokers. These locomotives
represented a significant evolution in technology from
the 2–8–2 and 2–10–2 class built just a few years earlier.
They could pull more freight than earlier locomotives
and required less heavy maintenance since they were

Photo 4 Baldwin Locomotive Works built this Lehigh Valley Railroad T-1 class 4-8-4 in 1932. It is seen here brand new at the Baldwin factory in Philadelphia before delivery. It is a good example of a modern state of the art freight hauling 4-8-4 of the late 1920s and early 1930s. Locomotives such as these would be the prime competition for the new diesels of the late 1930s. Courtesy of the Railroad Museum Of Pennsylvania (PHMC) H. L. Broadbelt Collection.

new. The labor savings from combining trains and need-
ing less heavy maintenance was considerable.

Like many railroads, the Lehigh Valley discontinued
many marginally profitable local and branch line passenger runs in the 1920s and 1930s. They also attempted
to revitalize long-distance and express runs with new,
streamlined equipment. Gasoline-electric rail motorcars
replaced steam locomotives and passenger coaches on
the surviving local and branch line runs. These motorcars did save money for the Lehigh Valley. On some runs
the motorcars were as much as 50 percent less expensive
to operate than comparable steam powered equipment.
The savings came not only from fuel and water but also
from labor, including both train and engine employees
and maintenance and shop forces. In 1925 the Lehigh
Valley estimated that the use of motorcars on five local
and branch line runs would save $122,820. The cost of
five motorcars and one trailer purchased from the newly
formed Electro-Motive Corporation was $183,700.[10] These
new motorcars would therefore pay for themselves in
approximately a year and a half. These motorcars gave
the railroad valuable experience with internal combustion motive power and electrical transmission as well as
establishing a business relationship with EMC.

At the same time as the introduction of the motorcars
into local service, the long-haul, express passenger service of the Lehigh Valley was revitalized with streamlined
equipment, new trains, and faster schedules. These new
streamlined trains were powered, not by diesel-electric
locomotives as on some other railroads, but by streamlined
steam locomotives. Even in the late 1930s, with the proven
efficiency of diesels for high speed passenger operation,
the Lehigh Valley opted for the steam locomotive. On the
Lehigh Valley the internal combustion engines would be
relegated to the branch lines and local runs, but the big
name trains would continue to be steam powered. This
policy did make sense from a cost standpoint. The Lehigh
Valley was never a major passenger road and other than
a few trains, did not devote substantial resources to passenger service. Instead of investing heavily in diesels for
streamlined passenger service, the Lehigh Valley took
existing 4–6–2 type locomotives and streamlined them
in its own shops. Gas-electric motorcars would pay substantial dividends but substantial investment in marginal passenger services on the main line simply was not

justified, especially in the tight times of the 1930s. The Lehigh Valley' primary competitors in passenger service also remained loyal to steam power until after the war. Since there was no primary competitor that embraced the diesel in the 1930s for passenger service, the Lehigh Valley did not feel the need to purchase diesels for competitive reasons like it did with the 4–8–4 locomotives.

Despite the conservative outlook of its management, the Lehigh Valley Railroad expressed an early interest in diesel-electric locomotives. The board of directors approved the "purchase of two 60 ton 300 h.p. gas-electric locomotives for use in New York City" on December 15, 1925.[11] They bought one from a consortia of Ingersol-Rand, GE, and Alco and one from Brill in 1926. This purchase followed on the railroad's positive experience with gas-electric motorcars, but may also have partly been in response to the purchase by a Lehigh Valley competitor, the Central of New Jersey, of the first diesel-electric switching locomotive built. This locomotive was also built by Ingersol-Rand, GE, and Alco and was placed in service in 1925.[12] The Lehigh Valley slowly bought more diesels and had sixteen on its roster by 1932. The manufacturers represented in this fleet included Alco, GE, Ingersol-Rand, Brill, Mack, and Electro-Motive Corporation. The reason behind these initial purchases lies with government legislation. These early diesels were used almost exclusively on the docks and yard tracks in and around New York City, which had passed various laws outlawing smoke producing steam locomotives within the city limits.[13] Despite the crude, almost experimental nature of many of these machines, they turned out to be durable and dependable, and were not retired from service on the Lehigh Valley until after World War II.

For switching operations, the Lehigh Valley purchased twenty-two locomotives over the four year period from 1937 to 1940. As the economy rebounded from the abyss of 1933, the Lehigh Valley had more traffic that needed to be handled and what better way to efficiently and cost effectively switch this traffic than with diesel switchers. These diesel switchers began to be used not just in the New York City area but in yards and terminals all over the system.[14] At this time many railroads realized the potential of the diesel-electric locomotive for switching duties. However, the Lehigh Valley was in the vanguard. Competing railroads such as the Central of New Jersey

and the Lackawanna did not invest in diesel switchers
to nearly the same extent as the Lehigh Valley. The CNJ,
after purchasing the first diesel-electric switcher, did not
purchase any more diesel locomotives until 1938 and did
not fully embrace diesels until after the war.[15] After being
initially forced to utilize diesels for reasons other than
cost of operation and efficiency, the Lehigh Valley management was starting to realize some of the cost saving
potential of the diesel locomotive in switching service.
However, the initial introduction of diesel power was due
not to its technical superiority or economic efficiency,
but because of legislative action and its perceived lack of
smoke pollution.

During the war, the dieselization drive of the Lehigh
Valley, and many railroads, was put on hold. Many railroads bought or built new steam locomotives to handle
wartime traffic. Some of these roads wanted diesel power
but had to settle for steam locomotives because of production controls. The Lehigh Valley was among this group,
purchasing ten 4–8–4's for fast freight service from Alco
in 1943. It likely would have purchased freight diesels
rather than steam locomotives if they were available.

After the war, the Lehigh Valley quickly decided that
the time was ripe to fully convert to a dieselized railroad,
the process being completed in 1951. The management
wasted no time in purchasing diesels and quickly retired
all steam locomotives. The first true road diesels on the
system were eight EMD FT's, purchased in January 1945
after War Production Board controls were eased. Again,
this was at least partly in response to the actions of neighbors and competitors. The Erie, Lackawanna, and New
York Susquehanna & Western were all embracing road
diesels.[16]

Other than the 4–8–4 locomotives, most steam power
on the Lehigh Valley was built in the late 1910s or early
1920s. By the time the war was over these locomotives
were approaching their twentieth, twenty-fifth, or even
thirtieth birthdays. These locomotives dating from the
first two decades of the century were small and inefficient
compared to modern steam power. They were generally
designed for slow speed movement of coal and not high
speed movement of manufactured goods and other time
sensitive merchandise. Maintenance costs were steadily
increasing for these locomotives which had been driven
hard for the war effort. Quite simply, they were old and

worn out. Of the 382 locomotives in service on the railroad in the fall of 1942, only 27 T class 4–8–4's, and six S class 4–8–2's could be considered truly modern. The rest were "low wheel type" locomotives not suited for high speed service. Eighty-five locomotives or almost a quarter of the total were twenty-nine years old or older.[17]

The FTs of the Lehigh Valley were initially put to use, not in main line, fast freight service which was what they were designed for, but in helper service, pushing trains up mountain grades between the Lehigh and Susquehanna River valleys.[18] They did offer substantial savings in labor and fuel costs over steam helpers. Also, helper work is relatively low speed and requires great tractive force, capabilities that diesel switchers had already demonstrated. The railroad used the new road diesels for a job which it knew from direct experience that they could perform well, rather than letting them haul heavy roadfreights. Keeping the diesels in one place also made fueling and servicing the new locomotives easier. Instead of building new diesel fuel facilities at several points across the railroad and training shop forces in many locations, only a few workers and only one fueling and service area needed to be constructed. Lastly it allowed the management to keep a close eye on the diesels performance.

Three years later in 1948, however, the situation had changed. With the overall verdict on the diesel in and with costs rapidly increasing, the Lehigh Valley decided to pursue dieselization with all possible speed and to dieselize the main line, scheduled fast freight trains as well as the express passenger trains with the eventual goal of complete replacement of steam locomotives. The steam tugboats that the railroad operated in New York Harbor were even replaced with diesel boats. With three years of operating experience with road freight diesels and many more years of experience with switchers, the management was well aware of the capabilities and potential cost savings of the diesel. It was estimated by the railroad that the dieselization of all main line fast freight trains would result in an annual saving, after depreciation, of $2.5 million.[19] This estimate was based "in part on study by Alco and EMD and in part on personal knowledge and operating experience of other roads."[20] Other studies put the annual savings at a lower, but still respectable, $1.9 million.[21] For perspective, the total operating revenue for the year 1949 was $69 million.[22] The savings included not only the fuel, labor, and probable servicing costs of the diesels, but also consolidation of some trains into longer ones that could not have been moved over the road by steam power in a timely fashion. These estimates, however, did not include new, permanent servicing facilities and specialized equipment for maintenance of the diesel locomotives.

To accomplish dieselization of the scheduled fast freight trains management decided to split its order for motive power between EMD and Alco. In October and November 1948, the Lehigh Valley ordered five main line freight locomotives from Alco and five from EMD.[23] This purchasing technique was clearly a carry over from steam days. A similar purchasing arrangement as was made in 1931 with the 4–8–4 order split between Alco and Baldwin. This split between manufactures was to characterize Lehigh Valley motive power purchasing for the rest of the railroad's existence.

There were many factors involved in the split order including the desire to reward an on-line manufacturer, Alco with some business, but perhaps the most critical was delivery time. EMD, Alco, and Baldwin all submitted bids to the Lehigh Valley for this order.[24] The costs were all roughly comparable but Baldwin had a delivery date of the fourth quarter, 1949. Alco and EMD could each deliver half of the ordered ten locomotives in October of 1948 and the rest later in 1948 or in early 1949. President Major stated, "Because the delivery of the Baldwin locomotives is about a year later than the other two and the savings would therefore be postponed for that period, the Baldwin bid is not attractive."[25] Perhaps the largest reason other than delivery time that Alco received part of the order was that Alco was an on-line customer of the Lehigh Valley, with its diesel engine plant located in Auburn, New York. The Lehigh Valley also had previous experience with Alco switchers and more importantly, road passenger locomotives.

From a maintenance standpoint it was more costly to split the order. The two types of locomotives ordered from two different manufacturers were fundamentally different, which necessitated keeping twice as many spare parts on hand, as well as learning two completely different systems. Alco locomotives used 4-cycle engines, while EMD locomotives used 2-cycle engines. All the internal systems were different, and the respective units could not operate together as a single locomotive controlled by one engineer in one cab. That is to say they could not Multiple Unit (M.U.) together.[26] If a train had locomotives of each type at the front, separate crews would be needed for operations.

Steam era thinking was illustrated in this split order. The flexibility that M.U.-capable diesels could bring to operations was not fully realized. Management continued to purchase locomotives solely for their initial intended tasks. If a situation arose where the EMD and Alco locomotives had to operate in concert, they would have to be manned by separate crews, which was how steam locomotives were operated. Even locomotives produced by the same manufacturer did not often have M.U. capability as standard equipment on early diesels because few people, railroad or manufacturer, foresaw its potential. As an option, M.U. capability, when offered, often cost extra. Manufacturers quickly realized their mistake, however, and by the late 1950s offered locomotives that could M.U. with locomotives from other manufacturers. The Lehigh Valley retrofitted some of their Alco FA/B units in 1956–1959 to become M.U. capable with EMD locomotives.

In 1948 the Lehigh Valley also decided to fully dieselize its passenger service which consisted mainly of long distance, New York to Pennsylvania and Buffalo, traffic. However, there were many shorter, branch line runs in Upstate New York and Pennsylvania served by gas-electric motorcars. Most of these unprofitable branch line operations were discontinued in the five to seven years after the end of the war. To remain even marginally competitive on the long haul routes, the Lehigh Valley had to dieselize operations. The Lackawanna, one of the Lehigh Valley's arch competitors, dieselized their premier passenger train, the Phoebe Snow, and also bought new, streamlined equipment for its flagship train. The Lehigh Valley, never a large passenger carrier, decided not to purchase new passenger cars but did dieselize operations to improve scheduling and maintain some degree of competitiveness.

Passenger diesels were more highly developed than freight diesels, having been in main line, revenue service since the Burlington Zephyr of 1934. Even though EMD was offering passenger diesels and had a long experience with them, the Lehigh Valley decided to look closer to home and purchased its passenger diesels from Alco.

Both models generated 2,000 horsepower, but the EMD version used two diesel engines driving separate generators, while the Alco model only used one larger engine. The Lehigh Valley evidently thought that the simplicity and potential maintenance savings of a one engine design, rather than the built-in reliability of having two engines, was more important. Alco had demonstrated its postwar passenger diesel, the PA, on the Lehigh Valley's premier, Black Diamond passenger train in 1946.[27] The management was impressed with the diesels, which did not require helper service on the mountain grades. This, combined with the on-line Alco facilities and prior relationship with Alco, was most likely the reason that the Lehigh Valley decided to dieselize passenger service with the Alco PA.[28] The Lehigh Valley also decided to modernize its sole remaining branch line passenger service, the Lehighton to Hazleton, Pennsylvania local. This service had been the province of EMC gas-electric motorcars since the early 1930s. In 1951 the Lehigh Valley purchased two Budd Rail Diesel Cars (RDC) to replace the aging EMC cars.[29]

The Lehigh Valley stands as a good example of many of the reasons why railroads chose diesels. They first used diesel switchers due to the smoke abatement policies of New York City but quickly discovered that there were other advantages in using them, namely increased availability and decreased costs of operation. Although they did not employ diesel streamliners in the 1930s as some other roads did they remained interested in the cost savings of diesel power for switching applications. When main line freight diesels became widely available after the war, the Lehigh Valley quickly embarked on a full-scale dieselization program. Diesels could help to control the rapidly escalating costs in the postwar environment and could also replace a steam fleet that was, for the most part, obsolete and worn out. Complete dieselization was achieved in 1951. In a highly competitive area, diesels would help the Lehigh Valley compete with other roads like the Lackawanna. Although the Lehigh Valley had substantial on line coal reserves, the perceived need to remain loyal to the coal industry was not a large concern. The coal reserves were all anthracite which was not well suited for burning in locomotives and the anthracite industry was already in a long slow decline. The Lehigh Valley was not the most healthy of railroads in the postwar era.

With rapidly increasing costs, competition from other rail-roads and from autos and motor trucks and the decline of the anthracite coal industry and general decline of heavy industry in the northeast, the Lehigh Valley jumped at the chance to control some of its costs with new diesels. However, its hasty decision would cause problems with its embrace of diesels by two different manufacturers, which would cause later maintenance and repair headaches. It finally fell under the control of the Pennsylvania railroad and would eventually, bankrupt and failing, be folded into the government created Conrail in 1976.

Delaware, Lackawanna & Western

The Delaware, Lackawanna & Western operated 966 miles of line from Jersey City through New Jersey, the anthra-cite region of northeast Pennsylvania, and on to Buffalo. It also had a network of branch lines in central and west-ern New York state and the Pennsylvania coal country. However, the Lackawanna was also burdened with exten-sive suburban commuter operations in northern New Jer-sey, something that the Lehigh Valley lacked. Some of this service was electrified in 1930 and operated by electric multiple unit cars. This electrification cut costs, increased efficiency and also eliminated smoke in the highly popu-lated areas of northeastern New Jersey. The Lackawanna operated the shortest route between New York City and Buffalo and was known for its massive engineering proj-ects and well maintained track. The huge Nicholson Via-duct, built in 1915, was the longest concrete bridge in the world for many years.[30] The Lackawanna suffered many of the same problems as the other anthracite-dependent roads during the 1930s and 1940s as anthracite coal use began to decline and competition from many sources increased. Since they possessed the shortest route between Buffalo and New York City, the road refocused on merchandise traffic. The Lackawanna was also the operator of many docks and port facilities in and around New York Harbor. Like the Lehigh Valley the Lackawanna was prodded by antismoke legislation to invest in diesel locomotives. It purchased two Alco-GE-IR switchers in 1926 for use on docks and yards in and around New York City.[31] Later, after the two experimental diesels had proved themselves both techni-cally and financially, the Lackawanna purchased fourteen

additional diesels from both Alco and GE. These locomotives began the dieselization of switching operations
and began to be seen outside of the New York terminal
area. Additional diesel switcher orders in 1935 and 1940
swelled the ranks of diesels on the railroad. The railroad
management realized early on that especially in switching applications, diesels could cut costs significantly due
primarily to their greater availability and lower maintenance costs.

In a pattern similar to the Lehigh Valley that was
repeated by many railroads, the Lackawanna was also
purchasing large steam locomotives during the same
period. To move freight and passengers faster and more
efficiently between the Buffalo gateway and northern New
Jersey, the Lackawanna invested heavily in modern steam
power. From 1927 to 1934, fifty-five state-of-the-art 4–8–4
types were purchased for high speed freight service. For
high speed passenger service the Lackawanna decided,
like many railroads, not to opt for the impressive but
expensive diesel streamliner but to stick with steam. The
Lackawanna purchased five 4–6–4 types in 1937 to speed
up passenger schedules. During the depths of the Depression, the Lackawanna kept shop forces working overhaul-
ing and rebuilding older locomotives into modern 0–8–0
switchers. Sixty were produced from 1929 to 1935.[32] This
would seem contradictory at first glance but such a policy
likely made good economic sense. New diesel switchers,
while cheap to operate, were expensive to purchase. With
available capital scarce during the Depression, it would
be better to employ skilled labor that otherwise might
leave the area by rebuilding steam locomotives. These
new steam switchers were more efficient than older locomotives and did save some money for the company.

By 1940 the Lackawanna was doing well as far as
motive power was concerned. Modern steam road power
was joined by updated modern steam switchers and an
increasing stable of diesel switchers. When the wartime
traffic boom hit the Lackawanna it found that it needed
additional power. By 1943 the choices open to the Lackawanna management were greater than they had been
just a few years before. The EMD FT was available and
was compiling an extraordinary record in heavy service
on other railroads. In mid-1943 the Lackawanna placed
an order for twenty FT units to be used for freight and
helper service. Production controls and a flood of orders

delayed delivery until May 1945. Once the new units arrived they quickly lived up to their exemplary reputation.[33] With modern freight diesels on the property, the Lackawanna and especially new president William White quickly realized the benefits of large scale dieselization especially the lower costs of operation and maintenance and embarked on a massive dieselization program. New locomotives were purchased in every year from 1946 to 1953 from EMD, Alco, and Fairbanks Morse. The Lackawanna completed dieselization in 1953.

The Lackawanna was similar to the Lehigh Valley in its reasons for adopting the diesel. Initially pushed to employ diesels by antismoke legislation, they quickly learned the cost saving advantages of diesel switchers. Under competitive pressure from other railroads as well as other modes of transportation, they modernized their steam fleet extensively in the late 1920s and even in the 1930s. With modern steam power and a lack of available capital in the cash strapped depression years, they chose to stick with steam in the 1930s for passenger service and even for some switching service instead of opting for expensive diesels. When freight diesels and capital became available after WWII the Lackawanna embarked on a large scale dieselization program not only to control costs but to keep up with the competition. They took a bit longer than the Lehigh Valley to completely dieselize and pursued a slightly more deliberate course rather than the overly hasty Lehigh Valley. While diesels were turning in savings, the Lackawanna was still not a healthy property. It was rebuffed in an attempt to merge with the Midwestern Nickel Plate Road in 1947 and finally succumbed to merger with the parallel Erie in 1960. Even this merger did not bring back prosperity to the property and, with the help of Hurricane Agnes in 1972 and the massive floods it generated, the bankrupt Erie Lackawanna was folded into Conrail in 1976.

New York, Ontario & Western

While the Lehigh Valley and the Lackawanna were anthracite-dependent railroads trying to maintain themselves in the rapidly changing postwar economic environment and the competitive New York to Buffalo fast freight market, other eastern roads had similar reasons for embracing the diesel. The New York, Ontario & Western was a small carrier with 569 miles of line that wandered its way from Weehawken, New Jersey, through the Catskills and into central New York State to the Lake Ontario port of Oswego. Of major importance was a secondary line to Scranton, Pennsylvania. Utilizing this line, the O&W tried to emphasize and capture bridge traffic between western connections and New England via Maybrook, NY and the Poughkeepsie bridge over the Hudson River. The Old & Weary or Old Woman as it was nicknamed was not a healthy railroad by the 1930s and 1940s. It was surrounded by larger and more prosperous railroads. The little on line passenger traffic to Catskills resorts was rapidly evaporating due to automobile competition, while other sources of revenue, namely milk from upstate New York dairies, was captured by motor trucks.[34] The little anthracite revenue generated by mines around Scranton was also declining by the 1930s. The steam power of the O&W was old and outdated by the late 1930s. Most locomotives had been built in the 1910s or before. Only a few 4–8–2 types purchased in the mid- and late 1920s could be called modern.

In this competitive environment the management of the Ontario & Western needed to cut costs and cut them fast and modernize its locomotive fleet, and what better way to do that than to replace the aging and outdated steam power with new efficient diesels. According to O&W historian Robert E. Mohowski, "In truth, the road had little choice in the matter since it simply could not afford continued steam operations."[35] Financing was readily available from banks as well as the large locomotive builders, especially EMD though the General Motors Acceptance Corporation or GMAC.[36] Without this financing it is unlikely that the O&W would have purchased any diesels. The O&W began experimenting with a few small GE switchers in 1941 and 1942. The big leap came, as with many other roads, with the delivery of several EMD FT locomotives in 1945. The FTs were quickly put to use and lived up to their billing by saving money for the bankrupt railroad. Dieselization was completed in 1948 with the purchase of more EMD F-units and several EMD switchers.[37] All steam was retired in the summer of 1948 making the O&W one of the first fully dieselized railroads in the nation.

Unfortunately for the O&W, this is not the end of the story. Diesels slowed but could not stop the flow of red ink. Indeed, they only prolonged the inevitable. As traffic continued to dwindle and the automobile and truck rose to dominance in the 1950s, the O&W fell on increasingly hard times. Only the war years of 1942 and 1943 were profitable for the railroad. Despite full dieselization and other cost cutting measures, the entire railroad was shut down in 1957.[38] Locomotives and rolling stock were offered for sale, and the rail was pulled up and scrapped. Diesels successfully saved money for the O&W, but they could not bring a moribund railroad back to life. Diesels may be much more efficient at hauling trains and cost less to fuel, service, and maintain, but they have to have freight and passengers to pull. If the traffic goes away, as it did for the O&W, even the newest, flashiest motive power will make little difference.

New York, Susquehanna & Western

The New York, Susquehanna, & Western was a small railroad of only 120 miles of line operating exclusively in northern New Jersey. It was primarily a freight carrier but it did offer rudimentary commuter passenger service with gasoline and diesel railcars. In some ways a large shortline, it was never a player with the larger roads like the Lehigh Valley, Lackawanna, or even the New York, Ontario & Western. Never-the-less, the Susquehanna has the distinction of being one of the first class I railroads to become completely dieselized doing so on June 2, 1945.[39] From forty-one steam locomotives in 1936, the Susquehanna was able to substitute only sixteen diesel locomotives and four rail motor cars by 1945.[40] Its roster of motive power was cut in half. One reason that the Susquehanna dieselized so early was that the steam locomotives that it owned were all at least twenty-seven years old, and many were closer to forty years old. The Susquehanna was in the market for new power and chose to opt for the diesel. Most of the work that the locomotives did was slower speed switching and freight service, an area where the diesel was particularly suited. The use of diesel railcars for the few commuters and other passengers also had the potential to drastically reduce costs. The cost advantages for the diesel were simply too great to ignore. By dieselizing so rapidly they could also abandon all the steam locomotive fueling and servicing facilities, saving more money. The Susquehanna was also able to dieselize so quickly because of its size. For both the Susquehanna and the Ontario & Western, controlling costs was the prime factor in dieselization.

Reading

The Reading Company, famous for its inclusion on the monopoly game board, was not a large carrier, geographically. All of its nearly 1,500 miles of line were within 115 miles of its namesake city of Reading, Pennsylvania. However, it served one of the most heavily industrialized and populated areas of the United States. The Reading was the largest carrier of anthracite coal from northeastern Pennsylvania, and its steam locomotives were custom designed to burn this clean, but slow burning fuel.[41] The Reading was also burdened with extensive commuter operations and terminal facilities in Philadelphia. To increase efficiency on its commuter lines, the Reading electrified most commuter operations in the 1920s. Freight and longer distance passengers still moved by steam. The Reading was part of the "Alphabet Route" for freight shipped between the Northeast and the Midwest. The route was so named for the number of initials of all the component railroads. The Reading joined the Central of New Jersey, Western Maryland, Pittsburgh and West Virginia, and New York, Chicago and St. Louis (Nickel Plate Route) to offer competitive freight service from the industrial cities of the Midwest such as St. Louis and Chicago to the New York–New Jersey metropolitan area.[42]

Reading steam power was a curious mix of older and more modern locomotives. For example, the railroad had hundreds of 2–8–0 types, the bulk of which were built before or during World War I. However, the Reading also built or bought seventy-five of the same type from 1922 to 1925. The 2–8–0 was a good locomotive for the many branch lines and terminal facilities on the railroad. For hauling long heavy trains of coal out of the Pennsylvania mountains, the Reading invested in the 2–10–2 type, acquiring twenty-one between 1927 and 1939. Passenger trains moved behind forty-five 4–6–2 Pacific types, many constructed in the Reading's own shops in its namesake city.[43] As the economy began to revive in the late 1930s, the Reading found itself with adequate power, especially for slow, heavy service. High-speed freight service was another matter, however.

The Reading was an early experimenter with diesel switchers and decided early on that they were well suited for urban industrial service with their high availability and high starting tractive effort. They also emitted much less bothersome smoke, a concern in heavily populated areas like Philadelphia. The first diesel on the Reading has the distinction of being one of the first diesel locomotives in operation on the continent. An Ingersoll Rand-Alco-GE boxcab like the pioneering CNJ 1000 was placed in operation in June 1926. The locomotive spent almost all of its life in and around the Reading Passenger Terminal in downtown Philadelphia.[44] A near copy followed in 1928. Ten years would pass before the next diesel purchase and again it would be switching power. Late 1937 brought six EMC switchers that were quickly followed by further offerings from Alco, Baldwin, and the first locomotive to be built by Fairbanks Morse. By the start of the war the Reading had a fairly large fleet of thirty-eight diesel switchers.[45] During the war it further dieselized switching operations and began to dieselize main line freight operations as well. Twenty five new switchers arrived on the property during the war. They were joined in early 1945 by twenty EMD FT units semi-permanently connected in two sets of two units each.[46] This is similar to the Lehigh Valley, DL&W and other railroads operating in the area. The Reading purchased FT types despite not being involved in the 1940 demonstration tour of the pioneering locomotive.

Despite these purchases, the Reading was not fully committed to the diesel until well after the war. In a pattern that was repeated with many other railroads, it built new steam locomotives in its own shops in Reading as late as 1948. In need of fast freight power in the late 1940s and with diesels being expensive and with long waiting times for delivery, the Reading took the boilers from thirty older 2–8–0 types and lengthened them while setting them on a 4–8–4 running gear arrangement. These T-1 types were quite successful and remained in service until as late as 1958.[47] The Reading also built ten modern Pacific types for passenger service in its own shops in 1948. This policy made financial sense to the Reading management. New diesels were quite expensive, and recycling older steam locomotive parts into new locomotives using existing facilities and skilled labor could give the railroad new locomotives with similar operational performance for a fraction of the price. There were also substantial tax advantages for rebuilding

Photo 5   This posed publicity photo shows "the diesel that did it," the EMC FT. The Reading purchased this four unit locomotive in February 1945. The four units seen here developed 5400 horsepower. Courtesy of the Railroad Museum Of Pennsylvania (PHMC) Reading Railroad Collection.

locomotives rather than purchasing new ones. The Reading also embraced steam for passenger service. Its streamlined Crusader train from Philadelphia to New York was operated by steam power and not by diesels until 1950. Complete dieselization was not achieved until the relatively late date of 1958, and even then several of the newest T-1 type 4–8–4's were kept in reserve just in case traffic levels necessitated their use.

The Reading is similar to many of the other roads analyzed thus far in its reasons for dieselization. Initial purchases were made in the 1920s due to government anti smoke legislation or other threatened action. Further switcher purchases were made in the late 1930s after the first locomotives had proven capable of cutting costs and improving operations and after revenues began to increase after the depths of the Depression. Freight diesels arrived and were put to good use during the later stages of the war. Where the Reading differs from its anthracite road brethren is in its continued embrace of steam after the war. Again this policy likely made economic sense for the Reading, which had the facilities, knowledge and shop forces available to construct new steam locomotives. It also had an oversupply of older 2–8–0 types no longer needed for hauling coal that were useful as raw material. Despite being a large coal hauler this likely had little impact on the decisions to dieselize. Anthracite was not well suited for locomotive use and the industry was in a long decline. The Reading dieselized but more slowly and deliberately than other railroads. It took its time and utilized the best of its existing resources to control costs and provide service after the war in a changing competitive environment. As late as 1948 it was not obvious that diesels would completely supplant steam so the Reading invested in both. The Reading was under the control of the Baltimore and Ohio railroad during the period of dieselization and adopted a similar approach to the diesel as its parent road. Like many of its neighbors though, the Reading, despite its differences in dieselizing, was also destined for bankruptcy and inclusion in Conrail in 1976.

Baltimore & Ohio

The Baltimore & Ohio Railroad (B&O) traced its origins back to the beginnings of railroading not only in the United States but in the entire world. By the middle of the twentieth century, the 5,658 miles of the B&O stretched from its name sake city north to Philadelphia and west to Washington, D.C., Harpers Ferry, West Virginia and Cumberland, Maryland. At this point the route split with one line heading directly west to Cincinnati and St. Louis. The other line veered north to Pittsburgh and continued across Ohio and Indiana to Chicago. Substantial secondary lines connected to Cleveland, Toledo, and Columbus, Ohio; Buffalo and Rochester, New York; and Springfield, Illinois. The B&O operated a large network of coal branches in the mountains of western Maryland and West Virginia. The B&O was a large railroad with 2,364 locomotives at the end of 1929.[48] However, it competed with larger and more successful roads like the Pennsylvania and New York Central for traffic, especially lucrative, long haul traffic from Chicago and St. Louis to the Eastern seaboard. The Great Depression hit the B&O harder than some of its neighbors. Although railroad operations remained solvent through the decade, the company as a whole was in the red for much of the 1930s.

The B&O was an early experimenter with diesel power. They rostered an early EMC boxcab type locomotive built in the summer of 1935. The locomotive was assigned to the Royal Blue, New York to Washington streamlined passenger train.[49] The Pennsylvania Railroad had recently electrified its New York to Washington main line and was operating fast and frequent trains between the two cities. To try to remain even a slight bit competitive, the B&O chose diesel power. The B&O did not stop there, they also operated the first E-unit built. In 1937 and 1938, while the Santa Fe was acquiring E-units to dieselize its new streamlined passenger service, the B&O also acquired twelve E-units for its passenger services.[50] The results were mixed. After the first diesel was installed, passengers did return to the rails of the B&O. In 1934 the railroad hauled slightly over 3 million revenue passengers. This increased to over 5 million in 1936 but declined to 3.8 million for 1939. More disturbing however was the revenue generated by these passengers, which remained relatively static for the 1930s at around $2.50 to $2.90 per passenger.[51]

Diesels for passenger service can easily be explained by competition with other railroads, especially the Pennsylvania, and by public relations and advertising reasons. A high profile diesel streamliner running in the heavily populated northeast would have benefits beyond just increased passenger loadings. Businesses and potential

freight shippers would hear of the train and then possibly look at the B&O for freight service. It is important
to remember that the vast majority of the revenue generated by the railroad came from freight. The B&O was one
of a few eastern roads and the only large coal hauler to
host the FT locomotive on its demonstration tour. Being
already familiar with diesels as well as with EMC, it is
no surprise that the B&O chose to embrace the FT. The
railroad ordered a total of twenty-four units, delivered in
1942 and 1943.[52]

Based on the above information, it would seem that the
B&O was an early convert to diesel power. This was not the
case. They also continued to develop new and advanced
steam locomotives well into the 1940s. Even as late as the
1947 annual report, passenger traffic is represented by
a chart with diesels pulling passenger trains of various
length to show the various passenger earnings while the
freight chart shows large modern steam locomotives pulling freight cars. This was despite freight diesels being
in service since 1942. The Baltimore Mt. Claire shops
experimented with water tube boilers and duplex drive
locomotives in the late 1920s and 1930s. Neither design
innovation was successful. Even while it was purchasing
a few FT units for evaluation purposes, the railroad was
purchasing new EM-1 type 2–8–8–4 locomotives from Baldwin. These huge locomotives were head and shoulders
above most others not only on the B&O but throughout the
eastern district in size as well as performance. It is likely
that the railroad purchased both the latest in advanced
steam power and new diesels to directly compare the two.
Wartime controls on the production of FT locomotives
also was a likely factor in the order for the massive EM-1
type. As technically impressive as the EM-1 locomotives
were, the railroad also needed smaller, fast freight types
during and after the war. The answer was not simply more
diesels but more steam as well. Baltimore's own Mt. Claire
shops built forty modern 4–8–2 locomotives from 1942 to
1948 to meet the need for speed. These were to be the
last new steam locomotives that the B&O would operate.
Again, the B&O decided, like the Reading, to utilize existing shop forces and equipment to produce needed fast
freight motive power rather than spending limited capital
on expensive new diesels. This was especially true during
the war when diesels were not only expensive but scarce
and difficult to obtain in large numbers. The railroad also

purchased used steam locomotives from other roads that had switched to diesels. For instance, ten 2–6–6–4 locomotives from the Seaboard Air Line were purchased by the B&O in 1947. That same year thirteen modern 4–8–2 locomotives were purchased from the Boston & Maine.[53] Used but modern steam locomotives could provide needed service at a fraction of the price of new diesels and were more efficient and cost effective than older steam locomotives. B&O management, like that of the Reading, decided that it made economic sense to stick with some steam for a while. Being a large coal hauler likely also had an impact on management to retain some steam power to placate the coal industry.

By the end of 1948, the verdict on the diesel was in. No more steam locomotives would be purchased new or used or built in company shops. The cost savings from diesels were simply too great to ignore. The B&O also realized that some increased operational efficiencies could be had with diesel operations. The 1948 annual report states, "Studies indicated substantial savings would accrue from the substitution of Diesel power for steam locomotives between Parkersburg and East St. Louis."[54] The report goes on to state, "The considerable reduction in number of trains and train miles required to move the traffic is resulting in a substantial saving in operating expenses."[55] The report also stated that considerable economies resulted from using diesels in yard switching duties. Despite this acknowledgment of the superiority of diesels not only in cost but in capability, most traffic on the B&O at the end of 1948 still moved behind steam. Only 17 percent of the freight ton miles and 45 percent of the passenger car miles were pulled by diesel locomotives.[56] At the end of 1950, the B&O had 512 diesel locomotives in operation but still had 1,460 steam locomotives.[57] The annual reports continued to chronicle the dieselization of the B&O. At the end of 1951, 596 diesels were in service. An even more strongly worded statement than the one in 1948 followed the statistics. "Diesel locomotives are much more efficient and economical than steam locomotives. They haul heavier trains at higher speeds, require less helper service over grades; fuel costs are considerably lower and availability higher." The report goes on to state that, "Economy realized from the greater use of diesels was the most important factor in partially offsetting rising costs of operation and maintenance. For that reason and to handle additional traffic and meet competition, it is essential to substitute diesel power for other types more costly to operate."[58] By the end of 1952 diesels were hauling the majority of traffic on the B&O. The 698 diesels in service at the end of the year handled 64 percent of the freight ton miles, 53 percent of the passenger train miles and 65 percent of the yard switching hours.[59] Steam power would not disappear completely from America's first railroad until 1958.

Like the Reading, the B&O appeared to be in both the steam and diesel camp for a significant time. One reason that the B&O may have been reluctant to take full advantage of the diesel is their reliance on the coal industry. In 1950 fully 44 percent of all tonnage on the B&O was bituminous coal.[60] Despite the substantial amount of coal that the B&O hauled, it could not ignore the economies of the diesel and devoted ever more effort to full dieselization after 1948. Many of the reasons for dieselization can be seen with the B&O. Competition with other railroads in passenger and freight service, costs, and improved performance all played a role in the dieselization of the B&O. As with other eastern roads however, the B&O, despite dieselization and other cost cutting measures, while not bankrupt was not a vibrant and healthy railroad by the late 1950s. The smaller but better off financially Chesapeake & Ohio took control of the B&O in 1962 and the two combined roads operated as the Chessie system until it became part of the larger CSX Transportation rail system in 1987.

Western Maryland

The B&O faced competition not only from the large trunk roads like the Pennsylvania but also from smaller roads even in its home state. The 837 mile Western Maryland (WM) extended from Baltimore west to Connellsville, Pennsylvania with extensive branches in the coal country of West Virginia as well as links to York and Shippensburg, Pennsylvania. For much of its route it ran on one side of the Potomac river while the B&O ran on the other. The WM was a major coal hauler but also did a brisk interchange business as part of the "Alphabet Route" from the Midwest to the East coast. The passenger traffic on the Western Maryland was minuscule. As a coal-dependent railroad it was no surprise that it burned what it hauled.

The steam locomotive fleet of the Western Maryland was optimized to haul this coal as efficiently as possible. The road purchased ever larger 2–8–0 types throughout the early decades of the century. The final group of these loco-motives were built between 1921 and 1923. These were not fast locomotives but were good at hauling coal. To handle the increasing time sensitive merchandise traffic of the late 1930s, the road ordered twelve advanced Challenger 4–6–6–4 types which were delivered in 1940 and 1941, just prior to the outbreak of the war.[61]

The Western Maryland began to experiment with die-sels about the same time that the new Challengers were being delivered. The first diesel on the property was a small Alco switching locomotive delivered in late 1941.[62] Several more switchers followed in the war years of the early 1940s. While the yards were increasingly the home of diesel power, the main line remained the domain of steam. The 4–6–6–4 locomotives were good, but more locomotive than what was needed on the eastern end of the railroad where grades were not as intense. The WM decided in 1947 to purchase modern 4–8–4 types for its fast freight service.[63] This marks the WM as one of a few railroads to purchase new steam after the war. While this decision may seem incongruous, for the WM it likely made sense at the time. Coal was readily available from the on line mines and relatively cheap.

Steam power did not live on long on the Western Mary-land. A few road-freight diesels were acquired beginning in 1947, even while the 4–8–4 locomotives were brand new. This is likely a move to compare the two types of motive power in service by the WM management. As seen with the Reading and B&O, as late as 1947 and even 1948, railroads were still considering both steam and diesel for motive power. The results of the comparison were exactly what would be expected. By 1950, a relatively few diesels were hauling 31 percent of all ton miles on the railroad.[64] Then the floodgates opened. With competitor B&O embracing the diesel and with costs of steam locomotive operation rising, the WM would have to as well. Large amounts of road diesels arrived from Alco, Baldwin, and EMD. The modern new 4–8–4 locomotives would not have a long life on the WM. They were all retired by the end of 1954 when complete dieselization was achieved.[65]

Although a large coal hauler, the Western Maryland railroad simply could not ignore the efficiencies and operating economies of diesels. Beginning with several wartime switching locomotives, the railroad embarked on a large scale dieselization program in the early 1950s. Again, costs were primary but competition with neighbors also necessitated a switch to diesels. To remain competitive on the alphabet fast freight route diesels were seen as a public relations necessity. With other neighboring roads and competitors embracing the diesel, the WM needed to show that it too was keeping up with technology and would use new technology to provide the best service to its customers or they would go elsewhere. The WM played it safe though and didn't fully commit to the diesel until it had direct experience with both modern steam and diesel operating on its own property. Like other roads, it too did not fully realize the potential for lower maintenance and servicing costs with adopting diesels from only one manufacturer.

Thus far, most of the roads analyzed have been Northeast or Mid-Atlantic roads that often had substantial mountain grades to battle and that many times served large coal mining regions. What about the cities and prairies of the Midwest? Would the diesel find as many converts there as it did further east? Did the different terrain and operating environment have an effect on the pace of dieselization? Were the coal industry or passenger operations major factors in the embrace of the diesel? These and other questions are addressed in the examples that follow.

Chicago & Eastern Illinois

The Chicago & Eastern Illinois railroad ran south from Chicago through eastern Illinois to connections in southern Illinois and southwestern Indiana. The 886 mile C&EI was an essential connection for southern and southwestern roads to the important interchange city of Chicago.[66] It also served important coal fields in southern Illinois and Indiana. The C&EI was not a financially healthy railroad, entering and exiting receivership several times prior to 1950, including, like many other railroads, during the Great Depression. Wartime traffic provided a huge boost to the C&EI, and it began the second half of the century firmly in the black. With the increasing industrial growth of the south and its role as an important connection between Chicago and the south the prospects for the C&EI looked good.

C&EI steam motive power was a hodgepodge of different locomotives from different manufacturers. The majority of locomotives were smaller types built during the first two decades of the century and were rapidly nearing their retirement dates by the late 1930s. The only exceptions to the above were twenty 2–8–2 types for freight service built in 1922 and 1923 and six modern Pacifics for passenger service also built in 1923.[67] During the Depression the railroad upgraded its existing steam locomotives but did not have the means, nor the reason to purchase new power. In 1937 the railroad ordered three small diesel switchers for service in the Chicago terminal area.[68] The switchers would reduce operating expenses but would also eliminate the smoke and cinders associated with coal fired steam locomotives, a large concern in the city of Chicago and a subject of increasing city agitation and legislative action. The switchers were a success, and four more were ordered in 1941 for service in other yards and terminals. Throughout the war more diesel switchers followed for service not only in Chicago but throughout the railroad. Of special note were four RS-1 road-switchers ordered from Alco in 1944.[69] This put the C&EI at the forefront of the movement to adopt multiuse roadswitchers and away from more dedicated single use power.

The C&EI was also interested in using diesels for passenger service, ordering three EMD E-7 passenger units in late 1944 and early 1945 as well as new passenger cars for the expected postwar boom in leisure travel.[70] The locomotives entered service in 1946 and were well received. By the end of the war the already aging steam locomotives were simply worn out. Replacements were needed. The C&EI had not decided to completely abandon steam, however, and was still spending money on upgrading existing steam power and servicing facilities. This changed on January 1, 1948 as a new president, John M. Budd, came to power. Budd, along with General Manager Downing B. Jenks hired in late 1949, transformed the C&EI into a completely dieselized railroad.[71] Thirty-four new freight and passenger units were purchased from EMD in 1947 and 1948. Included in this number were three BL models from EMD. This again shows that the C&EI was quick to recognize the value of the road-switcher type, purchasing even the flawed BL model. To complete dieselization the railroad ordered twenty EMD GP-7 locomotives in late 1949. The GP-7 was only introduced in October of 1949 and was still a new, relatively unproven design. However, the C&EI liked its road-switcher configuration so much that they became one of the first customers to purchase the new design. Unlike the ill-fated BL model, the GP-7 and further developments like the GP-9 and GP-18 were hugely successful. As the locomotives began arriving in the spring of 1950, steam power finally vanished from the railroad. With few exceptions, the C&EI embraced diesels from EMD. The railroad seemed to realize the inherent advantages that locomotives of a single manufacturer would provide in the maintenance and service department.

The C&EI dieselized for several reasons. Like the Lehigh Valley and the Lackawanna, it was initially prodded to try diesel switchers due to antismoke regulations. After some experience with these switchers in downtown Chicago, the railroad began to purchase more switchers, but this time for the cost savings and greater availability rather than the elimination of coal smoke. With many other railroads operating streamlined diesel passenger service, the C&EI purchased some diesel passenger units shortly after the end of the war. While cost savings was a likely concern, competitive pressures and the desire to have modern locomotives for new modern trains was also a large consideration. This whole time however, the C&EI continued to upgrade its steam locomotives. With a new president and general manager the C&EI quickly abandoned steam and wholly embraced the diesel. The new management was quick to realize the potential of the diesel to reshape operations and dramatically cut costs. When the decision was made to fully dieselize, the railroad forgot its conservative past and catapulted to the front of the pack. The flat Midwestern landscape did not have a noticeable effect on the dieselization experience of the C&EI although it would with other roads. Although the railroad served important coal mining areas, the C&EI did not feel the need to remain loyal to coal as a fuel to appease coal producers. One possible reason is that there were several new coal fired electric power plants coming on line in the area in the postwar years that served to ensure a market for local coal and a revenue source for the dieselized railroad. The C&EI embodies many of the reasons that railroads chose to dieselize, antismoke concerns, cost, and passengers. Unlike some of its eastern brethren, the C&EI did well financially in the 1950s. It was an attractive railroad for takeover as it was well run and provided access to the rail capital of Chicago. Consequently, in the 1960s the Missouri Pacific and Louisville & Nashville split the C&EI with each getting access to Chicago.

WESTERN DISTRICT

The western district was by far the largest district geographically but also the least dense in terms of traffic. The western roads were characterized by long hauls, as far as from Chicago to Los Angeles on the Santa Fe or Minneapolis to Seattle on the Great Northern and Northern Pacific. The West was still a growth area, especially during and after the war, so the prospects for the western roads were good. However, the West also had some of the most challenging weather and terrain with which to contend. Mountain grades and high passes, hot and dry deserts, and the cold and snowy northern plains made railroading a constant challenge.

Atchison Topeka & Santa Fe

The first western district railroad that wholeheartedly embraced the diesel was also one of the largest and most profitable, the Atchison Topeka & Santa Fe. With 13,073 miles of line stretching from Chicago to Los Angeles and Denver to Houston, the Santa Fe was a huge railroad, and a profitable one. By the end of the 1930s the steam fleet of the Santa Fe was quite diverse with 2–8–0 and 2–6–2 types from the turn of the century along side modern 4–8–4 types. The railroad invested heavily in steam power during the 1920s purchasing dozens of modern 4–6–2 and 2–8–2 types and even purchasing some 4–6–4 and 4–8–4 types for high speed freight and passenger service. In the late 1930s as traffic began to rebound from the nadir of 1932 and 1933, the road again invested in modern steam power including 4–6–4, 4–8–4, and 2–10–4 types. Even while it was purchasing modern steam in the mid and late 1930s, the road began to explore diesel power. The Santa Fe began its foray into diesel power in February 1935 with the purchase of a small Alco switcher, likely for antismoke reasons in the Chicago Terminal. While one small switcher did not cause a big splash, the next purchase did. The Santa Fe contracted EMC to build a high speed passenger locomotive to haul the new streamlined luxury train, the Super Chief. In August 1935 EMC delivered a unique pair of locomotives for the new train. Each unit contained two separate engines each with a rating of nine hundred horsepower for a total of 3,600 from four engines in two units. This was a big step for the small company, and all eyes were on the new units to see how they would perform in the demanding high-speed long-distance passenger service. The Santa Fe held off on major diesel purchases for almost two years while it evaluated the performance and costs of the new units, only buying one diesel switching locomotive in 1936. By early 1937 the verdict was in, and it looked good for the diesel as well as the folks at EMC. After the success of the Super Chief, the Santa Fe began to acquire more diesels for other passenger applications. Santa Fe purchased two E-1 units in 1937 followed by nine more in 1938 for other high profile passenger services.[72] Six more passenger units were purchased in 1939 and 1940 along with a plethora of switchers from Alco and Baldwin in addition to offerings from EMC.[73] These new passenger diesels allowed another streamlined train, the El Capitan, to enter service. Many of the switchers were used in downtown passenger terminal locations where smoke was a concern.

While there were only a relatively few diesels on the property, they were running off some impressive mileage. In 1940 the sixty-one passenger and switching diesels totaled slightly over 5 million miles or over 80,000 miles per locomotive. The 1,477 steam locomotives ran a total of over 49.5 million miles but this was only an average of 33,600 miles per locomotive.[74] What makes these numbers even more impressive is the fact that of the sixty-one diesels in service, forty-two were switchers that were usually confined to yards and terminals and would therefore not amass nearly the mileage as the nineteen elite passenger locomotives. The bright red, yellow, and silver passenger units were streaking across the plains and deserts from Chicago to Los Angeles on tight schedules. The Super Chief took just under forty hours to travel from Chicago to Los Angeles, a distance of 2,224 miles. This ambitious schedule would have been all but impossible to maintain with steam locomotives, not because they could not achieve high speeds, but because they required much more time spent in online fueling, watering, and servicing. The Santa Fe, unlike other railroads, was quick to recognize and capitalize on the advantages of diesel operation such as increased availability and less need for en route servicing.

While the Super Chief and El Capitan luxury streamliners were the high profile examples of the Santa Fe's experimentation with the diesel, passengers did not pay most of the company's bills, since passenger revenue was only about a tenth of total operating revenue.[75] Freight made up the bulk of the rest and freight is where the Santa Fe would be the first to put the diesel locomotive to work on a large scale. The Santa Fe is most notable for being the first railroad to opt for the EMC model FT. The Santa Fe, which had a long established relationship with EMC since 1935, consulted with EMC during 1938 and 1939 on the development of the FT locomotive. It was only fitting then that the Santa Fe hosted the demonstrator FT on its nationwide tour and was excited by the possibilities inherent in the locomotive. One reason for the recognition of the possibilities of the diesel in addition to the previous experience with streamlined passenger power was new vice president, Fred G. Gurley. Gurley had recently come to the Santa Fe from the Chicago Burlington & Quincy where he was deeply involved with the streamlined Zephyrs of that road. He was keenly aware of the benefits of diesel power and pushed for increasing use on the Santa Fe. The railroad quickly placed an order, and the first FTs began to arrive in December 1940. Between then and the end of the war in September 1945, the Santa Fe received 320 FT units of both A and B varieties.[76] This was vastly more units than any other railroad. The Santa Fe quickly put its new diesels to work on the most demanding stretch of the railroad in the desert southwest. Their primary territory was between Winslow, Arizona, and Barstow, California, over 450 miles of long and heavy grades and an area with little water for steam locomotives.[77] They were also used on the heavy mountain grades north and south out of Barstow with grades of up to 2.2 percent. This territory included some of the harshest environmental conditions on the continent. The diesels handled the wartime traffic boom better than expected and in no small way enabled the Santa Fe to keep up with the crush of men and material moving to the west coast from eastern and Midwestern states.

The wartime traffic was too great for the new diesels to handle by themselves. While they kept traffic moving across Arizona and the deserts of Southern California, more motive power was needed for other parts of the railroad. With diesel production restricted, the Santa Fe responded by ordering new steam locomotives. Baldwin built 40 modern 4–8–4 types from 1941 to 1944. These locomotives were joined by 25 huge 2–10–4 locomotives, also built by Baldwin in 1944. In pure horsepower terms one 2–10–4 was equal to an FT four unit set. The 1944 Baldwin 2–10–4 locomotives would be the last new steam power that the Santa Fe would purchase. Diesel promoter and enthusiast Fred Gurley would become president of the Santa Fe that year and no further steam locomotives were purchased.

In 1946 with the war over and costs rising, the Santa Fe, led by the fiscally conservative Gurley took a cautious approach, purchasing only 30 diesels for passenger service. The following year brought 25 more locomotives, 21 passenger and 4 switchers. Large-scale dieselization began in earnest in 1948 with 103 predominantly passenger locomotives purchased. Of special significance were several passenger locomotives that were also capable of use in freight service. They were off-the-shelf EMD F-Units equipped with steam generators for heating passenger cars. The years 1949 and 1950 brought large numbers of new freight diesels to the railroad, 100 in 1949 and 74 in 1950. By 1950 over 60 percent of gross ton miles were handled by diesel power, up from 30 percent in 1947 and 10 percent in 1943. By the end of 1952 the change was even more dramatic. Of the total volume of Santa Fe business in the month of December 1952, diesels handled 77 percent of freight gross ton miles, 93 percent of passenger car miles, and 95 percent of yard switch locomotive hours.[78] Despite these impressive gains, steam would soldier on in a few isolated places until 1957. In August of that year the last revenue steam run occurred when a 2–10–4 and a 4–8–4 worked as helpers in New Mexico.[79] With capable and relatively new steam on the railroad, Santa Fe management decided to use the steam locomotives in service to try to recoup as much of the initial investment as possible.

The Santa Fe dieselized for several reasons. Vice president and later president, Fred Gurley provided much of the top down push for diesels. His initial experience with diesels on the Burlington convinced him of the ability of the new form of motive power to cut costs and increase operational efficiency. After the initial efforts and especially after the introduction of the FT, the lower-level management and operating forces were impressed with the power, speed, and efficiency of the diesels. As they did elsewhere, the diesels cut costs for the Santa Fe. However, costs were far from the only reason that the Santa Fe dieselized. In the competitive Chicago to California passenger market, diesels would give the Santa Fe an edge, not only in speed and trip time, but in appearance and public relations as well. The Super Chief would have been less super with a steam locomotive on the front. What really made the diesels attractive to the Santa Fe was their lack of need for track side water facilities. The Santa Fe operated through arid country in New Mexico, Arizona, and California and finding and chemically treating the often alkaline water in the massive quantities needed for large steam locomotives was always a problem. In fact, the railroad had to ship tank car loads of water to some facilities because there was no local water available. The Santa Fe was also a successful railroad with the available resources to purchase and operate new diesel locomotives. There was little on line coal reserves or traffic on the Santa Fe so the coal industry was not a large player in the dieselization of the railroad. The Santa Fe did serve several oil producing regions and already had established relationships with major oil producers and refiners. This made it easy to embrace diesel as a fuel. The Santa Fe, as might be surmised, did very well in the postwar era and was a successful and profitable independent railroad until its merger with the Burlington Northern in the 1990s.

Chicago, Burlington & Quincy

The next Western district railroad analyzed is the Chicago, Burlington & Quincy (CB&Q), often called the Burlington or simply, the Q. The CB&Q stretched for over 8,800 miles from Chicago north and west to Minneapolis, Omaha, Kansas City, Denver, and Billings, Montana. At Denver a line extended south through Amarillo to Dallas and Houston. Officially lines in Colorado were part of the Colorado & Southern Railroad, while the lines in Texas were part of the Fort Worth & Denver Railroad. However, all were operated as one large system of nearly 11,000 miles. True to its motto of, "Everywhere West," The Burlington operated a huge network of branch and secondary lines. Iowa, Missouri, and Nebraska were covered with an extensive grid of these lightly built and lightly used agricultural branch lines.[80]

As with most other large roads, the Burlington had a great variety of steam power. At the beginning of the 1930s main line freight moved behind 2–8–2, 2–10–2 and eighteen new 2–10–4 types. Local and branch lines were the domain of smaller power like 2–8–0 and 2–6–2 types. Passengers were hauled by 4–4–2 types, many recently modernized by the railroad in its own shops, 4–6–0, 4–6–2, and 4–8–2 types. Despite the abysmal business conditions during the Great Depression, the Burlington purchased and built large, modern 4–6–4 and 4–8–4 types throughout the 1930s. Baldwin produced twelve 4–6–4 types and eight 4–8–4 types for the road in 1930. The large shops in West Burlington, Iowa built two 4–6–4 and twenty-eight 4–8–4 types from 1935 to 1940.[81] Again we see a road that utilized its own resources to provide low initial cost modern steam locomotives that would also generate efficiencies in operations by being more powerful and requiring less maintenance.

The Burlington is somewhat of a special case in the story of the dieselization of North American railroads. The Burlington made a huge splash with the introduction of the Zephyr streamlined diesel train in 1934. From that point on it continued to purchase flashy stainless steel clad EMC and later EMD passenger diesels as well as a few more prosaic switchers. The various Zephyrs were successful in cutting costs and in bringing passengers back to the rails, for a time. Much like the Reading and B&O railroads in the eastern district or neighbors and competitors Chicago & North Western and Chicago, Rock Island & Pacific, the Burlington continued to purchase and build new steam locomotives, long after the Zephyr and its siblings were polishing the rails of the Midwest. The Burlington sampled the FT on its 1940 demonstration tour but steam motive power on the Burlington was deemed sufficient to handle existing traffic so no orders were immediately forthcoming. Wartime traffic changed the mind of management and the first FT units were delivered to the Burlington in late 1943.

The experience with the FT during the war sealed the fate of steam on the Burlington. Once the FT entered service, no new steam locomotives were built or purchased. Many detailed studies were made chronicling the saving possible by using diesel power. Not only could the FT outperform even the mighty 2–10–4 by hauling twice as much tonnage on a particular grade, but sixteen FT units and fifteen switchers would only require thirty tank cars of diesel fuel per day compared with 512 cars of coal for the steam locomotives they displaced.[82] On a railroad choked with wartime traffic, the fewer cars needed for company service, the more cars available for revenue generating freight. The railroad began to purchase more diesels immediately upon cessation of hostilities with 159 new diesel units delivered between 1946 and 1949.[83] By the end of 1950, the railroad had 448 diesel locomotive units and 657 steam locomotives.[84] By the end of 1953 all regularly scheduled passenger trains and 95 percent of all freight trains were diesel powered.[85] Steam would continue to burnish the rails of the Burlington for some time, lasting until 1958.[86]

The Burlington embraced the diesel for many reasons. Initially the publicity value of the streamlined Zephyrs and the cost savings over steam powered passenger trains were the primary reasons. Competition with other railroads in passenger service was also part of the reason to choose diesels. The Burlington, while not faced with the arid deserts of Arizona and California like the Santa Fe, did have coal and water supply issues on its western and southern lines. Once freight diesels were available, the cost differences and the increased performance sealed the fate for steam on the road. The Burlington was also fortunate in that it had an upper management that was familiar with and receptive to diesels from the earliest days of the Zephyr. It also had a small but vital core of midlevel officials and trained shop forces. It is also no coincidence that the CB&Q decided to dieselize with EMC and EMD products as the railroad served the EMD manufacturing plant in suburban Chicago. Like most western roads, the Burlington did well financially during the war and in the immediate postwar period and had the available capital to spend on diesels and other improvements. While recognizing and embracing the diesel, the Burlington wanted to get its money's worth out of its modern steam locomotives as well and used its 4-8-4 and 2-10-4 types well into the 1950s. The Burlington served important coal producing areas in southern Illinois and Wyoming but was not a major coal hauler to the extent of some of the Appalachian railroads so coal industry interests were not a large factor. The Burlington survived the postwar era relatively well finally merging with the long time

affiliated Great Northern and Northern Pacific to form
the Burlington Northern in 1970.

St. Louis–San Francisco

While some western roads experimented with diesels
before the war, most did not. The St. Louis–San Francisco railroad, universally known as the Frisco, did not
roster a prewar diesel streamliner like the Burlington
and Santa Fe but was quick to dieselize after the war.
The 5,735 miles of the Frisco was shaped much like a
large X. One main line ran from Kansas City via Memphis, Tennessee to Pensacola, Florida. The other leg
ran from St. Louis to Tulsa, and Oklahoma City. The two
lines met at Springfield, Missouri, location of large yards
and shops. The Frisco also had an extensive network of
secondary and branch lines that extended to Dallas and
Paris, Texas; Wichita, Kansas; and Ft. Smith, Arkansas.
In spite of the name, its tracks never made it within 1,000
miles of San Francisco. The Frisco was one of many railroads to enter bankruptcy during the Great Depression.
It operated under receivership from 1932 to 1947. With
little spare capital and with major decisions scrutinized
by creditors, it is no wonder that the railroad followed
a conservative path and did not embrace the flashy and
experimental diesels in the 1930s.

The steam power of the Frisco in the late 1930s was relatively modern but not overly so. Freight was hauled by
2–8–0 types from the first decade of the century mingled
with large and capable 2–8–2 types built in the mid-1920s.
Passengers were pulled by standard Pacific types dating
from the 1910s as well as more modern and capable 4–8–2
Mountain types. As speed and efficiency became more
important in the 1930s and with capital scarce, the Frisco
looked to its own shops for faster and more capable locomotives. As with other railroads, using fully owned shop facilities allowed the Frisco to keep workers employed during
the Depression and therefore in town and to produce new
modern locomotives at less cost than a commercial builder.
There were also some tax benefits from rebuilding locomotives rather than purchasing new ones. The shops took
old and outdated locomotives and extensively rebuilt them
into modern fast 4–8–2 type power. The program continued
until 1942 when a total of thirty-four new locomotives had
been created. Increased wartime traffic created a need for

Photo 6 Birmingham, Alabama in June of 1940 is the location of this Frisco 4–8–2 or Mountain type. This locomotive was built by Baldwin in 1926 as a passenger locomotive for the Frisco and is a good example of modern, late 1920s passenger power. Courtesy of the Museum Of The Rockies, Ron V. Nixon Railroad Photography Collection.

even more locomotives so twenty-five modern 4-8-4 types were delivered from Baldwin in 1942 and 1943.[87]

As was typical of many railroads, the Frisco began to experiment with diesels during the war. The conservative Frisco management looked first to known locomotive suppliers. Baldwin supplied five diesel switchers in 1941 primarily for terminal service in St. Louis. By the end of the war there were forty-six diesel switchers on the property but no road passenger or freight locomotives.[88] Like other railroads, the Frisco took a break at this point and did not order any further diesels for a couple years. Road passenger units were the first post war diesels with six delivered in 1947. Neighboring roads and competitors in the passenger market were already dieselized or were dieselizing quickly. To remain competitive the Frisco needed to embrace the diesel for passenger operations. Road-freight units began arriving in 1948. By the close of 1950 there were 288 diesels in service alongside 363 steam locomotives.[89] While not yet a numerical majority, the diesels accounted for 73 percent of all train-miles in December 1950.[90] Further diesel orders in 1951 and 1952 enabled steam to be completely displaced by February 1952.[91] The Frisco is notable for being an early convert to the road-switcher type with several entering service beginning in 1950.

The Frisco dieselized for many reasons. Cost was the primary reason but competition with neighboring railroads was a large factor especially in passenger dieselization. Municipal smoke restrictions were likely also important, especially in the initial purchase of diesel switchers for operation at downtown passenger terminals. Never a large coal hauler, the Frisco felt no need to remain loyal to the coal industry for locomotive fuel. Indeed, most of its locomotives burned oil. The Frisco, once it emerged from receivership in 1948 aggressively dieselized and was quick to realize the advantages of the road switcher type. As it served the growing southwest in the postwar era, the Frisco did reasonably well financially and remained a relatively strong and independent road until merger with the Burlington Northern in 1980.

Missouri Pacific

A direct competitor of the Frisco was the Missouri Pacific (MP). The MP operated an extensive network of lines radiating south and west from St. Louis. They reached as far

west as El Paso, Texas and Pueblo, Colorado, northwest to
Omaha and Lincoln, Nebraska, and south to New Orleans,
Dallas, Houston, and the Mexican border at Laredo and
Brownsville, Texas. Operated as part of the nearly 10,000
mile Missouri Pacific system were the Texas and Pacific,
International—Great Northern, and Missouri–Illinois
railroads. Like the Frisco, the railroad went bankrupt
and fell into receivership during 1933 and remained
there for the rest of the 1930s. The steam power of the
Missouri Pacific was heavily modernized in the 1920s.
New 0–8–0 switchers were purchased along with 2–8–2
freight power and 4–6–2 and 4–8–2 passenger power.
Of special note were thirty 2–8–4 Berkshire types purchased from 1928 to 1930.[92] Because of the lack of traffic
and the lack of money, no new steam power would be purchased by the MP until the Second World War. Dieselization began with a group of six EMC switchers purchased
fairly early, in the summer of 1937. These pioneering six
were joined by forty-two others by 1942.[93] Clearly the MP
and its creditors were convinced of the cost savings of
using diesel switchers. Main line dieselization began in
1939 with two E-units from EMC. These two units were
earmarked for the new Eagle streamlined passenger
train and were adorned with a large, stylized stainless
steel eagle on the front of the locomotive. The first two
Eagle units were joined by five more before the attack on
Pearl Harbor.[94]

During the war the MP continued to dieselize purchasing more switchers as well as twenty-four EMD FT
units. After hosting the FT on its demonstration tour and
already familiar with diesels due to the passenger diesels in service, MP officials decided to purchase some
FT locomotives. Once the diesels began arriving on the
property in late 1943 they continued to impress operating crews and officials with their performance, especially
their speed and hill climbing ability. A mark of their ability is the nickname given to them by the operating crews,
"big jeeps."[95] Even while the MP was hosting the FT on its
demonstration tour, they were investing heavily in steam
locomotives. From 1940 to 1942 the MP took twenty-five
1930 built 2–8–4 Berkshire type locomotives and completely rebuilt them in its Sedalia, Missouri shops into
fast, powerful 4–8–4 types. In 1943 they were joined by fifteen new Baldwin built 4–8–4 locomotives.[96] Thus, by the
end of the war, the MP had not only state-of-the-art diesel

Photo 7   The Missouri Pacific purchased diesels from Alco as well as EMD. This is a set of Alco FA type locomotives. The FA was roughly equivalent in performance to the EMD F-3 type. Courtesy of the Union Pacific Museum.

locomotives, like the FT, but also modern advanced steam power. The Missouri Pacific, like railroads such as the B&O and Reading, seemed to have one foot planted firmly in both the diesel and steam camp. They needed motive power and steam made economic sense, especially with wartime production restrictions on diesels in place. Utilizing their own shops was also a money saving move as it enabled the railroad to produce high quality and well performing locomotives for a fraction of the cost of new steam or diesels.

With the war over, the Missouri Pacific began full scale dieselization in earnest. Beginning in 1946 and continuing well into the next decade, diesel locomotives arrived on the property by the dozen. Unlike other roads, there was no waiting period in 1946 and 1947 to see what the economy would do. New switchers were joined by new passenger power and freight units. By 1950 the Missouri Pacific system rostered 535 diesels and 870 steam locomotives.[97] Complete dieselization was achieved in 1955.[98] Diesels came to dominate the Missouri Pacific for similar reasons as other roads. Initial purchases were concentrated on flashy passenger diesels and on small switchers that would effect large economies and have smoke abatement utility. With the railroad operating in receivership cost savings were especially important. The FT comes along in 1940 and both its performance and economy of operation can not be ignored. The newly rebuilt 4–8–4 types would have a short life, doomed by the cost savings of the diesel. The post war traffic boom in the southwest along with the savings of the diesel allowed the MP to finally emerge from receivership in 1956. The MP, like some other railroads, did not fully appreciate the advantages of standardization on one locomotive manufacturer and purchased a large variety of different types. Standardization came in the 1960s. The Missouri Pacific, under the leadership of Downing Jenks, president from 1961 to 1972, would become a world class railroad and go on to become a major part of the expanded Union Pacific system upon merger of the two in 1982.

Chicago Rock Island & Pacific

The 7,610 mile Chicago, Rock Island & Pacific, the Rock Island line of song and story, was indeed a "mighty fine line" during the first half of the twentieth century. The

Rock Island extended from Chicago, St. Louis, and Memphis in the east to Minneapolis, Denver, Santa Rosa, New Mexico, and Galveston, Texas. At Santa Rosa it connected with the Southern Pacific forming a through route from California to the Midwest. The Rock Island served the agricultural heart of the nation with many branches from Texas to Iowa designed and built to serve agricultural producers. By the 1930s the steam locomotives of the Rock Island were a varied and relatively up to date bunch. Local freight moved behind 2–8–0 types from the first decade of the century while through freight had more advanced 2–8–2 types built in the 1920s for power. Passengers moved behind a mixture of older 4–4–2 and 4–6–0 types on branch lines and local trains while the through trains were pulled by more modern 4–6–2 and 4–8–2 types.

The Rock Island was an early convert to internal combustion power. It built in its own shops two gasoline electric locomotives for freight service in 1927. Several more small boxcab type gas-electric locomotives followed in 1929.[99] The first true diesel on the railroad followed a year later. This locomotive was an interesting beast. It was powered not directly off a generator driven by the diesel engine but by batteries. The batteries, in turn, were continually recharged by a constant speed diesel engine.[100] It was similar to others operated by the New York Central and Lackawanna. While there were efficiency gains to be had from the early experimental internal combustion locomotives, smoke abatement was a more pressing reason for their construction.

The Rock Island was an early adopter of diesels for streamlined passenger service. Its Rockets polished the rails of the heartland as early as 1937. The trains were powered, at first, by the unique to the Rock Island, EMC model TA. The TA was a small version of the normal EMC passenger power, the E unit. By the outbreak of the war these TA units had been joined by larger EMC E-units as well as Alco DL-109 types.[101] Other competing railroads, such as the Burlington, were embracing streamlined diesel motive power. Despite financial hardship, the Rock Island went bankrupt in 1933 and was operating in receivership, to remain competitive in the passenger arena it had to implement faster streamlined trains.

Like other railroads the Rock Island continued to purchase new steam locomotives and upgrade existing ones while promoting diesel passenger services. Sixty-five modern 4–8–4 locomotives were delivered in 1929 and

Photo 8 This Rock Island EMD E-Unit seen here leaving St. Paul, Minnesota in August 1946 is typical of the hundreds of E-units purchased and put into passenger service. Courtesy of the Museum of the Rockies, Ron V. Nixon Railroad Photography Collection.

1930. These locomotives were extensively modernized and upgraded in the late 1930s. During the war they were joined by ten more 4–8–4 types. The last delivery of this type of locomotive to the Rock Island was in 1946 when an additional ten were added to the roster.[102] Arriving at the same time as the last group of 4–8–4 locomotives was the first group of diesel freight locomotives, the EMD FT. After hosting the FT on its demonstration tour, the Rock Island ordered thirty-six FT units which were delivered in 1944 and 1945. On the line from Rock Island to Kansas City, the new diesels, when combined in four unit sets, were rated for 8,400 tons while the newest steam, the 4–8–4 types, were only rated for 5,000 tons.[103] Again we see a railroad, that despite much experience with diesel and internal combustion power for passengers and switching duties, remained somewhat loyal to steam power for freight. This policy likely made economic sense for the Rock Island especially during the lean 1930s. Utilizing existing resources instead of purchasing new units would preserve limited capital for other purposes. With the war over and costs increasing the days for steam were numbered. Huge numbers of diesels; switchers, passenger, and freight, as well as the new road-switchers flooded the railroad, especially after reorganization and the emergence from bankruptcy in 1948. Steam would last only until July 1953.[104] The Rock Island dieselized for many reasons. Initial experimental efforts were later followed by switchers destined for downtown terminal facilities and flashy streamliners. The diesel powered streamlined passenger trains kept the Rock Island in the public eye and matched the streamliners of neighboring competitors. The FT finally proved that the diesel could do to freight service what it could do to passenger service, namely cut costs and increase operating efficiencies. The Rock Island unfortunately would suffer a dismal fate unlike its neighbors and competitors. Its new diesels, a plethora of different types and builders, could not save the railroad although it did reasonably well throughout the 1950s and into the 1960s. The Rock Island was surrounded by larger and more prosperous roads, like the Burlington and the Santa Fe. When various merger and takeover bids of the 1960s were interminably delayed or outright failed, the Rock Island entered bankruptcy again in 1975 and ceased operation entirely in 1980. Many of its lines were acquired by other railroads however and remain in operation.

Chicago & North Western

Another Midwestern road like the Rock Island was the 9,569 mile Chicago & North Western. The C&NW was true to its name, extending north and west from Chicago through Wisconsin, Iowa, Minnesota, South Dakota, and Nebraska. The line reached its western-most point at Lander, Wyoming, over 1,200 miles from Chicago. Like the Rock Island and the Burlington, the C&NW was a "Granger road" with many lines built to serve agricultural producers. Although the vast majority of steam power on the railroad by the time of dieselization dated to the 1910s or before, the C&NW did have some capable modern power. The majority of freight moved behind 2–8–0 and 2–8–2 types. The railroad did have twelve Berkshire types, delivered in 1927. Two years later the railroad accepted thirty five modern 4–8–4 types from Alco. Passengers rode behind various 4–6–2 types. For high speed passenger service the C&NW purchased nine streamlined 4–6–4 Hudson types in 1938.[105] The Hudsons and 4–8–4 types were advanced and capable locomotives that were amongst the best in operation in the region.

Diesels came early to the North Western. Three box-cab switchers were purchased in 1926 and 1927. One more slightly larger locomotive was added in 1930.[106] These locomotives toiled away in relative obscurity spending most of their time in the Chicago terminal area due to antismoke concerns. The next diesels were to be very different from the small, workmanlike boxcab switchers. In the late 1930s in cooperation with the Union Pacific and the Southern Pacific, the C&NW purchased six EMC E-units for the new streamlined City of Los Angeles and City of San Francisco trains. Both of these trains were direct competitors with the diesel powered streamliners of the Santa Fe. More E-units and some new switchers joined the roster in the next couple years. By the outbreak of hostilities in 1941, the C&NW had twenty-three diesel units on the roster, mixed between high speed passenger units and switchers.[107] The war years would more than double the number of diesels on the railroad, from twenty-three in December 1941 to 103 in December 1945. Most of this increase was in switching locomotives but the C&NW did purchase a small number of EMD FT locomotives delivered in the summer of 1945 despite not having hosted the FT on its demonstration tour. However, neighbors and competitors the Chicago Milwaukee St. Paul and Pacific or Milwaukee Road and the Burlington were also

Photo 9 This husky looking 4-8-4 of the Chicago & North Western was built by Baldwin in 1929. It was extensively modernized in 1940 and again in 1946. There is no better example than this of state of the art steam power during the heyday of dieselization. It is seen here in 1952 passing beneath a coaling tower at DeKalb, Illinois. The large cylindrical object above the main headlight on the front is an oscillating warning light. Courtesy of the Museum of the Rockies, Ron V. Nixon Railroad Photography Collection.

operating FT locomotives. The North Western likely purchased some to try them out and to remain competitive.

Like the Rock Island and many others, the North Western had not given up entirely on steam power. While no
new steam locomotives were ordered after the 4–6–4 order
of 1938, the railroad continually modernized its existing
equipment. The huge 4–8–4 locomotives were extensively
modernized twice. The first time was in 1940 when they
received roller bearings and other improvements. After
the war the same locomotives were again extensively modernized in company shops including an entirely new cast
steel frame.[108] Again, the C&NW stands as an example of a
railroad in both the steam and diesel camp, at least until
1947 or so. Utilizing existing shops and labor to improve
performance of existing locomotives cost substantially less
than purchasing new locomotives but would not result in
the cost savings inherent in the operation of diesel motive
power. As with other roads, the turning point was 1947. With
postwar traffic and with years worth of direct diesel experience, 61 diesels were added in 1947 including the first
large order for road-freight power.[109] By 1950 the C&NW
was operating 376 diesels and 890 steam locomotives.[110]
The next three years saw almost 300 diesels added to the
roster. Steam finally disappeared from regular service in
May 1956. The rest of the 1950s and 1960s were relatively
prosperous times for the Northwestern under the progressive leadership Ben W. Heineman, chairman and CEO from
1956 to 1972. The C&NW acquired several smaller carriers
in the 1960s including the Chicago Great Western and Minneapolis & St. Louis and underwent a period of employee
ownership in the 1970s. Coal from Wyoming brought new-
found prosperity in the late 1970s and 1980s and enabled
the C&NW to buck the merger trend until the 1990s when it
finally became part of the expanding Union Pacific system.

There are many similarities between the railroads of the
Midwest in their response to the diesel. Many were initially
prodded to try the diesel for downtown terminal switching
by anti smoke legislation or agitation in the 1920s. This was
especially true in the city of Chicago. The 1930s brought
passenger streamliners and experience with main line diesels in high speed service. Many roads inaugurated streamlined service in an effort to not only increase passenger
revenue and decrease costs but to increase public aware-
ness and to remain competitive with neighboring railroads
and the ever increasing number of automobiles. Freight,

the bread and butter of the railroads, continued to move behind steam power. Many roads substantially modernized their steam freight power during the 1930s and early 1940s as finances allowed. Using company shops to build or heavily rebuild locomotives was often an economical alternative to purchasing new locomotives from a commercial builder like Lima, Baldwin or Alco. Roads that hosted the FT demonstrator generally purchased some after they were impressed with the performance and potential cost savings of the units. Even roads that did not host the demonstrator often embraced the FT. Although some roads purchased new or substantially upgraded their steam power immediately after the war, by 1948 the verdict was in. From that point on the roads pursued dieselization with all possible speed. The long term outlook for Midwestern roads was mixed. Some went on to become powerful and prosperous, like the Burlington and the Missouri Pacific while others became merger and takeover targets like the Frisco. The Rock Island stands as the extreme case with its bankruptcy and later dismemberment. Dieselization was not a panacea but, if done correctly and accompanied by other changes, it could breathe new life into a railroad.

Denver & Rio Grande Western

The 2,387 mile Denver & Rio Grande Western Railroad, while having a lyrical name, was cursed with some of the most difficult terrain in North America. It ran from Denver and Pueblo, Colorado west through the heart of the Colorado Rockies to connections at Salt Lake City and Ogden, Utah. It also had an extensive network of branch lines that served predominantly small mining communities in Colorado and northern New Mexico. Several of these branch lines were narrow gauge (three feet) and as such were operated almost as a separate railroad, detached from the national rail network. The Rio Grande's finances were as torturous as the terrain it traversed, and it was in receivership from the early years of the century until 1947. Despite these problems and the lack of available capital the railroad tried to modernize its fleet of steam locomotives in the 1920s and 1930s. Because of the severity of the grades it encountered, it needed massive and powerful locomotives.[111] Aptly named 4–8–2 mountain types were purchased in the 1920s for passenger service, while even larger and more massive 2–8–8–2 articulated locomotives were purchased to lug freight across the high mountain passes. While these locomotives may have been good at crawling up heavy grades, they were not high speed machines. With an increase of bridge traffic and war clouds on the horizon, high speed was just what the Rio Grande needed.

The solution to the speed problem was found in the 4–6–6–4 high speed articulated. The Rio Grande purchased ten such locomotives from Baldwin in 1937. To handle the wartime traffic crush eleven more were added to the roster in 1942 and 1943.[112] The war placed a huge strain on the Rio Grande, and its strategic route connecting the great plains with the far west was choked with more traffic than the available steam locomotives could bear. The Rio Grande began its experience with diesels in the same way that most railroads did, with a single small switching locomotive, purchased in 1941. The railroad was quick to realize the potential in the FT after it was demonstrated on the railroad in 1940 and placed an order for twelve units to be delivered in three sets of four units each in April 1941.[113] By the end of 1944, thirty-six more FT units would be on the railroad. The railroad, because of its strategic location as a bridge route between the Midwest and far west was allocated the locomotives by the war production board. The railroad was convinced; diesels were the way to go. On a mountain railroad diesels were able to showcase the high tractive effort that they developed at slow speeds, the dynamic braking and the lack of acrid coal smoke, a concern for a railroad like the Rio Grande with many tunnels. It would be twelve more years before steam would completely vanish from the standard gauge rails of the D&RGW but its days in main line fast freight and passenger service were numbered. At the end of 1950 the railroad owned 40 diesel switchers, 6 dedicated diesel passenger locomotives and 142 multi-use freight units. This total of 170 diesel units exactly matched the number of steam locomotives in service.[114] While the number of locomotives in service may have been equal, the utilization was anything but. In 1950 steam locomotives accounted for 498,073 freight miles, while diesel locomotives accounted for 1,423,637 freight miles, almost three times as much. The difference in passenger miles was even more extreme, 19,348 to 87,111.[115] By the end of 1956 the number of diesels on the property had risen to 244, while all standard gauge steam power had been retired.[116]

The Rio Grande dieselized for many reasons. Cost, as always, was a factor but many other variables came to play.

The extreme conditions of the line with its many grades and tunnels made the diesel with its unique abilities especially attractive. The railroad, impressed with the performance of the FT, was able to secure so many during the war because of its strategic importance in hauling war material. It was similar to the Santa Fe in this regard. The wartime traffic boom provided the traffic initially and as soon as the war was over, the Rio Grande, in order to maintain competitiveness with railroads that had routes not as geographically challenging, continued to embrace the diesel. Although it served several coal mining areas, the need to remain loyal to coal was not a factor in the dieselization of the Rio Grande. Coal from the Colorado and Utah mines served by the Rio Grande was increasingly destined for power plants and steel mills in the postwar industrializing west and not for the fireboxes of steam locomotives. The Rio Grande continued to do well in the postwar era and remained a strong and independent railroad until a merger with the Southern Pacific in the 1990s.

Western Pacific

One of the railroads the Rio Grande connected with on the west end and its primary interchange partner was the Western Pacific (WP). The 1,524 mile WP ran from Salt Lake City west across the Utah salt flats and the Nevada desert. It descended the Sierra Nevada mountain range through the scenic Feather River Canyon and served Sacramento, San Jose, and Oakland, California. It did not have many branch lines but did connect with the Great Northern via the "inside gateway route" to Bieber, California. The WP was primarily a bridge or through route for traffic from and to California. It generated little on line traffic. The WP was a latecomer to the western railroad scene and was completed in 1909. It promptly entered bankruptcy in 1915.[117]

In the 1930s, as speed became ever more important for railroads, the WP found itself, like the Rio Grande, in need of faster motive power. Also like friendly connection the Rio Grande and neighbor and competitor Union Pacific, the WP chose the 4–6–6–4 as the locomotive to move this fast freight across the mountains and deserts of Nevada and Utah. In the mountains of California several 2–8–8–2 types were used. While slower they were better suited for the heavy grades.[118] The other steam power of the WP ranged from 2–8–0 and 4–6–0 types built in the first decade of the century to more modern 2–8–2 and 4–8–2 types dating from the 1920s.

The WP likely would have purchased even more modern articulated steam as traffic returned in 1939 and 1940 except for one thing. The railroad had hosted the demonstrator model of the FT on its nationwide tour in 1940. While the performance of the four unit FT set was somewhat superior to the performance of the most modern 4–6–6–4 locomotives, what most impressed officials was the substantial potential savings in fuel and labor costs. The FT could also be used anywhere on the railroad, while large steam locomotives would be restricted in their operational territory because of size, weight, or service facilities.[119] The WP placed an order for twelve units arranged in three four unit sets in June 1941. The first set arrived on the property on December 7, 1941. By the end of 1944, forty-four more units would be hauling the heavy wartime traffic.[120]

The FT was not the first diesel on the Western Pacific. In a pattern seen with most other railroads, the first diesels were three small switching locomotives, purchased in 1939. These small switchers gave the WP valuable experience with diesels and also enabled the railroad to begin to forge new supplier relationships with Electro-Motive. As with other railroads, the switchers were used in terminal areas where steam locomotive smoke was a municipal concern. With the switchers and the FT, steam power was soon eliminated from the WP. With more orders for diesels after the war including road-switchers, by July 1953 the Western Pacific was dieselized.[121] The WP is quite similar to the Rio Grande in its reasons for dieselization. After the decisive demonstration tour of the FT, the railroad was able to get FT units during the war because of its strategic location. The diesels were better suited to the harsh operating conditions on the WP. After the war, continued dieselization enabled the WP, never a financially strong railroad, to better compete against its larger and more successful competitors, primarily the Southern Pacific. The small size of the WP, surrounded as it was by giants like the UP and SP, eventually did lead to its demise. In 1982 it was merged into the expanding Union Pacific system.

SOUTHERN DISTRICT

The southern district was home to many large railroads but seemed to have more than its share of small regional and short lines. Southern railroads generally did not have the traffic density of the eastern roads, especially the heavy coal and steel traffic and did not have the infrastructure to support such traffic. The exception to this rule were the large Appalachian coal hauling railroads which had some of the highest tonnage figures of any railroad. The unique dieselization experience of the short lines is examined in chapter 4.

The Gulf Mobile & Ohio Railroad (GM&O) in 1940 operated from St. Louis south to New Orleans and Mobile with secondary main lines to Memphis, Birmingham, and Montgomery. In 1947 the GM&O, under the leadership of the aggressive Ike Tigrett, acquired the Alton Railroad which extended the GM&O from St. Louis north to Chicago and west to Kansas City creating a 2,898 mile system. The GM&O served coal mines in Illinois but most traffic on the southern lines was not coal but agricultural, manufactured, and forest products.

The steam power of the GM&O was decidedly not modern. The bulk of locomotives in service in 1940 were built in the first decade of the century.[122] In that year, the GM&O was created by the merger of the Mobile & Ohio (M&O) with the Gulf, Mobile & Northern (GM&N). The M&O had purchased thirty-seven, 2–8–2 types in the 1920s for fast freight service and also ten light Pacifics for passenger service but nothing was purchased after 1928. The GM&N was probably in even worse shape as far as motive power was concerned with only twenty-one locomotives purchased during the 1920s. Of these newer locomotives, sixteen were 2–10–0 decapod types suitable only for slow, drag freight service. Only three locomotives could be considered remotely modern, a trio of 4–8–2 types delivered in 1927 for fast freight service.[123]

Under the leadership of the innovative Ike Tigrett, the GM&N experimented early on with the diesel streamliner, The Rebel in 1935. It was particularly notable not only for being the first diesel streamliner in the south but also for abandoning the articulation of the Zephyr and M-10000 for a more conventional arrangement.[124] This allowed the railroad to offer through service from St. Louis to both New Orleans and Mobile by splitting the train into two parts in Mississippi. The GM&N did not experiment further with early prewar diesel switchers or other passenger diesels, likely because of limited capital. The Alton railroad also had experience with early diesels, hosting an early EMC boxcab that pulled the Abe Lincoln train

Photo 10   The GM&O dieselized early and purchased a couple Alco DL 105 models in the early 1940s. One is seen here leading the Gulf Coast Rebel train at Mobile, Alabama. Collection of Robert F. Schramm.

between Chicago and St. Louis.[125] In the spring of 1945 the Alton purchased several EMD E-units for dieselization of its fast and frequent Chicago to St. Louis passenger service. Its Kansas City service was provided by a prewar gas-electric motorcar. The Alton railroad, like many others, purchased some diesel switching locomotives, primarily for passenger terminal switching in downtown Chicago during the war.[126]

After the 1940 merger of the GM&N with the M&O to form the GM&O, the railroad embarked on a program of further dieselization. The first additions were three Alco DL-109 types, two arriving in 1940 and one more in 1943.[127] The Alco units were put to work in express passenger service between St. Louis and the gulf cities of Mobile and New Orleans. Eleven Alco diesel switchers were also purchased during the war. While many railroads also purchased additional steam locomotives during the war to handle the traffic crush, the GM&O did not. As a north-south railroad traffic wasn't as severe as on the main east west trunk roads, although traffic to the port of Mobile increased greatly.

When diesels became more widely available after the war the GM&O was among the first to purchase large quantities of both EMD and Alco road-freight and passenger diesels. Beginning in 1946 and continuing after the GM&O-Alton merger, freight, passenger and switching units were added to the roster. The railroad was quick to realize the benefits of the road-switcher design and had several RS-1 units from Alco on the property immediately after the war.[128] The last regularly scheduled steam powered train was on October 15, 1949. This marked the GM&O as the first large railroad to be completely dieselized.[129]

The rate of the changeover was striking. In 1945 diesels contributed less than one half of one percent of total gross ton-miles. In 1946 diesels contributed 25 percent, in 1947, 84 percent, 1948, 95 percent, and for the first eight months of 1949, diesels contributed 99 percent of total gross ton-miles. During the same time period average train load increased 50 percent from 2,049 tons to 3,001 tons, and average train speed increased 10 percent from 17.2 mph to 19.0 mph.[130] Complete dieselization brought about a reduction in the number of locomotives. A diesel fleet of 231 units was sufficient to perform the work of 384 steam locomotives. These new diesels were not cheap, however. Combined investment in diesel locomotives

Photo 11 The GM&O was an early convert to the road-switcher type of locomotive like this Alco RS-1 built in May 1948. A testament to the ruggedness of the design is that it is seen here, in essentially unaltered form, in 1970 in Venice, Illinois. Photo by Robert F. Schramm.

was over $60 million.[131] In 1950, the first full year of diesel operations, the GM&O had a net income of $8 million on total revenues of $78.4 million. This compares with an income of $4 million and total revenue of $73 million in 1949.[132] The diesels, while a costly investment, were paying for themselves.

As may be surmised, the primary reason for dieselization of the GM&O was cost. The savings were simply too much to ignore. With ample early experience with the Rebel streamliner and then other passenger locomotives, the management was quick to grasp the possibilities inherent in the diesel. There are other reasons for the fast embrace of the diesel however. The southern end of the GM&O was cobbled together from several railroads that were not built to high standards. Many began as logging lines in the piney woods of Mississippi. Light rail and bridges and sharp curves precluded the use of large and heavy steam locomotives. Diesels and their lower axle loading weights could modernize the system without spending much money on heavier rail and new bridges. With this lightly constructed railroad came lighter and older steam locomotives. The large, powerful and advanced types of steam available in the 1930s did not exist on the GM&O. The Chicago to St. Louis mainline of the former Alton railroad was a major passenger route and served several other important on line cities such as the state capitol, Springfield, Illinois. Many other railroads offered passenger service between the two major Midwestern cities and diesels would not only allow the GM&O to cut costs but also to speed up schedules and attract more customers in this competitive corridor. Also important in the dieselization of the GM&O is president Tigrett. His aggressiveness and forward thinking resulted not only in the creation of the railroad itself but in an early embrace of the diesel.

Seaboard Air Line

The Seaboard Air Line Railroad or Seaboard (also SAL) was a major railroad in the southeastern states from Virginia to Florida and Alabama.[133] The SAL ran from Richmond and Norfolk, Virginia, south through the hilly Piedmont of the Carolinas to Atlanta and Birmingham and also south into Florida serving both the east and west coasts for a total of almost 4,500 miles of line. The SAL was the subordinate railroad in the region, always playing

second fiddle to the larger and more prosperous Atlantic
Coast Line, located on the easier terrain of the coastal
plain to the east. The competitive relationship between
these two railroads would shape the dieselization of both
and provide for the first large scale diesel operation in
the coastal southeast.

Steam power on the Seaboard was somewhat more modern than on the GM&O. The bulk of passengers moved
behind aging 4–6–0 and capable 4–6–2 types built in the
first two decades of the century. Freight moved behind
2–8–0, 2–10–0, and 2–10–2 types built during the same
years. The Seaboard also had some advanced power. Over
sixty modern 4–8–2 types were acquired beginning in
1914 for passenger service. In 1935, seeking to speed up
fast freight schedules over the up and down lines of the
Piedmont, the Seaboard ordered five 2–6–6–4 types from
Baldwin. Five more followed in 1937.[134] The locomotives
were a success but did not generate any further orders,
likely because the SAL was in receivership and working
capital was tight. Additionally in the 1930s there simply
wasn't much traffic to justify new locomotive orders.

The SAL was in second place in the lucrative Northeast
to Florida passenger market. Deciding that it had little
to lose and much to gain, the SAL took a gamble and purchased ten E-4 passenger locomotives from EMC in 1938
to dieselize the storied Orange Blossom Special passenger train. The units were even painted in citrus colors
of orange, green, and yellow to accentuate the connection to the warm vacationlands of Florida.[135] The newly
streamlined Orange Blossom Special was a hit, and the
SAL decided to invest in more diesel passenger power to
dieselize its other trains. It inaugurated the famous Silver Meteor streamliner in 1939. By the beginning of the
war most of the long haul passenger service had been
dieselized with twenty-two E-units. Eager to try diesels
in switching service as well, the Seaboard began to purchase diesel switchers in 1939. By the end of 1945 there
were twenty diesel switchers from EMD, Alco, and Baldwin on the railroad.[136]

Flashy orange, yellow, and green streamlined passenger
diesels may have been good for public relations and passenger counts, but it would take freight diesels to really
impact the bottom line. The Seaboard would not have to
wait long. In 1942, just as the wartime traffic crunch was
beginning to hit, the Seaboard took delivery of its first FT

Photo 12 One can only imagine the reaction of passengers and bystanders to this orange, green, yellow, and silver streamlined EMC E-4 of the Seaboard Air Line. It is seen here in Atlanta in 1940. Courtesy of the Museum of the Rockies, Ron V. Nixon Railroad Photography Collection.

units. The Seaboard did not host the demonstrator FT on its nationwide tour in 1940 but was so convinced by the published performance data and its experience with passenger E-units that it opted to purchase some anyway. By the end of 1944 there were forty-four FT's on the railroad. When the war ended the Seaboard quickly moved to dieselize remaining operations. With 348 units in operation at the close of 1950, all principal passenger and freight trains and more than half of all switching was performed by diesel power.[137] This 348 total included more than 150 road-switchers, marking the Seaboard as an early convert to this more flexible type of motive power. The ten modern 2-6-6-4 steam locomotives were sold to the Baltimore and Ohio in 1947 as they were no longer needed. The last steam in regular service was in 1953.[138]

In direct competition with the Seaboard Air Line and serving most of the same markets was the Atlantic Coast Line (ACL). The 5,155 mile ACL ran south from Richmond and Norfolk, Virginia across the easy terrain of the Carolina coastal plain to Georgia and Florida. Branches extended to Atlanta, Birmingham and Montgomery. The SAL and ACL were fierce competitors for freight and passenger business, although the ACL was generally the more successful and more conservative of the two railroads. The ACL was the self-described "standard railroad of the south" and did indeed live up to its motto.

The steam power of the ACL dated mostly from the 1910s and 1920s, generally more modern and capable than neighbor SAL. Passengers moved behind 4-6-0 and 4-6-2 types while freight was pulled by 2-8-2 and 2-10-2 types. The ACL was uncommon in also using 4-6-2 types for freight. Since it ran on the relatively flat coastal plain it had little reason for purchasing large and powerful steam locomotives. When the SAL inaugurated diesel streamliner service from the Northeast to Florida in 1938, the ACL responded with modern steam power, twelve 4-8-4 locomotives for fast heavy passenger service. They were far and away the most modern steam power on the line and were head and shoulders above the 4-6-2 classes built in the mid-1920s. The ACL then had a change of heart and decided to launch its own diesel streamliner with the Champion entering service in 1939.[139] To pull this new air conditioned streamlined train, the ACL copied arch competitor SAL and ordered two EMC E-3A units. To equal or even surpass the orange, yellow and green citrus scheme of the SAL, the two units were painted royal purple and silver that must have particularly impressed both passengers and those standing track side accustomed to dirty black steam locomotives.[140] While the SAL had decided to dieselize passenger service as much as possible, the ACL opted for a more cautious approach, trying out both modern steam and diesels for passenger service. The initial two E-3A units performed well and with the SAL purchasing more diesels the ACL decided to dieselize much more of their passenger service. There were also problems with the new 4–8–4 locomotives that made them hard on track. In late 1940 and early 1941 the railroad purchased fourteen E6A units and four E6B units. Also in 1940 two small switchers joined the ACL roster. Yard and terminal dieselization began in 1942 with several switchers purchased from not only EMD but also from Alco and Baldwin.[141]

To meet the demands of war traffic, the ACL invested in diesel freight power in 1943 and 1944. Once approval was given from the War Production Board, twenty-four FTA and FTB units were acquired from EMD and put to immediate use hauling fast freight trains. Like the SAL, the ACL did not host the demonstrator FT but with arch competitor SAL purchasing FT locomotives, the ACL felt compelled to. The ACL also purchased several more switchers from both Alco and Baldwin. While the railroad was purchasing many new diesel locomotives, steam locomotives were not being retired at a comparable rate. Most were kept in service to handle the crush of wartime traffic. When the war ended the ACL, like its competitor the SAL, quickly dieselized. By the end of 1950 they employed 280 diesel units. A year later the total was 545, which included 154 EMD GP-7 type road-switchers.[142] By 1952 diesels were handling 99 percent of the trains, passenger and freight, on the Atlantic Coast Line.[143]

The ACL-SAL story illustrates just how important interline competition can be in the dieselization story. The weaker railroad, the SAL, first tries the diesel to give it an advantage in the competitive northeast to Florida passenger market over its more successful rival. The rival, the ACL, then responds with diesels of its own in a desire to keep its position. This tit for tat continues from early passenger diesels through freight diesels and even to road switchers. While the diesels did save money and reduce costs for both railroads, this only added to the competition. One could not let the other get an edge in publicity, technology or finances. Neither road had substantial coal reserves on line so neither one felt a loyalty to coal producers. With only a few exceptions, both roads did not roster much modern steam power. The traffic boom of the war years and the relative good times of the late 1940s and early 1950s in the still industrializing south also gave both roads the available capital to purchase large numbers of diesels. As the 1960s dawned things did not look as good for either road. Much of the cream of the freight traffic was going to the ever increasing number of trucks on parallel Interstate 95, although passengers continued to ride the trains to Florida into the 1960s. The competitive relationship between the two would not stop the two roads from merging in 1967 into the Seaboard Coast Line, now an integral part of the larger CSX system.

Southern

The largest railroad system in the south was the Southern with over 6,300 miles of line. It extended from St. Louis, Cincinnati, and Washington, DC south as far as New Orleans, Mobile, and Jacksonville, Florida. In between the Southern served almost every sizable city including Atlanta, Savannah, and Macon, Georgia; Charlotte, Raleigh, and Asheville, North Carolina; Charleston and Columbia, South Carolina; Chattanooga, Knoxville, and Memphis, Tennessee; and Louisville, Kentucky. Traversing the Piedmont and southern Appalachians, the Southern was confronted with many grades. Of special note was the line from Cincinnati to Chattanooga, nicknamed the Rathole, for the many tunnels, grades, and curves on its route. The Southern was a system and was technically composed of several railroads including the Southern proper, the Cincinnati, New Orleans & Texas Pacific, New Orleans & North Eastern and others. However, it was operated essentially as one large railroad.

Like its smaller neighbor to the west, the GM&O, the steam power of the Southern was decidedly not modern. With the exception of some 2–8–2 types purchased in the 1920s, most of the steam freight power was 2–8–0 types that dated from before World War I. Of the 793 steam freight locomotives used by the Southern Railway proper at the end of 1939, 638 were built before 1920 and 357 were built before 1910.[144] The more modern and efficient locomotive types like the 2–8–4 and 4–8–4 were not pursued by the Southern. The passenger power was only slightly more modern. Of the 232 passenger locomotives available for service at the close of 1939, 187 were built prior to 1920 with 59 built prior to 1910.[145] For passenger power the Southern relied on 4–6–0 types for local trains and 4–6–2 and 4–8–2 types for longer distance expresses.[146] While capable locomotives they were not state of the art and were beginning to show their age by the late 1930s.

The Southern was not a large experimenter with prewar diesels but did have limited experience with self-propelled streamlined diesel rail cars, operating some in local passenger service beginning in 1939. The turning point for the Southern, as with other roads, was the demonstration tour of the EMC FT. The Southern hosted the demonstrator in August 1940 and by February 1941 had submitted an order for eight units to be delivered in two sets. The units were delivered and in service by July on the torturous Rathole line where they impressed operating forces so much that a further order was placed in November 1941.[147] By the end of 1945 the Southern system had seventy-six such units, the third highest total. Where other railroads had to purchase new steam locomotives to keep up with the wartime demands, the Southern performed the same job with new FT locomotives. Diesel passenger locomotives and switchers also joined the Southern during the early 1940s. By the end of 1945 the Southern Railway proper had forty-eight freight units, thirteen passenger and forty-four diesel switchers.[148] More diesels including some FT units were owned by subsidiaries like the Cincinnati, New Orleans & Texas Pacific and New Orleans & North Eastern.

During and after the war the southeast experienced a great deal of industrial development. This was music to the ears of the Southern management, for industries meant traffic. After the war the Southern continued to dieselize quickly. As of the end of 1950, the Southern railroad system including all subsidiaries owned 624 diesel units compared to 912 steam locomotives. However, the diesels achieved about 50 percent of gross ton-miles and passenger car-miles. In switching service diesels held an even greater percentage, more than 60 percent of all yard switching hours.[149] As of October 15, 1952 the Southern Railroad system had 834 diesels on hand and 45 more units on order. In September 1952, 96.9 percent of the gross freight ton miles, 99.5 percent of the passenger car miles and 94.2 percent of the yard switching hours were handled by diesels. These diesels were saving millions for the Southern. The railroad estimated that for 1951, diesels saved the railroad almost 35 million dollars in operating expenses. The railroad was quick to point out that not only was this good news for the stockholders, but it was good news for the government as well since a larger net income results in more income taxes paid.[150] The Southern was fully dieselized by the end of 1953, the largest railroad to fully dieselize to that time.

The Southern dieselized for many reasons. Cost savings, as always, was primary. The Southern system saved millions of dollars by converting to diesels. Cost was not the only reason though. The steam locomotive fleet of the railroad was old and obsolete. Impressed with the performance of the FT and serving a growing region, diesels were an easy choice, especially once the cost savings from diesel operation began to accrue. Another reason for the dieselization on the Southern was not just the age and condition of the steam locomotive fleet but the age and condition of the track and bridges. Twisty and hilly track with light rail simply could not accommodate the increased weight and long rigid wheelbase of new modern steam locomotives like heavy 4–8–4 types. Lightly built bridges and trestles, dating back to the nineteenth century in some cases, simply could not take the extra weight of modern steam. The lighter and more nimble diesel would allow the railroad to modernize without spending extraordinary amounts to straighten curves and strengthen bridges. Competition with other roads was also a factor. As its competitors to the east, the SAL and ACL converted to diesel, so did the Southern. The Southern did serve coal mines in the southern Appalachians and while the use of diesels to serve coal producing areas was a concern to management, it did not dissuade them from dieselizing quickly. The Southern survived the general downturn in railroad fortunes in the 1960s well, although it did chafe against the limits of ICC authority. It finally merged with the successful Norfolk & Western railroad in 1982 to create the Norfolk Southern.

Richmond, Fredericksburg & Potomac

Unlike many railroads, the Richmond, Fredericksburg & Potomac (RF&P) was accurately described by its name.

It was a single route railroad, running a well maintained double-track main line from Washington, D.C. south to Richmond, Virginia, a distance of only about 120 miles. While normally this would qualify as a large shortline, the RF&P was an integral part of the national rail system and a vital link between the northeast and southeast. At Washington it connected with the B&O and mighty Pennsylvania railroads, while at Richmond it connected with the ACL, SAL, Chesapeake & Ohio, and Southern railroads. The RF&P was the primary route for passengers and freight between the northeast and the coastal southeast. Passenger trains of both the SAL and the ACL used the RF&P to access Washington, DC. The railroad was owned equally by its connections, the Pennsylvania and Baltimore & Ohio to the north and the ACL, SAL, Southern, and Chesapeake & Ohio (C&O) to the south.

Since it had little online industry and no branches, the RF&P was primarily engaged in moving traffic from one railroad to the next. This so called bridge traffic was extremely time sensitive. For every day that a foreign line car remained online, the RF&P had to pay a charge. Because of this time-sensitive traffic the RF&P invested heavily in fast modern steam power. Freight and passengers alike moved at speed behind 4–6–2 types. The RF&P investigated electrification during the late 1930s but felt that future traffic levels did not warrant the investment. Principle northern connection and part owner Pennsylvania railroad had recently completed its massive electrification project. Had the RF&P management foreseen what traffic levels would have been because of the war they likely would have changed their mind about electrification. By 1942 the window for electrification had closed but more motive power was needed. To help handle the increasing volume of wartime freight traffic, it purchased ten 2–8–4 Berkshire types built by Lima in 1943. The RF&P was also a major passenger route. To handle passenger traffic as well as freight, the railroad purchased twenty-seven modern 4–8–4 types built by Baldwin beginning in 1937 and ending in 1945.[151] With this modern capable steam power, the RF&P chose not to dieselize during the war or immediately thereafter. Diesels did roam the rails of the RF&P however as both the SAL and ACL had run through agreements where their diesel passenger trains would run over RF&P rails from Washington to Richmond with diesel power. Despite the modern steam power the

RF&P decided to dieselize in 1949, after neighboring roads and all the owning roads had embraced the diesel, even the large coal hauling roads C&O and Pennsylvania. By the end of 1950 only a small fraction of either freight or passenger service was being handled by steam power.[152] By 1952 steam was gone from the RF&P.[153] Loyal to steam before and even during the war, the decision to dieselize was made well after diesels had transformed operations on other roads. Because of the relatively small size of the railroad, complete dieselization was achieved in a short period of time. Although not a large coal hauler, coal for fuel was readily available from the mines of Pennsylvania, Maryland and Virginia. The multiple ownership of the RF&P was likely a factor in dieselization. Where a progressive president could embrace a new technology on many roads, the multiple owners of the RF&P would be likely to choose a more conservative option. Competition with other roads was not a factor for the RF&P for the same reason.

Louisville & Nashville

The 5,250 mile Louisville & Nashville (L&N) railroad operated not in the Southeast but was a vital connection between the industrial Midwest and the mid and deep South. From New Orleans the L&N extended north through Alabama to Nashville, Louisville, Cincinnati, and St. Louis. Like many railroads, the L&N had a large network of secondary and branch lines that covered the states of Alabama, Tennessee, and Kentucky. Of special note were the extensive array of lines that served the coal mines of southeastern Kentucky and also lines to Memphis and Atlanta.

Coal and other freight on the L&N moved behind 2–8–0 and 2–8–2 types dating from the 1910s and 1920s, including many built by the railroad itself in its Louisville shops. Passengers were pulled by 4–6–2 types also built during the 1910s and 1920s. For heavy passenger service on hilly portions of the railroad, twenty-two 4–8–2 Mountain types were purchased from Baldwin in 1926 and 1930.[154] They were the last new locomotive purchases for several years. The L&N experimented on a small scale with diesel switchers just before and during the war. As was the pattern elsewhere, its first two diesels were purchased in 1939 to serve in the Louisville terminal area to reduce smoke that led to civic agitation.[155] Several more switchers arrived in 1941 and throughout the war and went to work in terminals and yards across the system. With traffic increasing in 1940 the road looked for more motive power. For passenger service the road seriously looked at modern 4–8–2 or 4–8–4 types. Their performance would have been more than adequate, but as with other roads there were problems with operating such large and heavy locomotives. Along the Gulf coast the L&N had miles of wooden trestles over the many swamps and inlets. These wooden trestles could not support the weight of a large modern 4–8–4. Instead of rebuilding miles of bridges and trestles, the answer to this problem appeared in the form of the lighter weight EMC E-unit. The board of directors authorized purchase of sixteen passenger diesels in September of 1941. All were in service by the fall of 1942.[156] The Southern, which competed for passengers in some markets was also exploring diesel passenger power at the same time.

However, while the L&N was purchasing E-units from EMC, it was still purchasing modern steam power. At the same meeting that the board authorized the purchase of the passenger diesels they also authorized the purchase of fourteen 2–8–4 types from Baldwin.[157] Between 1942 and 1949 the railroad purchased a total of forty-two modern 2–8–4 Berkshire types from Baldwin and Lima. These locomotives, nicknamed "Big Emmas" stayed predominantly in the Kentucky coalfields where fuel was cheap and readily at hand, although some were used in passenger service during and just after the war when traffic levels were high.[158] Coal made up nearly half of the tonnage and accounted for almost 30 percent of total freight revenue on the L&N so keeping the coal industry happy with coal burning locomotives was likely a factor in their purchase. Unlike neighbor and competitor the Southern, the L&N, which had more on line coal shippers, did not embrace the FT but stuck with tried and true steam power for freight.

The last order of steam in 1948 also marked the beginning of large scale dieselization of freight operations. Five EMD F-3 units were ordered at the same time and put to use as helpers in the coal fields. A downturn in traffic allowed the new diesels to be tested on other divisions of the railroad, most notably the roller coaster like line between Louisville and Cincinnati. The results

Photo 13 The 2-8-4 Berkshire type is well illustrated by this 1942 Baldwin product for the Louisville & Nashville. This "Big Emma" as the crews called them spent most of its life in the coal fields of eastern Kentucky and was likely scrapped only fifteen years after this builder's photo was taken at the Baldwin plant in Philadelphia. Courtesy of the Railroad Museum of Pennsylvania (PHMC) H. L. Broadbelt Collection.

were striking. The diesels could handle almost double the tonnage of the modern 2–8–4 types. Not only that but they could achieve that performance with less operating expenses, $77,000 compared with $95,000.[159] Although initially reluctant to embrace the diesel for freight service, the board quickly sized up these results and embarked on a large-scale dieselization program. By the end of 1950 there were 202 diesel units on the system compared with 640 steam locomotives.[160] Diesels continued to arrive in droves in the early 1950s. By the end of 1954 all passenger and all switching and yard services were dieselized with only 12 percent of freight gross ton miles hauled by steam.[161] Steam finally succumbed on a cold January day in 1957. The L&N is yet another example of a dual motive power philosophy railroad. Diesels were suitable for use on passenger streamliners but the bread and butter of the railroad, freight and especially coal, stayed with steam during and after the war until the railroad had direct experience of the savings that diesel freight power could bring. Competition with other railroads, while a likely factor in the passenger diesel purchase, was not a large factor in freight dieselization. The Southern and other railroads in the same area as the L&N were dieselizing freight service years before the L&N decided to give diesels a try. The influence of the coal industry is paramount as well. With readily available coal for fuel the railroad chose to remain with steam in that area until rapidly rising costs in the late 1940s finally forced them to embrace the diesel. In the south especially there was a greatly increasing demand for coal for use in generating electricity. This increase offset much of the decrease in demand for coal for steam locomotive fuel. The L&N, like its neighboring southern roads, fared reasonably well in the 1950s and 1960s. It merged the smaller Nashville, Chattanooga & St. Louis in 1957 and acquired not one but two connections north to Chicago with part of the C&EI and all of the Monon railroad in 1969 and 1971 respectively. The L&N had been controlled by the ACL since the early years of the century but was operated separately until the 1970s when operations were gradually consolidated under the Family Lines moniker. The L&N finally ceased to exist as a separate corporate entity at the end of 1982 when it became part of the larger CSX system.

There were a multitude of reasons why railroads chose to embrace the diesel. As can be seen by the examples above, some railroads quickly realized the savings in fuel and labor and the increased availability and other operational advantages that the diesel could bring. Although some may have been prodded into initially purchasing diesels because of antismoke regulations or other municipal concerns, many continued to experiment with diesels and made diesel switchers a part of their operations before and during the war. Streamlined diesel passenger trains held the promise of bringing passengers back to the rails and did so for many railroads. While some railroads invested in reliable road diesels as soon as they were available, thereby transforming operations and cutting costs, others chose to continue to utilize their modern steam locomotives until rapidly rising costs after the war and deferred maintenance on existing steam locomotives forced them to consider the diesel. However, as described above, each respective railroad did things differently depending on its own operational environment, competitive pressure, economic needs and management philosophy. Some roads maintained dual motive power strategies for several years, running diesels in some services and steam in others, while other roads simply took the record profits from the World War II years and invested it in diesels as fast as possible after diesels became widely available in late 1945 and 1946 and after the diesel had proven itself on other railroads during the war.

In many cases competition encouraged neighboring railroads to dieselize, as can be seen with the SAL-ACL story. There are few common factors between the roads except for cost, the primary motivation for dieselization. Dieselization was not a cure all. Many roads that embraced the diesel did not do all that well after dieselization. The O&W was the extreme, ceasing operations in 1957, while the GM&O, L&N, SAL, and ACL despite operating in the south and Midwest where industrial decline and road competition was not as severe as the northeast, all succumbed to mergers in the late 1960s and 1970s.[162] The Lehigh Valley and Reading, both bankrupt and disintegrating, were absorbed into Conrail in 1976. The western roads, with the exception of the Rock Island, bankrupt and dismembered in 1980, fared better. The CB&Q joined with long time friendly connections Great Northern and Northern Pacific to form the Burlington Northern in the early 1970s. The Western Pacific and Missouri Pacific were merged into the Union Pacific in the early 1980s. The mighty Santa Fe survived intact until a merger with the Burlington Northern in the mid-1990s.

4

Dieselization Deferred

DIESELIZATION, LIKE OTHER COMPLEX DECISIONS, WAS AFFECTED by a multitude of different actors and influences. Some of these pushed railroads to embrace the diesel as a new form of motive power. Chief among these were the costs of operation and maintenance of diesels compared with steam motive power. Other influences also pushed railroads to purchase diesels including competition, passenger service, and municipal antismoke regulation. However, there were also many actors that were pulling on railroads not to abandon steam power. One large reason mentioned previously was the influence of the coal industry as the largest shipper and a major supplier to many railroads. There were other reasons not to embrace the diesel, at least on some roads. These reasons to stick with steam vary from having a modern and capable steam fleet to the background and personal experiences of upper management. For some roads sticking with steam seemed to make economic sense, at least for a time while for other roads management was clearly emotionally connected with steam locomotives. This nostalgic look at the steam locomotive was a factor, although a hard to quantify one, for the dieselization experience of many roads. This chapter will further examine the decisions to dieselize of various railroads but paying attention to the actors involved in the reasons not to dieselize rather than the reasons to embrace the diesel. Instead of the push to dieselize, this chapter looks at the pull to stick with steam.

The decision to delay dieselization was based on many of the reasons that railroads decided to embrace the diesel. The high initial cost of diesels compared to steam locomotives was a factor in the dieselization decisions for some roads, especially roads that were bankrupt and operating in receivership or roads that were small and did not have much available capital to spend. Roads that had extensively modernized their steam rosters during the 1930s and early 1940s may have wanted to extract the maximum value from these investments and therefore postponed diesel purchases. Modern steam from the 1930s and 1940s did offer some gains in efficiency over older locomotives and made diesels less economically attractive. Roads with large modern steam also had likely invested in strengthened bridges, larger roundhouses and turntables, and modern servicing facilities. With such a large investment, roads would be loath to simply abandon many of the improvements by switching to diesels. Some roads were not fully convinced of the increased performance and cost savings of the diesel especially in the early years of dieselization before and during the war. Many large railroads simply could not dieselize quickly. While a small or midsized road with a few dozen locomotives like the RF&P or the GM&O could dieselize rapidly once the decision was made, roads with thousands of locomotives like the Pennsylvania or New York Central could not.

In addition many companies actively resisted diesel power, exploring alternatives such as steam turbines, gas turbines, and even electrification. The reasons for this resistance are many and vary between railroads but include both internal corporate culture and external political and economic factors. Managers that had almost literally been raised with steam locomotives were reluctant to dieselize and abandon the machine that had not only enabled their own personal success but had enabled the success of their railroad and, by extension, the country itself. This nostalgia for a simpler time before the complicated cold war competitive, regulatory and poltiical environment of the late 1940s and early 1950s undoubtedly was a factor in the dieselization experience for some railroads. A final reason to delay dieselization was coal. It is generally true that the more a railroad depended on the movement of coal for revenue, the less likely it was to embrace the diesel. Coal for locomotive fuel was a large source of revenue for some railroads that they did not want to lose. Because of their dependence on hauling coal, many roads sought to continue to use coal for fuel to maintain the existing relationships with their major shippers and suppliers. When they did dieselize, these roads generally purchased more road-switcher type locomotives like the GP-7 and GP-9 rather than cab units such as the EMD F-units and the Alco FA simply because the road switchers were the newest, most flexible and reliable locomotives then available. The decision to wait may have also been simply to wait for the next, and presumably better type of locomotive to come along. With the rapid changes in motive power from 1920 to 1945, some roads believed that further extreme changes, especially with the knowledge gained by wartime experience, would make the next generation of motive power even more efficient and cost effective than the first few production runs of diesels. As in chapter 3, we begin our examination in the eastern district, continue to the western district and end in the southern district.

Eastern District

In the eastern district, the two largest railroads, the Pennsylvania and New York Central, were both reluctant to fully adopt the diesel until after the war. When they did dieselize they did so primarily to control rapidly increasing costs but interline competition and other influences were also factors. After decisions were made new diesel locomotives from all manufacturers arrived amazingly fast, arguably too fast. Both roads purchased locomotives from all major manufacturers and were later burdened with inefficient and maintenance intensive types.

New York Central

The New York Central (NYC) at midcentury was a huge transportation machine stretching from Montreal, Boston, and New York City in the east to Chicago and St. Louis in the west. Its lines covered its name sake state and it served almost every large city in Ohio, Indiana, Michigan, and Illinois. Important secondary lines penetrated the coal producing areas of central Pennsylvania and West Virginia. The NYC was a huge railroad, the third largest in the country in terms of route mileage in 1950 with almost eleven thousand miles of line.[1]

The year 1929 was the last really good year for quite some time for the NYC, with a net railway operating income of over $64 million. Ten years later the net railway operating income was slightly more than $37 million. This was a marked increase from 1938 which saw an income of only $15.5 million and a net deficit for the company after all charges were included. The war years brought traffic and income to the railroad. Operating revenue peaked in 1944 at over $700 million with net income peaking in 1943 at over $60 million. While the railroad was earning much more than it had just a few years before, costs were also increasing rapidly. The costs finally outpaced income growth in 1946 with the New York Central posting a net deficit of over $10 million, although direct railway operations did stay in the black. The company was back in the black in 1947 and 1948 but the increase in costs was a constant theme in the annual reports of the era. Net income was still markedly below the levels of 1929. As with other companies, the New York Central was facing high and increasing costs, especially labor and materials, while freight and passenger rates, while up from the prewar average, were not keeping pace. The 1951 annual report states that hourly wage rates were up 142.9 percent over the 1935–39 average. Materials likewise were up 139.5 percent. Revenue per ton mile for freight was up merely 53.8 percent while for passengers the increase was only 27.9 percent. This compares to an overall cost of living increase by 1951 of 85.9 percent.[2] By 1950 the New York Central had to cut costs and cut them fast.

The NYC began experiments with alternative motive power in the first few years of the century. With the construction of Grand Central Terminal in New York City and its underground approach tracks, electric motive power was extensively used. This third rail electrification would extend as far north as Croton-Harmon, New York, 32.7 miles from Grand Central.[3] Operations in Detroit and Cleveland were also electrified, primarily for smoke abatement reasons although the added efficiency that electric operations would bring was a factor. The NYC was also an early user of internal combustion power. In the late 1920s the railroad worked with Alco to construct three experimental diesel-electric locomotives. One was a three power switching locomotive designed to use either diesel, batteries, or third rail electric power. The second locomotive was designed from the outset as a road-freight locomotive. This marks it as the first true road-freight diesel locomotive in the country.[4] It was soon joined by a similar locomotive designed for road passenger service. Both of these locomotives were specifically designed for service on the Putnam division, a suburban commuter line north out of New York City. Since the line operated in heavily populated areas and in the city, smoke from steam locomotives was a concern. The New York Central could have electrified this line like it did others in the area but wanted to see if using diesels would be cheaper than electrification with its high first cost and extensive infrastructure. The freight locomotive was successful and remained in service for eighteen years. The passenger locomotive was somewhat less successful and only lasted until 1936. The New York Central possessed almost 3500 locomotives at the end of 1929. Of this total only three were classified as "Oil electric Diesel" types.[5] With other concerns during the depression no further orders for similar diesels were forthcoming from the New York Central during the 1930s. Nevertheless, this experiment shows the NYC management was interested in the diesel and curious about its performance. However, the fact that there were no further orders for locomotives similar to these also illustrates that the management, while willing to experiment with diesels during good economic times, was not willing to embark on a large-scale dieselization program during the dark years of the 1930s. While no new passenger or freight diesels were seen on the NYC during the 1930s, by the later part of the decade the NYC began to invest in increasing amounts of small diesel switchers. There were forty-six diesels on the property at the end of 1938. During 1939 they were joined by thirty-two more for a total of seventy-eight.[6] These were the only locomotives that the NYC added to its roster in 1939. While some of these locomotives were likely purchased for reasons other than simply economic efficiency such as smoke abatement, the relatively wide spread adoption of diesel switchers indicates that the NYC saw the value of employing diesels in this area. Despite the switchers joining the railroad before the war, the NYC remained firmly committed to steam power for road freight and passenger trains, designing new steam locomotives even while road diesels were proving themselves on railroads around the country.

The NYC system had some of the most modern steam power available. The Berkshire type was named for the Berkshire mountains in western Massachusetts that the NYC subsidiary, Boston and Albany battled. It should be no surprise that the railroad ordered 55 2-8-4 types between 1926 and 1930.[7] If a four wheel trailing truck would work on a freight engine, what would it do to a passenger engine? The answer was the 4-6-4 type, appropriately named the Hudson. Again, the NYC was the first user of the type. In the eleven years from 1927 to 1938, 275 Hudsons joined the fleet.[8] This was the most of this type on any railroad on the continent. The railroad was also a

Photo 14 The New York Central 4-6-4 Hudson was the archetype for the modern passenger steam locomotive from the 1920s to the 1950s. Here one is seen with a short train approaching Cleveland, Ohio in May of 1940. The overhead wires are for the Cleveland Terminal Electrification of the New York Central. Courtesy of the Museum of the Rockies, Ron V. Nixon Railroad Photography Collection.

large user of modern 4–8–2 types. The first batch began arriving in 1916. To handle wartime traffic 115 modern versions were purchased between 1940 and 1944. These Mohawk types were found to be equally suited for fast freight or passenger service.[9]

The crown jewel of NYC steam power was the magnificent 4–8–4 Niagara class. During the war existing passenger trains, especially the luxurious 20th Century Limited were getting too long and heavy for even the best Hudsons to handle. With the expected postwar boom in passenger traffic, something larger and more powerful was needed. The answer was delivered in March 1945, a huge and powerful 4–8–4 type from Alco. Even before this first model was delivered the railroad ordered twenty-six more.[10] To conserve weight the locomotives had aluminum cabs and running boards. The boiler was so large that the smoke stack could only be seven inches high. The Niagara was the largest steam locomotive that existing facilities and clearances would allow. According to locomotive historian Philip Atkins, the Niagara, "may be regarded as the ultimate development of the basic conventional simple expansion reciprocating steam locomotive."[11]

The performance of the new Niagaras was equally impressive. In tests they achieved a maximum horsepower of 6,600 at eighty-five mph. In late 1946 the management of the NYC decided to test its new super steam power against the best diesels then available, the EMD E-7, in high-speed, long-distance passenger service. The results of these tests would have a direct bearing on the future of steam power on the railroad. Both the diesels and the Niagaras received preferential treatment at servicing facilities and the steam locomotives also received higher grade coal.[12] The results were quite close. In overall performance the two challengers were roughly equivalent. Both were able to maintain the demanding schedules of the flagship passenger trains. Steam had a sizable advantage in first cost, costing less than half of what a comparable set of diesel locomotives would cost but required $.41/mile in fuel to the diesels $.28/mile. Total operating expenses gave a slight edge to the diesel, $0.9896/mile verses $1.1307/mile for steam.[13] While the costs may have been somewhat similar, availability was not. Barring unforseen emergencies, steam was unavailable for service a minimum of twenty-eight days a year compared to twelve for the diesel.[14] However, pure economics was not the only consideration. The test period was disrupted for thirteen days while coal miners were on strike in December 1946.[15] The susceptibility to outside disruptions and possibility of higher coal prices caused the upper management of the railroad to have second thoughts about continued steam locomotive development. The mighty New York Central, railroad of the Vanderbilts, would not be held hostage by United Mine Workers president John L. Lewis and his striking miners.

Flaws in the boilers of the almost new Niagaras in 1947 doomed continued steam locomotive development on the New York Central.[16] The railroad began dieselization in earnest, but to replace thousands of steam locomotives would take time. From 1942 to 1946 the New York Central acquired 92 new steam road locomotives, including the Niagaras and 131 diesel switchers. Switching was increasingly the domain of the diesel while the vast majority of freight and passengers moved behind steam. None the less, by the end of 1946 and with a deficit on the ledger books, the New York Central could no longer afford to ignore the efficiencies of the diesel for road service. Ten road freight units and 12 passenger units were in operation with 66 more road freight and passenger units on order.[17] The 1947 annual report heralds a massive "233 million dollar" improvement program with a goal of reducing operating costs and improving service. Integral to this program was the continued investment of over $45 million in diesel power. However, the report also states that $6 million of this program was for the Niagara locomotives.[18] The New York Central, while recognizing the cost savings of the diesel, was still bragging to stockholders about the mighty Niagaras. Much more space in the report was devoted to new passenger and freight cars and other improvements such as new coal and ore docks at Toledo, Ohio. By the end of 1947 the railroad had 46 diesel freight units in operation, 41 diesel passenger units and 241 diesel switchers for a total of 330 diesels. They still had over 3,000 steam locomotives on the roster.[19] In contrast, the 1948 report specifically addresses dieselization. Under the heading "Dieselization is Progressing," the report states that the New York Central system ordered more than $33 million worth of diesels in 1948. About 13.5 percent of road freight and 19.4 percent of passengers were pulled by diesel power by the end of the year. Diesel switchers accounted for about 28 percent of all switching hours.[20] Far from bragging about its new Niagaras, the report goes on to explain to stockholders that despite the relatively low percentage of dieselization, that the NYC was actually in the forefront of the diesel movement and would have almost one million diesel horsepower by the time the current orders were delivered. A photo of EMD e-units on passenger trains is accompanied by the caption that diesels have "many advantages, such as added flexibility in power utilization, fuel economies, and greater production of mileage per unit."[21] However, far from the photo of streamlined diesels at the end of a paragraph that talks about dynamic balancing of wheels and reducing freight car weight is a sentence that states, "and the Central, in cooperation with other railroads, is continuing the exploration of the potentialities of a coal-fired gas-turbine locomotive as a form of railroad power."[22] The NYC, which was a major coal shipper, was not yet entirely ready to give up on the coal burning locomotive, even if the gas-turbine under study was a far cry from the traditional steam locomotive. At the end of 1950 the railroad had 828 diesel units but still rostered 2,522 steam locomotives.[23] While the diesel and its ability to control costs and effect greater operating efficiencies continued to be stressed in the annual reports for the next several years, more and more space was devoted to issues of public policy and competition such as freight rate increases and potential threats like the publicly funded St. Lawrence Seaway. Diesels were controlling costs and helping the railroad remain solvent but by the late 1950s management knew that more was needed than simply technological improvements if the New York Central was going to survive its second century as well as it had its first. The mighty Niagaras, which had fought the new diesels to a near tie in cost and performance, would be out of service by the end of 1956, with the final steam run on the railroad in the spring of 1957.[24]

The New York Central had a history of innovation with regards to motive power, both with steam power and electrification. It developed and was a major user of advanced steam power like the Berkshire and Hudson types. It even experimented with passenger and road freight diesels in the 1920s. However, when later diesels became available in the late 1930s and during the war, the New York Central decided to stick with steam and to continue to develop the steam locomotive with the Niagara type. There are many

reasons for this decision. The railroad had a huge investment in modern steam and wanted to get its money's worth
out of the locomotives. There is also an element of corporate pride involved. The New York Central was a large
and prosperous railroad that was accustomed to having
its own designs built by builders like home town builder
Alco. It was not accustomed to and resented the new, mass
produced diesels becoming available from EMD as there
was very little input that the railroad had in the building
process. None the less, the NYC did quietly purchase two
FT sets for evaluation in 1944. The FT had demonstrated
on the NYC back in 1940 but the railroad had shown little
interest at the time. With neighboring roads purchasing the
FT the NYC decided to give it a second look. While other
roads quickly embraced the diesel, the New York Central
waited until several years of cost and performance data was
amassed. With capable and efficient modern steam there
was no urgent need for increased diesel purchases, at least
until the rapidly increasing costs and competition of the
late 1940s began to bear upon railroad decision makers.

Pennsylvania

The primary competitor of the New York Central was the
immense Pennsylvania Railroad.[25] Like the NYC, the Pennsylvania or PRR covered its name sake state with a vast
network of lines. The PRR also operated the high-traffic
northeast corridor line from New York City to Philadelphia,
Baltimore, and Washington, D.C. The PRR served much of
the same territory as the NYC in the states of Ohio, Indiana, Illinois, and Michigan including most major cities. The
Pennsylvania railroad was an enormous transportation
machine. In the 1920s, one of every ten steam locomotives
in the country was owned by the Pennsylvania.[26] Where
other railroads rostered perhaps a couple dozen of a single locomotive type, the Pennsylvania operated hundreds.
It standardized its steam locomotive fleet much more than
most railroads.

The Pennsylvania railroad was a huge and prosperous
railroad. In 1929 for instance net income, after interest on
debt and other fixed charges was deducted, was over $100
million.[27] The Pennsylvania, while operating less than 5
percent of the total mileage of all class I railroads in the
United States in 1929, generated over 10 percent of the revenue ton miles and over 19 percent of the passenger ton

miles. It also had 11 percent of the total number of railroad employees, 12 percent of the freight cars and almost 15 percent of the passenger cars. Almost 11 percent of the total number of locomotives on Class I railroads were on the Pennsylvania where they generated 12.4 percent of the total tractive effort of all locomotives. These locomotives used a massive amount of coal, almost 15 million tons in 1929 alone.[28] The depression hit the Pennsylvania hard but it managed to avoid using the red pen for the 1930s, unlike many railroads. Net railway operating income fell from a high of $134 million in 1929 to $49 million in 1932. Small gains were made in the rest of the decade but by 1939 net railway operating income was only $77 million or roughly equal to what it had been in 1924.[29]

The Pennsylvania was unique in many ways other than just size in the annals of North American railroading. The self described, "Standard Railroad of the World" was anything but standard in operating and motive power policies and practices. For example, the PRR was a large user of 4-4-2 types and 2-10-0 types and continued to improve them long after they had been replaced by more modern types on other roads. The PRR had a huge manufacturing complex in Altoona, Pennsylvania that was able to manufacture almost anything that the railroad would need, including locomotives and cars for both passengers and freight.[30] The Pennsylvania designed its own locomotives and only rarely looked to outside builders, usually home town builder Baldwin, to manufacture them. The Pennsylvania standardized its steam power much more than other railroads. For example the New York Central had dozens of different classes of 2-8-2 types while the Pennsylvania had only two different classes. By the end of the 1920s, most freight and passengers moved behind locomotives of only five different types, the E6 class 4-4-2, K4 class 4-6-2, L1 class 2-8-2, I1 class 2-10-0, and M1 class 4-8-2. The I1 and M1 classes shared the same boiler and other components.[31] This standardization of steam power forecast the standardization that diesels would bring to the railroad industry. However, the standardization of steam power resulted in the PRR resisting diesels when first available precisely because they were different and did not fit into the standard scheme of motive power thus far developed.

The PRR was successful financially during the 1920s and invested much of this record profit into new locomotives and other improvements. More than 1,200 new steam

locomotives joined the roster during the decade.[32] At the
end of 1929 the road had 6,152 locomotives on the property
with all steam except for about 70 electrics.[33] Passengers
on the Pennsylvania moved behind 4–6–2 Pacific types on
express trains and behind smaller but capable 4–4–2 and
4–6–0 types for local and commuter trains that were not
electrified. Freight moved behind 2–8–0 types for local
and branch line work and behind 2–8–2 and 4–8–2 types
on the main line. The 4–8–2 types in particular were capable locomotives and able to move freight at speed. Heavy
freight like coal and ore moved behind large and powerful but slow 2–10–0 and 2–10–2 types. The new locomotives
and other developments enabled the Pennsylvania to make
some impressive gains in efficiency during the 1920s. From
1921 to 1929 average cars per freight train increased from
forty-one to fifty-seven. Net tons per train increased from
839 to 1,095 and pounds of coal per 1,000 gross ton miles
decreased from 145 to 125. The railroad was moving more
freight with less coal. Similar gains were seen in passenger
service with pounds of coal per passenger train car mile
falling from 17.1 to 15.9.[34] The PRR used almost fifteen million tons of coal in 1929 so even small gains in efficiency
could result in large savings in fuel costs. These locomotives
were capable designs but were not state of the art and were
technologically outclassed by the 1930s. While competitors
were purchasing 2–8–4, 4–6–4 and 4–8–4 types, the Pennsylvania ignored further steam locomotive development. One
reason for the lack of steam locomotive development on the
PRR during the late 1920s and the Depression was the large
scale electrification program then underway. Beginning in
1928 and extending for ten years, the PRR electrified the
high-traffic New York to Washington main line as well as
from Philadelphia to Harrisburg, Pennsylvania. This huge
capital expenditure, undertaken during the depths of the
Depression, cost over $250 million.[35] The newly electrified
territory needed new electric locomotives, many of which
were constructed in the Juniata shops in Altoona, taking
up space and using labor and engineering resources that
could have been used for steam locomotive production. As
electrification progressed, steam locomotives displaced
from newly electrified lines found assignments on other
portions of the railroad. With this surplus of locomotives
extra attention to steam development was unnecessary.
    By the late 1930s with the electrification project wind-
ing down the PRR management was beginning to again

pay attention to its steam locomotive needs. While the massive electrification project had released hundreds of steam locomotives for use elsewhere on the system, they were older types not suitable for high speed heavy service. To maintain a sixteen hour schedule from New York to Chicago on its premier passenger trains, it was necessary to use two K4 type Pacifics from Harrisburg, the end of the electrified territory, west, over the mountains to at least Crestline, Ohio, a distance of over five hundred miles. This was in marked contrast to competitor New York Central which was hauling its premier passenger trains on similar schedules behind only a single advanced 4–6–4 Hudson. The PRR could have designed and built a modern 4–6–4 or 4–8–4 but instead chose to push the envelope and designed a huge 6–4–4–6 duplex type, called the S-1 in company documents. It announced its decision in August 1937.[36] In deciding to build the duplex locomotive the PRR illustrates that corporate pride can be a significant factor in motive power decisions. It would not be acceptable for the mighty Pennsylvania railroad to merely duplicate already existing locomotives, especially one named after a river that its arch competitor paralleled. They would have to come up with a design that was larger and more powerful than any other passenger locomotive on the rails, especially those of the New York Central. The Pennsylvania, the self proclaimed "Standard Railway of the World" would not play second fiddle to anyone. The new locomotive was so large and fast that the existing track was unable to let it fully meet its potential. It also spent much of its time in the shop with maintenance problems. Diesel power, such as that operating on the Santa Fe and Union Pacific streamliners, was not considered for this application. The PRR itself had observed passenger diesels in a trial by EMC of its 511–512 boxcab type locomotives in 1936. These locomotives were similar to pioneering units purchased by the Santa Fe and the B&O. For eighteen days in March 1936 the experimental diesels worked passenger trains across the PRR system. The PRR was careful to publicly state that this was just a test and that they had no intention of purchasing any diesels for such service.[37] Operations officials were impressed with the diesels and their superiority over the K4 Pacific types then working passenger schedules. Notwithstanding the positive evaluation of the locomotives, a 1936 proposal by EMC to dieselize the premier Broadway Limited was

Photo 15 The unique styling of the Pennsylvania railroad T-1 class duplex 4-4-4-4 types is unmistakable. This locomotive would have an operating life of less than ten years. Courtesy of Railroad Museum of Pennsylvania (PHMC) Pennsylvania Railroad Collection.

politely refused by the PRR.[38] Although no records exist to confirm it, the trials were likely at least partly to determine what acceptable performance levels should be for the new duplex locomotives then in the design stages.

While the S-1 was a huge and powerful locomotive the PRR management realized that it was too large for the physical plant. Downsizing the S-1 resulted in the T-1, 4-4-4-4 type. It was designed to pull 880 tons at one hundred miles an hour rather than the 1,200 tons of the S-1. Design work was completed in the early 1940s with the first prototype delivered from Baldwin in April 1942.[39] The war intervened and prevented large scale production of the new type until the end of hostilities. The PRR was impressed with the performance of the two prototype T-1s and eagerly approved construction of fifty more in the fall of 1945. The order was split between Baldwin and the company shops in Altoona. They were to be the last steam locomotives built in Altoona and the last steam locomotives added to the PRR roster.[40] The management of the PRR was determined to place its own design in service even as late as 1946. Diesels had proven themselves in passenger service long before this date. Neighbor and competitor B&O had been using diesel power in passenger service for almost a decade by this time and even the New York Central was exploring use of passenger diesels.

The decision of the PRR to stick with its home grown T-1 is even more curious since the railroad had already approved the purchase of passenger diesels. In December 1941 the PRR approved the purchase of two EMC E-units for the South Wind passenger train between Chicago and Miami. This train was operated in conjunction with the Louisville & Nashville and the Atlantic Coast Line railroads. This may partly explain the reason for the interest in diesel power as both roads were making use of passenger diesels at this time. To remain competitive and to keep the image of the Pennsylvania railroad as an innovative company the use of diesel power was necessary. Diesels may have also been easier to swallow on this route as it was between Chicago, Indianapolis, and Louisville, far from the home territory and coal fields of Pennsylvania. The war intervened and the order, officially placed on December 9, 1941 was cancelled only to be later reinstated once War Production Board controls were relaxed. The locomotives were finally delivered in September 1945.[41] Further orders for thirty more E-units followed in late 1945 but the units did not arrive until 1946. Thus, although the railroad may have had at least a slight interest in passenger diesels, they did not have much direct operating experience with them at the time that the order for full scale production of the T-1s was issued.

New freight locomotives would also be needed now that traffic was beginning to rebound from the abysmal levels reached in the early 1930s. The PRR again decided to push the envelope and developed advanced duplex drive freight locomotives, the unsuccessful 4–6–4–4 and the much better 4–4–6–4 types. Altoona manufactured 26 of the Q-2 class 4–4–6–4 types in 1944 and 1945. The Q-2 types were fast and powerful but complicated and doomed to a short life. They equaled the performance, at least on paper, of the EMC FT. They were retired earlier than less powerful but simpler to maintain locomotives. The wartime traffic surge was too much for the existing locomotives to handle and the complex duplex drive locomotives were not yet fully operational. With the War Production Board restricting new locomotive designs the PRR looked south to the C&O and its modern 2–10–4 type for an interim heavy freight locomotive to meet the pressing need for more power. Altoona built 125 of these 2–10–4 types between 1942 and 1944. These interim locomotives outlasted their supposed replacements, the Q-2 types with many in service until the end of steam on the PRR.

The duplex drive locomotives were a manifestation of the corporate culture of the Pennsylvania railroad and its engineering and motive power departments. Impressive and complicated machines they none the less failed to live up to the expectations of officials. The lessons learned by locomotive designers a generation before, that extra cylinders may make for powerful and efficient locomotives but the complexity that they brought along was not worth the trade off in additional maintenance, was lost on the designers of the duplexes. The PRR, the standard railway of the world, simply had to have motive power that was worthy of its self appointed position. The duplexes would be the embodiment of this idea. They were designed and built in house and burned locally mined coal. The railroad could rightfully take full credit for these engineering masterpieces. The electrification of the lines between New York and Washington was also part of this self-assured corporate vision. Only the mighty Pennsylvania railroad with its resources could embark on and complete such a massive undertaking, especially during the dark days of the depression. Diesels that were mass produced by an outside company and with little direct railroad input did not fit this corporate vision. It was almost inconceivable that the Pennsylvania would operate a locomotive that was the same as locomotives on neighboring railroads. Were it to do so the superiority and distinctiveness of the Pennsylvania would cease to be.

The first diesels on the Pennsylvania were, not surprisingly, switchers. Unlike other roads like the New York Central, the PRR did not experiment with diesels during the 1920s with the exception of a single abortive home built test unit.[42] Despite studies throughout the early 1930s and even tests of various diesels in yards in Philadelphia and Baltimore, the PRR was diesel free until 1937. This is in spite of numerous favorable impressions of the various diesels tried out in switching service including a ringing endorsement by the Vice President of Traffic, Charles Young which stated that, "The Diesel switch engine has definitely proven its great economy over any type of steam locomotive yet developed."[43] The PRR finally purchased an EMC model SW for $69,950 in 1937. The reason behind the purchase was that the large General Motors plant at Linden, New Jersey required diesels to switch it allegedly for fire insurance reasons. GM subsidiary EMC was only too happy to provide a suitable locomotive.[44] The PRR resisted this purchase and tried to get GM to agree to the use of at first a regular steam locomotive and then a gasoline electric locomotive. Not surprisingly, GM stated that such locomotives were unsuitable and that only a diesel, like the SW would be appropriate. The PRR next tried a diesel, but one made by Fairbanks-Morse. Not surprisingly GM found this locomotive too was unsatisfactory. The PRR reluctantly agreed to purchase a single SW type locomotive of six hundred horsepower from Electro-Motive but even then seemed less than pleased with it. The diesel was delivered painted completely black with no identifiable railroad ownership markings. They were added by the Pennsylvania itself rather than Electro Motive. The PRR was determined to keep some control over its motive power policies, even if it was only the paint scheme. Two more EMC switchers were ordered in 1941 for service at other GM automotive plants. This initial use of diesels must be seen for what it was, GM essentially forced the Pennsylvania to use its own diesels to switch its own plants as a way of hopefully opening the door to further diesel purchases by the Pennsylvania. During the war fifteen more diesel switchers entered service with the railroad, many for special operating reasons like the above locomotives.[45] These fifteen diesels, all from home town builder Baldwin, mark the first time that diesels were freely chosen by the PRR. They were all destined for service in and around the New York and Philadelphia terminal areas.[46] With heavy wartime traffic stressing the railroad and the available motive power and with costs increasing, midlevel operating officials began to be more and more convinced of the benefits, especially to the bottom line, of using diesel switching power. By the end of 1946 there were fifty-one diesel switchers in service or on order for the railroad. They were being purchased no longer for specific environmental or legal reasons like the GM plants or antismoke legislation but for the general efficiency and cost effectiveness that they embodied.[47]

Despite using diesel switchers, the PRR remained wedded to coal fired steam power during and after the war. It did not host the EMC FT locomotive on its demonstration tour and displayed only a casual interest in contemporary diesel developments of the time. Even while its duplex drive locomotives were entering service and with teething problems, the PRR began experiments with coal burning steam turbine locomotives. It built the only mechanical steam turbine locomotive to operate in the United states and was exploring steam-turbine-electric locomotives as well. While the project began as a large conventional reciprocating design, it quickly became a mechanical turbine and finally a steam turbine electric. As the railroad began to experience increasing financial difficulties after the war, the project was first shelved and finally cancelled altogether.[48]

The PRR took its first real look at the diesel for use beyond switching service and a few high profile passenger runs in 1946. With the cost of coal increasing, president Clement directed his staff to come up with ways to control this increasing cost. Vice president of operations J. F. Deasy simultaneously requested input from the other officials on what types of locomotives the railroad should procure. While increased use of diesels would be an easy suggestion for both, it was not stressed. The report generated in response to both inquires emphasized that seventy-five more Q-2 freight duplex locomotives would enable greater efficiencies and that twenty-five more passenger diesels would enable the PRR to remain competitive in the passenger arena. The report stressed that diesels should be used in switching service where the PRR had more direct operating experience and where they knew by mid-1946 that diesels could cut costs and effect greater operating efficiencies.[49] Freight diesels were not even considered.

The reason that the seventy-five Q-2 locomotives were not built and freight diesels began to appear on the Pennsylvania lies with James Symes, vice president of the Western Region with a home office in Chicago, not Philadelphia like most of the rest of the officials. Being in Chicago, home of the EMD manufacturing plant and also the location of the main offices for many railroads that were using diesels in large numbers, like the Burlington and the Santa Fe, Symes likely had more exposure to and experience with diesels. In an October 1946 memo in response to the above report, Symes questioned the superiority of the Q-2 locomotive and stated in no uncertain terms that diesels would do a better job than the much vaunted duplex. He went further by bringing competition into the argument by reminding officials that the PRR's competitors in time sensitive freight between the east coast and Chicago, the New York Central, Erie, and B&O, were all making use of freight diesels. Last but not least he questioned whether coal mining interests were keeping the company from embracing the diesel. Symes had explicitly stated and questioned what many had felt, a loyalty to the coal industry. Shortly after he wrote his groundbreaking memo he was promoted to the specially created position of deputy vice president of operations out of the home office in Philadelphia. Once arriving in Philadelphia he undertook a detailed study of modernizing all though freight service west of Harrisburg that directly addressed areas that the diesel had a sizeable advantage in such as elimination of helpers and the expense of delivering coal for locomotive consumption. The study also specifically addressed coal revenue should the PRR shift to diesel power. The conclusions were self evident to those that cared to examine the issue. Steam had no further place on the Pennsylvania railroad from an operational and accounting perspective and that regardless of what the PRR chose to burn in its locomotives, the coal industry would face challenges as other railroads increasingly chose to use diesel motive power.[50] The PRR would not suffer excessive declines in coal revenue by switching to diesels. President Clement was receptive to Symes's recommendations and urged that

Photo 16   The replacements for the T-1 duplexes on the Pennsylvania were EMD E-Units like these. The worker at the ash pit on the right and the oil can in the center will both soon be unnecessary as more diesels replace maintenance intensive steam locomotives in passenger service. Courtesy of the Railroad Museum of Pennsylvania (PHMC) Pennsylvania Railroad Collection.

more diesels, including freight diesels, be acquired. The first small order was placed in December 1946, before the final report was even ready.[51]

The final report was released in the spring of 1947. In the space of six months the PRR had gone from contemplating building 75 more Q-2 freight locomotives to embarking on a large scale freight dieselization program. Large orders were placed so that by the end of 1948 the PRR rostered 82 freight units, 63 passenger units and 449 diesel switchers. The 1947 annual report chronicled these purchases under the heading of "new equipment" and included a somewhat understated endorsement of the new locomotives, "This class of motive power is proving satisfactory from the standpoint of economy and service performance."[52] The PRR had finally decided to fully embrace the diesel. The decision was made in no small part because of the high costs and problems being encountered with the various duplex drive steam locomotives. The PRR was also hard up financially. While weathering the Depression without once using the red pen, the railroad found itself hemorrhaging money by 1946, its centennial year due to greatly increasing costs. For the mighty Pennsylvania to be in the red in its centennial year was an embarrassment that was felt at all levels of the organization. Expensive and unproven steam designs simply could not promise the cost reductions and potential savings that the diesels could. Corporate culture and management change also played a large role in the decision of the Pennsylvania to first stick with steam and then to fully embrace the diesel. President Clement who had a firm operations background and was familiar with steam, was not replaced until 1948 but J. M. Symes, who had overseen operations of the western division came east to assume the role of vice president in charge of operations. After his promotion in 1947, steam was all but dead on the PRR. The coal industry, or allegiance to it was a major factor in the initial reluctance of the PRR to dieselize and the efforts to develop advanced coal burning locomotives, be they steam turbine or gas turbine. This allegiance to the coal industry was an integral part of the corporate culture of the PRR but was not based firmly in economic and statistical data. Once data became available combined with the increased cost of coal in 1946 and 1947 and after a series of miners strikes, the PRR lost some of its loyalty to the coal industry and quickly embraced the diesel for its cost advantages.

The PRR dieselized in a rush, buying almost anything that promised cost savings. This would later come back to haunt them as they purchased several unreliable models from Baldwin for example. In 1946 2.7 percent of the yard switching hours were performed by diesel while only .5 percent of the passenger car miles and .1 percent of the freight ton miles were handled by diesels. By 1950 well over half of the yard switching hours at 57.4 percent was handled by diesels. The majority of passengers and freight still moved behind steam but the diesel percentages were climbing, 30.8 percent of freight ton miles were behind diesels and 44.7 percent of the passenger car miles were diesel hauled.[53] Out of a total of 3800 locomotives on the railroad at the end of 1950, an astonishing 1,175 were diesels. By 1952 diesels handled 82 percent of freight traffic, 97 percent of passenger traffic and 91 percent of switching outside of the electrified territory. The last year for heavy overhauls of steam power at the Juniata shops in Altoona was also 1952.[54] Steam was gone in a remarkably short time for such a large railroad with the last steam run occurring in late 1957.

While they may have been arch competitors, there were many similarities between the dieselization experiences of the New York Central and the Pennsylvania. Both roads were large, powerful and prosperous but were facing challenges in the post World War II economy. Both had a tradition of innovation in motive power. Both used electric power and were cognizant of the advantages it brought. The New York Central was less reluctant than the Pennsylvania to experiment with diesels and adopted diesel switching locomotives earlier but both roads did not see any need to purchase large numbers of passenger or freight diesels until after the war. Corporate culture also played a large role in the dieselization experiences of both roads. The Pennsylvania, at the top of the railroad pyramid, was complacent and did not embrace the diesel until it was jarred out of its complacency by the looming deficits of 1946. The New York Central, the perennial number two in the eastern railroad arena, may have been more eager to embrace the diesel to try to give it an edge over its competitors. Both railroads, once they started to dieselize, competed with each other to try to dieselize faster and place more diesel horsepower in service. Both railroads dieselized quickly, perhaps too quickly and did not give adequate thought to long term diesel use and maintenance. The modern steam power of the New York Central such as the Hudsons and Niagaras and the duplexes of the Pennsylvania exist only in photos and memories. Neither road preserved any examples. Other earlier examples of steam power from both roads did get preserved. It is almost as if both roads were embarrassed of their devotion to steam and sought to eliminate from history the offending locomotives while earlier locomotives found a place in museum collections.[55] Both railroads also found that despite the efficiencies of the diesel, the profitability of the 1920s could not be recaptured. While the annual reports of both railed against unjust federal transportation policy, unfair taxation, and predatory labor unions in the late 1940s and 1950s, they found few that would listen. By the late 1950s the two railroads were exploring a merger in a further effort to control costs. The merger into the Penn Central occurred in 1968 and bankruptcy promptly followed. The declining industrial base in the Northeast combined with poor management, rising costs, declining passenger traffic and heavy handed regulation led to the largest bankruptcy the US had seen to that time. Had either road dieselized differently, either earlier or later, the results likely would have been similar. Buying large amounts of FT units and abandoning the Niagara and duplex projects earlier would have made scant difference.

Nickel Plate Road

While the Pennsylvania and New York Central had few competitors in their name sake states, once they got out into the fields of the Midwest things were different. Not only did they compete with each other but also with several other railroads. One in particular, the New York, Chicago & St. Louis Railroad, more commonly known as the Nickel Plate Road (NKP), was well known for its fast freight service.[56] The 2,192 miles of line of the NKP served the heart of industrial America. From an eastern terminal at Buffalo it stretched westward along the southern shore of Lake Erie to Chicago, Peoria, and St. Louis. Secondary lines connected to Toledo, Ohio, Indianapolis, Indiana, and Wheeling, West Virginia. The NKP prided itself on moving freight at speed and emblazoned "the Fast Freight Route" on its cabooses and in advertising. Passengers brought little to the bottom line.

The Nickel Plate came under the control of the Cleveland based Van Sweringen brothers in 1916. The Vans were real estate developers who also became interested in railroads. During the early 1930s they held a controlling or substantial interest in not only the Nickel Plate but also the Erie, Chesapeake & Ohio, Pere Marquette, and Missouri Pacific. John Bernet, formerly a vice president with the New York Central, became the new president of the Nickel Plate in 1916, moved to the Erie in 1927 and then to the C&O in 1929.[57] He promulgated the use of modern motive power for moving heavy trains at speed. All of these roads were extensive users of modern freight power, especially the 2–8–4 type. Although the Vans lost control of their empire during the 1930s, the motive power decisions made under their direction would continue to be felt for the next twenty years.

The steam power of the NKP was quite modern. Freight that had moved behind 2–8–2 Mikado types built in the late 1910s and 1920s was increasingly pulled by fast modern 2–8–4 types. After good experiences on the Erie, the first Berkshires arrived from Alco in 1934. With war traffic placing a strain on the railroad fifty-five more locomotives were ordered from 1942 to 1944 from on line Lima. The Berkshires performed efficiently and exactly as designed and regularly moved long trains of time sensitive freight at speeds of sixty miles an hour across the plains of Ohio and Indiana. Many railroads purchased new steam to handle wartime traffic, but few continued to purchase steam after the war. After trying the latest products from EMD, the Nickel Plate decided to stick with the capable Berkshire, purchasing ten new 2–8–4 types from Lima in 1949.[58] By standardizing their fast freight power with one type of locomotive from one builder, the Nickel Plate received some of the advantages of standardization that the diesels would later bring.

With little passenger traffic and no reason for diesel streamliners, dieselization began on the NKP, as it did on most other railroads, with a few small switchers. By the end of 1942 there were ten small diesel switchers of several models and from both Alco and EMD on the railroad.[59] These switchers went to Buffalo and Chicago and served in the yards and terminal facilities located there. Again, smoke abatement was a likely factor in some of these initial purchases. The next exploration of diesel power came at the conclusion of the war. Passenger service on the Nickel

Plate, what little there was of it, was handled by a handful of lightweight 4–6–2 and 4–6–4 types, the newest of which dated from 1929.[60] These locomotives were beginning to show their age, especially after being worked hard in the war years. They also were not powerful enough to handle the expected increase in passenger service after the war. To remedy the situation and to remain even slightly competitive, in 1947 the NKP purchased eleven Alco PA passenger units to dieselize all main line passenger service.[61] Switcher purchases resumed after the war, and by the middle of 1949 the railroad had fifty-seven switchers that had essentially dieselized several major yards on the system.[62] The railroad had recognized the efficiencies of at least diesel switcher operation and likely main line passenger operation as well.

As the economy continued to rebound after the postwar transition period, the NKP found itself short of power in 1948. While other railroads were ordering diesels by the dozen, the NKP decided to test the newest offering from EMD against their modern steam power. EMD was happy to supply four F-3 units to the NKP for test purposes. After extensive testing between Chicago and Buffalo in the summer of 1948, the results were mixed. The diesels had better low speed performance but above forty mph the opposite was true. The steam locomotive also slightly bested the diesel in the time it took to move trains from one terminal to the next. The 513 miles from Chicago to Buffalo were covered in twelve hours forty five minutes with steam and thirteen hours thirty minutes with diesels. Fuel costs were virtually identical, $.179 per one thousand gross ton miles for both forms of power.[63] The EMD diesels were sent packing and the road promptly ordered its last ten 2–8–4 types from Lima. Steam was cheaper than diesel in initial cost and the railroad already had dozens of similar Berkshire types in operation so maintenance forces would be familiar with the new steam locomotives. EMD would try again in 1949 with its newer F-7 type of locomotive. Again the Nickel Plate decided not to opt for new diesels. Note however, that the railroad did not fully examine maintenance, servicing, and availability issues, all areas where the diesel held a large advantage. In performance at least, modern steam could equal the diesel. At the end of 1950 there were only 82 diesels on the railroad, mostly switching locomotives compared to 392 steam locomotives. There were no main line freight diesels, yet.[64]

The year 1950 was a turning point for the Nickel Plate. In July EMD demonstrated its new GP-7 type road-switcher for the NKP. The third time was a charm for the diesel builder, and the NKP ordered several units to begin dieselization of main line freight service.[65] The flexibility of the road switcher type of locomotive over the previous F-units was likely a significant factor in the decision by the Nickel Plate to adopt road diesels. Diesel switchers continued to replace steam in most terminals and yards. While diesels were now dominating passenger and yard service, the opposite was still true for freight. As of February 1953 out of a total of 152 diesel locomotives, only 23 were in main line freight service.[66] The bulk of freight still moved behind the capable 2–8–4 locomotives. Diesels began to arrive in ever increasing quantities over the next few years and began to bump even the mighty Berkshires from freight service, the last one being retired in 1958. The remaining steam operation on the railroad was a lowly switcher.[67]

The Nickel Plate seemed to follow a conservative path. They were clearly aware of the advantages of the diesel, with many operating in yard and passenger service, but they could not justify the purchase of expensive diesels for freight service when there were advanced and capable steam locomotives around. The physical plant of the railroad was optimized for modern steam with the Berkshires operable over the whole of the railroads main lines. The Berkshires were ideally suited for their task of moving freight quickly and efficiently across the plains of the Midwest. The relative standardization of the type, almost all were built by Lima to the same design, enabled the road to enjoy some of the benefits of standardization in maintenance and servicing. Only when more flexible road switchers became widely available did the Nickel Plate begin to dieselize freight service. Coal was not a major factor in the decision making process of the Nickel Plate with a couple exceptions. The railroad served few on line coal producing areas with the exception of the former Wheeling & Lake Erie lines, acquired in 1949. However, ample supplies of coal were readily available and just a short distance south and east of the railroad's main lines. Coal therefore was easily accessible and transportation costs for coal for locomotive fuel would have been small. The Nickel Plate survived the 1950s in good shape financially but succumbed to a merger with the Norfolk &

Western in 1964. The Wabash, which served many of the same areas as the Nickel Plate, was also merged by the N&W at the same time.

WESTERN DISTRICT

Union Pacific

The western district also had some railroads that experienced both forces pushing for adoption of the diesel and forces advocating for continuation of steam power. Like the eastern district, the railroads thus effected included some of the largest of the western roads. The Union Pacific (UP) is arguably the most famous name in railroad history. From its early days as the transcontinental to its famous streamliners and huge steam locomotives, it has a unique place in the pantheon of North American railroads. The Union Pacific of midcentury was a large and expansive road that stretched from Omaha and Kansas City west through Denver and Cheyenne, Wyoming to the Great Salt Lake. Here the line split with one main heading northwest through Idaho to Portland, Oregon and Seattle. The other main headed southwest to Las Vegas and the Los Angeles basin of California. A small collection of secondary and branch lines extended the railroad's reach in Kansas, Nebraska, Idaho, Oregon, and Washington.

The UP has long been known for its large and impressive steam motive power such as 4-8-8-4 Big Boys and 4-6-6-4 Challengers. However, in the mid-1930s, neither of these huge steam locomotives existed. At the end of 1935, the UP owned 1,445 locomotives. The newest had been delivered in 1930. The largest single class were the 368 2-8-0 types, closely followed by 359 2-8-2 types. The only moderately advanced locomotives on the roster were the 88 immense but maintenance intensive 4-12-2 types built a few years before.[68] While the 2-8-2 and especially the 4-12-2 types were capable machines, they were optimized for pulling power, not speed. For passenger service 145 4-6-2 Pacifics were joined by 60 4-8-2 Mountain types.[69] The UP, a wealthy railroad with substantial land holdings, significantly modernized its steam motive power as the economy slowly recovered in the late 1930s. The first to arrive were 15 4-6-6-4 Challenger types in 1936. They were quickly joined by 25 more in 1937. The Challengers were put to use in fast freight service. For passenger service the UP purchased 20 4-8-4 types in 1937. Fifteen more followed in 1939.[70] As war clouds gathered, the UP continued to modernize its steam locomotive fleet. In 1940 Otto Jabelmann, vice-president of research and mechanical standards, designed the huge 4-8-8-4 Big Boy type.[71] For the UP to be purchasing substantial numbers of steam locomotives for both passenger and freight service in the late 1930s was notable but not unusual when compared with other railroads, especially those with the available capital.

The UP had ample experience with internal combustion motive power for many years prior to full dieselization. The railroad was one of the largest users of the early gasoline-mechanical McKeen motor cars. Indeed, William McKeen developed his self propelled motorcar with substantial help from the UP including the use of the Union Pacific's Omaha Shops. While the McKeen cars were less than a huge success, the UP was poised to make a big splash with its next internal combustion project. In 1933 the UP began the streamliner craze with its M-10000, the City of Salina. While the three-car articulated train was powered by a spark ignition distillate engine, its offspring were diesels. Throughout the rest of the 1930s the UP purchased, sometimes jointly with other railroads, several custom built diesel locomotives and train sets for streamlined passenger service.

By the late 1930s the UP knew well the capabilities of the diesel for fast passenger service. It is somewhat curious then that the railroad chose also to expend valuable capital on new 4-8-4 type passenger locomotives during the same time period. This is especially notable when competitors like the CB&Q and the Santa Fe were dieselizing ever increasing numbers of their passenger trains. The conservative management of the UP felt that diesels were still in an experimental stage and that a large investment in diesels would not be wise until they had been further developed. Diesels were good for a few lightweight streamliners and the public relations benefits that they brought but were not judged to be up to the rigors of heavy duty, day to day railroading. Also of note is that the monstrous Big Boy was designed after the EMC FT had made its barnstorming demonstration tour and after competitor Santa Fe had already expressed an interest in the pioneering units. On the UP, diesels seemed to be useful on some of the flashy streamliners, but freight, the bread and butter of the railroad, would continue to roll behind steam locomotives.

This course of action becomes clearer when we look at the leadership of the railroad. Newly installed in October 1937, President Jeffers was a veteran railroader who worked his way up exclusively through the UP operating department. "An old fashioned man in a newfangled world," he knew and understood steam power.[72] He even justified the order of more 4–8–4 types in a letter to the board of directors in New York: "I appreciate that recommendations for purchase of steam power for passenger service should be conservative in view of developments of Diesel and other types of power, but in event steam is superseded by other types to any considerable extent, the locomotives recommended can be used most advantageously in freight service."[73]

The UP would remain almost entirely steam powered through the war years, even though other western roads and competitors like the Santa Fe, Western Pacific, Rio Grande, and others were purchasing diesel freight power. To keep the wartime traffic moving the railroad ordered more of its most advanced locomotives, 4–8–4, 4–6–6–4 and 4–8–8–4 types.[74] These locomotives were among the largest and most powerful locomotives built not only in North America, but in the entire world. The 4–8–4 types could easily sustain one hundred miles per hour across the flat lands of Kansas and Nebraska with full passenger trains. The Challenger and Big Boy locomotives were also very capable machines and were a quantum leap in performance over earlier types. President Jeffers partly explained his steam policy in a letter to Woody Charske, chairman of the executive committee, "As you know, I have not been too enthusiastic over the purchase of heavy duty Diesel freight locomotives, because I was convinced that, due to improvements brought about by the emergency of the war, the present heavy duty Diesel freight locomotive would be obsolete within the next few years."[75] Jeffers also criticized the EMD FT then in service in large numbers with the Santa Fe and other railroads, "It is my considered judgement that the 5400 H.P. unit now being manufactured by Electro-Motive is not an entirely satisfactory heavy duty freight unit and that there is no need for four units."[76] Jeffers seems to have thought that the available diesels would soon be superseded by more capable and better performing units including possibly gas turbines, and that the UP should wait for these new locomotives. He also demonstrated steam-era thinking with his preoccupation on the number of units.

The war years did see the purchase of a few diesels, however. While the main line trains moved behind huge steam locomotives, small diesel switchers were beginning to make their presence felt in the yards and terminals across the system. The board approved an expenditure of $86,600 on March 12, 1940 for the purchase of one EMC diesel switcher. It was to be used in the Omaha terminal area, literally just down the street from headquarters. This way management could keep a close watch on the new form of motive power to see if it would live up to all its promises. The reasons for recommending listed on the authority for expenditure include eliminating smoke and cinder nuisance and reducing fire hazards and more importantly, "Diesel switching locomotives will contribute to greater utilization and adaptability and more freely negotiate curves on industrial trackage."[77] Potential cost savings or return on investment was estimated at 12.4 percent compared to comparable steam power. Several more switchers followed in 1940 and 1941. Pure hard headed accounting was not the only reason for the purchase of these additional diesels, however. In a letter of December 1, 1940, President Jeffers stated that it was necessary to transfer three diesels from Omaha to Los Angeles to use at a new Douglas Aircraft plant, "where we are obligated to the use of Diesel switch engines."[78] In addition, diesels were required in Salt Lake City due to a local antismoke ordinance.[79] Competitive pressure also played a role in the decision to use diesels in Salt Lake City. Another letter states, "In view of the anti-smoke ordinance and the fact that the D.& R.G.W. has complete Diesel operation, we would consider it desirable to provide complete Diesel switching at Salt Lake City."[80] Thus, the Union Pacific adopted diesel switchers not only for the savings that they could generate but also for legislative and competitive reasons.

After the end of the war, the Union Pacific invested in new passenger diesels to meet the expected postwar surge in passenger travel. In addition to a surge of passenger business, the beginning of 1946 also saw a change in leadership for the railroad. President Jeffers retired on January 31, 1946. The new president was George F. Ashby. Unlike the quintessential railroad man Jeffers, who had ample operations experience, Ashby's background was statistics and

accounting.[81] By the end of the year Ashby was initiating
a large scale modernization and improvement program,
designed to correct the years of deferred maintenance
that the railroad experienced during the Depression and
war years. Part of this modernization program was the
purchase of substantial numbers of freight diesel motive
power. In a letter to the board of directors explaining that
past motive power purchases were not well spent, Ashby
stated, "I have been slow to suggest conversion of operations from steam to diesel, but I am now convinced that
we should make a substantial start in that direction."[82] The
first order for 133 total units, 21 passenger units and 112
freight units, was approved in December 1946.[83] This was
the first order for diesel freight units for the railroad.

The late 1946 order for freight diesels meant that the
days were numbered for steam power, but steam would
still be used more than a decade later. The UP, blessed
with online coal reserves on company property and powerful, modern steam power, used this power to its fullest
even while dieselizing. The modern 4–8–4, 4–6–6–4, and
4–8–8–4 types were relocated to keep them close to the
coal mines in Wyoming and main steam shops in Cheyenne. Older and less powerful steam locomotives were
retired as they suffered large component failures and as
more diesels came online. The UP dieselized the western most areas of its system first, partly because of the
difficulty and expense of transporting coal fuel and the
difficulty of providing adequate water in the deserts of
California, Nevada, and Oregon. By 1953, after seven
years of dieselization, steam still moved a large amount
of the passengers and freight on the railroad. In that year
steam was used on 68.7 percent of freight train mileage
and 36.1 percent of passenger train mileage.[84] The next
couple years would see continued diesel deliveries and
large scale steam retirements, including some of the modern types mentioned above. By 1957 steam was used only
occasionally during the fall peak traffic season. The next
year again saw use of steam during the heavy traffic fall
harvest season. A few locomotives were fired up during
the summer of 1959, but the delivery of new diesels combined with a steel industry strike that negatively affected
traffic levels led to the end of steam power on the Union
Pacific in July 1959. The railroad kept several locomotives
ready in case they were needed for the 1960 season, but
they were not.

Photo 17 This publicity photo graphically illustrates the unique motive power philosophy of the Union Pacific Railroad. Beneath the scenic hills of Green River, Wyoming sits at right, an EMD F-3, in the middle a 4-8-8-4 "Big Boy," and on the left a General Electric gas turbine locomotive. The Union Pacific was the only railroad in the world to operate both the Big Boy and the gas turbine. Courtesy of the Union Pacific Museum.

The Union Pacific stands as a good example of many of the factors of dieselization. Early experiments with streamliners and difficult operating conditions gave the railroad impetus to embrace the diesel. However, other factors kept the road operating steam power. Blessed with online coal reserves and adequate revenues during the 1930s, the railroad invested heavily in large and powerful steam locomotives. A powerful but old fashioned president who was wary of the diesel also played a big role. Even during the war years with neighboring railroads purchasing FT locomotives by the dozen, the UP remained committed to steam for its main line freight. After a management change after the war, dieselization began in earnest with the railroad proceeding slowly and cautiously, dieselizing by division and keeping the best steam in service, generating revenue. This cautious strategy helped the UP to survive the postwar years in good shape. Experiments with other forms of motive power in the 1950s and 1960s ended by 1970. With long hauls and the booming west, the UP did not experience the problems that many railroads experienced in the 1960s and 1970s. It began to expand in the 1980s, merging first the Western Pacific and Missouri Pacific, followed by the Missouri–Kansas–Texas, and in the 1990s the Chicago and North Western and Southern Pacific came into the system. The Union Pacific is unique among the railroads analyzed in that it still exists under its original name.

Southern Pacific

The other western road that delayed dieselization was the operating successor of the other half of the original transcontinental, the Southern Pacific (SP). Second in mileage only to the Santa Fe, the 12,441 mile SP was a huge, powerful, and prosperous railroad. It and its wholly owned subsidiaries such as the Texas & New Orleans, stretched from New Orleans across Texas and the southern parts of Arizona and New Mexico to Los Angeles and San Diego. From L.A. the lines stretched north serving the rich agricultural central valley of California as well as the cities of Sacramento, Oakland, and San Francisco. The lines continued north to Portland, Oregon and also east, along the original Central Pacific route to the interchange point of Ogden, Utah. The SP was cursed with some of the most difficult operating terrain on the continent ranging from deserts to snowbound mountain passes. Of special note was the western ascent on the Sierra Nevada, a 104-mile 2.2 percent climb from Roseville, near Sacramento, to the summit near Truckee, California.[85]

Similar to the Union Pacific, the SP was interested in internal combustion power early. Like the UP, the SP invested in many McKeen motor cars during the early years of the century. Also like the UP, the cars proved to be less than ideal, and most were removed from service in the 1920s.[86] The SP experimented with larger gasoline-electric motor cars in the 1920s and 1930s. These cars were used in service ranging from San Francisco commuter service to the Arizona desert to the isolated, Northwestern Pacific line in northern California.[87] SP management was also interested in what the diesel could do, especially for the bottom line. SP president Julius Kruttschnitt was in contact with Baldwin as early as 1922 about diesel locomotive developments.[88] Kruttschnitt was eager to get a new experimental Baldwin diesel locomotive out to the west coast for a trial on SP lines. Little became of these negotiations, not due to disinterest on the part of the SP, but because the diesel locomotive was not a high priority at Baldwin. When finally built, the locomotive proved unsatisfactory. Krutschnitt remained interested in diesel motive power and said so on numerous occasions.[89] He retired in mid-1925 and died soon afterward, thus ending the SP's pioneering effort at dieselization.

The next diesel operations on the SP would be over a decade later. A change in leadership again had an impact on the motive power policies of the railroad. New president Angus McDonald who took office in 1932 was devoted to reclaiming some of the passengers whom had been lost to the automobile and the Depression. Many other railroads were also trying to recapture passenger traffic and were doing so with streamlined trains. The famous UP M-10000 pioneering streamliner was exhibited on the SP system in several places including San Francisco.[90] The huge crowds that turned out to view the futuristic train evidently made an impression on the SP management as they began to develop their own plans for streamlined service. The UP, fresh from its success with the M-10000, inaugurated several other streamlined trains including the City of Portland, City of Los Angeles, and City of San Francisco. The trains began in Chicago and ended their respective journeys in their namesake cities. However, the UP did not directly serve Chicago or San Francisco. The eastern connection from Omaha to Chicago was made via the rails of the Chicago and North Western Railroad, while the western connection from Ogden, Utah to San Francisco was on the SP.[91] The new streamliner would cut the travel time from Chicago to San Francisco from sixty hours to slightly less than forty hours, an impressive achievement.[92] The success of the streamliner caused the operating railroads to inaugurate a larger and more luxurious City of San Francisco in 1938. However, diesel power would not expand to other passenger runs on the SP, despite proposals to the contrary. The new Daylight streamliners between Los Angeles and San Francisco were powered not by diesels but by streamlined 4–8–4 steam locomotives.[93] The SP was interested in the new diesels but preferred to have other railroads do the experimenting, especially in the tight times of the Depression.

While the streamlined luxury trains were grabbing the public attention, President McDonald began to think of dieselization of more than just fancy streamliners. For several years the efficiencies of diesel switchers in yard work had been well known. McDonald started the SP down the road to freight dieselization in 1939 with the evaluation and purchase of several small switching locomotives from both EMC and Alco. An EMC SW-1, purchased April 1, 1939 and numbered 1000, was the first fully SP-owned diesel locomotive.[94] By the outbreak of the war, the SP owned fifty diesel switchers operating in yards and terminals across the system.[95] This illustrates that by the war the SP had generally accepted diesel switching locomotives, even if some were purchased for reasons other than purely economic efficiency.

While the switchers and streamliners were bringing diesel power to the SP, management continued to purchase new and advanced steam locomotives. For passenger and high-speed freight service the SP adopted the 4–8–4 type beginning in 1930. By 1940 there were thirty of this type on the system. The war years brought more, with forty added by 1943.[96] Freight power was modernized during the beginnings of dieselization as well. The many mountain grades and desert conditions placed an extra burden on railroad operations. The SP responded to this challenge by designing large and powerful locomotives custom built for particular assignments. The most famous of these were the several classes of 4–8–8–2 cab forwards. The ascent from Sacramento over the Sierra Nevada to Reno was an arduous climb of greater than 2 percent for over one hundred miles. Not only were there steep grades and tight curves but there were many long tunnels and snowsheds.[97] To keep crews from literally suffocating on the smoke, the SP and Baldwin came up with the cab forward design. They took a conventional steam locomotive and turned it around so that the cab was at the front. The tender was still behind the locomotive. Pipes carried the water and oil fuel from the tender to the locomotive. The first of the type arrived in 1909. Baldwin continued to build the unique locomotives for the SP for the next twenty-five years with 105 modern versions added to the roster from 1928 to 1939.[98]

The war placed a heavy burden on the SP, heavier than on many other railroads. Because the railroad served several Pacific coast ports as well as important military production, assembly, and training sites in California and Texas, new power was needed. The SP hosted the EMC FT demonstrator in May 1940, but no orders were forthcoming.[99] Operating officials were impressed by the diesels' admittedly superior performance but, as with passenger diesels earlier, were cautious about committing to the new and expensive units. Instead of adopting the diesel for heavy road-freight service, like neighbor and competitor Santa Fe, the SP stuck with steam and ordered many more huge modern steam locomotives. They even built a new heavy shop for steam locomotives at Sparks, Nevada near Reno to service the new locomotives.[100] In this regard the SP was similar to its other large neighbor and competitor, the Union Pacific. Even while dozens of massive new 4–8–8–2 cab forward types were entering service, dieselization of yard and terminal facilities continued. By the end of 1944 there were 130 diesel switchers on the property with 29 added in 1944 alone. Also added that year were ten new 4–8–8–2 cab forwards.[101] These would be the last new steam locomotives purchased by the SP.

With the war over and the capability of the diesel proven by the demands of wartime traffic on other railroads including neighboring Santa Fe, the SP began to purchase more diesels. The railroad hosted the EMD F-3

Photo 18 Steam locomotives required large shops for servicing and maintenance. The larger the locomotives, the larger the shops required. Seen here in the ample Sparks, Nevada shops of the Southern Pacific are two 4-8-8-2 cab forward types. The front of both locomotives is at left. The 4192 was a 1939 Baldwin product while the 4260 was built during WW II. Both were out of service by 1958. Courtesy of the Union Pacific Museum.

demonstrator units in December 1945, and officials were impressed with the performance.[102] Even before the on line test, in October of that same year the railroad ordered eighty 1,500 horsepower units to be assembled into sets of four.[103] Twenty-eight 6,000 horsepower four-unit locomotives were available for use by the end of 1947.[104] This marked the beginning of main line freight dieselization on the SP. That year also brought twenty-three new switching locomotives and new passenger units. Perhaps more telling, it also saw the retirement of eighty steam locomotives, although none of the modern 4–8–8–2 or 4–8–4 types were withdrawn from service.[105] The immediate postwar years did see continued investment in steam servicing facilities including a testing lab at the huge Sacramento shops complex.[106] The new diesels were put to use in through freight service on many parts of the system but were concentrated on routes out of Los Angeles where environmental conditions most favored the diesel. While the diesels were able to save the railroad money, the management of the SP realized that to truly take advantage of the cost savings inherent in the diesel they had to get rid of steam locomotives completely. This would enable the railroad to abandon the steam servicing and repair facilities rather than maintaining dual steam and diesel facilities. It was reported in the trade press at the time that complete dieselization of a single operating division would enable greater savings than system wide limited diesel use.[107]

In 1948 the railroad drew up a comprehensive ten-year motive power plan that would provide the blueprint for dieselization for the entire Southern Pacific System. It was a slow and deliberate plan that retained the best steam power for use, although in ever declining duties. It put diesels on assignments where they would use their unique operational characteristics to do the most good, such as mountain districts. Steam would be gradually confined to the flat lands of the California Central Valley and the San Francisco Bay area. Of special significance was the proposed retirement of steam locomotives. The most modern 4–8–4 and 4–8–8–2 types built from 1937 to 1944 were not scheduled for retirement in the ten years outlined in the survey.[108] The report stated that, "Economies for diesel operations are principally due to: (a) fuel, (b) locomotive repairs, (c) elimination of helper districts, and (d) more tons per train on some of the districts."[109] It also detailed by district what the costs and savings would be for substitution of diesel motive power. For instance, on the tortuous mountain division from Roseville, California, to Sparks, Nevada, a 6,000 horsepower diesel freight locomotive was able to haul the same train as a modern 4-8-8-2 steam locomotive, 8,000 tons east and 6,400 tons west.[110] However, the use of helpers was noticeably different. The diesel would not require any help westbound and would require another 6,000 horsepower diesel for the eastbound trek. The steam locomotive would require one additional 4-8-8-2 westbound and two additional 4-8-8-2 types eastbound. Total diesel savings per year on this run alone were estimated at $269,120. Diesels had a distinct advantage in most costs. While crew wages were roughly the same, the diesel eliminated the use of two helpers which saved wages for their crews. Fuel costs for the diesel were calculated at 112.5 cents per train mile. Steam fuel costs were 393.9 cents per train mile with the heavy residual oil that the steam locomotives burned. Repair and servicing costs also greatly favored the diesel. Repairs were calculated as 108.6 cents per train mile for the diesel and 292.6 cents per train mile for steam.[111] Results varied by district. For instance, between El Paso, Texas, and Tucumcari, New Mexico, the diesel, while still superior, did not have quite the edge. Total diesel savings on this run per year were estimated at $249,100. Diesels were able to pull a significantly heavier train, 9,000 tons eastbound as opposed to 6,500 tons for steam. However, the steam locomotives used on this district were coal fired as opposed to oil fired. This gave steam somewhat less of a cost disadvantage when comparing fuel costs. Even with cheaper fuel for steam locomotives, diesels managed an average cost per train mile of 60.2 cents while coal fired steam managed 117.6 cents per train mile.[112]

On the flat lands of the California central valley and San Francisco Bay area the diesel savings were not as extreme. For instance, from Fresno to Bakersfield a three thousand horsepower diesel was calculated to save $114,300 per year compared to a 1920s vintage 4-8-2 steam locomotive.[113] Passenger dieselization savings were also documented. These savings ran from $205,000 per year on the run from Tucumcari to Los Angeles to only $5,000 per year on the local passenger train from Tucson to Nogales, Arizona.[114] Not coincidentally, the Tucumcari–Los Angeles run was scheduled for dieselization in 1950, while the passengers heading to Nogales were scheduled to ride behind steam until 1957 or more likely until the route was abandoned.

The SP generally followed the recommendations in the report and transformed itself into a diesel rather than a steam road. At the end of 1953 there were 1,037 steam locomotives on the system and 1,401 diesel units.[115] Diesels accounted for 71.4 percent of all locomotive mileage. For the year of 1953 diesels pulled 73.9 percent of gross freight ton miles and 50.8 percent of passenger train miles.[116] By this time the Salt Lake division from Ogden, Utah to Sparks, Nevada was completely dieselized. The plan was to progressively dieselize each division beginning at the northern and eastern ends of the system and progressing toward the San Francisco area.[117] A revised plan called for 127 steam locomotives to be left at the end of 1957 with all officially retired by 1960. However, with perhaps the traffic crunch of World War II and the Korean conflict fresh in their minds, the report recommends that, "a number of selected types of steam locomotives be retained for any unusual heavy traffic demand above normal requirements."[118] The selected locomotives included twenty-five small switchers, twenty-five 4–8–4 types and fifty of the modern 4–8–8–2 cab forwards. SP management just could not bear to part with its most modern steam.

The end of the line for steam came roughly on schedule. At the end of 1957 there were but 113 steam locomotives left compared with 1,991 diesel units.[119] However, none of these locomotives were in service. The last steam freight run was in November 1956 and the last steam passenger run, a San Francisco commuter run, was in January 1957.[120] The Southern Pacific, like the Union Pacific, illustrates many of the influences on dieselization. A forward thinking chief executive began inquiries in the 1920s but his death ended the early flirtation with diesels. Later a few diesel streamliners in the 1930s were accepted, but only because they increased passenger revenues. Like the UP, freight would move behind steam power until after the war. With modern steam and the custom designed cab forwards, the SP felt it did not need diesels. After the war with not only the diesel's usefulness in freight service proven by neighbor and competitor Santa Fe but with rapidly increasing costs, the diesel became the only real option available to the railroad. Coal was not a factor in the dieselization of the SP as most of its locomotives

Photo 19 The massive cab forward locomotives of the SP were replaced with locomotives like these, EMD F-7s. These four units could produce 6,000 horsepower and could easily out pull a cab forward and do so for much less operating expense. Courtesy of the Union Pacific Museum.

burned oil, readily available from the oilfields of California and Texas. Since the railroad was not only accustomed to burning oil and had the facilities for storage and transport of the liquid fuel but also supplier relationships with oil companies, when the shift occurred from steam locomotive fuel oil to diesel fuel, the road was easily able to make the substitution. Like neighbor and future merger partner Union Pacific, the Southern Pacific did well in the postwar years, mostly because of the booming economies of states served by the SP like Texas and California.

SOUTHERN DISTRICT

The next three roads analyzed are the three southern district pocahontas region coal roads. While they all operated in the same region and were dependent on coal for the bulk of their traffic and revenue, they responded to the diesel in different ways. All delayed dieselization primarily because of their allegiance to the coal industry but many other factors, especially management change and corporate culture, played a role.

Norfolk & Western

Of all the railroads that resisted the diesel, the most famous would have to be the Norfolk & Western (N&W). The N&W was the most extreme case of those railroads that chose to defer adoption of the diesel locomotive as it was the last wholly steam powered large railroad in North America.[121] The 2,126 mile N&W was built to haul coal, and it did it well. It stretched from tidewater at Norfolk, Virginia, west to Roanoke and the coal-filled hills of West Virginia. It also ran northwest from the coalfields to Columbus and Cincinnati, Ohio. Coal moved both ways to the furnaces, factories and steel mills of the industrial Midwest as well as to Norfolk for transfer to ships and export. The N&W and coal were inseparable. In 1950, fully 74 percent of all tonnage and 55 percent of all operating revenue was from coal.[122]

Moving long trains of coal out of the mountains of West Virginia required large and powerful locomotives. In the early 1910s, the railroad began to purchase several 2–6–6–2 and 2–8–8–2 compound articulateds for heavy mountain service. By the end of the 1920s, the railroad had 185

2–6–6–2 types and over one hundred 2–8–8–2 types of various classes.[123] Faced with obsolete power and the need to speed up schedules in the mid-and late 1930s, the N&W responded. Like many other railroads, they chose new steam power. In 1936 the N&W built the first of its forty-three A class 2–6–6–4 locomotives in its own shops in Roanoke, Virginia. The locomotives were a complete success and are widely recognized as being a high point of steam freight power. The war years of 1943 and 1944 brought twenty-five more A class 2–6–6–4 types to the railroad. While the class A was a remarkable locomotive, it was not designed for slow speed, heavy haul service. To modernize its heavy steam power, the N&W began to further refine the 2–8–8–2 Y type in 1930. From 1936 to 1940, thirty-five Y6 types were produced, again in the shops in Roanoke. During the war sixteen more locomotives were produced.

Up to this point the N&W seems not very remarkable. Many railroads bought or built new steam power in the late 1930s and continued to do so during the war years. However, most railroads had abandoned further development of the steam locomotive by the end of the war or shortly thereafter and many were well down the path to dieselization, even those, such as the Pennsylvania, SP, and UP, with modern steam purchased only a few years before. The N&W stands as the only large railroad to not embrace the diesel in the late 1940s. After the war, the N&W returned to producing and operating its modern steam power. For fast freight service eight more A class 2–6–6–4 types were constructed in 1949 and 1950. For slow drag freights and mountain service thirty more 2–8–8–2 types were built from 1948 to 1952.[124] Even passenger service remained behind steam. Eleven J class 4–8–4 types were built during the war. They were joined by three more built in 1950. Switchers too remained steam. The N&W built forty-five 0–8–0 types from 1951 to 1953.[125]

Did economics somehow not apply in the hills of West Virginia? Why did the N&W, alone among North American railroads, decide to stick with steam? The answer is complex but a big part of it can be stated in one word, coal. It was the lifeblood of the railroad from the earliest days and was far and away the largest single commodity in terms of tonnage and revenue. The mines served in West Virginia produced some of the highest quality steam coal on earth. This coal, in addition to being high quality, was also relatively cheap. The railroad could purchase coal literally at the mine mouth, and did not have large coal transportation costs.

N&W management also was fully committed to steam power. President Robert H. Smith knew steam and the railroad well. He began his career on the N&W in 1911, and worked his way up to the presidency in 1946.[126] Along the way he held many operating positions including roadmaster, division superintendent, and general manager.[127] With cheap local coal, skilled workers and shops, and the finest and most efficient steam locomotives on the continent and probably on earth, the N&W was perfectly content to stick with steam. The railroad was not completely static however. The N&W continued to perfect steam locomotive technology and operations in search of ever greater efficiency. For example, one weakness of steam locomotives was the extensive servicing required. The N&W went to work on this problem after World War II and came up with the lubritorium. Instead of heading off to the roundhouse when in need of service, the locomotive would instead head to the lubritorium, a specially constructed building with tracks down the middle. Once inside, several hoses hanging from the ceiling would be used to lubricate the many moving parts. While the locomotive was being lubricated, workers in the inspection pit between the rails would be inspecting bearings and brake components.[128] Facilities were also designed so that locomotives could take on coal, water, and sand simultaneously. These improvements meant that the N&W achieved the best utilization of steam locomotives of any railroad. George Drury states that these facilities "gave N&W's steam locomotives an availability record that compared favorably with diesels of the day."[129] By investing in modern steam servicing facilities, the N&W partially negated a large advantage of the diesel, higher availability.

In 1952 the N&W accepted the offer of EMD to test its new F-7 type of diesel locomotive. The rest of the railroad world watched to see if the best of steam could compete against the diesel. However, both sides tried to stack the deck in their favor. Both EMD and the N&W added small enhancements to their respective locomotives to boost performance.[130] Since both parties engaged in this deception, the end results were most likely not greatly affected. The results of the test showed that the modern steam power on the N&W was practically the equal in performance and fuel costs to the EMD F-7. Maintenance and availability were not addressed. The diesel did have a slight advantage on the most mountainous of districts but this advantage evaporated when the terrain flattened out. Needless to say, no order for diesels was forthcoming from the N&W in 1952. The N&W did have an ace in the hole that it was banking on to keep the diesel off of the railroad's rails for the foreseeable future. The aptly named *Jawn Henry* was about to be unveiled. This steam-turbine-electric locomotive would combine the features of electric traction with a coal-fired steam boiler. The development of this locomotive is examined in greater detail in chapter 5.

Steam made good economic sense for the N&W in the early 1950s. The railroad was continually among the five most profitable railroads in the country and earned operating returns of near 30 percent.[131] However, even President Smith was not immune to the advantages of the diesel. In early 1955 the N&W quietly placed an order for eight diesel locomotives, four from Alco and four from EMD. When questioned, President Smith stated that these locomotives were destined for the lightly trafficked branch line from Durham to Lynchburg, Virginia. The use of diesels would permit greater flexibility and permit the large steam power that had been assigned to the branch to be better used on the main line. Smith remained loyal to steam however. He stated, "this does not mean that we have changed our view that our modern coal burning steam locomotives can handle the major part of our traffic economically."[132] Once the diesel began operating and turning in savings of over 30 percent from the former steam power, the results could not be denied. More orders for diesels followed in the fall of 1955 and early 1956. Other branch and secondary lines were being dieselized but steam still reigned supreme out on the main line in the heart of coal country. Even at this point the N&W had no immediate plan to fully dieselize. At the end of 1957 despite 168 diesels on the property, more than 95 percent of all passenger miles and the bulk of freight tonnage east of the service facility at Williamson, West Virginia, was steam hauled.[133] Change would come soon however. In April 1958, President Smith stepped down and Stewart Saunders became the new president. Saunders did not have an operating background like Smith but came out of the accounting department. On June 25, 1958, Saunders announced that the N&W would be completely dieselized by the end of 1960.[134] The end came quickly with the bulk of steam, dozens of locomotives, out of service within a year. The last steam run on the N&W, the last steam powered large railroad in the United States, occurred on May 6, 1960.[135]

The N&W exemplifies many of the factors that combined to delay the adoption of the diesel. The importance of the coal industry to the railroad can not be overstated. This importance led upper management, including President Smith, to believe that diesel power was anathema to the primary task of the railroad, hauling coal. With a capable engineering staff and with the necessary facilities and skilled labor to build and operate its locomotives efficiently, the railroad saw no need to embrace the diesel in the immediate postwar period. By the late 1950s the economies from diesel operation could no longer be denied. Upper management at first delayed and then, after a presidential change accelerated the process but even on the N&W, the days were numbered for steam. The N&W remained a profitable railroad, no matter what pulled its long coal trains out of the hills of West Virginia. After other mergers had been announced in the east including the Erie Lackawanna and the Penn Central, the N&W acquired the Midwestern Nickel Plate Road and Wabash to become a major powerhouse not only in coal but in all sorts of freight traffic. It merged as equals with the Southern in 1982 to become the Norfolk Southern and acquired roughly half of Conrail in the 1990s to become one of the two large eastern systems.

Chesapeake & Ohio

The Chesapeake & Ohio stretched from tidewater at Newport News, Virginia west through Richmond to the coal rich mountains of West Virginia and then north to the industrial cities of Cincinnati, Toledo, and Chicago. The C&O was a larger railroad than the N&W but was similar in many respects. In 1947 the C&O merged with the Pere Marquette Railroad of Michigan to create a system of over five thousand miles of track with a large network of lines covering the lower Peninsula serving several important automotive and manufacturing cities such as Detroit, Flint, and Grand Rapids. The C&O originated more coal traffic than any other railroad in the United States, 63 million tons in 1950. This was equal to a staggering 1/8th of total bituminous production.[136] However, because of the former Pere Marquette lines the railroad was also a large merchandise freight hauler and was not as dependent on coal as was the Norfolk & Western.

Hauling coal out of the hollers of West Virginia was hard work and required powerful locomotives. The C&O rostered some of the largest and most powerful steam locomotives ever built. From the 2–8–0 type, the standard freight locomotive at the turn of the century, the C&O quickly moved up to the 2–8–2 and 2–10–2 with dozens on the railroad by 1920. The C&O needed powerful locomotives that could navigate the rickety track on isolated lines to mines. A long wheelbase 2–10–2 simply would not do. The answer came in the form of the 2–6–6–2 articulated, which was first tried out in 1910. Even more powerful 2–8–8–2 types were added in the 1920s.[137] By the end of the decade speed was becoming more important. The ponderous articulateds could pull almost anything but not at competitive speeds. The answer for the C&O was the 2–10–4 type, with forty purchased from Lima in 1930. Passengers, never a major source of revenue on the C&O, were moving behind 4–6–2 and 4–8–2 types.

In the late 1930s and the beginning of the 1940s with increasing traffic and the challenges of rearmament and then war, the C&O again needed to upgrade its fleet. Longer passenger trains were taxing the existing 4–6–2 types, so the C&O followed the lead of other railroads like the New York Central and embraced the Hudson 4–6–4 type for high speed passenger service. In the mountains where more pulling power was needed the railroad adopted the 4–8–4. To help handle the expanding wartime traffic, the railroad looked to locomotive builder Lima for additional 4–8–4 types as well as capable 2–8–4 types and the immense 2–6–6–6. After the war the railroad continued to purchase steam locomotives. Many more 2–8–4, 4–8–4, 4–6–4, and 2–6–6–6 types joined the fleet from 1945 to 1948. To work the branches to the coal mines, the C&O ordered an updated version of the venerable 2–6–6–2 in 1949. These locomotives were not markedly different from the first 2–6–6–2 of 1910 and were the last steam locomotives built by Baldwin for service in the United States.[138]

Up to this point the C&O sounds somewhat like its neighbor the Norfolk & Western. However, the similarities are not as great as may be supposed. The C&O was dependent on outside builders for locomotives unlike the N&W, which built most of its modern steam in its own shops. The C&O also inherited twenty-five diesels when it purchased the Pere Marquette in Michigan. This number had increased to forty-five units by the end of 1948, mostly yard switchers and EMD passenger diesels.[139] This gave them experience with diesels as well as the shops and labor necessary to maintain them. Although the C&O did own a few, mostly inherited diesels in 1947 and 1948, They were more interested in steam turbines. Working closely with Baldwin, the C&O designed and purchased three coal-burning steam-turbine-electric locomotives for high speed streamlined passenger service. The first was delivered in the summer of 1947 with the other two following in early 1948.[140] The turbines were huge machines and, like the N&W's *Jawn Henry* to follow, destined to a short life. While they worked they proved to be expensive and time consuming to maintain and had an insatiable appetite for increasingly expensive coal. In the fall of 1948 the passenger train that they were supposed to haul was cancelled and the locomotives themselves were quietly scrapped a short time later. The fall of 1948 also saw a change in leadership for the C&O. Walter J. Touhy, an executive who had cut his teeth in the coal industry and not on the railroad, assumed the presidency.[141] With a president from their own industry, the coal shippers on the C&O had less to fear from dieselization. The first large order for diesels followed in May 1949.

The C&O shows that while coal may be a major factor in the decision to delay dieselization, it could be overcome. By having a chief executive from the coal industry the coal shippers on the C&O had one of their own at the top. Ths alleviated many concerns that the shippers would have about the railroad remaining loyal to their industry. The C&O also shows the lengths that railroads would go to to avoid dieselization. Even with diesels turning in exemplary service in Michigan, the railroad still chose to purchase additional steam locomotives and even to build the steam turbines in an effort to remain a coal fueled railroad.

Virginian

The Virginian railroad was the most coal dependent of all the roads mentioned thus far. It was essentially a 545 mile conveyor belt for coal from the mountains of West Virginia to tidewater at Norfolk. In 1949 for instance, almost 80 percent of the total revenue was from coal.[142] Like other coal dependent roads with cheap on-line supplies, the Virginian stayed with steam power well into the 1950s. The Virginian was a relatively young railroad, having been built in the first decade of the twentieth century. As such, it was built to the highest standards and expressly for large heavy motive power. The smallest steam locomotives on the railroad were 0–8–0 switchers and 2–8–0 types. The 2–8–0 types were all retired by 1933, replaced with ever larger locomotives.[143] The Virginian was a user of large articulated power from the outset with 2–6–6–0 and 2–8–8–2 types lugging coal over heavy mountain grades. In a quest for ever more tractive effort, the Virginian in the 1910s pushed the envelope of steam locomotive development. In 1916 they accepted a 2–8–8–8–4 triplex type. It was a dismal failure and reportedly never made one successful trip. In 1918 they got it right with the 2–10–10–2 type. This huge but slow locomotive was perfectly suited to lugging long trains of coal east out of the mountains to tidewater at Norfolk. From 1923 to 1945 the Virginian did not purchase any new steam locomotives but instead devoted money and attention to electrification of the most severe mountain grades.[144] While this may seem out of character for a coal dependent railroad, the electric generating plants necessary for the electrification were themselves burning low cost locally produced coal delivered by the Virginian. The efficiency gains by operating electric locomotives over the steepest grades were substantial.

After World War II the Virginian was in need of new motive power and something faster than the ponderously slow articulateds. Neighbor C&O was having good luck with its 2–8–4 and 2–6–6–6 types so the Virginian ordered five and eight, respectively. The last steam locomotives added to the roster were fifteen 0–8–0 switchers purchased second hand from the dieselizing C&O in 1950.[145] New electric locomotives arrived in early 1948 to supplement the now aging originals from the 1920s.[146] By the mid-1950s even neighbor N&W was beginning to purchase diesels and the C&O was well down the path to full dieselization. The little Virginian, home of large and unique steam and electric motive power decided to dieselize in a unique way as well. The road conducted an extensive survey of the existing diesel locomotives and decided to dieselize fully with only two types and from only one manufacturer, Fairbanks-Morse. The maintenance savings by employing locomotives from only one manufacturer were evident to the management. From 1954 to 1957 the road purchased forty sixteen hundred horsepower units and twenty-five larger twenty-four hundred horsepower units.[147] The last steam locomotive run was in the fall of 1956. The diesels were more flexible than the older steam power. They could be used on mine runs in the hills or on fast freight across the coastal plain of southern Virginia with equal aplomb. The diesels worked in concert with the electric locomotives to move freight, mostly coal. After an abortive effort in the 1920s, the N&W and the Virginian merged in late 1959. Electric operation only lasted a few years longer as the newly merged railroad combined the best track from both railroads to eliminate most heavy grades; grades that the electrics had been designed to conquer. Coal was still king on the Virginian, no matter what motive power was used. Even after dieselization, more than 85 percent of total traffic was coal.[148]

Illinois Central

The final southern district road does not fit many of the patterns presented thus far. The Illinois Central (IC) has roots that extend back to the early days of railroads in the Midwest. It was also one of just a handful of roads that operated in all three districts, Eastern, Western, and Southern.[149] The Illinois Central of midcentury was a 6,539 mile system that described itself as the, "Main line of Mid-America" and with good reason. It was a large railroad with a main line that extended from Chicago south to New Orleans. A huge network of secondary and branch lines covered Illinois and Mississippi. The IC also had secondary main lines that stretched eastward into Alabama, Kentucky, and Indiana as well as west into Louisiana, Iowa, and South Dakota. Unlike most railroads, the predominant traffic pattern on the IC was not east-west but was north-south. The Illinois Central also served many important coal mining areas in southern Illinois and western Kentucky. In 1950, the IC carried twenty-seven million tons of coal which accounted for 38 percent of total tonnage.[150] This was not as high as the Pocahontas roads like the N&W but still a major commodity.

Like many roads, the IC undertook a major upgrading of physical plant and motive power during the 1910s and 1920s. Its standard freight locomotive was the 2-8-2 type with over five hundred acquired between 1911 and 1924.[151] Passengers moved behind 4-6-2 types built during the same period. The IC was an early convert to the 2-8-4 type, purchasing the demonstrator from Lima in 1924. Fifty copies followed in 1926. The 1920s also brought 2-10-2 types for heavy drag service and 4-8-2 types for heavy passenger service. While there were no large articulateds or speedy Hudsons or 4-8-4 types on the railroad, such locomotives were simply not needed on the easy terrain of the plains of the Midwest and Mississippi valley. By the end of the 1920s the railroad was well equipped with modern power. The 1920s also saw the electrification of its suburban commuter operations on the south side of Chicago, primarily for antismoke reasons but also for added efficiency.

The Illinois Central was an early user of diesel power, operating both switchers and streamlined passenger diesels in the 1930s. The flashiest would have been the Green Diamond. It was a short articulated diesel powered train similar to the Zephyr of the CB&Q. However, where the Zephyr was a silver streak of stainless steel, the Green Diamond was green with chrome accents.[152] It entered service in early 1936 between Chicago and St. Louis.[153] It was quickly joined by several diesel switching locomotives including a massive two thousand horsepower transfer locomotive built by GE in 1936.[154] The switchers were for service in Chicago with its antismoke ordinances. Other smaller switchers followed in the late 1930s, most confined to the Chicago yards and terminals as well. While the switchers may have been performing a useful and vital service, they could not match the exposure of passenger trains. In the late 1930s and continuing through the 1940s the Illinois Central purchased streamlined passenger locomotives from EMC and EMD for its long distance passenger services. Famous trains like the City of Miami, Panama Limited, and City of New Orleans were all moving behind diesel power shortly after World War II.

The above would seem to indicate that the IC was quick to embrace the diesel. After all, the N&W and PRR did not purchase flashy diesel streamliners or small diesel switchers in the 1930s. However, the IC stands

Photo 20 The Illinois Central was known for rebuilding locomotives at its Paducah, Kentucky shops. One product of Paducah was this 4-8-2 type seen at Memphis in June of 1940. It is likely fresh from the shops and was a capable and efficient locomotive especially for fast freight on the flat lands of the Mississippi valley. Courtesy of the Museum of the Rockies, Ron V. Nixon Railroad Photography Collection.

apart from many of the patterns developed previously. While the railroad was purchasing diesel switchers and passenger locomotives it was simultaneously rebuilding older steam locomotives into newer types in its own shops for freight service. Beginning in 1934 and lasting for almost ten years, 434 steam locomotives were extensively rebuilt. Some were simply modernized and upgraded while retaining their existing wheel arrangements, while others were practically new locomotives with different wheel arrangements, new boilers, frames and other parts.[155] With the rebuilt locomotives proving fast and powerful the IC was in good shape for increasing wartime traffic and the economic revival of the postwar period. Diesels may have found a permanent place in the yard and at the head of passenger trains but steam ruled the freights. As late as 1950 all freight moved behind 617 steam freight locomotives. That same year there were 107 diesel switchers and only 26 diesel passenger units.[156] The IC seemed to have struck a happy balance between diesels and steam. This policy made economic sense to the conservative management of the Illinois Central headed after 1945 by president Wayne Johnston. Johnston, who had worked his way up through the administrative ranks of the IC, was known for his fiscal conservatism. In the tight 1930s the use of existing shop assets and labor to modernize steam locomotives instead of heavily investing in new and somewhat still experimental diesels was sound. In the war years with diesels regulated by the War Production Board the use of steam also made sense.

For many years after the war freight still moved mostly behind steam, even while most passengers were traveling behind diesels. The IC continued to dieselize its passenger service. By May 1952 all through passenger services were dieselized, almost exclusively with orange and chocolate brown E-units from EMD.[157] This dual motive power strategy began to change in 1952. Tests performed that year established that EMD GP-7 type locomotives could operate over the road and produce, "savings somewhat more than had been anticipated."[158] The added operational flexibility of the road switcher design combined with the other cost advantages of the diesel made them too attractive to pass up. Dieselization of road-freight traffic began in earnest in 1953 with thirty-five GP-7 units. The units were assigned to the portions of the railroad farthest from the coal fields of southern Illinois and western Kentucky where coal fuel transport costs were highest. The conservative IC would not opt for fancy colors for the utilitarian freight units. They were painted a simple black with white numbers and a small Illinois Central green diamond herald. More units arrived the following years but as late as 1955, 51.7 percent of freight train miles were behind steam as opposed to 4.1 percent of passenger train miles and 18.6 percent of switching hours.[159] Complete dieselization was achieved in May 1959. However, steam would have one last gasp on the IC. From October 1959, to April 1960, steam power was again used in the western Kentucky coal fields to handle a boost in traffic.[160] This late use of steam power marks the IC as one of the last railroads to use steam in everyday service. Curiously, they were among the first railroads to employ the diesel in yard and passenger service.

With the efficiencies of the diesel proven in yard and passenger service, why did the railroad not pursue dieselization with all due speed? A conservative management headed by president Johnston that wished to make best use of existing assets is one reason. Diesels were expensive. They may have been useful in switching where their high availability made steam uneconomic and passenger service where the demands of competition and public relations made diesels attractive. Steam locomotives, overhauled and rebuilt in the expansive Paducah shops could do the job hauling freight for much less first cost than diesels, even if they were more expensive to operate and maintain. Continued use of steam would also not require extensive new facilities for the maintenance and servicing of the locomotives like the use of diesels would. The railroad had a well deserved reputation for fiscal conservatism. This reluctance to spend money on new diesels when there were perfectly good steam locomotives around helps to explain the persistence of steam power on the IC. All three of the former Harriman roads, the IC, SP, and UP were noted for conservative management and were among the last railroads to dieselize. Another part of the answer is the relatively modern steam power of the railroad. The Paducah, Kentucky, shops were one of the most advanced locomotive shops on any railroad and were more than capable of keeping the steam power modern and up to date. The extensive rebuilding program in the late 1930s and 40s resulted in modern efficient power well suited for the conditions of the railroad.[161] The geography of the region also played a small part in the decision of the IC to stick with steam. The flat lands of the Mississippi valley simply did not require locomotives with extensive low speed lugging ability, like diesels. The history of the Illinois Central in the fifty years after it dieselized is also unique. It remained intact until 1972 when it merged the Gulf Mobile and Ohio to create the Illinois Central Gulf. The ICG spun off many lines in the 1980s, including most former GM&O lines and returned to using the Illinois Central name. After an abortive merger with the Kansas City Southern it was finally purchased by, of all roads, the Canadian National and made a part of the CN system. This led to such incongruous sights as red and black Canadian National diesels in Mississippi and New Orleans, a long way from Canada.

There are many similarities that can be identified among the railroads that chose to delay dieselization. Often they were large railroads with many hundreds or thousands of locomotives. It would take time to change such a large fleet from steam to diesel. Many of the later dieselizers were also major coal shippers and did not want to alienate such a large shipper by refusing to use their product. A further characteristic of the railroads that chose to defer full adoption of the diesel is that all of them had invested in modern, powerful steam in the 1930s, 1940s, or even in the case of the Norfolk & Western, the early 1950s. With relatively new and efficient steam power some of the cost impetus for dieselization was lacking. The personalities of the top management of the railroads also was a factor in many cases. Presidents and other officials who cut their teeth on steam were reluctant to replace it for emotional and nostalgic reasons.

SHORTLINES AND TERMINAL ROADS

While the railroads analyzed above have run the gamut from behemoths like the Pennsylvania to smaller regional roads like the Lehigh Valley or Virginian, they all had several characteristics in common. All had a mixture of freight and passenger operation, and all had a balance of main line through freight, local, and terminal service. All the railroads were designated as Class I carriers by the ICC.[162] The vast majority of railroads fell into the above categories. However, not all railroads can be so easily compartmentalized. Short lines and terminal railroads made up a small but sizable chunk of the railroad business. Because of their unique characteristics, they dieselized in a much different fashion than the railroads above.

Terminal roads were just that, railroads that operated almost exclusively in one city or terminal area. Often only a few miles in length, they nonetheless could have a large volume of traffic shuttling back and forth from local industries and customers to line-haul railroads. Some terminal railroads were used to interchange traffic between various line-haul railroads operating in a particular area. Railroads that served only one large industry, like steel mills or oil refineries, would also be classified as terminal roads. Terminal roads varied from small, one locomotive lines to large, heavy traffic roads like the Belt Railway of Chicago and the Terminal Railroad Association of St. Louis.

Terminal roads faced vastly different needs than the typical line-haul railroad. Speed, the impetus behind much advancement in steam locomotive technology in the 1920s and 1930s, was simply not an issue with terminal roads. Much more important was pulling power or tractive effort. Other considerations also influenced the motive power choices of terminal roads. Operating in confined city environments and on industrial trackage with tight clearances meant size and weight was a concern. A huge 2–8–8–2 might have had more than enough tractive effort for a large terminal road, but it simply would not fit in the confined urban industrial environment. Because most terminal roads operated in urban areas smoke was also a concern. Terminal roads rarely operated any form of passenger service so public relations oriented design like styling and streamlining were not concerns. However, in some instances terminal roads did perform switching of passenger cars at major urban stations. This required some locomotives to have the necessary equipment to provide steam to the cars for heat. Many terminal roads were owned by the larger class I roads that entered a particular city. As such they could be influenced by the motive power policies of the owning railroads. With combined ownership, as in the case of the RF&P, terminal roads generally had a conservative motive power strategy and did not experiment with new sources of motive power until they had proven themselves.

The first terminal road analyzed was also one of the largest, the Terminal Railroad Association of St. Louis or the TRRA. St. Louis was second only to Chicago in importance as a railroad gateway city. Eastern roads like the B&O, Pennsylvania, and New York Central interchanged traffic there with western roads like the CB&Q, Missouri Pacific, Frisco, Missouri-Kansas-Texas, and others. Other important carriers like the Illinois Central, Gulf Mobile & Ohio, Wabash, Southern, and Louisville & Nashville also interchanged in the metropolitan area. With this huge number of carriers in such a small area, interchange between them could be chaotic. To facilitate smooth flow of traffic, several of the railroads together formed the TRRA to serve as the interchange carrier for all of them.

As may be expected the TRRA had extensive yard facilities on both sides of the Mississippi river as well as connections with every railroad that entered the St. Louis area. These yards required many switchers to perform the seemingly endless shuffling of cars. The TRRA was also responsible for switching passenger trains at St. Louis Union Station. Steam power on the TRRA was confined to two types, the 0–6–0 and 0–8–0. Between 1912 and 1925 the TRRA purchased seventy-six new steam locomotives for its expanding operations.[163] After 1925 the railroad assembled several 0–8–0 types in its own shops with the last one emerging in 1930. The 0–8–0 locomotives were exactly what the TRRA needed, and were able to negotiate tight curves, provide traction on the many short but sharp grades and assist in moving the increasingly longer and heavier trains.[164] During the Depression with the decrease in traffic the TRRA was able to get by with its existing motive power. While some roads purchased new locomotives during the 1930s for higher speed service, this was not a concern on the TRRA or any terminal road. Neither was streamlined passenger service as the TRRA did not have any passenger service.

Dieselization began on the TRRA in 1940. In June and July of that year, ten diesel switchers from three different manufacturers arrived on the property.[165] Eight of the ten were relatively small, six hundred horsepower machines,

Photo 21   The needs of a terminal railroad like the TRRA of St. Louis were different than a line haul railroad. A small switching locomotive like this Baldwin was ideal for the low speed work of a terminal road. Courtesy of the Railroad Museum Of Pennsylvania (PHMC) H. L. Broadbelt Collection.

probably destined for passenger switching service at St. Louis Union Station where smoke was a concern. As traffic continued to improve and as war became a distinct possibility, 1941 saw thirteen more diesel switchers, most of them one thousand horsepower models well suited for freight switching. The incredible volume of traffic moving through the St. Louis gateway during the war caused a need for even more motive power. The TRRA added substantially to its diesel fleet during the war, with thirty-five units joining the railroad. After the war dieselization continued, but somewhat slowly. No new diesels joined the railroad in 1946 and 1948 with fourteen added during 1947.[166] By the close of 1952 the railroad owned 109 locomotives, and steam was all but gone. It would be several years however before steam power was completely replaced by diesel. The last steam locomotive run was in the summer of 1955.[167] With the wartime traffic crunch of World War II and Korea fresh in their minds, the managers kept some steam locomotives around, just in case. Of interest is the fact that the TRRA purchased diesels from all five major manufacturers, EMD, Alco, Baldwin, Fairbanks-Morse, and Lima. This seems to illustrate that the railroad was still thinking of locomotives in a steam setting as individual units and did not seem to realize the maintenance benefits that could come with owning locomotives of only one manufacturer. However, it must be stated that the way that these locomotives were used may have helped to contribute to the variety of manufacturers. In switching a locomotive is not subjected to prolonged high speed service and the stresses that accompany it. While Alco, Baldwin, and Fairbanks-Morse freight and passenger units had maintenance troubles on line-haul railroads, the switchers did not experience the same degree of difficulty on the TRRA. This is evidenced by the service life of these units. Most lasted twenty years or more in service, the average design life of unrebuilt diesel locomotives. The TRRA, while large, was typical of terminal roads. With the economies of diesel switcher operation well known by the late 1930s and with their advantages in operation in urban environments, the TRRA began to replace its steam before the war and added more diesels when finances and traffic allowed. Diesel switchers were not purchased earlier due to the ample supply of capable steam locomotives and the lack of available capital during the Depression, even though it was widely known by the

mid 1930s that diesel switchers could provide adequate
service while saving money.

Also in the St. Louis area was the Alton & Southern
railroad. It was owned by two of its principal interchange
partners, the Chicago & North Western, and the Missouri
Pacific. While not as large as the TRRA, the A&S was an
important terminal road and provided yard facilities for
many of the railroads entering the area from the east. It
had no passenger service. The A&S got through the war
years with hand me down steam locomotives from its
owners. Once the economy stabilized after the war and
with costs increasing, the dieselization of the A&S began
in 1947 with the purchase of several Alco RS-2 type locomotives.[168] Unlike the TRRA the A&S would remain with
Alco for all their diesel purchases until the late 1960s.
This shows that they realized the benefits in maintenance
and servicing that a one manufacturer fleet would generate. By the summer of 1949, twenty-four of the Alco road-
switchers were handling most, if not all, assignments. The
A&S seems to have realized the inherent efficiencies in
having a locomotive roster from only one builder. As such
it was more typical of other terminal roads and shortlines.
Its later dieselization, only after it was clear that the diesel would completely supplant the steam locomotive, also
is more typical of most terminal roads and shortlines that
seemed to adopt a wait and see attitude. Both the TRRA
and the A&S still exist as terminal carriers in the St.
Louis area. While ownership has changed due to the multiple railroad mergers and consolidations in the post war
era, the two roads still go about the task that they were
initially created for, shuffling endless strings of cars for
the major line haul railroads.

SHORTLINES

Terminal roads were confined to large cities or industrial
areas, usually in the northeast or Midwest. Shortlines,
however, covered the continent. Few generalizations can
be made about this diverse lot but a few conclusions can
be drawn. Shortlines were nicely described by their name.
They were short, ranging from a hundred or so miles to only
a couple. Shortlines were different from terminal roads in
that they generally connected two or more towns or cities rather than operating wholly in one. Shortlines almost

always were short, not only in mileage, but in revenue. Even the largest and most successful could only manage a couple million dollars a year in total operating revenue, less than one percent the revenue of many larger roads. The lack of revenue manifested itself in many ways at the various shortlines. Shortlines were forced to be creative in making the best use of their limited capital. Shops and maintenance facilities were small and often not fully equipped. Often they operated with second hand steam locomotives purchased from neighboring larger railroads rather than purchasing new locomotives outright. While these older and less efficient locomotives may have been obsolete in service on the large railroads, they were often just what the shortlines required. Shortlines, because of the lack of capital, also generally had light track and bridge work. This track would have buckled under the weight of a large 4–8–4 type but was perfectly suited for a lightweight 2–6–0 built around the turn of the century.[169] This lightweight construction would play a role in the dieselization of these railroads. In some cases special lightweight diesels were specially created for this market. Shortlines were generally freight carriers exclusively. What passenger service was provided on some was purely local. High speeds were unheard of on shortlines, even the passenger trains would operate at thirty miles per hour. This low speed service also affected dieselization. High speed streamlined diesels, freight or passenger, were simply not needed. What was needed were lightweight, versatile units that could be called upon to perform most any sort of duty.

While shortlines operated in all areas of the country, the south had an abundance of them. The Mississippi Central had its origins in logging railroads built to exploit the southern pine forests after the civil war. Several of these railroads were cobbled together and upgraded to higher standards to form the Mississippi Central. It served the timber industry in south central Mississippi but also interchanged with several larger railroads including the Southern, Illinois Central, and Gulf Mobile & Ohio. The road ran almost due west from Hattiesburg, Mississippi to Natchez on the Mississippi River. Here a connection was made to the Louisiana Midland Railroad via a car ferry. The Mississippi Central was one of the largest and most successful of shortlines, serving not only local traffic but also competing for overhead or bridge traffic between the southeast and southwest.[170]

The Mississippi Central was interested in internal combustion power early. Mr. R. K. Smith, vice president and general manager wrote to the neighboring Southern railway in February 1912 inquiring about the possibility of inspecting a gas-electric motor car recently put into operation.[171] Several other letters to other railroads were written inquiring about experiences in gas-electric operation. By the early 1920s there was at least one such motorcar and trailer in operation on the Mississippi Central providing passenger service to the many small towns along the route.

Beginning in 1921 the railroad began to purchase new steam power to replace the small and inefficient power it was then using. While other railroads were exploring new wheel arrangements, the small Mississippi Central opted for the capable but not overly large 2–8–2 Mikado type, purchasing five in 1921. An equal amount followed in later years so that by 1929 there were ten relatively modern freight steam locomotives on the property.[172] These locomotives, together with three older 4–6–2 types carried the railroad through the Depression and war years ably. Passenger service was abandoned by 1941 although some troop trains were handled to Camp Shelby, just south of Hattiesburg during the war.

While neighboring roads such as the Gulf Mobile & Ohio and Southern explored diesel power in the late 1940s, the Mississippi Central stuck with its tried and true steam power. Beginning in the early 1950s the railroad began to explore complete dieselization. Since they had only a handful of locomotives, they could dieselize completely with one purchase. They did not have to ease into diesel operation like larger roads. The Mississippi Central solicited bids from Baldwin-Lima-Hamilton, EMD, and Alco. All were extremely detailed and included not only the costs and characteristics of the diesel locomotives but also details on train operations and even maintenance procedures and facilities. For instance, the Alco study began with an airbrushed photo of a diesel locomotive in a proposed Mississippi Central paint scheme, and included maps, financial statistics, several pages on how diesels would transform operations including time and distance charts and graphs, and several appendices. The Alco study concluded that the railroad "could realize a 42.7 percent reduction in operating expenses and show a return on gross investment of 14.1 percent."[173] The other builders all suggested similar savings. Baldwin claimed savings of $204,413 per year with a return on investment of 13.83 percent for its primary plan of dieselization.[174] EMD was the most ambitious, projecting a savings of $256,214 per year with a return on investment of 24.4 percent.[175] The Mississippi Central opted for the largest anticipated savings and ordered ten SW-9 type diesels from EMD. The first unit was placed in service May 9, 1953 and the last revenue steam run was just a couple weeks later on May 26.[176] In addition to the superior estimated savings of the EMD products, the Mississippi Central was able to take advantage of the financing of the General Motors Acceptance Corporation, or GMAC. With a 10 percent down payment of $10,625 per unit the railroad would pay a monthly installment of $795 per locomotive for 120 months.[177] With the power of credit from GMAC, the EMD bid was that much more attractive to the railroad. To put things into perspective, total net income for the railroad in 1950 was just slightly over $200,000 on total operating revenues of $2,430,663.[178] By the 1960s the railroad was facing increasingly hard times and was looking for salvation. It was purchased by the Illinois Central in 1967.

Because of their unique characteristics, shortlines and terminal roads had different requirements for motive power. Terminal roads especially needed locomotives that were adept at switching rather than at moving trains over the line at speed. High tractive effort was of much greater importance than high speed. Availability was also important to the terminal roads. For terminal roads that switched passenger terminals, like the TRRA, smoke was a concern. Finally, size and weight were considerations. Many terminal roads had to switch industrial plants and other locations where space was tight. Tight curves and short but steep grades were also common. Large locomotives of any type would simply not fit. Shortlines had similar requirements for their motive power. Many shortlines were built cheaply with light rail and bridges. A large heavy locomotive designed for optimum use on a high speed main line would literally tear the track apart on most shortlines. A final determinant in shortline and terminal road dieselization was financial. Because of their size many roads did not have the necessary capital to purchase new diesel locomotives but instead soldiered on with outdated steam power until more money came along or, more likely, the line was abandoned. For those that could afford to purchase new locomotives the size of the railroad often enabled dieselization in one fell swoop rather than over a period of time as was the case with larger railroads. Available financing, as in the case with the Mississippi Central could be a key factor in the dieselization of small shortlines and terminal roads.

The experiences of the above railroads show that dieselization was a complicated process that was influenced by much more than simple economics. While costs of operation were the primary factor, they were only one of many elements in dieselization. The influence of the coal industry, or more technically the loyalty of the railroads to the coal industry was a major factor in the dieselization of many roads, especially the Appalachian coal roads like the C&O and N&W. Management change was a factor as well with many roads including the UP and N&W. Municipal legislation often brought diesels to urban centers and some roads chose diesel streamliners for the public relations benefits that they could bring but many of these same roads eschewed diesels for freight service. A characteristic of most of the roads that chose to delay full dieselization was the employment of modern steam motive power, be it home built articulateds like on the N&W, high speed Hudsons on the NYC or flawed duplexes on the PRR. With modern efficient steam performing as it was designed, roads were reluctant to dieselize, both because the savings would be less than it would have been with older and less efficient steam power and because many roads were loath to abandon practically new locomotives.

5

The Routes Not Taken:
Alternatives to Dieselization

THE DIESEL-ELECTRIC LOCOMOTIVE WAS NOT THE ONLY ALTERNATIVE available to railroads looking to modernize their motive power and control costs. Gas turbine, steam turbine, straight electric, free-piston gasifier, and even nuclear locomotives were proposed and studied.[1] All promised more efficient operation and potential cost savings over traditional steam motive power and some even promised savings over diesels. The first three were seen to be real alternatives to diesels. For railroads that were major coal haulers and for those concerned about the relative scarcity of oil fuel compared with coal, coal burning turbines were especially attractive. The turbines held the possibility of using coal as a fuel while electrification could use coal as a fuel at central power stations. There were also experiments with other types of diesel locomotives such as diesel hydraulics that did not have the complicated and expensive electrical gear that the diesel electrics had. With all of these proposals, whether coal burning steam turbine or diesel hydraulic, the age old themes of design versus operation and thermodynamic efficiency versus maintenance come to play. While many of the proposals were indeed much better performers than steam and could even out perform traditional diesel electrics, they generally lacked the standardization and maintenance benefits of the standard diesel.

Of all the alternatives to steam and diesel motive power, electrification was the oldest and the most widely used, having been employed to move passengers and freight since the 1880s. Many of these early electric railroads were streetcar lines, interurbans, and trolleys, and were not viewed as the same ilk as the steam railroads. The ICC even classified them differently, and they had different rules and regulations to follow, from fares and rates to safety.[2] The technology of these electric railroads varied but all fall into a pattern. First, power plants, either railroad owned and operated or run by local utilities, generated electricity. Electricity, either AC, or more commonly, DC was then delivered to the locomotive or self propelled cars. There were generally two ways to deliver this electric current, via overhead wires or a third, electrified, rail. Locomotives or self-propelled cars then transformed this electricity into motion via traction motors located on the axles or in the car bodies. Most streetcar and interurban lines used relatively low voltage DC and overhead wiring systems. For heavier applications like subways, DC systems used the third rail system to carry the large current load while AC systems used higher voltage and sometimes elaborate overhead wires. Most urban subway systems standardized more or less on six hundred volts DC and a third rail system although the actual specifications could vary slightly from system to system. There was no standardization for other electrification projects.

The electrified streetcar and interurban systems were quite varied, from small systems of only a few cars and miles of track in small cities, to large regional systems that served not only large cities but outlying areas as well. Streetcar and trolley systems generally describe systems that operated mostly or wholly within a city or urban area. Interurban systems, as the name suggests, operated between cities. Interurbans often had a large commuter component but traveled longer distances and at higher speeds than streetcars. Interurbans likely had their own private right of way, unlike the aptly described streetcars which operated in public roads and streets. One of the most successful passenger oriented interurban systems was the Pacific Electric operation in the Los Angeles region. Founded in the early years of the century, this system operated 575 miles of track by 1929. It stretched from the San Fernando valley north of Los Angeles south to Long Beach and Orange County and from the shoreline in Santa Monica west to San Bernardino. It was a huge influence on the settlement and development patterns of the LA basin during the first half of the century.[3] The Pacific Electric, like most streetcar and interurban lines, served a niche that the steam railroads did not. Steam roads were optimized for longer distance travel and movement of freight. The early electric systems were designed for local passenger travel with freight only as a secondary consideration. Since they were primarily serving local passenger traffic, the streetcars and especially the interurbans were especially susceptible to automobile and motor bus competition. The interurban had a short life with most abandoned by the Great Depression. A few, the Pacific Electric included, soldiered on into the 1950s. Streetcar systems too were abandoned in increasing frequency during the Depression. A short respite came during WWII but by the mid 1960s only a few large cities such as Philadelphia and Pittsburgh had streetcar lines.

Some of the larger interurban systems competed directly with the steam railroads for not only passengers but freight as well. Among the most successful of these large regional systems was the Illinois Traction System, later the Illinois Terminal Railroad (IT). The IT was, by the Depression, a successful railroad operating from St. Louis, Missouri to the Illinois cities of Decatur, Peoria, Springfield, Danville, Bloomington, and Champaign. Many smaller communities were also served. The IT not only had a strong passenger service but a strong freight service as well. This allowed the IT to survive well beyond the time that most interurbans were abandoned as their traffic began to drive the ubiquitous model T.[4] The Illinois Terminal survived as an independent railroad much longer than most of the former interurbans, although it abandoned passenger service in the early 1960s, dieselized and concentrated purely on freight service. It was finally merged into the Norfolk and Western system in the early 1980s.

These eclectic streetcar and interurban lines did offer advantages in operation over traditional steam power. Electric power was clean with no smoke, a real concern in cities. It also offered faster acceleration and a higher density of service, also advantages on streetcar and commuter lines. Costs could be lower than with steam power, even with the huge initial expense of building the electrical generation and distribution system. These advantages were widely recognized by the large steam railways and many embarked on electrification projects of their own, especially for commuter service.

The first large scale electrification of a main line by a steam railroad was on the Baltimore and Ohio in its hometown, Baltimore, Maryland. The reason for electrification was a long tunnel with a hefty grade underneath the middle of Baltimore. Smoke belching steam locomotives and long tunnels did not mix well. The smoke and fumes could asphyxiate the crew, to say nothing of passengers. Begun in 1895, this pioneering effort was the first true main line freight and passenger electrification effort in the United States. It used small electric locomotives that operated on six hundred volts DC gathered from a third rail, similar to emerging heavy city transit systems. Electric locomotives would couple on to the front of trains and the steam locomotive would not uncouple but would simply not pull the train but be towed through the tunnel.[5] This pioneering electrification attempt was successful and operated until the electric locomotives were replaced by diesels in 1952. While it worked, it was not cheaper to operate than conventional steam in its early years. Therefore, the B&O did not electrify any other portions of its system. In a pattern that would be repeated on several railroads, electrification was confined to areas where its unique operational capabilities were necessary, such as long tunnels. Other long tunnels were converted to electric operation to reduce smoke. The Great Northern electrified its Cascade tunnel in Washington State in 1909, the Boston & Maine electrified its Hoosac Tunnel in western Massachusetts in 1911 and the New York Central and Canadian National electrified tunnels under the Detroit and St. Clair Rivers in 1910 and 1908 respectively. While electrification promised substantial gains in efficiency, it was the operational constraints of tunnel operation that led to the first adoption of electric power on main line steam railroads.

The first large scale electrification projects on the main line steam roads for true efficiency reasons were the massive New York City terminal projects. The New York Central was facing large increases in passenger traffic in and out of New York at the turn of the century. This combined with dirty steam locomotives and a two mile long smoke filled tunnel led the New York Central to adopt electric power for service into its new Grand Central Terminal. Although it was already considering electric power and a new passenger terminal, the city forced the hand of the railroad by outlawing steam locomotive operation on Manhattan Island after a deadly accident in the smoke filled tunnels leading to the station. Beginning in 1906, the NYC embarked on the largest electrification project to date. It not only built the huge new terminal station but electrified track out as far as Croton and White Plains, thirty-four and twenty-four miles from Grand Central Terminal. By 1913 the electrification was essentially complete. The New York Central chose low voltage DC power (six hundred volts) and a third rail system for its electrification similar to subways and elevated mass transit lines then being constructed in major cities.[6]

The New York, New Haven & Hartford railroad, known as the New Haven, used the tracks of the New York Central to access New York City. When the New York Central electrified, the New Haven had to as well. The New Haven chose to also electrify out to the end of commuter train territory at Stamford, Connecticut, some thirty miles from Grand Central Terminal. Later this electrification would be extended to New Canaan, Danbury and New Haven itself for over one hundred miles of electrified line. The New Haven chose not to employ the third rail low voltage DC system of the NYC but chose a higher voltage AC system with overhead wires. The initial electrification project was complete by 1908. The Pennsylvania railroad and its subsidiary the Long Island railroad was next with its monumental undertaking to build Pennsylvania Station and tunnel under the Hudson and East rivers for direct Manhattan access from both the east and west. Construction began in 1904 and proceeded in phases for several years until completion in 1910. This initial Pennsylvania electrification was also low voltage DC. By 1914 New York City's railroad connections had been transformed from smoky steam locomotives and ferry boat links to state of the art modern electric power with two spectacular new center-city passenger terminals to show for it. Electrification made huge increases in passenger traffic possible and led to the continued growth of New York City and its suburbs.

Perhaps taking a cue from the successful interurban and streetcar lines and the successful New York City electrification efforts, other steam railroads electrified portions of their commuter lines. For example, the Delaware, Lackawanna & Western railroad electrified many of their commuter lines in suburban New Jersey. Likewise the Reading and Pennsylvania electrified their commuter lines radiating from Philadelphia and even the Illinois Central electrified its commuter territory running south from Chicago. All of these systems were quite similar in operations. For instance, they all utilized not electric locomotives pulling conventional coaches, but individually powered cars, similar to the interurban cars but beefed up to steam road standards. These so called M.U. (Multiple Unit) cars were quite successful and operated well into the 1970s.[7] While the operations were similar, the technology was not. The Illinois Central and Lackawanna

Photo 22 This electric locomotive of the New York Central's Cleveland Union Terminal subsidiary is a good representation of electric locomotives of the 1920s and 1930s. Electric locomotives were quiet, powerful and efficient. The largest drawback was the necessity for miles of complex and expensive overhead wiring. Courtesy of the Museum of the Rockies, Ron V. Nixon Railroad Photography Collection.

electrifications used 1,500 and 3,000 volts DC and overhead wires respectively while the Reading and Pennsylvania systems used high voltage (11,000) AC. While the elimination of smoke in urban areas was a major concern of these electrification projects, gains in efficiency and flexibility and reduced costs were the primary reason for most of these electrification efforts. All of these electrified commuter lines are still in operation although with updated equipment.

There were other attempts at main line electrification but most occurred in mountainous territory where steam locomotives consumed huge amounts of coal and water and where the low speed torque of electric motors conveyed a distinct operating advantage. These electrification efforts were, like the pioneering Baltimore and Ohio installation, often accompanied by long tunnels which were difficult to operate through with steam locomotives. During the 1910s and 1920s, the Norfolk & Western and Virginian railroads both electrified portions of their main lines in West Virginia and southwest Virginia to help them conquer the Blue Ridge mountains and to ease the flow of loaded coal trains from the mines of West Virginia to tidewater at Norfolk.[8] The N&W was first with fifty-five miles of electrified track by 1924. The system was high voltage AC and was designed only for the eastbound movement of loaded coal trains. Westbound empty trains and passenger and non coal freight would continue to move behind steam power. The Virginian had more mileage, 134, under wire by the mid 1920s. It too was a high voltage AC operation. While it may seem unusual for such coal dependent railroads to adopt electric motive power, the roads had to build and maintain their own, coal burning power plants to provide the necessary electricity. Therefore they still burned what they hauled although in a stationary location rather than in the fireboxes of steam locomotives. The electrification projects of both roads enabled them to move coal more efficiently and to control costs.

The Chicago, Milwaukee, St. Paul & Pacific or Milwaukee Road and Great Northern railroads also jumped on the electrification bandwagon by electrifying portions of their main lines through the Rocky and Cascade Mountains in the northwest. The Great Northern electrified its new 7.8 mile long Cascade tunnel and significant lines on either side in 1929 while the Milwaukee Road electrified hundreds of miles of line from Montana to Puget Sound.[9]

The Great Northern system was high voltage AC while
the Milwaukee system was three thousand volts DC. The
Milwaukee road electrification stands out as the longest
mainline electrification project in the United States with
663 miles of line, although not the one with the most traffic.
The Milwaukee electrification project saved the railroad
substantial amounts of money over using contemporary
steam power. In 1920 alone for instance, the net savings
from electrification was $1.9 million.[10] By 1938 the US had
over 2,400 miles of line and 6,300 miles of track electrified, over 20 perdent of the world total.[11]

While electrification was certainly a viable challenger
to steam power, especially in locations where the smoke
from steam locomotives was a problem or in mountainous
territory where steam locomotives used large amounts
of fuel and water, it was not immune to the challenge of
the diesel. Most of the electrified track of 1938 has been
de-electrified and in many cases, abandoned altogether.
The Norfolk & Western electrification was the first to go,
being discontinued in 1950 with a new tunnel and less
steep grade operated with steam locomotives. This is the
only instance of steam power replacing electric power.
After WWII the electric locomotives were old and worn
and needed replacement. Much of the rest of the electric
infrastructure was also in need of modernization and
replacement. Instead of investing in costly new electric
locomotives and other equipment, the railroad built a
new tunnel at a lower elevation and relocated much of
the line on the heaviest grades to eliminate the need for
electric locomotives. When the project was complete in
1950, the railroad abandoned electric operation in favor
of its advanced and capable steam fleet. Its neighbor the
Virginian did purchase new electric locomotives after
the war and operated under the wires until 1962 when
because of merger and dieselization, the electrification
was abandoned.[12] The merger of the N&W and the Virginian enabled the resulting railroad to utilize the best lines
of both to eliminate the heaviest grades that the electrics
were designed for. The Great Northern electrification was
discontinued in 1956 when diesels replaced steam power
on that portion of the railroad. Diesels, although they did
emit exhaust, were able to operate though the long Cascade tunnel. The Milwaukee road electrification lasted
until 1974 when it was finally replaced with diesels.[13] By
this time the Milwaukee Road was in dire financial straits

and simply could not afford the maintenance on the 1920's vintage power system and locomotives. Upgrading to current standards was out of the question. The fact that most of the freight oriented electrifications were abandoned illustrates a great weakness of electrification. Unless an entire system is electrified, a short electrified segment requires stopping and starting trains, adding and removing locomotives and reduces, rather than enhances flexibility in operations. While this was not a large concern during steam days as steam locomotives had to often stop for fuel, water and servicing and were regularly switched in and out, it was a large negative when diesels entered the picture. Diesels could run over an entire system with little need for on line service other than fuel. The efficiency gains from electric operation were negated by the efficiency losses of adding and removing locomotives and the other rigidities involved in electric operations..

Of all the examples of large scale main line electrification one clearly stands out as the largest and most successful, the Pennsylvania Railroad's northeast corridor from New York to Washington, D.C. with a connecting line from Philadelphia to Harrisburg, Pennsylvania. Its lines between Washington and New York were some of the heaviest traveled railroad lines on the continent. After much study and experimentation the PRR, in several stages, electrified most of its high density passenger and freight lines in the region with high voltage AC. Electrification enabled more and better service to keep up with the increasing passenger and freight traffic of the growing industrial eastern seaboard. Electric locomotives could accelerate faster, reach higher speeds, and reduce travel time. They were also more powerful and generally required less maintenance. For example, the GG-1 type of electric locomotive which entered service in the 1930s lasted in high speed daily service until the early 1980s, a life span of almost fifty years.

Begun in 1915 and finished in 1938, just in time for World War II, the Pennsylvania electrification stands apart in scale and scope. Hundreds of miles of main and yard track were electrified and hundreds of electric locomotives purchased or built to move passenger and freight trains in the electrified territory. Only a railroad with the financial resources of the mighty Pennsylvania could afford such a monumental undertaking. Much of the work was completed during the Great Depression which actually worked in the Pennsylvania's favor as material and labor costs were lower and rail traffic that would be impacted by construction was less. The results were impressive. In 1938, after the Harrisburg extension was fully operational, the PRR calculated that electrification saved over 7.7 million dollars in operating, maintenance and repair costs to motive power. Electric locomotives cost from one half to one third as much to operate per mile as did modern steam locomotives.[14]

Electrification had and has advantages and disadvantages. The advantages were numerous and can be compared to some of the advantages of diesel-electrics. When compared to steam locomotives the most obvious advantage was the lack of smoke. This concern over smoke, whether in long tunnels or crowded urban areas was a major reason for electrification of city passenger terminals, commuter lines and long tunnels. Electric locomotives had all the advantages of the electric transmission on diesels like high starting tractive effort and the capability for dynamic braking. However, electrics had further advantages. Instead of dissipating excess energy as heat as diesels do when using dynamic braking, electrics could actually pump this electricity back into the wires where it could be used by other trains. This is called regenerative braking. Electric locomotives, since they had fewer moving parts, were also more rugged and tend to last longer in service. Electric locomotives of the Pennsylvania and New York Central railroads served for more than fifty years and required fewer repairs than steam or diesel locomotives. Since they required less time out of service for repairs, electric locomotives had a higher availability record than either steam or diesel locomotives. Electric locomotives could also accelerate faster than steam or diesel locomotives because they were not limited to the power that they could generate on board but by the power they could pull from the overhead wire. Electrics could potentially achieve higher speeds than steam or diesel locomotives and could haul heavier trains. When produced in quantity, electric locomotives were often cheaper than diesels because of the lack of the complex diesel engine prime mover.

There were, and still are, substantial barriers to electrification. The largest disadvantage was the huge initial cost. Electrification could not be eased into slowly like dieselization with a few locomotives. Electrification, if it was to provide the most benefits, had to encompass a large area and all trains operated over the electrified trackage. Stringing miles and miles of wire as well as acquiring the specialized locomotives was quite a challenge in itself, but many roads had to go one further and set up their own electrical generating plants and distribution networks, especially in areas of the west and south that were not fully electrified. The Pennsylvania could purchase commercial power but the Norfolk & Western and Milwaukee Road had to build their own powerplants. Another major disadvantage of electrification for large railroads was the operational headache of changing from steam or diesel power to electric power. For example, if a tunnel or mountain grade was electrified all trains would have to stop, the steam locomotive would have to uncouple itself and an electric locomotive would have to couple to the front of the train. Brake tests would have to be performed and then the train could go on its way. The above procedure may have only taken a few minutes but every minute stopped is a minute wasted. Multiply those few minutes by hundreds or even thousands of trains a year and the time and labor adds up. The logistical constraints of having many different types of specialized motive power also added challenges to railroad mangers in areas other than operations. Further disadvantages to electrification that the PRR encountered were increased vandalism and weather related difficulties, especially from lightning. Neither of these problems were insurmountable however.

A last substantial disadvantage of electrification was that it wedded the railroad to a large and expensive infrastructure. When time came for improvements or replacement, the costs could be staggering. This institutional inertia is a major disadvantage of electrification and is a large reason for the lack of electrification in the United States. Instead of just replacing a few locomotives here and there, the entire electric system would have to be upgraded or replaced. The combination of replacement cost and operational inflexibility were the leading factors in the abandonment of electric service in most mountainous regions. Even on the former Pennsylvania northeast corridor, electric freight service was abandoned by Conrail in the 1980s and only electric passenger service under Amtrak remains. Electrification is theoretically a better way to move trains but its high initial cost will likely preclude it from being adopted by railroads in North America except where government regulation or other government enticements help with the construction costs.[15]

Electrification was a real alternative to steam power especially in mountainous regions or high traffic urban areas but its advantages lessened in the face of the diesel. Diesels could deliver many of the advantages of electrification including dynamic braking, high starting tractive effort and lower fuel and maintenance costs. In the stressed financial environment of the late 1940s and early 1950s when most roads chose to fully dieselize, devoting huge amounts of capital to a massive electrification project simply wasn't possible. The necessary capital wasn't there to begin with and most roads were wary of becoming wedded to a particular technology. The fast pace of technological development, especially during the war, led many railroad decision makers to believe that newer more efficient motive power than even the diesel might be only a few years away. A massive electrification project might be outdated and obsolete by the time it was completed, as had happened with some of the most modern steam locomotives built in the 1940s. Diesels were the immediate solution to increasing costs and promised a good return on investment as well as increased performance. While the potential benefits from large scale electrification projects were great, the costs and risks were simply too sizable. Electrification has been contemplated since the 1940s, especially in the 1970s with increasing oil prices but none of the studies resulted in new wire being strung except for a couple of isolated mine to power plant coal hauling roads that are operated separately from the national rail network. The only electrification projects since the 1950s on the national rail network have been relatively small scale expansions of existing electrified commuter lines. The one exception is Amtrak's electrification from New Haven to Boston to enable high speed electric passenger service from Washington DC, through New York to Boston. This is the exception that proves the rule in that it was completed for passenger service only and with substantial government investment.

Mechanical engineers and locomotive designers had known of the advantages in efficiency and operation of turbines since the early 1900s. A turbine has fewer moving parts and is much smaller than a conventional piston engine of the same power. A turbine also lacks the reciprocating motion of pistons and rods that causes stress and requires more robust manufacture. The basic principle of the turbine had been known for thousands of years. Windmills are a simple form of turbine as are children's pinwheels. There were two different types of turbines that were used in railroad locomotives, the steam turbine and the gas turbine. The steam turbine was driven by high pressure steam produced in an external boiler similar to conventional steam locomotives while the gas turbine was driven by the combustion gasses from the burning of fuel internally. The steam turbine has found a permanent home in large commercial power plants. The variant of the gas turbine that most people are familiar with is the jet engine although they too have been used in stationary and marine applications. The gas turbines used in the locomotives were more akin to helicopter engines than the ones on the wings of a 737 in that they were designed for a shaft output rather than maximizing airflow.

Steam turbines found a place in stationary and marine applications before they were tried for railroad service. By the first World War, many of the ships of all the navies involved were steam turbines. Electric power plants also began to convert to steam turbines. The turbines proved remarkably adept at operating at steady speeds for long periods of time, a characteristic of stationary and marine engines. Just as the diesel was employed first in stationary and marine use because of its need for cleaner surroundings and its ability to operate at a steady speed, so was the steam turbine. By the later 1920s and 1930s railroad locomotive designers both in North American and Europe began to explore the steam turbine for rail use. The Europeans produced a few experimental locomotives but the only relatively successful production steam turbines were a few Swedish models designed for heavy freight haulage. The experience of the Europeans, and especially the British with steam turbines was widely reported in the trade press on the other side of the Atlantic.

The Chesapeake & Ohio, Norfolk & Western, Union Pacific, and Pennsylvania railroads all experimented with steam turbines and other types of advanced coal burning locomotives well after the diesel had proven itself more than capable. True to form, the Pennsylvania Railroad chose the most conservative path. It developed a geared, direct drive steam turbine locomotive, the only one ever in operation in the United States. The Pennsylvania Railroad steam turbine locomotive, designated S-2 was built by Baldwin in 1944 with a conventional boiler and looked much like a conventional steam locomotive but with a unique 6–8–6 wheel arrangement. It contained two turbines, one for forward and one for reverse. Both multistage turbines were directly connected via a geared transmission to conventional steam locomotive drivers.[16] It was tremendously powerful, with 6,900 maximum horsepower and could attain speeds in excess of one hundred miles an hour but used inordinate amounts of fuel and water when idling and at low speeds. The conventional boiler when mated with the turbine also experienced problems resulting from pressure fluctuations. While it was one of the most powerful locomotives operating on the continent at the time it was in service, it was not considered successful and only one example was built. It spent a few years pulling passenger trains between Chicago and the division point of Crestline, Ohio, before it was pulled out of service and quietly scrapped in 1952. It almost certainly spent more time in the shop than out on the main line pulling passenger trains, not a good characteristic for a locomotive.[17] The experience of the S-2 shows a fundamental problem with all turbines. They operate best and achieve their highest efficiencies at a constant high speed, a characteristic not generally encountered in railroad service.

The PRR also designed a steam-turbine-electric locomotive that was called the V-1 type or the triplex. The design went though many iterations and was never built but final plans called for a conventional boiler that burned coal and a coal bunker housed in a streamlined exterior shell. The coal bunker would be at the front, followed by the cab and the boiler, mounted backward from traditional steam locomotive practice. A tender for water trailed the locomotive. The boiler would generate steam by burning coal. This steam would then be conducted to the turbine which would in turn spin a generator to produce electricity for traction motors on the wheels. It was an effort to combine the coal burning steam locomotive together with the electrical transmission system of the diesel electric all in one unit. As may be surmised it was a complicated design and was cancelled when the PRR decided to fully embrace the diesel and stop all steam locomotive development in 1947.[18]

The Chesapeake & Ohio (C&O) decided to go one better than the Pennsylvania and actually build a steam-turbine-electric and combine the tried and true technology of the coal burning steam locomotive with the advantages of electric transmission. Three locomotives were built for the C&O railroad in early 1947 by Baldwin. They looked similar to the design of the V-1 by the Pennsylvania with a forward coal bunker followed by a cab for the crew and a reverse mounted boiler. Water was carried in a separate tender. The locomotives were intended to power a new streamlined passenger train called the Chessie that would run on a daylight schedule between Washington D.C. and Cincinnati. The train was never put into service however and the locomotives spent their short life pulling other passenger trains. They functioned as designed and were thermodynamically efficient, but the maintenance required was more than conventional steam locomotives and much more than diesels. They were considered technical successes in that the design worked but practical failures. The steam turbines required more maintenance since they had a conventional fire-tube boiler and all of its maintenance headaches as well as complex electrical equipment all housed in a hard to access streamlined shell. Coal dust and cinders played havoc with the electrical equipment. They were impressive looking machines and could run at one hundred miles per hour, but spent much more time in the shop than on the main line. Like the complex compound cylinder locomotives half a century earlier, maintenance and serviceability won out over pure efficiency. All three were scrapped in 1950 after only three short years in service.[19]

The Norfolk & Western steam turbine electric, *Jawn Henry*, was slightly more successful than the C&O turbines. It was built in May 1954 by Baldwin-Lima-Hamilton with a marine type, water-tube boiler that required significantly less maintenance than the more conventional fire-tube type. It had automatic controls adapted from marine practice that promised less maintenance and enroute servicing. The different type of boiler also made higher boiler pressures possible which increased efficiency. The N&W and Baldwin learned some lessons from the ill-fated C&O turbines. *Jawn Henry* was designed for easier maintenance than the C&O turbines, but still retained the same inherent weaknesses of all coal burning steam locomotives, lack of flexibility and reliance on track side coal and water facilities. The locomotive was a remarkable machine and could out pull just about

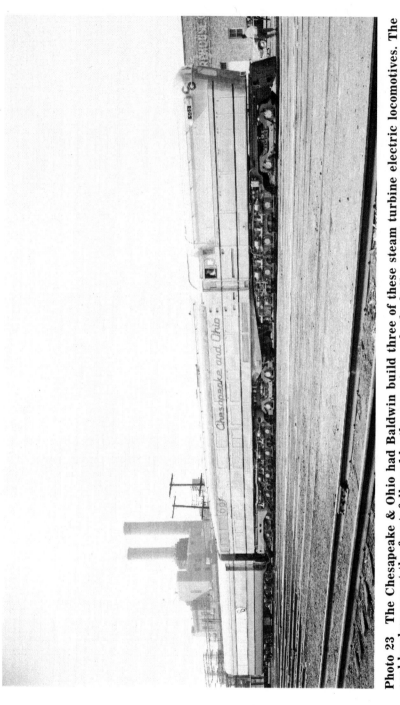

Photo 23 The Chesapeake & Ohio had Baldwin build three of these steam turbine electric locomotives. The coal bunker was at the front, followed by the operators cab, the boiler and then the electrical generating gear. The tender on the extreme left carried water. Courtesy of the Railroad Museum Of Pennsylvania (PHMC) H. L. Broadbelt Collection.

anything, including diesels, when it worked correctly. It was designed for freight and had a maximum speed of sixty miles per hour. It performed well in tests pulling long trains of coal out of the mountains of West Virginia but was destined, like its namesake, to live a short life. After just over three years in service it was set aside in December 1957 and scrapped the next month.[20] Some sources assert that the N&W mechanical department wished to order several more copies of the *Jawn Henry* but were overruled by upper management. By 1956, even on the N&W, coal burning steam, whether turbine or not, simply could not compete against the diesel.[21]

One can speculate that the engineers and management of the N&W may have surmised that the *Jawn Henry* would fight a noble but losing battle against a new technology and chose its name to reflect this. The mythical steel driving man raced the steam drill and won but it cost him his very life. The locomotive could out pull a diesel but it too would not live long. By 1954 the diesel had clearly and decisively shown its superiority in operations, maintenance and costs over steam locomotives, be they conventional or turbine. Despite the advantages of the electrical transmission, the steam turbines of the C&O and N&W were still tied to wayside coal and water facilities and required much greater maintenance than the diesels. They also lacked the flexibility of diesels. If traffic was light the turbines had power to spare while if traffic was unusually heavy they had to augmented with extra steam or diesel locomotives. Any number of diesel units could be coupled together to meet the tonnage requirements for any train, no matter how long or short the train was. The steam turbines illustrate not only a loyalty to the coal industry and to steam power but also a continuation of steam era thinking of designing, building and operating the largest and most powerful single locomotive possible.

The two Union Pacific steam-turbine-electric locomotives were the most ambitious and technologically advanced locomotives to have traveled American rails to that point. Even by today's standards they were impressive. They also had perhaps the shortest operational career of any locomotive documented thus far, six months. Built by General Electric in 1938, they contained a 1,600 pounds per square inch oil fired, water-tube boiler, the highest boiler pressure of any locomotive ever built. They were the only condensing steam locomotives ever in service in North

Photo 24 The Jawn Henry of the Norfolk & Western was similar in appearance to the ill fated C&O steam turbines although it contained a more advanced marine type watertube boiler. Courtesy of the Railroad Museum of Pennsylvania (PHMC) General Collection.

America. The steam, instead of being exhausted out the stack, was condensed in large radiator type condensers and recycled. They were essentially a full fledged oil fired steam electric generating plant on wheels. They looked impressive as well with highly streamlined and stylized exteriors including polished chrome accents and neon lighting. They were designed for passenger service, and during tests reached speeds well in excess of one hundred miles an hour. As can well be imagined, they were extremely complex and required much specialized maintenance. They went on many exhibition tours around the country but actually hauled few revenue trains. Due to the unreliability of the locomotives as well as their relatively high maintenance they were returned to General Electric less than six months after delivery. GE leased them out briefly during World War II to the Great Northern and New York Central railroads to help with the wartime traffic surge but they were more useful to the war effort as raw material and were soon scrapped.[22] GE, a long time electric locomotive builder, did not, in the 1930s and 1940s, have the necessary expertise to fully develop a diesel locomotive although its electrical gear was used on locomotives built by Alco. This experimental oil fired steam turbine was an effort to find a niche where they could use existing company proficiency to compete with the diesel and modern reciprocating steam. The wealthy Union Pacific under its old fashioned president was designing ever larger conventional steam to respond to the challenge of the diesel. It was the natural customer for the new GE steam turbines.

The Union Pacific was not done with turbines after their brief fling with the GE steam turbines in the late 1930s. They were unique among North American railroads by using large gas turbine-electric locomotives in daily service throughout the 1950s and 1960s. These locomotives burned heavy grade, bunker C type fuel oil in the turbines. The turbines in turn drove a generator that produced electricity for traction motors on the axles. They therefore embodied the advantages of the electrical transmission but replaced the diesel prime mover with a gas turbine. There were three distinct types of gas turbine locomotive in service on the UP. The first was a single GE and Alco product of 1948. The second were a group of twenty-four, 4,500 horsepower GE turbines produced from 1952 to 1954. These were the first truly operational turbines in the United States. The final group of gas turbines on the

Union Pacific were the monstrous 8,500 horsepower "Big Blow" turbines built from 1958 to 1961. These were the largest and most powerful single locomotives in the world when produced and have not been matched in raw power to the present.[23] Other railroads than just the UP were interested in gas turbines. For a time in the late 1940s the gas turbine was seen by engineers and designers as the locomotive of choice for the future because of its fewer moving parts and its high thermal efficiency. Westinghouse built a single experimental gas turbine prototype locomotive but, unlike GE, no orders followed its trials on various lines.

During the same time period that they were acquiring the oil fueled gas turbines, the Union Pacific also experimented with a coal burning gas turbine locomotive that was probably the largest and ugliest single locomotive to have ever trod the rail in North America. This monstrosity was built from a converted diesel locomotive and a converted electric locomotive, and furnished with a modified turbine from the earlier gas turbines. Instead of buring heavy grade oil, it was designed to burn powdered coal inside the turbine. This turbine had many more difficulties than the earlier turbines and was purely experimental.[24] This experimental coal burning gas turbine was the only example of its type to actually pull trains, however there was a long running research project in the late 1940s and early 1950s, funded by several large coal hauling railroads and equipment manufacturers to build a coal burning gas turbine locomotive. The technical problems were too great to overcome with existing technology and no prototype was ever built.[25]

The Union Pacific gas turbines, with the exception of the coal burning turbine, were much more successful than the earlier steam turbines but still were not an unqualified success. They consumed large amounts of fuel at idle and at low speeds. They were loud, and could only be operated in rural and isolated areas. The same problems of flexibility that affected the steam turbines also affected the gas turbines. They were soon operating in multiple with other turbines and diesel locomotives. What finally doomed the turbines was rising fuel costs. The bunker C fuel oil that they were designed to operate on became much more expensive toward the end of the 1960s than it had been in the late 1940s and 1950s.[26] There were also the obvious problems of keeping two types of fuel at terminals as well as the many specialized parts and expertise that the turbines required. While the gas turbines did provide a useful service and moved many millions of tons of freight over their roughly ten year life spans, the fact that they were retired and not replaced with other turbines is telling. The diesel had vanquished yet another challenger.

To what can we attribute the costly experiments of the steam and gas turbines? Likely the primary reason was a management that was unwilling or unable to grasp the potential, inherent in the technology, of the diesel-electric locomotive. Whether it was the C&O, PRR, or the UP, managers were operating in a steam era mindset that dictated how they designed and acquired new motive power. Instead of realizing the advantages in flexibility, operation, and maintenance that the diesel locomotive offered, they were preoccupied in having the largest and most powerful single locomotive, clearly a carryover from the steam locomotive days of the early twentieth century. Engineering forces at the railroads that tried turbine power were preoccupied with theoretical efficiency and power rather than with availability, maintainability, and serviceability. While the turbines could and did in some cases operate efficiently and cost effectively, they simply could not match the mass produced diesel in availability, reliability, and maintainability.

In addition the Pennsylvania, C&O, and N&W railroads were trying to appease their largest single shipper, the coal industry. By utilizing a locomotive that burned what it hauled the railroads would maintain the existing relationship that they had already established with the coal companies rather than having to forge new supplier relationships with oil companies. Turbines would also preserve the existing relationship with locomotive builders that the railroads enjoyed. The PRR essentially designed its S-2 and V-1 turbines itself with help from long time partner Baldwin. This contrasted with the off the shelf purchase style of diesel locomotives. The C&O and N&W likewise utilized significant in house expertise in the development of their turbine locomotives, something that was not necessary or available in diesel manufacture.

The Union Pacific likely embraced the turbines because of a unique corporate culture that was accustomed to and prided itself on operating large and unique locomotives. The UP was the only railroad to operate the 4–12–2 type of locomotive and was the only railroad to operate one of the largest steam locomotives in the world, the Big Boy 4–8–8–4 type. The Union Pacific was also accustomed to custom designing locomotives for specific requirements. Their famed Big Boys were designed to lug trains through the Wasatch mountain range east of Salt Lake City. The turbines were designed for similar custom duties where diesels could have fulfilled any duty on the railroad. The UP was a railroad with the capital necessary to invest in large and powerful motive power. The "big engine" culture remained at the UP as they went on in the late 1960s even as the turbines were retired, to purchase large single unit diesels that were only utilized, for the most part, by the UP.

Since the earliest diesel experiments of the 1920s and including the famous streamliners of the 1930s, North American diesel locomotives had been equipped with electric transmissions. There was another way, a hydraulic transmission, not unlike the automatic transmission on an automobile but vastly scaled up and more powerful. Hydraulic propulsion for railroads has a long history. Initial developments were made in the early twentieth century in both Europe and the United States. It would be some time however before a truly practical hydraulic transmission was developed. Europe was first with the development of small switching locomotives in the 1920s and 1930s in Britain and Germany. The famous 1935 Flying Hamburger diesel express train of the German Railways also used diesel-hydraulic propulsion.[27] The diesel hydraulic promised even better performance than the diesel electric, especially at low speeds. It also held the potential to cost less to purchase and maintain, due primarily to the lack of expensive electrical gear.

In North America the hydraulic transmission was less used. Despite small scale experiments in the 1920s there was no large scale use of diesel-hydraulic propulsion until after World War II. In 1947 the Budd company, a manufacturer of passenger rail cars including the famous Zephyr, came out with the Rail Diesel Car or RDC, a self-propelled passenger car. Each RDC had two, 275 horsepower diesel engines under the floor of the passenger compartment, each connected to a hydraulic transmission which was, in turn, connected to the drive axles. The RDC was successful with more than three hundred sold. A few remain in operation.

Throughout the rest of the 1950s there was interest in diesel-hydraulic propulsion from many quarters. EMD produced two experimental diesel-hydraulic switching locomotives in 1951 and 1954 but both failed to generate any orders from railroads. Baldwin-Lima-Hamilton, trying to salvage the last of its rapidly diminishing locomotive market, proposed a line of diesel-hydraulic locomotives in the mid-1950s. All that resulted were three experimental passenger locomotives for the New Haven and New York Central railroads that were quickly removed from service due to mechanical problems and a quickly declining passenger market.[28]

The most successful effort at diesel hydraulic locomotives was on the Southern Pacific. With dieselization nearing completion but with costs still increasing, the SP was looking for ways to increase its operating efficiency. In the late 1950s the Southern Pacific sent its research director, Frank Kurz on a fact-finding trip to Europe to view operations of diesel-hydraulic locomotives. He studied the diesel-hydraulic locomotives operating in Britain and Germany and developed a close relationship with locomotive builder Krauss Maffei, located in Munich. After a long study period, Kurz and his supervisor, Paul Garin, Manager of Mechanical Engineering and Research, recommended to the Southern Pacific leadership the purchase of a few diesel-hydraulic locomotives to evaluate their performance under American operating conditions and procedures. The board approved and in 1959, contracted with Krauss Maffei to build three, 4,000 horsepower diesel-hydraulic freight locomotives.[29]

The diesel-hydraulic had several advantages over the diesel-electric according to Kurz. These advantages included a high starting tractive effort and a higher factor of adhesion, 33 percent compared to 25 percent for diesel-electric power.[30] The capability for hydrodynamic braking was also important to the Southern Pacific with their many steep mountain grades. The diesel-hydraulic was supposed to have reduced maintenance costs because of the inherent simplicity of the mechanical nature of the drive system.[31] As with steam locomotives, maintenance and servicing concerns were just as important, if not more so, than performance issues. According to the Southern Pacific, most failures of diesel-electric locomotives were electrical system failures, not engine failures. The Southern Pacific hoped that the diesel-hydraulic would be more reliable than the diesel-electric since it did not have complex electrical control and propulsion systems.

If diesel-hydraulic propulsion was so great, why wasn't everyone using them? The answer, at least partly, lies with Southern Pacific corporate culture, and specifically with Frank Kurz, Research Director. Being fluent in German and a frequent traveler to Europe made Kurz more receptive to European technology. Had it not been for Kurz it is likely that there would have been no diesel-hydraulics operating on the Southern Pacific. Kurz and Garin, as engineers, were impressed with the technical sophistication and theoretical efficiency of the diesel-hydraulic.

The Southern Pacific was one of several railroads operating in the western United States. It was competing against other large and profitable railroads like the Union Pacific and the Atchison Topeka & Santa Fe. They saw the Union Pacific especially as an arch rival. The Union Pacific was also faced with the problem of using many low horsepower units to achieve the needed horsepower to move trains at speed. They chose a different solution and invested in large gas turbine locomotives, including the monstrous 8,500 horsepower "Big Blow" turbines. According to internal documents the Southern Pacific did not choose turbines because of efficiency concerns, limited operating range and noise issues.[32] More important to the diesel hydraulic story, the Union Pacific was involved with locomotive manufacturer EMD in a research program to upgrade existing, low horsepower (1,500–1,800) diesel locomotives by turbocharging them. By 1958 these experiments had born fruit, and the Union Pacific was acquiring 2,400 horsepower turbocharged EMD locomotives.

The Southern Pacific was concerned about these developments by its competitor. A letter written by Southern Pacific President D. J. Russell speaks volumes: "It is distressing to learn that our own people are not out in front in a situation such as this one. Has there been any falldown on our part or on that of the manufacturer in not getting the higher horsepower locomotives on our property at least simultaneously with, if not ahead of, the Union Pacific tests?"[33] To keep the Southern Pacific at the forefront of motive power development it needed to eclipse the Union Pacific's latest advancements. The diesel-hydraulic was supposed to do just that.

The first of the three unit order was under construction in Munich in 1960 under the watchful eye of Frank Kurz.

These locomotives were a curious blending of European and North American technology. Some parts were metric while others were American standard measures. The wheels for instance, were standard forty-two inch locomotive wheels, while the diesel engines were metric sized Maybach engines unlike anything on American rails. The locomotives incorporated many advanced design features that did not show up in domestic manufacture until much later. For instance, the engineer's position was behind a desktop rather than at a conventional control stand. Domestic manufacturers did not offer this design until the 1980s. The cab of the locomotives, where the crew sat, was also built as a separate component and was isolated from the rest of the unit by sound and vibration absorbing material. This innovation did not appear until the 1990s on domestic locomotives. The crews of the units would also enjoy the best visibility of any locomotive then on North American rails.

The locomotive was tested extensively on the Semmerling line between Munich and Vienna in July 1961 with a large number of officials on board. Although this line had many curves and a grade of up to 2.75 percent, it was not as arduous as the Southern Pacific assault on the Sierra Nevada. The locomotive performed well in its European tests and along with the others was shipped to Houston, Texas, in October 1961.

The units lived up to much of their promise, at least initially. They were put to work on the grueling assault on the Sierra Nevada from Roseville, California, to Sparks, Nevada. The three units could do the work of eight 1,500 horsepower F-7 type locomotives. One trip in particular deserves note. The three units pulled a train uphill at one mile an hour following a trainman walking the track looking for possible rock slides. Such a trip by conventional diesel-electric power would have quickly overloaded the electrical gear and required a complete replacement of all traction motors.[34]

Despite the testing in West Germany and Austria the locomotives developed problems when placed in service in the United States. The first and most serious resulted in several damaged engines. In long tunnels and snowsheds the air intake on the locomotives would ingest the hot exhaust gasses. This led to scorched pistons and burned intake valves and necessitated a field design change. Shop forces quickly altered the locomotives with extra duct work to draw air in from lower levels, closer to the ground where it would be cooler and not damage the diesel engine.[35]

The Southern Pacific was intrigued with the new power despite the minor problems. However, for a true test they would need more than three locomotives. Therefore, in 1962 the Southern Pacific requested bids for several additional diesel-hydraulic locomotives from domestic and foreign builders. Krauss Maffei and Alco were the only bidders. In the specifications, Southern Pacific sought to correct many small problems that the first units experienced. Krauss Maffei was to build fifteen of the new units while Alco was to manufacture three. Both would use the same hydraulic transmission but the Alco units would have their own domestic built 251 diesel engine rather than the fussy German Maybach. These locomotives were of a more conventional hood configuration rather than the streamlined carbody configuration of the first order. The locomotives were delivered to the Southern Pacific in 1964.[36] Now the railroad had enough locomotives to perform a real long term test of their operating ability.

Despite the advanced cab facilities of both the first and second order of Krauss Maffei units, the operating crews were not fond of them. The windows leaked and occasionally enough water leaked in that it damaged the instrumentation. The large expanse of glass acted like a greenhouse and made the southwest deserts seem that much hotter. Crews were also nervous about having a drive shaft transferring 2,000 horsepower directly underneath the cab floor. Although there were no failures, the crews were not enthusiastic to be sitting directly on top of so much power. When paired with other locomotives, the Krauss Maffei units were often relegated to trailing position, even though the crew accommodations were what one author called, the Mercedes-Benzes of locomotives.[37]

While the operating forces may not have cared too much for the locomotives, management was more worried about the consistent maintenance problems. The German built Maybach engines were well designed but were described as delicate and fussy. The engines were of such tight tolerances that they had to be heated up to ninety-five degrees Fahrenheit before they could even be started.[38] The transmissions were also incompatible, not with American track or train size, but with American maintenance practices or the lack thereof. In Europe, locomotives would often return to maintenance facilities nightly for care. In contemporary North American operations, diesel would likely see many miles and months between visits to a shop for anything more than toping off the oil and coolant and checking the operation of vital components. To have a diesel-hydraulic with great performance but that required much more shop attention would essentially negate one of the large advantages of the diesel-electric, the lack of extensive routine maintenance.

Much of the reason for the diesel-hydraulic locomotives was the higher horsepower that they were able to pack into one unit. At least this was true when the program began in 1959. In that year the most powerful domestic diesel-electric locomotive generated 2,400 horsepower. However, a horsepower race was about to begin. General Electric entered the large locomotive market in 1960 with a 2,500 horsepower unit that joined Alco and EMD offerings at 2,400 horsepower. By 1966 EMD was offering 3,000 and 3,600 horsepower units. Alco and GE followed suit each bringing their own 3,000 and 3,600 horsepower units out by 1967.[39] These units generated this power with only one large diesel engine, not two like the Krauss Maffei units. The Southern Pacific purchased hundreds of these new high horsepower locomotives. The horsepower justification for ordering the diesel-hydraulics in 1959 had disappeared just a few years later.

With the German built units out of service because of maintenance difficulties and the three Alco built units staying close to their maintenance base, Southern Pacific management decided to end the decade long experiment. On February 13, 1968, the Southern Pacific officially announced the end of the diesel-hydraulic program. The need for large powerful units was being met by domestic, mass-produced diesel-electrics, not exotic, maintenance intensive diesel-hydraulics.

We can learn several lessons from the experience of the Southern Pacific and its diesel-hydraulic locomotives. Perhaps one of the most important is a lesson that we have seen many times before, the difference between operational ability and maintainability. The older, less technically sophisticated domestic diesel-electric power was not able to even approach the performance of the diesel-hydraulics. However, the domestic power was there when it was needed and ran. A similar lesson was learned with the steam turbines a decade or more before. While they were able to equal or even surpass the performance of diesel-electric locomotives, they required much more maintenance. An old adage in railroad operating circles is that the most expensive locomotive is the one that just sits. By this measure the Krauss Maffei diesel-hydraulics were an expensive investment. In addition, the thought of American railroads turning to overseas suppliers for their locomotives, no doubt encouraged the domestic manufacturers to proceed with development of higher horsepower locomotives.

This story also illustrates the differences between European and North American operating and maintenance routines. The German built units were able to easily adapt to the operations of the Southern Pacific, including some of the most demanding conditions in the world. This was despite the many differences in European and North American general operating practices. Where the new locomotives were not able to adapt was in the maintenance aspect. Specialized procedures with the German engines could not compete against the standardized robust engines of the domestic manufacturers. Finally, this story provides an interesting glimpse into the role of individuals and the corporate culture of the Southern Pacific Railroad. While steam had been gone from the railroad for several years, the management still thought in a steam mindset with a preoccupation on large, single unit locomotives and a desire, like in steam locomotive times, to have a say in the design and manufacture of its locomotives. A German speaking research director and a president who was determined to regain his technological bragging rights combined to create a motive power experiment that was unique among North American railroads.

The exotic turbines and other proposals were perhaps the ultimate expression of the battle between efficiency and operations that was waged since the late nineteenth century. Locomotive designers and railroad motive power officials came up with compounding, feed water heaters, superheating, and ultimately the steam and gas turbines in a constant battle to increase the efficiency and power of locomotives. The operational forces and the railroad accountants cared little for the continual improvements in efficiency. They just wanted a locomotive that would work reliably and move the trains cost effectively. Both parties finally got their wish in the efficient and reliable diesel-electric. Electrification is somewhat different as it is generally regarded as a more efficient solution to the problem of moving trains both from a technical perspective and from an accounting one. However, the huge initial cost of electrification and the specialized locomotives and operational headaches that it entailed have limited electrification in North America to isolated lines or government supported passenger operations.

6

Shoveling Oil:
Labor and Social Effects

THUS FAR THE FOCUS OF THIS STUDY HAS BEEN ON THE TECHNOL-ogy of steam and diesel locomotives and the business and operating decisions of railroad management. However, there were many other players in the dieselization drama. Regardless of the locomotive used or what it burned, it needed skilled workers to operate, service and maintain it. The changes detailed so far have not taken into account how these workers and the unions that represented them responded to technological change and a restructuring industry. In this chapter, the highly unionized railroad industry during the period of dieselization is analyzed to determine how workers, as well as management, and government responded to diesel locomotives, coupled with reduced growth and even decline due to increased competition and heavy regulation. Workers lived in larger communities that were also affected by technological change. The impact on these communities is also addressed. Entire small communities grew up around maintenance and servicing facilities for steam locomotives. When the steam locomotive disappeared, these communities had to find a new reason for being or risk disappearing as well. The complex labor relations and convoluted work rules of railroads are more difficult to decipher than horsepower and tractive effort but are key to understanding the full impact of the diesel locomotive.

From the late 1930s to the end of the 1950s the American railroad industry was transformed by the introduction and large scale use of diesel-electric locomotives. During this time railroads also felt greatly increased competition from other forms of transportation; most notably automobiles and motor trucks. The change in railroad motive power technology had far reaching repercussions in many areas of the industry, especially labor. The largest single cost for railroads during this time was labor. In 1946, for instance, labor accounted for a full 52.1 percent of Class I railroad's total operating revenue. With more powerful and less maintenance intensive internal combustion motive power many positions became redundant or at least underutilized. By the completion of dieselization in 1960 labor costs accounted for 49 percent of total operating revenue.[1] This relatively small change is indicative of the restrictive union work rules of the time. Train and engine crews were the same in 1960 as they had been fifteen years before, even though the steam locomotive demanded much more en route care. Shop forces had begun to decline with the elimination of the steam locomotive but greater declines were in store. Many workers, from locomotive engineers to boiler makers, mechanics, and dispatchers were affected by dieselization but none more graphically than the locomotive fireman.[2]

In steam locomotives the fireman was responsible for the upkeep of the fire, usually fueled by coal, needed to produce steam. A fireman could shovel as much as fifteen or twenty tons of coal each shift. Firemen were more than simply brawny laborers. It was a highly skilled position and required much more than simply physical strength. In addition to feeding the fire, the fireman had to make sure the fire was burning correctly and producing enough steam to meet the requirements of the locomotive. Too much fuel could smother the fire while too little would not generate enough heat. In addition to keeping the fire, the fireman helped with the servicing of the locomotive, from taking on coal and water to oiling and greasing parts when stopped. The fireman was also supposed to help the engineer look for obstructions, signals, and generally act as another pair of eyes in the engine. With diesel-electric locomotives the fueling was automatically controlled, and there was no necessity for enroute maintenance or upkeep as with a steam locomotive. The engineer, in contrast to the fireman, was responsible for driving the locomotive and all the associated duties that this entailed such as looking out for signals and other train traffic.

As steam locomotives became larger and more powerful in the early decades of the century, the job of the engineer and fireman did not change much. If anything, larger locomotives required more work from the fireman and engineer as the larger and more powerful engine demanded more coal, water and lubrication than earlier smaller machines. The addition of efficiency enhancing appliances throughout the 1910s and 1920s raised the workload of engine crews. A major development of the

1920s that directly affected the fireman in particular was the introduction and widespread use of the automatic coal stoker. With a stoker, the fireman no longer had to shovel all the coal into the firebox. The stoker could provide coal at a rate surpassing that of even the most brawny fireman and enabled larger fireboxes and hence, larger and more powerful locomotives. The stoker did not make the fireman obsolete, for he still would shovel coal at times, direct the placement of coal by the stoker, tend the fire, and make sure that it was burning properly. This took much skill and was not a job that could be learned easily. The fire had to be varied to meet the conditions that the locomotive was liable to meet. For instance, if there was a large grade ahead the fire would have to be stoked and made hotter. Similarly, if the locomotive was coming into a terminal, the fire would need to be tended to reduce smoke. Railroad management generally sought to minimize the smoke from their locomotives. Thick black smoke consists of small particles of unburnt or partially burnt coal in addition to exhaust gasses. Therefore a locomotive trailing a thick, black plume of smoke would literally be exhausting good fuel up the stack.

The fireman was regarded as an engineer in training and viewed almost as an apprentice engineer. An individual would hire on to the railroad as a laborer or possibly directly as a fireman. The fireman would shovel coal but also be instructed in the overall operation of the locomotive by the engineer. Several years, depending on labor conditions, would be spent as a fireman, learning the ins and outs not only of locomotive operation but also of the route. By the time firemen would have the opportunity to become engineers, they knew their particular division like the back of their hand. All the grades, curves, bridges and other features of the home territory were memorized. The engineer and the fireman acted as a team in steam locomotives. Both were necessary for the operation of the machine and its timely movement of freight and passengers over the railroad.

The multitude of highly technical and complex tasks required to keep a locomotive running, particularly a steam powered one, led to over a dozen major craft designations among railroad workers. Each of these crafts had their own strong union. The two organizations that are of the most concern for direct, on board operations of locomotives were the Brotherhood of Locomotive Engineers

(BLE) and the Brotherhood of Locomotive Firemen and Enginemen (BLF&E).[3] Together with the Brotherhood of Railroad Trainmen and the Order of Railway Conductors the BLE and BLF&E represented the majority of employees on trains. Both the BLE and BLF&E were founded prior to 1880 but constrained their business to mainly fraternal and beneficial society activities up until that time when they started to play a more active role in labor disputes.[4]

Despite the efforts of Eugene Debs in the Pullman strike of 1894 to promulgate his American Railway Union, industrial unionism did not catch on in the railroad industry. The craft unions did however work together on many issues that affected the industry and its workers as a whole, especially in the twentieth century. The four train service unions often presented a united front when negotiating with railroad management over wage and job issues. Despite consolidation attempts in the late 1920s and again in the mid-1940s the BLE and BLF&E remained separate organizations until 1956 when they finally merged. All labor relations on the railroads during the period of dieselization and up to the present, were governed by the 1926 Railway Labor Act, with subsequent amendments. Railroads were apart from most other industries and had their own system of labor relations due to the differences in federal regulations. The Railway Labor Act specified the process of collective bargaining and authorized when and how federal involvement could take place.

The history of wages in the railroad industry is also a long and complex story that defies easy summary. However, some background is necessary to understand the controversies that would erupt with the introduction of new forms of motive power. In the nineteenth century there were three prevailing basis of pay, the monthly wage, the daily wage, and the trip system in which the hours, mileage, and other local conditions established the wage. Over time the trip system evolved into the mileage system which was based purely on the miles traveled. This last system came to prevail for engine and train employees.[5] A full day's work was defined as one hundred miles, which was the typical distance that a late nineteenth or early twentieth-century freight train would cover in roughly ten hours, and was also the typical distance between engine terminals. Wages for engine employees were also governed by the weight of the locomotive with the heavier locomotives presumably being more difficult to operate and therefore deserving of higher levels of compensation. Differences were also drawn between passenger, road-freight, and switching duties.[6] Different geographic conditions also led to differences in the rate of pay. Mountain divisions generally had higher pay rates than flatter divisions for instance.

The situation on American railroads of the late 1920s was dynamic but typical of a mature industry with well defined boundaries, goals, and players. The relationship between the unions and management, although antagonistic at times, was forged over the preceding fifty years and was well understood by all participants.[7] After the 1926 Railway Labor Act, the devastating strikes that had characterized the industry over the previous fifty years were gone, replaced with a complicated mediation process. Railroad operations were also dynamic but again with well understood players and limitations. Jobs and skills were well defined. An example would be the crew of a typical freight train. The crew consisted of an engineer responsible for the operation of the locomotive; a conductor responsible for the overall operation of the train and the man in overall command; a fireman responsible for fueling and tending the fire in the locomotive, and two trainmen or brakemen responsible for other aspects of train operation. The engineer and fireman, and sometimes a brakeman, would ride in the locomotive, while the conductor and the other brakeman would follow in the caboose.

If a train required two or more locomotives due to length of the train or heavy grades, each locomotive would be outfitted with an engineer and fireman. On steam locomotives this was necessary for operation. To try to eliminate this extra expense, railroads, in conjunction with locomotive builders, began development of more powerful and technologically sophisticated locomotives that could do the same amount of work as two, or even three, older locomotives. These new locomotives incorporated many of the incremental improvements in technology such as stokers and superheaters, detailed in chapter two. The development of more powerful locomotives necessarily lessened employment of train service personnel in the 1920s. This trend was mentioned explicitly in an article in the February 1930, BLF&E magazine. "Modern machinery has been constantly displacing wage earners and increasing the number of the unemployed, and in this connection the railroad industry is no exception. Due to ponderous locomotives with tremendously increased tractive power three trains are now being hauled in one, with the consequent displacement of two engine crews and two train crews for every full capacity tonnage train."[8]

While this editorial may be somewhat overstating the case, there was a definite trend toward larger and more powerful locomotives in the 1920s and 1930s that did eliminate many train service jobs. Since the fireman was the junior man in the engine, his job was in greater jeopardy from this technological change than was the engineer. An engineer displaced from his job by train consolidation could go back to work as a fireman while a fireman would no longer have employment.

To help secure employment for their members as well as to further the cause of safety, the unions agitated for adoption and strict enforcement of full crew laws and train limit laws in a number of states. Attempts at full crew laws at the federal level were unsuccessful but many states did enact various full crew laws. Full crew laws necessitated a crew of five or more men on each and every train regardless of length, while train limit laws capped the length of freight trains at around seventy cars, and passenger trains at fourteen to sixteen cars. Train limit laws were pitched at the railroads and the public to be purely safety oriented. In the days before two-way radio, the crew of a long train would have difficulty communicating with hand signals from the engine to the caboose and longer trains were much more difficult to control. As of mid-1930 twenty-one states had full crew laws or regulations on the books. In an important decision of October 1929, the legality of these state, full crew laws was upheld by the United States Supreme Court.[9] Most of these full crew laws remained on the books well after 1960 and full dieselization. Train limit laws were generally less successful, with only a few states such as Nevada and Louisiana enacting such laws.[10] Even after enactment of the laws they were generally ineffectual due to protracted court struggles. The Nevada law was eventually struck down by the US Supreme Court on the grounds that it violated the commerce clause and the due process clause of the fourteenth amendment.[11]

The first great challenge to the status quo in railroad labor relations came from rail motorcars. Beginning in the mid-1920s rail motorcars replaced steam locomotives and passenger coaches on local and branch line runs. They were not officially listed as locomotives on most railroads. The reason that motorcars were not listed as locomotives was most likely to circumvent the labor agreements regarding locomotive and train operation. For instance, a small, branch line local passenger train powered by a steam locomotive would have to have a full crew consisting of an engineer and fireman in the locomotive, and a conductor and usually two trainmen in the passenger coaches. Motorcars could be operated, and in fact were designed to be operated, by one engineer and with one conductor to take tickets and perform various other duties. In many respects the motorcars, in physical structure and operational intent, were more akin to streetcars or interurbans than steam powered passenger trains.[12]

The train service brotherhoods, led by the BLF&E, inaugurated a concerted effort to gain the employment of a second person in the cab of these motorcars. Discussions with the railroads were not fruitful so in many cases the unions opted to get the government to intervene. The government, at the local, federal, but especially the state level was an integral player in railroad labor relations well before it entered the organized labor arena in general during the New Deal. Due in part to union agitation, the attorney general of Texas declared in 1929, that motor driven trains had to have full crews just like steam powered trains while operating in that state. In a two page article in the BLF&E magazine of January 1930, the essentials of the decision are spelled out.

1. A motor car which runs on a railroad track on regular schedule and transports United States mail, baggage, and express and passengers, is a train.
2. The Full Crew Law applies to all passenger trains, regardless of the form of energy employed to propel them.[13]

The Attorney General goes on to mention the role of the locomotive fireman in detail.

That a fireman does not have the same duties to perform on a motor-driven locomotive that would be necessary on a steam-propelled engine, is entirely probable and true. The same method of fueling is not employed. The necessity, however, for performance of the same duties with reference to the safety of the traveling public exists. It is the duty of the fireman on all trains to keep a lookout for danger on the track, to keep and compare the correct time with the engineer, to familiarize himself with the orders governing the movement of trains, and keep check on the engineer as to the proper observance of said orders, to take charge of the engine in event of death or disability of the engineer, to blow the whistle, ring the bell and notify the engineer upon the appearance of danger, to notify the conductor when the engineer fails or refuses to observe orders, and numerous other duties all designed, in part, for the safety of the traveling public.[14]

The unions had decided to use safety as their bargaining tool. Even with this small but potentially precedent setting victory, the fight was far from won for the place of locomotive firemen on rail motorcars. The railroads applied for and received a restraining order, suspending this executive order. It was anticipated that this case would go to the Texas Supreme Court and perhaps even the US Supreme Court before a final outcome would be reached. Similar challenges by the unions were initiated in Ohio and Nevada also with limited immediate success.

The second challenge to the status quo in the railroad industry came in the form of the Great Depression that greatly reduced revenues. The Depression, which exacerbated the trends already mentioned from the modernization of steam motive power and consolidation of trains, especially affected train service crews. Firemen, being the junior members of the engine crew, were the first to be let go. Engineers, because of seniority rules, could be forced to return to the ranks fo the firemen. The Depression also expedited the shift to rail motorcars on local and branch lines that continued to run passenger services.

With the Depression cutting deeply into earnings, an even greater effort was made by the railroad companies to reduce expenses while still providing service and generating income. In an effort to bring passengers back to the rails as well as to cut costs, fast, diesel-powered streamlined trains were developed, the most famous being the Burlington Zephyr. This ground-breaking train was designed for, and initially operated with, a single engineer at the throttle. This high profile train, popularized in the period Hollywood movie, "Silver Streak," was a perfect target for the train service brotherhoods. In a scathing September 1935, editorial, the BLF&E took

full aim at the Burlington: "Any railroad that must subordinate safety to financial success is a failure as a business institution. To risk a railroad horror involving the
destruction of the lives of travelers and employees, in
order to realize the wage saving incident to dispensing
with the services of a needed train employee is a policy
so shortsighted, so calloused, so mercenary as to demand
vigorous determined action thru any and every available
agency with a view to its termination."[15] This concerted
effort to gain a second crewman in the cab of the Zephyr
was eventually successful, although it took the threat of a
strike and eleventh hour negotiations to win this conces-
sion.[16] Since the Zephyr was only one train, the Burlington case itself only affected a small number of firemen,
but set the precedent that diesel-electric streamliners
should have firemen in the cab. After the Burlington victory, the BLE and BLF&E found the going much easier
with railroads from the Boston & Maine to the Santa Fe
agreeing to employ a fireman in the cab of diesel locomotives employed in high-speed, streamlined passenger
service.[17] The railroads rightly perceived that safety was
an important issue and one that could be publicly humili-
ating. The railroads often saved enough money by utilizing diesel streamliners that they could afford the extra
expense of a firemen in the cab along with the engineer.
Lastly, in the early 1930s, with concerns about technological unemployment already strong, the railroads could ill
afford the negative publicity that further crew reduction
would bring.

Emboldened by their successes with motorcars and
streamliners, the BLF&E in late 1936 decided to take on
the railroads over the one man operation of all diesel,
gasoline, and distillate locomotives, not just high-speed
streamliners. By this time diesels had made significant
gains, especially in yard and terminal service, and were
beginning to be used more regularly in passenger service. Since they were fast becoming much more than
curiosities, the BLF&E decided to try to negotiate a settlement with the railroads as a whole rather than on a
case by case basis as they had done before. This illustrates a change in thinking by the union. Wages were traditionally determined by this method while grievance
concerns were necessarily limited to one railroad and
one location. Diesels were becoming so widespread that
they needed blanket agreements, not simply negotiations

on a case by case basis. On February 28, 1937, the BLF&E and hundreds of railroads, including many of the major carriers across the country, signed an agreement that placed firemen on almost all locomotives and motorcars.[18] Article one of this agreement stated, "A fireman (helper) taken from the ranks of the firemen shall be employed on all types of power used in road, yard, or any other service."[19] There were some self-propelled vehicles that were excluded from this agreement, most notably locomotives and motorcars that weighed less than ninety thousand pounds and self-propelled cranes, ditchers, weed burners, and other maintenance of way equipment. This ninety thousand pound rule led to a market for small, forty-four ton diesel switching locomotives that was met by many manufacturers.

This precedent setting agreement secured the place of the fireman in the cab along with the engineer, no matter what type of locomotive was employed. The engineers and firemen had joined forces to argue that, for safety's sake and for the purpose of training future engineers, a fireman was needed in the cab. Since the fireman's next step up the job ladder would be to engineer, it was necessary for a fireman to ride in the cab simply to observe the engineer and to learn his craft. This landmark agreement was to come under increasing pressure due to war, changing technology, and increased business. All of these circumstances forced reevaluation of the role of the fireman.

In the discussions over the fate of the fireman the BLE was a minimal player. In the monumental 1937 agreement the BLE was not present at the negotiations. They were vociferous in wage negotiations as well as pushing for train limits and other legislation, but remained rather noncommittal in the battle over the fate of the fireman. They endorsed the position of the BLE&F but did not play an active role in the negotiations. Even with new diesel streamliners, switching locomotives, and motorcars, there had to be an engineer operating the vehicle. These technological changes did not put the engineer's job in immediate jeopardy. In fact, the engineers of the new diesel streamliners were paid quite well and were greatly admired in the profession and by the public. The relative safety of the engineers' jobs when compared to the firemens' would change drastically when the brotherhoods next confronted the railroads over the so-called, diesel question.

Up until 1940, most diesel locomotives operated singly or, on a few specially designed large passenger streamliners, in tandem. This all changed with the introduction of practical freight diesels, most notably the EMC model FT. The FT was the first truly practical freight diesel and was designed from the start to be flexible. Any number of 1,350 horsepower units from one to three, four, six, and beyond, could be assembled into essentially one uniformly acting and centrally controlled locomotive. The potential market was huge and included virtually every freight train operating on the main line. After a whirlwind demonstration tour in 1940, many railroads realized the potential of the FT and began to order them.[20]

The BLE and BLF&E both wanted crewmen on each unit, implying that they were separate locomotives. The diesel operating changes were contained in a large package of wage and rules changes proposed by the train service brotherhoods. The rationale behind the decision to employ extra crews was that the crew members would be required to monitor the equipment and make adjustments enroute, as they would have had to do with a steam locomotive. The BLE was insisting upon a fully qualified engineer to ride in the engine compartment while the BLF&E thought that this was a natural job for the fireman who traditionally looked after the machinery of the locomotive. Referring to their demands, the June 1941 issue of the BLF&E magazine states, "in the multiple unit operation of other than steam locomotives, a fireman (helper) taken from the seniority ranks of the firemen will be employed on each unit."[21]

When the jobs of their members were in immediate danger the unions found it much more difficult to work together as they had in the past. Rather they chose to fight among themselves over the increasingly shrinking labor pie. Because of the inherent differences in the technologies, the diesel locomotives did not require any sort of enroute maintenance or care taking. Safety was not an issue in this case since the added employee would be riding in the engine compartment or in following units and would be unable to help call out signals and spot dangerous situations on the track ahead. It would seem that this was simply an effort by the unions to secure employment for all of their members.

Since any number of diesel units could be controlled from the lead unit, the management position was that the number of units coupled together did not matter; there was essentially only one driving locomotive and, therefore, only one crew was needed.[22] As early as 1934, the BLE had been discussing these changes in correspondence with various railroads, but there were never any agreements reached. In addition to a man on every unit, they wanted new pay classifications for these units. Since it was wartime, this labor dispute went to federal Emergency Board hearings in 1943, where the status quo with regards to employment of extra men was upheld. The issue of men in the engine compartments and men on each unit was taken up again by the unions and was not totally decided until 1948.[23] The existing agreement was continued at that time with firemen necessary for diesel powered trains but no extra firemen or other employee necessary for multiple units. This would be the accepted procedure for the manning of diesel locomotives for the period of dieselization although several other conflicts would occur.

Railroad management gave in to the BLF&E demand to keep a fireman in the cab for safety reasons as much as anything else, and extended the pay rate structure for the new locomotives, but management won in its desire to have only one crew for any number of units. An extra crewman in the engine spaces and an entire extra crew for each unit was not truly needed and did not come about. Rate of pay was to be determined by the weight on drivers as it was with steam locomotives and any mileage over one hundred miles per day was regarded as overtime and deserved appropriate compensation. This compromise allowed the railroads to save some costs by consolidating trains and moving trains over the road faster but not by the wholesale elimination of large numbers of firemen. The idea of new and more powerful motive power forcing train consolidation and therefore reduction in employment was not a new concept to either management or labor. Both seemed to adopt the strategy that they had maintained since the 1920s.

Unlike the 1937 decision on the place and role of the locomotive fireman, the 1943 and later disputes were much more controversial. In the Depression public opinion favored the firemen, especially with safety of the traveling public as a major issue in the debate. By the 1940s, with the Depression gone and unemployment no longer the concern it had been just a few years prior, efficiency and productivity were paramount in public discussion, especially during the war. Articles and editorials in business and mainstream magazines such as *Barron's* and *Readers Digest* asserted that the railroad unions were "featherbedding" and were hampering the war effort. For example, the articles asserted that on some runs engineers and firemen earned up to three days of pay for working barely eight hours. "The crew in the cab of the B&O's *Royal Blue* (italics in original) between New York and Washington may work only one day in three."[24] The article derided the movement by the unions to have a crew for each diesel unit as being simply a make work device. Antiquated terminal rules and regulations are also assailed by the article. Most of the regulations dated from the Depression when railroads and unions were trying to spread around what little work there was to do. During wartime however, some of the regulations resulted in terrible inefficiencies.

The article and others like it caused a storm of letters to the editor by union officials and working firemen and engineers. Regarding the employment of a fireman in the cab, an engineer and union organizer on the Union Pacific stated, "a team of pilot and co-pilot is no less necessary to the safe operation of a passenger airplane or a Flying Fortress than are two men in the cab of a locomotive."[25] Other letters point out that the select cases in the now infamous "featherbedding" article represented less than one tenth of one percent of railroad workers and that many workers were putting in up to sixteen hours per day, everyday, including Sundays to further the war effort.[26] Perhaps the most influential response to the controversy came from Joseph B. Eastman, director of the Office of Defense Transportation and former ICC commissioner. In an appearance before the House Military Affairs Committee quoted in the *Locomotive Enginemen's Magazine* he stated, "From the actual average of 50.6 hours per week now being worked by railmen, you can see that they are not loafing on the job and are surpassing the performance in most other industries."[27] He also stated that the regulations that were under fire were initiated by and continued in force because of the railroad managements. This is at least partially accurate in that the regulations were negotiated with and agreed to by railroad management and unions.

It would seem that these hard fought decisions secured the place of the fireman in the cab of diesel locomotives but that was not the case. The role and duties of the fireman as well as the other junior members of the train crew, trainmen and brakemen, were under constant assault by the railroads to cut costs. As the 1950s drew to a close and as costs and competition continued to drain away traffic from the railroads, the managements of various railroads began to revisit the fireman issue. The Canadian Pacific forced the issue in 1958. After a Royal Commission study Canadian railroads were allowed to discontinue hiring new firemen.[28] The existing firemen jobs would be gradually eliminated by attrition. American railroads were emboldened by the Canadian decision but such an easy and swift agreement was not to be had. After acrimonious negotiations and a very public campaign on both sides, a presidential commission in 1962 came to essentially the same conclusions as the Canadian commission, that no new firemen should be hired and that the existing jobs would slowly decline due to attrition. The unions strenuously objected and a new round of fruitless negotiations began. Binding arbitration followed in 1963. The conclusions again were that there was no inherent reason for firemen on a diesel and that, in a compromise to employees, no existing jobs would be eliminated but no new firemen would be hired. Agreement was finally reached in 1964 after the personal intervention of President Johnson. As before, railroads would not hire new firemen and the position would gradually die out. The presidential emergency board findings were only valid for two years though and renewed union agitation began in 1966. While no large scale national show downs were forthcoming, the firemen issue would continue to be a contentious one for the next two decades.

Not all railroads participated in the national negotiations. Railroads in the south especially preferred to negotiate separate agreements on work rules issues, likely because unions generally were not as strong in the south and the railroads thought that they could get a better deal by separate negotiations than by joining their northern and western brethren. The Southern railway system was known for its strict management especially in regard to labor relations. It was one of the first to break the status quo on firemen in the early 1960s. Noting that there was no requirement to replace firemen that died, quit or retired, the Southern hired no new firemen from 1959 to 1963, until ordered to do so by the National Railroad Adjustment Board to fulfill the rule agreed upon in 1948, a firemen in the cab with every engineer on every train. The Southern hired about one hundred new firemen to meet the obligations of the federal decision. To make the point that firemen were unnecessary, the Southern stated, "Since Firemen have no duties at all to perform, no skills, training, physical standards or education are required. In the circumstances it seemed reasonable to employ unskilled elderly people who are having a hard time finding jobs."[29] Capitalizing on the racial tension in the early 1960s in the south, the Southern hired aged African-American men with no prior railroad experience. It was a brilliant public relations move for several reasons. It exposed to the public that there really was no need for firemen on diesel locomotives and also exposed the racism of the BLF&E which prohibited African-Americans from becoming members.[30] While drawing renewed attention to the issue, the fate of the fireman was thrust back into the courts for years to come.

Firemen were gradually eliminated from the cabs of diesel locomotives beginning in the 1960s and continuing into the 1970s and 1980s. Many were eliminated through attrition, a method that railroads and labor both found agreeable. There was no national agreement in the late 1960s and early 1970s but individual railroads were often successful in negotiations with the unions on the firemen issue. A national agreement in 1978 allowed railroads to go to three man crews via attrition, with the elimination of not only the fireman but also one of the two trainmen or brakemen. The details would be worked out on the local level. Crews were further trimmed in 1991 with a national agreement to reduce crews to only the engineer and conductor for most through freight and passenger trains.[31] Gone was the caboose, the office of the conductor and brakemen. On freight runs the conductor now rides in the locomotive cab, taking the place of the fireman while many passenger trains are operated solely by an engineer as the conductor is busy with ticket taking and other duties in the passenger coaches. It may have taken almost fifty years but the fireman's place finally vanished, just like the steam locomotives that initially gave life to his occupation.

The fireman, due almost entirely to the strength of the BLF&E and the other railroad unions, outlived his reason for being for a generation. As late as 1980 there were still firemen in the cabs of diesel locomotives on roads where steam had been gone for over twenty-five years. The

statistics tell the tale. In 1952 there were 255,009 employees in train and engine work including engineers, firemen, brakeman, and conductors. By 1960 this had fallen
to 199,522. Most of this decrease was not due to new work
rules but do to train consolidation and other reasons. The
crew of a train in 1960 was composed of the same jobs as
in 1952 or 1938. From 1960 to 1970 the number of train
and engine employees continued to fall to 164,697. Much
of this was due to further consolidation and reduction in
trains but some was due to the reduction in the number
of crew members. By 1980 there were 135,741 in train and
engine service. With deregulation in 1980 and the other
decisions detailed above, the number of train service
employees continued to drop. By 1984 there were 95,873
train service employees with the fireman all but gone.[32]

While the firemen were waging a battle to preserve
their place on board diesel locomotives, other railroad
employees faced similar and perhaps even greater challenges. As previously mentioned, steam locomotives were
labor intensive machines. They required regular, daily
care, and periodic light and heavy maintenance. All but
the smallest shortlines had extensive maintenance and
shop facilities to maintain the fleet of steam locomotives.
These facilities were divided into two basic types. The
first were the maintenance facilities needed for daily
and other basic regular servicing and maintenance. Anywhere from less than ten to hundreds of workers would
be employed at these facilities depending on the size. The
other type of facility were the large heavy maintenance
facilities or the railroad shops. Typical railroad shops
would employ hundreds of workers. The largest facilities,
such as the Pennsylvania Railroad's gargantuan shop complex at Altoona, Pennsylvania employed many thousands.
With the introduction of diesel locomotives, many of these
workers, from hostlers and engine wipers at basic service
facilities to pipefitters, foundrymen, and the like at the
large heavy shops, found their skills no longer needed.

The steam railroad system had substantial service
facilities for daily and periodic maintenance at regularly
spaced intervals. The daily service a steam locomotive
needed would include fuel, water, sand, and extensive
manual lubrication of rods, bearings and other moving
parts. The basic daily maintenance included emptying
ashes, washing town boilers and tanks and performing any
minor maintenance. Locomotives also needed to be kept

hot with small fires so that they would be fully steamed up and ready to go when next called on for duty. Even when just sitting a locomotive needed attention. Most sizable cities with yards and industries served by railroads had engine houses, coal, water and sand towers, and other servicing facilities to perform the above work. Service facilities were also located roughly every one hundred miles on mainlines to serve through freight and passenger trains. Water and coal towers were located even more closely together with water towers as close together as tens of miles, depending on conditions. These city or mainline service facilities would generally consist of a roundhouse or other engine house to house locomotives during basic daily and periodic maintenance. This included tending fires, cleaning, lubrication and small repairs and adjustments. At selected facilities, roughly every two hundred to three hundred miles, more extensive repairs would be performed such as replacing boiler tubes and steel locomotive tires. The roundhouse would be paired with a turntable to turn locomotives along with coal, water and sand towers for replenishing these respective supplies. These facilities did not have the tools necessary for heavy overhauls of steam locomotives. In automotive terms, these roundhouses would be like tire and lube businesses where general maintenance tasks like oil changes are performed and new tires, batteries and the like are installed. The average roundhouse in a railroad division point or major city would employ from several dozen to a couple hundred people in various jobs from skilled pipefitters and boilermakers to general laborers to clerks.

Most railroads also had one or more large shops where heavy overhauls and even building of locomotives was performed. Small railroads would likely have one such shop installation while larger ones would have several at locations around the system. These larger shops would not only have the roundhouses and coal towers of the standard maintenance facility but would have extensive back shops or erecting houses often with large overhead cranes for lifting boilers and other heavy locomotive parts. Many times a foundry, machine shop, blacksmith shop, paint shop, power house, and other buildings would be located at the large shop complexes. Almost all the large shops could perform heavy repairs to locomotive boilers and running gear while the largest of these shop complexes could manufacture new steam locomotives from scratch. In automotive terms these large shops would not only be equivalent to the full

Photo 25 Steam locomotive servicing and maintenance facilities were large. This aerial photo of Cheyenne, Wyoming in the early 1950s illustrates what a typical major steam terminal would contain. Easily visible at the center is the roundhouse where daily and routine servicing would be done. Directly in front of the round house are large coaling and water towers. Behind the roundhouse are rectangular buildings. These are the backshops where more extensive maintenance was carried out. Courtesy of the Union Pacific Museum.

service auto repair shop where engine overhauls can be performed but also to the most fully equipped machine shop and foundry where new and replacement components can be cast, milled, and constructed by skilled workers. In 1914 there were 1,362 railroad shops listed in the US Census of Manufacturers with an average employment of 249.3. Most shops employed less than 250 but there were sixty-two shops that employed over 1,000 workers.[33] While some of these were car shops that built and maintained freight and passenger cars, the majority were likely locomotive shops. While some consolidation did occur due to more efficient and powerful steam locomotives in the 1920s and poor business conditions in the 1930s, the characteristics of steam locomotive repair and maintenance did not change.

The new diesels were mass produced machines that did not need the continual and custom care that steam locomotives required. The daily maintenance required on a steam locomotive simply was not necessary for diesels. No emptying of ashes, banking of the fire, cleaning out cinders, or manual lubrication of rods and bearings was needed. All that was really needed on a daily basis was fueling. The periodic servicing was greatly reduced. Diesels were mass produced and new replacement parts were available from the manufacturers. The extensive foundry and machine shop of the steam era were no longer needed. Diesels did require oil changes and parts replacement but did not require parts manufacture like the steam locomotives. With the end of this maintenance came the end of many jobs around the roundhouse and heavy shops. Since diesels did not need to stop as often for enroute maintenance and fuel and required no water those facilities were eliminated and the jobs that went with them. Diesels could easily run for hundreds or thousands of miles before even basic maintenance was required. The necessity of a locomotive service center every one hundred miles evaporated with the coming of the diesel.

These local roundhouses and servicing facilities were among the first to feel the impact of the diesel. The hundreds of jobs in a division point roundhouse were reduced to twenty to thirty and then to zero as the service point was abandoned altogether. The examples are numerous and stretch across the railroad system. Crestline, Ohio, a major locomotive service center on the PRR mainline between Pittsburgh and Chicago, saw its employment reduced by 90 percent before it was closed completely in

1968. From a labor force of at least 250 men in 1945 there were only about 30 by the dieselization of the PRR in the late 1950s.[34] Bellefontaine, Ohio suffered a similar fate as Crestline. Bellefontaine was at the crossing of two major New York Central lines, one from Cleveland to St. Louis and the other from Cincinnati to Toledo and Detroit. In 1945 with steam power the 36 stall roundhouse supported a work force of roughly 500 men. By 1963 and full dieselization this was reduced to only 28. Most locomotives no longer stopped in Bellefontaine at all but ran through to the large terminal cities.[35] Hundreds of other locations experienced similar declines. While the roundhouses built for steam may have been used for housing diesels for a time the many workers that tended to the steam locomotives were no longer there. Once vibrant and dynamic industrial locations were turned into near ghost towns by the diesel.

The impact of the diesel on the large shop complexes was more complicated. Most railroads had large heavy shops that could literally tear a locomotive down to the wheels and rebuild it. These facilities did not immediately become obsolete with the introduction of the diesel. Many railroads adapted these large shops to perform heavy diesel repair work. While extensive numbers of boilermakers, pipefitters and machinists were no longer needed, new jobs were opened up for electricians to service the extensive electrical gear on diesel electric locomotives. The large steam erecting shops with heavy duty overhead cranes could be used to lift diesel engines out of locomotives for extensive overhaul. Several railroads adapted their heavy steam shops to diesel work. For example, the Illinois Central Paducah, Kentucky, shops, famous for rebuilding steam locomotives in the 1930s and 1940s, retooled and performed major overhauls and upgrades on diesel locomotives in the 1960s and 1970s. The former Pennsylvania Railroad shops in Altoona also retooled to perform heavy diesel work. These shops even assembled new diesel locomotives from parts shipped in from the manufacturer. While some large shop complexes did transition from steam to diesel locomotive heavy repair, much less work was performed on diesels. The number of large shops that were fully equipped to handle heavy overhaul of diesels was a few dozen at the most. Many smaller railroads did not invest in the new equipment necessary for heavy overhaul of locomotives and instead sent the

Photo 26   While diesels did require servicing and maintenance, they did not require the labor intensive daily care that steam locomotives did. Smaller diesel terminals would look like this example from the Gulf Mobile & Ohio in South Joliet, Illinois in the early 1970s. The large vertical cylinder is for sand while fuel is stored in the horizontal tank on the right. Photo by Robert F. Schramm.

locomotives back to the manufacturer for heavy overhaul and remanufacturing.

While diesels did eliminate many jobs, they created new ones as well. Fixing diesels required workers with substantial electrical knowledge, an area in which most railroads lacked experience. However, a few electricians did not offset the hundreds of boilermakers, pipefitters, and other workers that lost their jobs due to dieselization. The number of workers engaged in maintenance of equipment and stores dropped from 345,531 in 1952 to 184,006 in 1960. In less than ten years the number of shop workers was cut almost in half, almost wholly due to the diesel. Further reductions followed in the 1960s and 1970s. In 1970 there were 123,546 workers in railroad shops while by 1980 the total had fallen to just 99,614.[36] The percentage of the total number of railroad workers represented by shop workers also fell from over 28 percent in 1952 to 23.5 percent in 1960 to 22 percent in 1970. The results are even more dramatic when one remembers that a substantial part of the total shop employment was in car shops that built and repaired freight and passenger cars. These car shop jobs, while in decline along with the general railroad industry in the 1950s, were not adversely effected by dieselization. The diesel, contrary to what may be first assumed, did not immediately cause the elimination of the fireman but did cause the elimination of most of the jobs in locomotive servicing and maintenance.

Overall railroad employment also suffered with the introduction of the diesel. (See table 6 in appendix) In 1928, US class I railroads employed over 1.6 million workers. In 1946 this number had fallen to about 1.3 million. However, by 1960 when complete dieselization was achieved, the number of railroad workers was about 780,000 or slightly more than 57 percent of the number in 1946.[37] Not all of this was directly diesel related. As railroads abandoned branches and closed stations many jobs were eliminated that were not directly diesel related. As passenger trains were discontinued the jobs of the crew as well as ticket agents and the passenger traffic staff were in jeopardy. Maintenance of way forces were also extensively mechanized during the postwar period and many track worker positions were eradicated. The fact that diesels were easier on track and weighed less than steam did lead to less wear and damage to track and bridges did lead to a small diesel related reduction in these forces. Estimates are that approximately 40 percent of the total job losses from 1945 to 1960 were diesel related.[38]

If shop workers were losing their jobs due to dieselization, what was the effect upon the communities where these shops were located? Again the results were complex but generally negative. Most every town of any size that had rail service had a roundhouse to perform daily and other light maintenance on steam locomotives. Larger heavy shops would be located at division points with some railroads centralizing all heavy work at one or two facilities.[39] The small roundhouses in outlying communities and at one hundred mile intervals were among the first to go. With diesels all that was needed was a fuel and sand station and perhaps a shed to keep the locomotives out of the weather. Daily maintenance was practically nonexistent. If a locomotive required further care, such as replacing a cracked cylinder, it could be sent to a regional shop. One such small division point with a roundhouse was the community of Newburg, Missouri, halfway between St. Louis and Springfield on the main line of the St. Louis–San Francisco railroad. Newburg was created as a railroad town. There were no other large industries in or near the community and the Ozarks were not a heavy agricultural area, although logging and some cattle ranching did occur. The majority of the working population of Newburg was employed by the railroad or in services dependent on the railroad. As the Frisco dieselized, trains were able to run from St. Louis to Springfield directly without stopping. Stopping at Newburg was no longer required to service the locomotives. Since the town was a division point, stops were still made to exchange crews. The roundhouse was closed after dieselization and eventually torn down. Other rail facilities in the town were also closed. The town itself suffered greatly because of the loss of railroad jobs. The population of Newburg declined from 1,056 in 1940 to 949 in 1950 to 884 in 1960, an overall decrease of over 16 percent in twenty years.[40] Other communities had declines even greater than Newburg. From 1950 to 1960 Brunswick, Maryland, location of a roundhouse and other facilities on the Baltimore & Ohio main line west from Washington DC, declined from 3,752 to 2,352 or a decline of over 37 percent. Again, the vast majority of workers in Brunswick were employed in the B&O facilities. The Ohio communities of Crestline and Bellfontaine examined earlier did better than most other railroad dependent communities.

Both experienced small increases in population from 1950 to 1960, the bulk of the dieselizaiton period on the New York Central and Pennsylvania Railroads respectively. The increase was 5 percent for Bellfontaine and 14 percent for Crestline. However, part of this increase was due to annexation of additional housing to the cities.

The regional shops also suffered with the introduction of the diesel. No longer were extensive shop facilities with blacksmith and foundry installations needed for each division. Many were closed or phased out while maintenance was consolidated at other facilities. Examples abound. The Southern Railway system is an example. Its extensive shops in Spencer, North Carolina were closed in the early 1950s shortly after dieselization and all heavy diesel repair work was shifted to specially constructed diesel repair shops in Chattanooga, Tennessee. As would be expected, the population in the town of Spencer fell from 3,242 in 1950 to 2,904 in 1960, a decline of over 10 percent. The neighboring larger community of Salisbury experienced a slight population growth of 1 percent with an increase from 20,102 to 20,324 during the same period. Even shops where diesel work supplanted steam suffered decreases in employment as diesels simply were not as labor intensive. Cleburne, Texas, about thirty miles south of Ft. Worth, was the site of major shops for the Texas lines of the Santa Fe. With dieselization many smaller roundhouses and engine facilities were abandoned and the railroad consolidated heavy diesel repair work at the shops in Cleburne. This huge complex was among the very few railroad owned shops to perform substantial upgrading and rebuilding of diesel locomotives. While the shops were still in use, they simply needed fewer people to perform the work on the diesels. The population of the town of Cleburne fell almost 5 percent from 1950 to 1960 from 12,905 to 12,289. The Santa Fe shops at Cleburne would remain one of the three large system shops along with Topeka, Kansas and San Bernardino, California until further consolidation closed the shops in 1989.[41] The massive Altoona shops complex, while still performing heavy repair work on the thousands of diesel locomotives of the Pennsylvania railroad, needed far less workers. The population of Altoona declined from 86,614 in 1950 to 83,058 in 1960 or 4.1 percent as a result.[42]

The effects on the surrounding community could be dramatic. While a city like Chicago or Buffalo could absorb the closing of a railroad shop and the unemployment of

its few dozen to few hundred workers with minimal dis-
ruption, smaller cities were in many cases company towns
where the railroad employed most of the workers and
was the dominant economic engine of the community. In
places like Altoona, Pennsylvania, the railroad was such
a large employer and had such substantial facilities that
it was politically impossible, at least in the 1950s, to simply leave. The Altoona shops retooled and cut workers,
but did not completely eliminate the workforce as would
happen down the line in Crestline, Ohio. Other large
shops such as the Illinois Central shops in Paducah were
similar. Smaller communities were not as fortunate. An
example of such a community was Caliente, Nevada. This
division point on the Union Pacific line from Salt Lake
City to Southern California is examined in a short article
from the June 1951, *American Sociological Review.* Caliente was in many ways an ideal choice for a study. The
town existed, "to serve the steam locomotive. So long as
the steam locomotive was in use, Caliente was a necessity.
With the adoption of the diesel it became obsolescent."[43]
The author, W. F. Cotrell goes on to detail how shop forces
as well as train and engine employees both lost due to
the introduction of the diesel. The greatest losses were
among the senior nonoperating or shop forces, such as
boilermakers.[44] However, the losses were by no means
confined to the railroad employees. Local merchants, the
local churches, and homeowners all paid. Those with little stake in the community and most willing to relocate
paid the least while those most involved, financially and
socially, in the community paid the most.[45] The population of Lincoln County, Nevada, of which Caliente was the
only incorporated place, fell from 4,130 in 1940 to 2,431 in
1960.[46] The Caliente experience was repeated nationwide
in hundreds of railroad division points some of which
have almost ceased to exist as communities.[47]

The impact of the diesel on railroad labor and on the
communities track side was large and complex. Locomotive firemen were able, through strong union agitation
and federal and judicial involvement to keep their jobs
on diesel locomotives, although in ever decreasing numbers. Railroad roundhouse and shop workers were less
fortunate. As their jobs became unnecessary with the
introduction of the diesel hundreds of small roundhouses
and other local servicing facilities were closed. Tens of
thousands of workers from skilled machinists to unskilled

labors were out of work. Some larger shops retooled to perform diesel work but the new hires of electricians in no way made up for the loss of machinists, pipefitters, blacksmiths and other workers. As jobs were eliminated in roundhouses and shops nationwide many communities suffered. Small towns that had been built around local railroad shops were the most affected, in some cases losing most of their residents and becoming little more than ghost towns.

The saga of the locomotive fireman as well as that of Newburg, Missouri and Caliente, Nevada, serve to remind us that all technological and business decisions have repercussions. These repercussions may be positive or negative and may, like ripples on a pond, extend far from the initial disturbance. It also illustrates how the adoption of the diesel locomotive had consequences far removed from tonnage ratings and revenue statements. Diesels and their uses were shaped by much more than technical concerns over horsepower or tractive effort. Likewise pure economic analysis does not fully describe the dieselization of American railroads and the many impacts it wrought, both in the boardrooms and in the roundhouses.

7

Red Markers and Conclusions

STEAM LOCOMOTIVES AND RAILROADS WERE INSEPARABLE. THE entire railroad system from the earliest days was built around the peculiar requirements of the steam locomotive. These requirements; fuel, water, sand, and daily maintenance, determined what the railroad network would look like and what employees would do. After the American rail network reached relative completion in the early decades of the twentieth century, railroads found that they had to refocus their efforts. In a heavily regulated environment where organized labor was also a major player, railroads were greatly limited in ways to increase their revenue or control costs. Rate increases for passengers or freight had to be approved by the ICC, and any labor concessions would have been hard fought. With the 1920 Transportation Act and the 1926 Railway Labor Act the federal government was now a major player in the railroad business. These developments left controlling costs in the transportation area as one of the few alternatives open to railroad management. Expansion into new markets was no longer the goal. More efficient and cost effective transportation in existing markets became essential. To achieve greater efficiency in moving trains, and therefore to control costs, railroads began to demand larger and more powerful steam locomotives. These new steam locomotives achieved gains in efficiency and started the railroads on a continuing quest for ever greater efficiency and cost effectiveness.

The Great Depression severely curtailed railroad revenue and made cutting costs of operation and maximization of revenue even more important. While World War II brought huge amounts of traffic, and revenue to railroads, it also brought greatly increased costs, especially in the immediate postwar period. To control these rapidly escalating costs and to effect greater operating efficiencies many railroads turned to the diesel, proven by war, for their motive power. While the diesel did save money for the railroads in the 1950s, the continual erosion of traffic to highway competition, the heavy handed regulatory environment and the gradual shift away from heavy manufacturing all combined to cause more difficulties for railroads.

By reading the above one would conclude that diesels were simply a natural progression of the search for ever greater efficiencies in moving freight and passengers. However, as the preceding chapters illustrate, this was not the case. While cost of operation may have been the primary reason for dieselization on many roads, it was far from the only one. There were many other motives in dieselization than simply economic ones. The initial spark for dieselization came not from economic motivation at all but from government regulation. The antismoke crusades of the 1920s and before in many major cities, but especially in New York, forced the railroads to look to less visibly polluting forms of motive power such as the diesel. Once some railroads purchased diesels for these smoke abatement reasons they discovered that the diesels could actually save them money and operate more efficiently than existing steam powered switchers. Despite this knowledge, railroads as a whole did not engage in wholesale dieselization of switching tasks in the 1920s and 1930s.

Another lesson that we can take away from this study is that no railroad or industry is immune from larger historical forces, in this case the Great Depression and World War II. The Depression hit railroads hard and virtually eliminated locomotive purchases for a time. Traffic that had seemed so plentiful a few years before was nowhere to be found. In a bid to recapture some of this lost passenger traffic, some railroads in cooperation with EMC and a few other builders inaugurated the streamliner era. The Zephyr and others like it did bring passengers back to the rails, for a time, and also saved the railroads money over comparable steam powered passenger trains. These pioneering streamliners also acquainted some railroads with the capabilities of diesel power more generally. As the economy slowly improved in the mid 1930s, some railroads invested more heavily in diesel streamliners while others discovered that modern steam at the head of a streamlined train could bring in similar increases in traffic without the high first cost and experimental nature of the diesels. After the "Roosevelt Recession" of 1937–38 and with increasing defense related traffic, some railroads embarked on modernization programs for their steam locomotive fleet. Massive 4-8-4, 4-6-6-4, 2-10-4, and other types began to be seen on the rails much more frequently. They were soon joined by the behemoths of steam, the 4–8–8–4 and 2–6–6–6 types. While these were extremely powerful and efficient locomotives, they were rapidly approaching physical size and weight limitations.

As war clouds were gathering on the eastern and western horizons another fateful event was happening, the introduction of the EMC FT, the first real main line diesel freight locomotive. The FT went on to prove itself during wartime by hauling huge amounts of traffic under demanding conditions on many railroads but most notably on the Santa Fe. At the war's end with diesels now proven in heavy freight service as well as passenger and switching service, it would seem it was only a matter of time before the diesel sent the steam locomotive off to the scrapyard. For some roads this was the case. With steam locomotives that dated from the 1920s or before and suffering the effects of deferred maintenance, many roads found it easy to embrace the diesel. Beginning in 1947 and continuing for a decade diesels by the thousands were manufactured by several builders and joined the rosters of hundreds of railroads from huge systems like the Santa Fe to small shortlines and terminal roads. By 1960 the steam locomotive was no longer found on the rails of the major railroads of the United States.

However, again the story was complicated. Many railroads had vested interests in keeping steam alive and in service. For some railroads like the Union Pacific the reason was a corporate culture that prided itself on steam locomotive design and operation. For others like the Norfolk and Western it was an allegiance to the coal industry, a major shipper. For others still like the Nickel Plate it simply did not make economic sense to replace locomotives built in the late 1930s and 1940s with new diesels when the steam locomotives were in many cases less than ten years old and perfectly capable of performing their jobs efficiently and relatively cost effectively. In many cases individual railroad presidents dictated motive power policy and either advanced or retarded the adoption of the diesel by years.

The coal industry, a major reason for the delay in the adoption of the diesel by some railroads, was not as severely impacted by the diesel as some feared. At the beginning of dieselization national coal output was roughly split three ways between use in electrical generating plants, transportation, commercial and residential use, and industrial use such as coke works and steel plants. As coal use declined in the residential and transportation areas, it greatly increased in the electric power generation area. In 1949 70.2 million tons of coal were consumed in transportation use, including railroads and steamships. By 1960 this was down to 3 million tons. In the same period coal consumption by electric power plants jumped from 84 million tons to 176.7 million tons, more than offsetting the decrease in coal consumption by transportation companies. Total coal production, while lower than during the war years, remained relatively stable in the 1950s. In 1943 590.2 million tons were produced. This fell to 457.3 million tons by 1953 and remained about the same, 458.9 million tons in 1963.[1]

Even after complete dieselization was achieved, some railroads continued to operate in a steam-era mindset. The capabilities of the diesel were not fully realized. Diesels could travel the length of the system without being refueled and had no need for extensive coaling and watering facilities. They could therefore move traffic faster than the steam locomotives. The speed and lack of enroute servicing of the diesels was a greater advantage the further they traveled. However, most diesels initially were not operated this way but were merely substituted for steam locomotives in shorter runs. The physical layout of the railroad remained stuck in the steam era.

Admittedly, to restructure completely the railroad system to take advantage of all the aspects of the diesel would have taken great effort and time and would have made contentious relations with organized labor even worse, but in many cases management and the operating employees did not even attempt to utilize the full potential of the new locomotives. Small operational changes such as helper service and some consolidation of trains occurred, but conservative management and operations staff did not transform the railroad system into a true diesel age network. In some ways the railroads are still stuck in a steam mentality with many crew districts based on the historical steam districts of sixty years ago. Engineers and conductors are still generally paid, not by the hour or a set salary, but by the trip, again a hold over from the early days of the century.

One major goal of this study has been to show the diversity inherent in the American railroad industry during the time of dieselization. Hundreds of companies ranging in size from the immense Pennsylvania and Santa Fe railroads to regional roads such as the Lehigh Valley and Gulf Mobile & Ohio were joined by terminal roads and shortlines in making up the railroad system. To discount these differences in size, location, or corporate structure reveals but a superficial understanding of the whole. Each road approached the challenges of increasing costs and reduced revenue differently. Some chose to dieselize as fast as possible. Others chose to slowly introduce the diesel and keep steam on in certain jobs while others still resisted the diesel until management change or red ink on the bottom line forced them to consider diesel motive power.

That said there are generalizations and conclusions that can be drawn. Railroads were reluctant to fully embrace diesel power until someone else had proven its capabilities. This reluctant, "look before you leap" style of management is typical of large organizations experiencing exceptional technological change. Often times an outside influence, generally government, must provide the initial spark to encourage the conservative managements to take the initial risk and embrace the new technology, especially when they were unfamiliar with it and had in many cases literally grown up with its predecessor. Many other students of technological change in large organizations, from Thomas Hughes to Steve Usselman to Al Churella come to similar conclusions.

Dieselization was not a forgone conclusion or an inevitable event. There were alternatives available that would have fit the bill technically. This refutes the technological determinism argument that diesels won out because they were the superior technology. They may have been superior to steam power in most technical instances, but there were other alternatives that were also serious contenders. The reason the alternatives were not adopted had less to do with technological failures than with political and sociocultural reasons. Electrification was, and is, a "better" alternative than diesels for many reasons, including operating cost and performance issues, but was not chosen in the United States due primarily to its high initial capital cost, a cost so high that only governments could bear it. Steam and gas turbines were also tried and could have been a real alternative to the diesel had the will to develop them further been evident.[2]

Technological innovation does not occur in a vacuum. Diesels were not designed and built solely on a technical basis but reflect the social and cultural milieu of the time.

As such diesels were a symbol of modernity. Bright stainless steel or aluminum streamliners rocketing across the plains or brightly painted and streamlined freight locomotives stood as a symbol of the bright future that technology could bring to a nation suffering the ravages of first Depression and then global war. It also showed that the railroad, a technology steeped in American history and mythology and familiar to everyone, could be a modern and progressive force in society as it had been during the great days of westward expansion.

Just as the railroads of the 1880s and 1890s spelled the end of the bison and the plains Indian, the diesel would also spell the end of the way of life for many workers whose raison d'etre was the steam locomotive. With no fire to tend, the role of the fireman was in doubt. That firemen remained in cabs of diesel locomotives for another thirty to forty years is a testament to the power of organized labor. Many shop forces and the towns where those shops were located were less lucky than the firemen. Hundreds, if not thousands, of locomotive servicing facilities in towns from Maine to California were rendered obsolete by the diesel. Many towns lost their largest employer and tax payer in the process. This reminds us that all technological change has impacts, positive and negative, on workers, communities, and society at large.

At the heart of this study is a story. The story had many actors and stretched over almost forty years. The story began in the glory days of the 1920s with a few awkward looking experimental units, and progressed through the hard times of the Depression when flashy streamliners entered the picture. With the challenges of global war new characters entered the narrative, freight units. With the war won and America as the new global power, although not without rivals, the diesel emerged as the new face of railroading, although it too had its own rivals.

Appendix

Table 1   US Railroads in 1920; All classes (I, II, and III)

Mileage Operated	252,845 miles
Locomotives Owned (note 1)	68,942
Average Tractive Effort	36,365 pounds per locomotive
Freight Cars Owned	2,388,424 cars
Passenger Cars Owned	56,102 cars
Revenue Tons Originated	1,362,999,000 tons
Revenue Ton Miles	413,698,749,000 ton-miles
Freight Revenue	$4,420,833,000
Freight Revenue per Ton-Mile	1.069 cents
Passengers Carried	1,269,913,000 passengers
Passenger Revenue	$1,304,815,000
Revenue per Passenger Mile	2.755 cents
Number of Employees	2,076,000
Total Employee Compensation	$3,754,281,000
Total Operating Revenue	$6,310,151,000
Total Operating Expenses	$5,954,394,000
Net Operating Income	$12,101,000

The vast majority of these locomotives were steam. A small number, less than 1 percent were electric or gasoline. There were no diesels.

From 1920 to 1955, class I railroads had annual operating revenue of $1 million or more. The ICC changed this to $3 million in 1956. From 1920 to 1956, class II railroads were designated as having revenues from $100,000 to $1 million with class III railroads having revenues below $100,000. Class I railroads operated over 90 percent of all trackage and earned well over 90 percent of all revenue during the period under study.

Table 2	Total Operating Revenue, Expenses,
and Net Operating Revenue

All US railroads (Classes I, II, and III), 1920–1946 Class I railroads, 1947–1960.			
Year	Total Operating Revenue	Total Operating Expenses	Net Operating Revenue
1920	$6,310,151,000.00	$5,954,394,000.00	$355,757,000.00
1921	$5,632,665,000.00	$4,668,998,000.00	$963,667,000.00
1922	$5,674,483,000.00	$4,509,991,000.00	$1,164,492,000.00
1923	$6,419,210,000.00	$4,999,383,000.00	$1,419,827,000.00
1924	$6,045,252,000.00	$4,608,807,000.00	$1,436,445,000.00
1925	$6,246,884,000.00	$4,633,497,000.00	$1,613,387,000.00
1926	$6,508,679,000.00	$4,766,235,000.00	$1,742,444,000.00
1927	$6,245,716,000.00	$4,662,521,000.00	$1,583,195,000.00
1928	$6,212,464,000.00	$4,508,606,000.00	$1,703,858,000.00
1929	$6,373,004,000.00	$4,579,162,000.00	$1,793,842,000.00
1930	$5,356,484,000.00	$3,993,621,000.00	$1,362,863,000.00
1931	$4,246,385,000.00	$3,273,906,000.00	$972,479,000.00
1932	$3,168,537,000.00	$2,441,814,000.00	$726,723,000.00
1933	$3,138,186,000.00	$2,285,218,000.00	$852,968,000.00
1934	$3,316,861,000.00	$2,479,997,000.00	$836,864,000.00
1935	$3,499,126,000.00	$2,630,177,000.00	$868,949,000.00
1936	$4,108,658,000.00	$2,973,366,000.00	$1,135,292,000.00
1937	$4,226,325,000.00	$3,165,154,000.00	$1,061,171,000.00
1938	$3,616,072,000.00	$2,762,681,000.00	$853,391,000.00
1939	$4,050,047,000.00	$2,959,438,000.00	$1,090,609,000.00
1940	$4,354,712,000.00	$3,131,598,000.00	$1,223,114,000.00
1941	$5,413,972,000.00	$3,709,921,000.00	$1,704,051,000.00
1942	$7,547,826,000.00	$4,653,705,000.00	$2,894,121,000.00
1943	$9,138,419,000.00	$5,714,804,000.00	$3,423,615,000.00
1944	$9,524,628,000.00	$6,345,035,000.00	$3,179,593,000.00
1945	$8,986,954,000.00	$7,115,391,000.00	$1,871,563,000.00

(continued)

Table 2   (continued)

Year	Total Operating Revenue	Total Operating Expenses	Net Operating Revenue
1946	$7,627,650,517.00	$6,357,415,175.00	$1,270,235,342.00
1947	$8,684,918,252.00	$6,797,264,686.00	$1,887,653,566.00
1948	$9,671,721,893.00	$7,472,035,344.00	$2,199,686,549.00
1949	$8,580,142,406.00	$6,891,819,289.00	$1,688,323,117.00
1950	$9,473,093,146.00	$7,059,276,243.00	$2,413,816,903.00
1951	$10,390,610,786.00	$8,041,277,137.00	$2,349,333,649.00
1952	$10,580,762,001.00	$8,052,518,337.00	$2,528,243,664.00
1953	$10,664,168,861.00	$8,135,228,716.00	$2,528,940,145.00
1954	$9,370,825,506.00	$7,384,499,431.00	$1,986,326,075.00
1955	$10,106,329,593.00	$7,646,418,260.00	$2,459,911,333.00
1956	$10,550,942,886.00	$8,108,352,851.00	$2,442,590,035.00
1957	$10,491,389,960.00	$8,227,521,638.00	$2,263,868,322.00
1958	$9,564,568,052.00	$7,543,842,172.00	$2,020,725,880.00
1959	$9,825,060,205.00	$7,704,815,314.00	$2,120,244,891.00
1960	$9,514,294,063.00	$7,565,335,771.00	$1,948,958,292.00

Results before and after 1947 are not directly comparable. The 1920–46 results are for all railroads while 1947–60 are for class I railroads only. However, class I railroads operated approximately 95 percent of all trackage and earned about 98 percent of all operating revenues.

Data from *Statistics of Railroads of Class I in the United States*, AAR, various years. *Railroads in this Century*, AAR, 1947.

Table 3　New Locomotive Additions
US Class I Railroads

Year	Steam	Diesel	Electric
1920	1017	note 1	
1921	1330		
1922	1226		
1923	4360		
1924	2786		
1925	1600		
1926	1882		
1927	1542		
1928	1017		
1929	1229		
1930	728	56	21
1931	126	4	52
1932	40	4	54
1933	1	10	11
1934	61	9	13
1935	37	16	88
1936	70	30	0
1937	357	75	5
1938	148	107	16
1939	76	203	17
1940	120	280	20
1941	157	469	6
1942	276	412	28
1943	438	438	15
1944	326	918	1
1945	115	760	2
1946	86	624	5
1947	69	1328	0
1948	86	2254	8
1949	57	2827	0

(continued)

Table 3   (continued)

Year	Steam	Diesel	Electric
1950	12	3191	12
1951	18	3490	6
1952	19	3035	2
1953	15	2122	0
1954	0	1110	0
1955	0	1070	26
1956	0	1198	12
1957	0	1011	4
1958	0	342	0
1959	0	848	0
1960	0	376	1

The 1920–29 Steam locomotive figures are total for all locomotives. The records did not make a distinction in locomotive type. The vast majority (90 percent or more) are steam locomotives.

Table 4   US Railroads in 1947
Class I

Mileage Operated	227,927 miles
Locomotives Owned (note 1)	41,719
Average Tractive Effort	Steam: 54,506 pounds Diesel: 56,524 pounds Electric: 58,816 pounds
Freight Cars Owned	1,758,144 cars
Passenger Cars Owned	38,770 cars
Revenue Tons Originated	1,537,545,786 tons
Revenue Ton Miles	654,728,304,000 ton-miles
Freight Revenue	$7,041,184,941
Freight Revenue per Ton-Mile	93 cents
Passengers Carried	703,279,582 passengers
Passenger Revenue	$963,322,178
Revenue per Passenger Mile	2.10 cents
Number of Employees	1,326,906
Total Employee Compensation	$4,350,229,295
Total Operating Revenue	$8,684,918,252
Total Operating Expenses	$6,797,264,686
Net Operating Income	$780,694,270

There are 35,108 steam locomotives or 84.15 percent, 5,772 diesel or 13.84 percent, 821 electric or 1.97 percent and 18 other.

Table 5 Railroad Employees and Compensation
All US Railroads (Class I, II, and III), 1920–45
Class I Railroads, 1946–60

Year	Number of Employees	Total Compensation	Average Yearly Compensation per Employee
1920	2,076,000	$3,754,281,000.00	$1,808.00
1921	1,705,000	$2,823,970,000.00	$1,656.00
1922	1,670,000	$2,693,292,000.00	$1,613.00
1923	1,902,000	$3,062,026,000.00	$1,610.00
1924	1,795,000	$2,882,658,000.00	$1,606.00
1925	1,786,000	$2,916,193,000.00	$1,633.00
1926	1,822,000	$3,001,804,000.00	$1,648.00
1927	1,776,000	$2,963,034,000.00	$1,668.00
1928	1,692,000	$2,874,429,000.00	$1,699.00
1929	1,694,000	$2,940,206,000.00	$1,736.00
1930	1,517,000	$2,588,598,000.00	$1,706.00
1931	1,283,000	$2,124,784,000.00	$1,656.00
1932	1,052,000	$1,535,066,000.00	$1,459.00
1933	991,000	$1,424,392,000.00	$1,437.00
1934	1,027,000	$1,541,313,000.00	$1,501.00
1935	1,014,000	$1,666,229,000.00	$1,643.00
1936	1,086,000	$1,873,819,000.00	$1,725.00
1937	1,137,000	$2,013,677,000.00	$1,771.00
1938	958,000	$1,771,083,000.00	$1,849.00
1939	1,007,000	$1,889,130,000.00	$1,876.00
1940	1,046,000	$1,990,631,000.00	$1,903.00
1941	1,159,000	$2,360,369,000.00	$2,037.00
1942	1,291,000	$2,966,062,000.00	$2,297.00
1943	1,375,000	$3,556,189,000.00	$2,586.00
1944	1,434,000	$3,897,755,000.00	$2,718.00
1945	1,439,000	$3,900,928,000.00	$2,711.00

(continued)

Table 5   (continued)

Year	Number of Employees	Total Compensation	Average Yearly Compensation per Employee
1946	1,358,838	$4,107,163,790.00	$3,069.00
1947	1,351,961	$4,350,229,295.00	$3,218.00
1948	1,326,906	$4,768,827,602.00	$3,594.00
1949	1,191,444	$4,419,433,316.00	$3,709.00
1950	1,220,784	$4,620,518,211.00	$3,785.00
1951	1,276,000	$5,336,197,599.00	$4,182.00
1952	1,226,663	$5,338,175,195.00	$4,352.00
1953	1,206,312	$5,326,316,057.00	$4,415.00
1954	1,064,705	$4,855,099,734.00	$4,560.00
1955	1,058,216	$4,993,662,226.00	$4,719.00
1956	1,042,664	$5,324,672,032.00	$5,107.00
1957	986,001	$5,358,043,915.00	$5,434.00
1958	840,575	$4,929,905,512.00	$5,865.00
1959	815,474	$4,986,252,831.00	$6,115.00
1960	780,494	$4,893,558,158.00	$6,270.00

Results are not directly comparable before and after 1945 due to the omission of Class II and III railroads from 1946 to 1960. In 1946 the number and compensation of employees on Class II and III railroads was approximately 1 percent of the total.

Data from *Statistics of Railroads of Class I in the United States*, AAR, various years. *Railroads in this Century*, Association of American Railroads, 1947.

Notes

Introduction

1. Chief of Motive Power files, Motive Power Department, Pennsylvania Railroad Records, Hagley Museum and Library, Wilmington, DE.

2. P. W. Kiefer, *A Practical Evaluation of Railroad Motive Power* (New York: Steam Locomotive Research Institute, Inc., 1947). Kiefer was the Chief Engineer of Motive Power and Rolling Stock for the New York Central System. The book details the results of a comparative test of diesel-electric, steam, and electric locomotives in various types of service.

3. To draw a parallel, the American automotive industry could be analyzed as an industry and many overarching conclusions would be valid. However, when looking at the success of the Mustang and the failure of the Pinto, the level of analysis must be reduced to look at the unique business and corporate culture of the Ford Motor Company. The railroad industry from 1920 to 1960 had not three major companies but over one hundred.

4. For example, different railroads had individual signal systems where identical indications meant entirely different things as well as different operating rules, different standard engineering designs for structures and bridges, different locomotive and car designs, and even different designs and standards for the rails themselves.

5. The eastern region was roughly everything east of Chicago and the Mississippi river and north of the Ohio and Potomac rivers. The southern region was everything south of the Ohio and Potomac and east of the Mississippi, while the western region was everything west of Chicago and the Mississippi. Railroads could operate in more than one region. Robert Selph Henry, *This Fascinating Railroad Business* (Indianapolis, IN: Bobbs-Merrill Co., 1946), 467–96.

6. The Pocahontas district was defined as Virginia and West Virginia and was specifically designed to encompass the large coal hauling roads. While it was within the southern region, it was set up to recognize the particular operating differences of the large coal haulers. Ibid., 475–76.

7. *Railroads in this Century* (Washington, DC: Association of American Railroads, 1947), 14, 16.

Chapter 1. Shiny New Things

1. On steep grades many trains required extra motive power to get over the grade. Helper locomotives generally pushed a train rather than pulled it, but the determination of which position to use was complex. Train size, cargo, weight, terrain, and whether the caboose had a wood or steel frame were all factors. Different railroads had

289

different operational practices for helpers as well. Fred Carlson, Air Brake Engineer for Association of American Railroads interview by author, July 1994. For a good general introduction to present day railroading, see John H. Armstrong, *The Railroad, What It Is, What It Does*, 3d. ed. (Omaha, NE: Simmons Boardman Books, 1993). For a popular introduction to railroading in the age of dieselization, see Robert Selph Henry, *This Fascinating Railroad Business*, 3d. ed. (Indianapolis, IN: Bobbs-Merrill Co., 1946). He deals with helper or pusher locomotives on 53.

2. Unless specifically stated otherwise, the terms diesel and diesel-electric are used interchangeably and refer to the diesel-electric type of locomotive. More technical details are presented in Chapter 2.

3. There are many good works on general railroad history, especially during the nineteenth century. See, for instance, John F. Stover, *American Railroads*, 2d. ed. (Chicago: University of Chicago Press, 1997). Social and cultural impact is analyzed in Sarah H. Gordon, *Passage to Union: How the Railroads Transformed American Life, 1829–1929*, (Chicago: Ivan R. Dee, 1996).

4. See, for instance Gabriel Kolko, *Railroads and Regulation, 1877–1916* (New York: W. W. Norton and Co., 1965) and Albro Martin, *Enterprise Denied, The Origin of the Decline of American Railroads, 1897–1917* (New York: Columbia University Press, 1971). For a period look at the complexities of railroad rate regulation, see William Zebina Ripley, *Railroads Rates and Regulation* (New York: Longmans, Green and Co., 1912). William Ripley went on to lead the ICC consolidation plans in the 1920s.

5. Mark H. Rose, Bruce E. Seely, and Paul F. Barrett, *The Best Transportation System in the World: Railroads, Trucks, Airlines and American Public Policy in the Twentieth Century* (Columbus: Ohio State University Press, 2006), 4–5.

6. Richard Saunders, Jr., *Merging Lines, American Railroads, 1900–1970* (De Kalb: Northern Illinois University Press, 2001), 43–44.

7. Ibid., 65–66. The ICC finally announced its plan in late 1929. It consisted of twenty one roughly equivalent sized systems. Some were relatively unchanged such as the Southern Pacific and Pennsylvania while others were curious amalgamations such as the Chicago & North Western, Chicago & Eastern Illinois, and Mobile & Ohio. It may have worked if implemented in the mid 1920s but after the stock market crash, it was simply out of date.

8. Railroads did have more passenger-miles during the war years but this is due to the length of the journeys taken, not the number of people traveling.

9. *Railroads in this Century* (Washington, DC: Association of American Railroads, 1947), 12.

10. "Santa Fe's New Diesel Makes Record Run," *Railway Age* (November 9, 1935): 595–97.

11. A.I. Lipetz, "Possibilities of the Diesel Locomotive," *Railway Age* (October 12, 1935): 473.

12. "Why the Diesel Engine is a Good Railroad Tool," *Railway Age* (October 26, 1935): 534.

13. J. L. Ryan, "Suggestions for the Improvement of Steam Locomotives," *Railway Age* (July 20, 1940): 106–109.

14. For example, J. S. Newton and W. A. Brect, "A Geared Steam-Turbine Locomotive," *Railway Age* (February 17, 1945): 337–40, and "Pennsylvania Tests Duplex Drive Locomotive," *Railway Age* (May 26, 1945): 925–29.

15. *Railway Age* (December 14, 1940), 29.

16. *A Review of Railroad Operations in 1960* (Washington, DC: Association of American Railroads, Bureau of Railway Economics, 1961), 10.

17. Ibid., 13. Trailer on flatcar traffic (TOFC) is sometimes referred to as "piggy-back" or trailvan traffic. It consists of truck trailers riding on railroad flatcars. The great increase in this traffic also illustrates the increase in commercial truck traffic.

18. Ibid., 10.

19. John Stover takes this view in his *History of the Baltimore and Ohio Railroad* (West Lafayette, IN: Purdue University Press, 1987) as do many of the individual railroad historians. The narrow, cost accounting analysis looks at some, but not all, of the respective operating costs of steam and diesel locomotives. The differences in operational capabilities that result from the introduction of new technologies are often overlooked. These histories are generally more business and finance oriented than operation or technology oriented.

20. For example, Maury Klein, "Replacement Technology: The Diesel as a Case Study," *Railroad History* 160 (Spring 1990): 109. Also "The Diesel Revolution," *American Heritage of Invention and Technology* 6 (Winter 1991): 16.

21. Thomas P. Hughes, *American Genesis* (New York: Penguin Books, 1989), 460–61. See also Thomas P. Hughes, *Networks of Power: Electrification in Western Society* (Baltimore: Johns Hopkins University Press, 1983), and "Evolution of Large Technological Systems," in *The Social Construction of Technological Systems*, ed. Wiebe E. Bijker, Thomas P. Hughes, and Trevor Pinch (Cambridge, MA: MIT Press, 1989), 76–80.

22. Steven W. Usselman, "Air Brakes for Freight Trains: Technological Innovation in the American Railroad Industry, 1869–1900," *Business History Review* 58 (Spring 1984): 31.

23. Steven W. Usselman, *Regulating Railroad Innovation: Business, Technology and Politics in America, 1840–1920* (Cambridge: Cambridge University Press, 2002).

24. Ibid., 7.

25. Ibid., 8.

26. Instead of using the term railroad buff, I will refer to these amateur historians as they refer to themselves, railfans.

27. The journal, *Railroad History* contains many such rosters or lists of locomotives as do the railfan locomotive news magazines, *Extra 2200 South* and *Diesel Era*. There are many books that also include locomotive rosters, most often with photos and sometimes with other primary source material as well. Many are mentioned below and throughout the text.

28. There are a few railfan works that do stand out as exceptionally well done. They include, John Bonds Garmany, *Southern Pacific Dieselization* (Edmonds, WA: Pacific Fast Mail, 1985), Robert E. Mohowski, *New York Ontario and Western in the Diesel Age* (Andover, NJ: Andover Junction Publications, 1994), and John B. McCall, *Santa Fe's Early*

Diesel Daze, 1935–53 (Dallas: Kachina Press, 1980). There are others mentioned throughout the text.

29. Fred Cottrell, "Death by Dieselization: A Case Study in the Reaction to Technological Change," *American Sociological Review* 16 (June 1951): 358–65.

30. Richard Paul Hydell, "A Study of Technological Diffusion: The Replacement of Steam by Diesel Locomotives in the United States" (PhD. diss., Massachusetts Institute of Technology, 1977), 304.

31. Steam locomotives required daily service and were not available to pull trains for a sizable percentage of each day due to maintenance. Diesels did not require this daily maintenance and were therefore available for work a larger percentage of the time.

32. Hydell, "A Study of Technological Diffusion," 304.

33. For example, Robert Charles Bingham, "The Diesel Locomotive: A Study in Innovation," (PhD. diss., Northwestern University, 1962) and Thomas Marx, "The Diesel-Electric Locomotive Industry: A Study in Market Failures," (PhD. diss., University of Pennsylvania, 1973).

34. John K. Brown, *The Baldwin Locomotive Works, 1831–1915* (Baltimore: Johns Hopkins University Press, 1995), 230. Brown's work is exemplary and sets the standard for future works.

35. Ibid., 232.

36. Ibid., 231.

37. Albert John Churella, "Corporate Response to Technological Change: Dieselization and the American Railway Locomotive Industry During the Twentieth Century," (PhD. diss., Ohio State University, 1994), 9–10. Also, Albert J. Churella, *From Steam to Diesel* (Princeton, NJ: Princeton University Press, 1998).

38. Ibid., 153.

39. Mark G. Mapes, "Losing Steam: The Decision-Making Process in the Dieselization of the Pennsylvania Railroad," (PhD. diss., University of Delaware, 2000).

40. Ibid., 4.

41. The PRR motive power policies were different than most other north American railroads. For example, the PRR was one of only a handful of railroads to make widespread use of the Belpaire type firebox on its steam locomotives. It also was a user of large and heavy 4-4-2 and 2-10-0 types, again almost unique among American railroads. It was one of a very few railroads that completed a large scale electrification project. No other North American railroad matched the scale and scope of the Northeast corridor electrification of the PRR. Its massive Altoona works were easily a step or two above the shop facilities of other railroads both in size and capability. The PRR was clearly uncharacteristic of north American railroads.

CHAPTER 2.　CARE AND FEEDING

1. John H. White Jr, *A History of the American Locomotive: Development, 1830–1880* (New York: Dover Publications, Inc., 1968), 46. White's work is essential reading for early American steam locomotive development. There are several ways to measure the output of steam and diesel locomotives. The two most common are horsepower and tractive effort. Tractive effort is simply the pulling force that a locomotive is able to exert expressed in pounds. Both vary with speed. Most figures quoted are initial or starting tractive effort.

2. George H. Drury, *Guide to North American Steam Locomotives* (Waukesha, WI: Kalmbach, 1993), 55. Drury's handbook is a great pocket guide to post-1900 steam locomotive development and also provides detailed roster information for most major railroads.

3. Ibid., 216–17.

4. White, *History of the American Locomotive*, 4.

5. In the typical nineteenth-century steam locomotive, a maximum of 4 percent of the heat was converted to usable work. This ratio, work performed / available heat, is known as thermodynamic efficiency. An efficiency of 100 percent is impossible to achieve but ratings of 70–80 percent are routinely achieved by modern steam turbines located in electrical generating plants. Internal combustion engines achieve an efficiency of about 15–30 percent. Yunus A. Cengel and Michael A. Boles, *Thermodynamics: An Engineering Approach* (New York: McGraw-Hill, 1989), 204–5.

6. Alfred W. Bruce, *The Steam Locomotive in America* (New York: W. W. Norton & Co, 1952), 152. Bruce deals mainly with post-1900 technical and engineering developments in steam locomotive design.

7. Locomotive boilers came in essentially two varieties, fire tube and water tube. Fire tube boilers were used on all but a very few experimental locomotives. Water tube boilers were more efficient and found a permanent place in marine and stationary applications but were not successful in railroad service due to less robust construction and added maintenance.

8. Drury, *Steam Locomotives*.

9. Fred Carlson, interview by author, July 1994. Spacing could vary greatly depending on local conditions and railroad. For example, the New York Central chose to emphasize coal rather than water space in its locomotive tenders and therefore had more widely spaced coaling facilities. They also had track pans that enabled specially equipped locomotives to replenish water at speed with scoops located below the tender. The description of a "jerkwater" town comes from the jerking of the waterspout down to water a locomotive. The reason for the town's existence was the water stop.

10. Just as hard water will leave scale deposits inside a tea kettle or coffee maker, hard water would do the same in steam locomotives. Railroads preferred water from surface sources due to its lower mineral content, but when they used ground water they often had to put a treatment plant at the site to de-mineralize the water.

11. Many of these maintenance concerns were addressed during the 1930s and 1940s. Roller bearings and centralized lubrication systems eliminated many of the maintenance headaches. However, the rods still had to be lubricated by hand. For example, the Norfolk & Western J class 4–8–4 locomotives built in 1949 and 1950 incorporated all of these evolutionary advances. They even had roller bearings on the bell. One of these locomotives, the 611, is preserved at the Virginia Museum of Transportation. Drury, *Steam Locomotives*, 304–5.

12. Richard Paul Hydell, "A Study of Technological Diffusion: The Replacement of Steam by Diesel Locomotives in the United States" (PhD. diss., Massachusetts Institute of Technology, 1977), 228. Hydell uses data from the Erie railroad and determines that due to the age of the locomotive fleet, dieselization followed a rational modernization policy. However, he errors in assuming that the Erie was typical of all US railroads.

13. A division point was the boundary between two regions of the railroad. Generally locomotives and crews only operated on their home divisions.

14. Drury, *Steam Locomotives*, 222–23.

15. Ibid., 347.

16. The Mikado was so named because the first railroad to operate the type was the Japanese Government Railways in 1897. During the Second World War there was an unsuccessful movement to rename the type MacArthur. Bruce, *Steam Locomotive in America*, 296, 298.

17. Average freight train speed in 1923 was just 10.9 mph. By 1930 it was up to 13.8 mph, and by 1939 it was 16.7 mph. *Railways of the United States, Their Plant, Facilities, and Operation* (Washington, DC: Association of American Railroads, 1940), 42. Not all roads needed the extra speed. For instance, the major coal roads did not have to worry about spoilage of coal or speed of delivery. Therefore they followed a different path, concentrating on larger and ever more powerful but slow locomotives. The ultimate development of this trend would be the 2–10–10–2 compound articulateds of the Virginian railroad.

18. Drury, *Steam Locomotives*, 284–85. The New York, Chicago and St. Louis, or "Nickel Plate Road," achieved great success with their many Berkshires and employed them until 1958. Some have been preserved.

19. For the definitive popular history of Lima Locomotive Works of Lima, Ohio, the smallest and in many ways most progressive of the steam locomotive builders, see, Eric Hirsimaki, *Lima* (Edmonds, WA: Hundman Publishing, 1986).

20. Drury, *Steam Locomotives*, 34–35. One Pacific, a Southern Railroad Class Ps-4, has achieved immortality by being enshrined in the American History Museum of the Smithsonian. A British Pacific, the Mallard, holds the land speed record for steam locomotives at 126 mph and is preserved at the National Railway Museum in York, England.

21. Ibid., 186–87. One Mountain, St. Louis-San Francisco Railroad number 1522, is preserved at the Museum of Transport in St. Louis and occasionally runs excursion trips.

22. Some railroads south of the Mason-Dixon line were not keen on having locomotives named Northern so they changed the name to better suit their region. Other railroads chose names more significant to their operating regions. For example; Dixie (Nashville, Chattanooga & St. Louis), Greenbrier (Chesapeake & Ohio), Potomac (Western Maryland), Niagara (New York Central), Pocono (Delaware, Lackawanna & Western), Wyoming (Lehigh Valley), Golden State and General Service (Southern Pacific). Ibid. 314–15.

23. Articulated locomotives will be examined in detail below. They consisted of two or more engines acting independently, underneath and fed by one boiler.

24. Drury, *Steam Locomotive*, 174. One wonders why they even purchased it.

25. Lloyd D. Lewis, *Virginian Railway Locomotives* (Lynchburg, VA: TLC Publishing, 1993), 32, 40–41.

26. Drury, *Steam Locomotives*, 84, 399. Two Alleghenies and several Big Boys are preserved but not in operating condition.

27. Eric Hirsimaki, *Black Gold–Black Diamonds: The Pennsylvania Railroad and Dieselization*, vol. 1 (North Olmstead, OH: Mileposts Publishing, 1997), 108.

28. Ibid., 151.

29. Drury, *Steam Locomotives*, 26.

30. Ibid., 328.

31. "Market Study" EMD, 2, John "Jack" F. Weiffenbach Papers, California State Railroad Museum Library, Sacramento.

32. The Pennsylvania railroad was especially noted for this. For example, see Brown, *Baldwin Locomotive Works*, 226, 230.

33. For information on Diesel himself and the early development of the diesel engine see, Donald E. Thomas Jr., *Diesel: Technology and Society in Industrial Germany* (Tuscaloosa: University of Alabama Press, 1987). For a history of the engine itself, heavy on the technical details, see C. Lyle Cummins Jr., *Diesel's Engine*, vol. 1, *From Conception to 1918* (Wilsonville, OR: Carnot Press, 1993).

34. Typical compression ratios for contemporary gasoline engines were around 8:1, while for locomotive diesels the ratio was closer to 20:1. *Diesel: The Modern Power* (Detroit, MI: General Motors Corporation, 1936), 8–9. See also, John B. Heywood, *Internal Combustion Engine Fundamentals* (New York: McGraw-Hill, 1988), 27.

35. Two cycle engines produce power on every other stroke of the piston. Examples would be engines used on chainsaws and outboard motors. Four cycle engines produce power every fourth stroke. Almost all automobile engines were four cycle engines. Two cycle engines are generally more efficient, but in the locomotive field, neither type had a clear advantage over the other. EMD diesel locomotives contained two-cycle prime movers, while all Alco, Baldwin, and General Electric locomotives contained four-cycle prime movers. Locomotives produced by Fairbanks-Morse were split between the two engine types. *Diesel: The Modern Power*, 8–9 and Louis A. Marre, *Diesel Locomotives: The First 50 Years* (Waukesha, WI: Kalmbach Publishing, 1995).

36. Fred Carlson, interview by author, July 1994. Also John Bonds Garmany, *Southern Pacific Dieselization*, (Edmonds, WA: Pacific Fast Mail Publications, 1985), 322–45. EMD produced one experimental diesel-hydraulic switch engine in 1954, but it was not successful. 271, 29. The Europeans, and especially the Germans, have had much more success with diesel-hydraulic locomotives. For more details, see chapter 5.

37. *EMD F-3 Locomotive Operating Manual* (La Grange, IL: General Motors Corporation, 1948), 639. All locomotives equipped with dynamic brakes used the same general system, regardless of the builder. Dynamic brakes did have limitations and could not be used at slow speeds.

38. Cummins, *Diesel's Engine*, 686.

39. Ibid., 689.

40. Ibid., 691.

41. For similar reasons the Caspian Sea also saw some of the first experiments with oil as a fuel for steam ships.

42. Cummins, *Diesel's Engine*, 694.

43. Marre, *Diesel Locomotives*, 138.

44. Number of passengers carried peaked at 1,269,913,000 in 1920. Passenger revenue (excepting the war years of 1943–1945) also peaked in 1920 at over $1.3 billion. *Railroads In This Century: A Summary of the Facts and Figures With Charts* (Washington, DC: Association of American Railroads, 1947), 16–17.

45. Lehigh Valley Railroad Annual Reports, 1920–1960. Other Railroad Annual Reports, 1920–1950. The New York, New Haven & Hartford railroad was also heavily passenger dependent.

46. 46. Richard W. Jahn, "Lehigh Valley Railroad Gas-Electrics," *Flags Diamonds and Statues* 6, no. 1 (1985): 4–21. Also Edmund Keilty, *Doodlebug Country* (Glendale, CA.: Interurban Press, 1982).

47. Somewhat surprisingly, other than a chapter in Churella's work, there has been little attention paid to these pioneering efforts other than railfan oriented works, mainly of a pictorial nature.

48. Maury Klein, *Union Pacific: The Rebirth, 1894–1969* (New York: Doubleday, 1989), 296.

49. Debra Brill, History of the J. G. Brill Company (Bloomington: Indiana University Press, 2001), 147–158.

50. *Our GM Scrapbook* (Milwaukee: Kalmbach, 1971), 14.

51. Lehigh Valley Railroad Company minutes, meeting of May 26, 1925. Pennsylvania Historical and Museum Commission (PHMC), Harrisburg, PA.

52. CNJ 1000 currently resides in the Baltimore & Ohio Museum in Baltimore, Maryland. For more info see Marre, *Diesel Locomotives*, 207–8.

53. John A. Droege, *Freight Terminals and Trains* (1925; reprint, Chattanooga, TN: National Model Railroad Association, 1998), 446.

54. Much has been written on the famous Zephyr. The best account remains that of Richard Overton, *Burlington Route: A History of the Burlington Lines* (New York: Knopf, 1965), 393–406. For general information, see David P. Morgan, *Diesels West: The Evolution of Power on the Burlington* (Milwaukee, WI: Kalmbach, 1963) and Margaret Coel, "A Silver Streak," *American Heritage of Invention & Technology* (Fall 1986): 10–17. Also look at Franklin M. Reck, *On Time* (La Grange, IL: General Motors Corp., 1948).

55. Distillate was a fuel similar to kerosene, somewhere between gasoline and diesel fuel in consistency but without detergent and other additives. The engine was similar in size to a diesel but operated with spark ignition. See "Union Pacific Installs Light-Weight High-Speed Passenger Train," *Railway Age* (February 3, 1934): 184–96. Later Union Pacific streamliners used diesel engines.

56. *Our GM Scrapbook*, 27.

57. The New York Central and Pennsylvania railroads, the two largest railroads in the northeast and among the largest in the world, both had fleets of streamlined steam passenger locomotives. The streamlined Hudsons of the New York Central are especially famous. For more information, see Eric H. Archer, *Streamlined Steam* (New York: Quadrant Press, 1972).

58. Marre, *Diesel Locomotives*, 207–8. These small switching units were quite successful, and at least one remained in service into the 1970s. A few railroads also purchased unique three-power locomotives from General Electric. These custom units contained a diesel that operated at a constant speed charging large banks of storage batteries. These batteries were in turn connected to the traction motors. These locomotives also contained either pantographs or third rail shoes so that they could operate in pure electric mode. They were used to switch coach yards and passenger terminals in large cities like New York, Chicago, and Detroit and also to serve industrial trackage and spurs off of electrified main lines.

59. For example, from 1931 to 1939 Alco produced 79 six hundred horsepower standardized switchers for a variety of railroad and industrial customers. EMC produced their first switcher in 1935 and quickly became a leading producer with 122 six hundred horsepower switchers produced by January 1939. From early 1937 to January 1939 they also produced 50 nine hundred horsepower switching locomotives. These early EMC switchers also marked EMC's entrance into the field as an actual builder of locomotives. Prior to this time all locomotives and motor cars produced by EMC were actually assembled by a variety of manufacturers including St. Louis Car Company and Bethlehem Steel. Baldwin began producing switchers in 1937 but few were sold until 1939. Marre, *Diesel Locomotives.*

60. The first E-units were twelve EA and EB units built in 1937 for the Baltimore and Ohio Railroad. They were quickly followed by eleven E-1 units for the Santa Fe that introduced the famous red, yellow, and silver "war bonnet" paint scheme. The Union Pacific, Southern Pacific, and Chicago and North Western, not wanting to be out done by the Santa Fe, quickly ordered six E-2 units for the newly constructed joint City of San Francisco and City of Los Angeles streamliners.

61. A note on terminology. Units with crew cabs and full controls were classified as A units. Units without crew cabs but with all other equipment were classified as B units. B units generally could not be moved without receiving control from a connected A unit. There were exceptions to this rule, and some B units were built with small control stands for moving the units around engine facilities and yards.

62. Actual designations varied from DL-103b through DL-105, 107 and 109 to DL-110. All were similar in appearance and internal characteristics. Marre, *Diesel Locomotives,* 279–80.

63. *Our GM Scrapbook,* 50. Morgan, a most eloquent writer, also compared the FT's impact on railroading to that of the jet engine to aviation and the nuclear age to the Navy.

64. *The Revolutionary Diesel, EMC's FT* (Halifax, PA: Diesel Era, 1994), 7.

65. Alco was allowed to produce a limited number of DL-109 dual passenger and freight locomotives for the New Haven and all builders were allowed to do limited research and development work.

66. Marre, *Diesel Lococmotives,* 90. The transitional F-2 and much more widely used F-3 packed 1,500 hp in each unit instead of the 1,350 hp of the FT.

67. 67. Ibid., The F-7 packed 1,500 hp per unit but had improved electrical equipment. The F-9 introduced in 1954 contained an upgraded diesel engine that boosted the horsepower up to 1,750 per unit. It did not sell as well with only 241 sold.

68. Ibid., 43.

69. Horsepower was raised to 1,600 in 1950 and production continued to 1959. Marre, *Diesel Locomotives,* 274.

70. PA locomotives were produced until 1953. While EMD needed two engines in one E-unit to produce sufficient horsepower, Alco only employed one large 2,000 hp engine in its PA. There were advantages and disadvantages to this decision. If one engine failed in an E-unit the locomotive could limp in to a shop facility using the other one. However, if the engine failed on a PA the locomotive, and all the passengers on the train behind it, were stuck. Of course, the maintenance forces would probably have rather dealt with one engine per

locomotive than two and the necessary twice as many spare parts, oil changes, broken cylinder liners, and so on.

71. Marre, *Diesel Locomotives*, 231–32.

72. The 2000 number includes many variations of the same general locomotive including locomotives with both four and six wheel trucks. Ibid, 241, 245, 247.

73. Ibid., 292–99. The switchers ranged from 660 to 1200 hp.

74. It was a modular design and was to have eight separate V-8 diesels each driving one traction motor on one axle. Only four engines were ever fitted and the locomotive was cut up in 1945. It would have been a maintenance headache of the highest order.

75. Marre, *Diesel Locomotives*, 320. Only three customers were found for the units, the Pennsylvania railroad, a long Baldwin customer, the Seaboard Air Line, and the National Railways of Mexico.

76. Ibid., 326. The most successful model was the distinctively styled RF-16 1600 hp locomotive with 150 sold from 1950 to 1953.

77. Robert Ronald Rohal, "The Erie's 300-mile Division," *Trains* (June 2000), 52–53.

78. Marre, *Diesel Locomotives*, 334. The switchers came in 1000 and 1200 horsepower varieties and were purchased by a number of different railroads including the Santa Fe and the Nickel Plate Road.

79. Ibid., 350.

80. Ibid., 355. Most of these locomotives were switchers from 750 to 1,200 hp, although they also produced a road-switcher and a large, twin engine, 2,500 hp transfer locomotive.

81. Some of these builders include Whitcomb, Plymouth, Davenport, Porter, and even Mack Truck. Ingalls shipbuilding of Pascagoula, Mississippi proposed a complete line of large diesel electric locomotives immediately following World War II. Only one was ever built. It was sold to the Gulf Mobile & Ohio where it was used for many years.

CHAPTER 3.   DIESELIZATION DECIPHERED

1. For example, different railroads had different signal systems where identical indications could mean entirely different things as well as different operating rules, different standard engineering designs for structures and bridges, different locomotive and car designs and even different designs and standards for the rails themselves.

2. Interstate Commerce Commission, *Annual Report on the Statistics of Railways in the United States*, various years.

3. Unless otherwise stated, mileage figures are for 1950 and are taken from Robert G. Lewis, *Handbook of American Railroads* (New York: Simmons-Boardman, 1951). Mileage is stated as miles of line, not miles of track. Miles of line counts only main track while miles of track counts all trackage including double track, sidings and yard track.

4. Robert F. Archer, *Lehigh Valley Railroad: The Route of the Black Diamond* (Berkeley, CA: Howell-North Books, 1978).

5. The Lehigh Valley even owned a fleet of lake boats until forced to divest itself from them by the Panama Canal Act.

6. Lehigh Valley Railroad Annual Reports, 1921–45.

7. The first railroad to operate 4–8–4's was the Northern Pacific, purchasing some from Alco in 1927. Bruce, *Steam Locomotive in America*, 89.

8. Lehigh Valley Railroad Company minutes, 1931. PHMC, Harrisburg. The Depression hit the Lehigh Valley hard but not nearly as hard as other railroads and industries. The Lehigh Valley finished in the black in 1934 and 1935 and had done quite well in the 1920s. Therefore, it could afford to invest in new locomotives and the service and maintenance changes necessary for the operation of these locomotives. Lehigh Valley Railroad Annual Reports, 1920–39.

9. Archer, *Lehigh Valley Railroad*, 242.

10. Lehigh Valley Railroad Company minutes, PHMC, meeting of May 26, 1925.

11. Ibid., 1925, 122. During the early days of diesel-electric locomotives, they were often referred to as oil-electric and sometimes even confused with gasoline-electric locomotives. The terminology did not become clearly defined until the mid-1930s when oil-electric was dropped in favor of diesel-electric.

12. Both the CNJ and LV diesel-electrics manufactured by Ingersol-Rand, GE, and Alco were successful and were in service until after World War II. The Brill built diesel was not considered satisfactory and was stored until 1931 when it was rebuilt by Alco with a new engine. With its new engine it too lasted until after the war.

13. These antismoke ordinances were also a major reason for the electrification of many rail lines into and out of the New York City area such as the New York Central, Lackawanna, and Pennsylvania. See chapter 5.

14. Archer, *Lehigh Valley Railroad*, 261.

15. Central Railroad of New Jersey, Annual Reports, 1930–50.

16. "Erie Cuts Tops Off Hills with Diesels," *Railway Age* (August 16, 1947): 62–64.

17. Lehigh Valley Railroad Company minutes, 1942. PHMC. It is somewhat curious that the large drivered, K class, 4–6–2 passenger locomotives are referred to as "low wheel type" locomotives. They were not as modern and efficient as the T class, 4–8–4 and S class, 4–8–2 locomotives but were well suited for passenger service.

18. Archer, *Lehigh Valley Railroad*, 261. The FT locomotives were designed for main line fast freight and proved to be capable of out performing even the most modern steam power on their 85,000 mile demonstration tour in 1939–40 as well as in service on many railroads during the war including eastern region roads like the Erie, Baltimore & Ohio, Boston and Maine, Lackawanna, and Reading. *Revolutionary Diesel.*

19. Lehigh Valley Railroad Company minutes, Report of Dieselization Committee, April 28, 1948. PHMC.

20. Ibid.

21. A. H. Candee, "Report on the Use of Diesel Electric Motive Power for Symbol Freight Train Services" Westinghouse Electric Corp. collaborating with Baldwin Locomotive Works, May 1948. Symbol freight trains were the scheduled fast merchandise freight trains as opposed to nonscheduled, extra movements or coal trains. Symbol refers to the letter designation of the trains. For example, train AS-1 would run from Allentown to Sayre, PA.

22. Lewis, *Handbook of American Railroads*, 126.

23. Lehigh Valley Railroad Company minutes, May 25, 1948. PHMC. While ordering ten locomotives, there were four units making up each locomotive. Twenty of these units were "A units" (ten Alco,

ten EMD) with cabs and controls for the crew while twenty were "B units" with no provision for independent control. Each unit was, in actuality, a separate locomotive with diesel engine, fuel system, electrical system, and other systems necessary to operate.

24. A bid was solicited from Fairbanks-Morse, another locomotive builder, but no response was received by the date of the committee report.

25. Lehigh Valley Railroad Company minutes, Dieselization Committee Report, April 28, 1948. PHMC.

26. M.U. is an abbreviation for Multiple Unit. In railroad industry usage it functions as a noun, verb, and adjective.

27. "Road Tests Completed on New 4,000-h.p. Alco-G. E. Diesel," *Railway Age* (August 17, 1946), 308. During the crippling 1946 coal strike, the diesel powered PA was one of the few locomotives moving on the railroad and was put to use hauling freight. This no doubt also played a role in the management decision to purchase diesels.

28. Richard W. Jahn, "PA: Lehigh Valley Style," *Flags, Diamonds, and Statues* 7, no. 2 (1987): 5.

29. Archer, *Lehigh Valley Railroad*, 275. One of these RDC's is preserved at the Railroad Museum of Pennsylvania in Strasburg.

30. Lewis, *Handbook*, 77.

31. *Revolutionary Diesel*, 54.

32. Drury, *Steam Locomotives*, 153

33. *Revolutionary Diesel*, 54.

34. Robert B. Shaw, "A Brief History of the New York, Ontario & Western Railroad," *Railroad History* 175 (Autumn 1996): 115.

35. Robert E. Mohowski, *New York Ontario & Western in the Diesel Age* (Andover Junction, NJ: Andover Junction Publications, 1994), 7.

36. The same GMAC that provides financing for consumer purchase of automobiles provided financing for locomotives.

37. Shaw, "Brief History," 131.

38. Mohowski, *New York Ontario & Western*, 24–25.

39. "Susquehanna Abandons Steam Power," *Railway Age* (June 30, 1945): 1132.

40. Ibid.

41. The Reading developed the Wooten firebox in the late nineteenth century. Named after its inventor, the Wooten was a large, wide and shallow firebox specifically designed to burn anthracite. Other railroads that burned anthracite coal such as the Lehigh Valley and New York, Ontario & Western also used the Wooten firebox.

42. The route westbound was CNJ, RDG, WM, P&WV, and NKP, hence the Alphabet route moniker.

43. Drury, *Steam Locomotives*, 333.

44. Dale W. Woodland, *Reading Diesels, vol. 1: The First Generation* (Laury's Station, PA: Garrigues House, 1991), 31.

45. Ibid., 166.

46. Ibid., 105. The Reading took such pride in its new diesel freight units that for the first several years the company required that they be waxed to maintain a clean appearance.

47. Drury, *Steam Locomotives*, 331. A few of these locomotives have survived and are in museums or operate in tourist service.

48. Annual Report of the Baltimore and Ohio Railroad Company, 1929. Hagley Museum and Library.

49. The train ran on the tracks of the Reading railroad from Philadelphia to New York as the B&O did not directly serve New York City.

50. Marre, *Diesel Locomotives*, 114. The shell of one of these locomotives is preserved at the B&O Railroad Museum in Baltimore.

51. Annual Report of the Baltimore and Ohio Railroad Company, 1939. Hagley Museum and Library.

52. *Revolutionary Diesel*, 28.

53. Drury, *Steam Locomotives*, 40–41.

54. Annual report of the Baltimore and Ohio Railroad Company, 1948, 8. Hagley Museum and Library.

55. Ibid., 9.

56. Ibid.

57. Lewis, *Handbook*, 19.

58. Annual Report Baltimore and Ohio Railroad Company, 1951, 7. Hagley Museum and Library.

59. Ibid., 1952, 9. Of interest is that steam locomotives appeared on the cover of B&O annual reports as late as 1948. The 1945 and 1946 covers featured steam locomotive photographs exclusively. By 1955 the cover was a copy of a B&O financial bond.

60. Lewis, *Handbook*, 19.

61. Drury, *Steam Locomotives*, 426.

62. Patrick H. Stakem and Patrick E. Stakem, *Western Maryland Diesel Locomotives* (Lynchburg, VA: TLC Publishing, 1997), 8.

63. Drury, *Steam Locomotives*, 426.

64. Stakem and Stakem, *Western Maryland Diesel Locomotives*, 5.

65. An interesting aside is the story of the marine fleet of the Western Maryland. To move freight cars around Baltimore Harbor, the railroad maintained a small fleet of barges and tug boats. This fleet was also dieselized beginning in 1940. Ibd., 60.

66. The Southern, Louisville and Nashville, and Missouri Pacific among others utilized the C&EI for traffic bound to and from Chicago.

67. Drury, *Steam Locomotives*, 441–42.

68. Ray Curl, "In Comes the C&EI–The Switcher Fleet," in *Missouri Pacific Diesel Power*, Kevin EuDaly (Kansas City, MO: Whiteriver Productions, 1994), 94.

69. Ibid.

70. The C&EI, although it did not have a lot of on line passenger traffic, was an important segment of the route for through trains from Chicago to Nashville, Atlanta, Florida, and other points in the South.

71. Ibid., 100.

72. The famous "war bonnet" red, yellow, and silver paint scheme was designed by EMC and inaugurated on these units. It is probably the most recognizable railroad paint scheme and has even come to symbolize streamlined passenger trains as a whole.

73. John B. McCall, *Santa Fe's Early Diesel Daze, 1935–1953* (Dallas, Kachina Press, 1980), 251.

74. *Forty-Sixth Annual Report of the Atchison, Topeka and Santa Fe Railway Company for the Year Ended December 31, 1940*, 39. California State Railroad Museum (CSRM), Sacramento, CA.

75. For example, in 1937 total operating revenue was $170,669,945 while passenger revenue was $17,526,621. Passenger revenue would increase dramatically during the war with over $100 million generated from passengers in each year from 1943 to 1945. After the war was over

passenger revenue quickly fell back to about a tenth of total operating revenue. In 1948 out of total revenues of $526 million passenger revenue accounted for $53 million. *Atchison, Topeka & Santa Fe Railway Company, 63rd Annual Report for the Year Ended December, 31 1957*, 38–39. CSRM.

76. *Revolutionary Diesel*, 11. Because of the strategic significance of the line, the Santa Fe had priority on wartime orders of the FT.

77. *Fiftieth Annual Report of the Atchison, Topeka and Santa Fe Railway Company for the Year Ended December, 31 1944*. CSRM.

78. *The Atchison, Topeka and Santa Fe Railway Company 58th Annual Report for the Year Ended December 31, 1952*, 9. CSRM.

79. Drury, *Steam Locomotives*, 14.

80. The single best source for information on the Burlington is Richard Overton, *Burlington Route: History of the Burlington Lines* (New York: Knopf, 1965). This lengthy study stands as one of the first, and best of the individual railroad histories.

81. Drury, *Steam Locomotives*, 106.

82. *Revolutionary Diesel*, 43, 44.

83. Overton, Burlington Route, 523.

84. Lewis, *Handbook*, 55.

85. Overton, Burlington Route, 561.

86. Drury, *Steam Locomotives*, 106. Determining the final date of steam operations on the CB&Q is more difficult than most because the road operated an extensive steam powered passenger excursion program in the late 1950s and 1960s. While embracing the diesel, Burlington management acknowledged the role of the steam locomotive in the history of not only the railroad but the land which it served and the emotional attachment many employees and members of the public had with it. Discounting these excursions, steam in revenue service lasted to late 1957 or 1958.

87. Ibid., 342–43.

88. Louis A. Marre and John Baskin Harper, *Frisco Diesel Power* (Glendale, CA: Interurban Press, 1984), 19.

89. Ibid., 21. Data from Annual Reports.

90. Lewis, *Handbook*, 195.

91. Marre and Harper, *Frisco Diesel Power*, 13.

92. Drury, *Steam Locomotives*, 254.

93. Kevin Eudaly, *Missouri Pacific Diesel Power*, 20–23. These early switchers were an odd mix with several unique locomotives represented. At least seven different manufacturers were represented: Alco, EMD, Baldwin, GE, Whitcomb, Porter, and Davenport. The latter four manufactured small, low-power switchers much better suited for industrial purposes than main line railroading.

94. Ibid., 27.

95. *Revolutionary Diesel*, 78.

96. Drury, *Steam Locomotives*, 250.

97. Lewis, *Handbook*, 146–49, 220.

98. EuDaly, *Missouri Pacific Diesel Power*, 10.

99. *Our GM Scrapbook*, 17.

100. Louis Marre, *Rock Island Diesel Locomotives, 1930–1980* (Cincinnati, OH: Railfax, 1982), 19. Similar locomotives are currently in production for efficiency and air pollution reasons.

101. Ibid., 73–78.

102. Drury, *Steam Locomotives*, 126.

103. *Revolutionary Diesel*, 51–53.

104. Drury, *Steam Locomotives*, 124.

105. Ibid., 97.

106. Paul K. Withers, *Diesels of the Chicago & North Western* (Halifax, PA: Withers Publishing, 1995), 7.

107. Ibid., 300.

108. Drury, *Steam Locomotives*, 96.

109. Withers, *Diesels of the Chicago & North Western*, 300–301.

110. Lewis, *Handbook*, 51.

111. The Rio Grande had several mountain grades of 2 percent or greater and some main line grades of 3 percent. Its main crossing of the Continental divide was at Tennessee Pass, Colorado at an altitude of more than 10,000 feet, the highest main line in North America.

112. Drury, *Steam Locomotives*, 157.

113. *Revolutionary Diesel*, 57.

114. *The Denver and Rio Grande Western Railroad Company: Information Pertaining to Its Properties and Their Improvement; Traffic; Territorial Development; and Results of Operations* (Office of the President, Denver, Colorado March 1951), 57. Collection of Colorado Railroad Museum, Golden, Colorado.

115. *The Denver and Rio Grande Western Railroad Company Annual Report, 1950*, 38. Collection of Colorado Railroad Museum, Golden, Colorado.

116. Ibid., *1956*, 39. The narrow gauge lines did not succumb to the onslaught of the diesel. Since there were no mass produced domestic narrow gauge diesels that would be suitable, the old steam power soldiered on. The narrow gauge lines were also not profitable and were being abandoned as fast as the ICC would allow. Reluctant to spend money on custom built diesels for a money-losing enterprise that would only last a few more years, the Rio Grande kept the steam power in service. Tourists began to discover the steam-powered narrow gauge lines in the 1950s, and after much effort two segments, from Durango to Silverton, Colorado and from Antonito, Colorado to Chama, New Mexico, were saved. Many of the original narrow gauge steam locomotives survive and even make a profit pulling carloads of tourists through picturesque mountain scenery.

117. Drury, *Steam Locomotives*, 428.

118. Ibid.

119. Virgil Staff, *D-Day on the Western Pacific: A Railroad's Decision to Dieselize* (Glendale, CA: Interurban Press, 1982), 20. While a railfan oriented book, this is one of the best individual railroad studies of dieselization that I have seen to date. While not extensively documented the author consulted original company documents and conducted interviews with former employees.

120. Joseph A. Strapac, *Western Pacific's Diesel Years* (Muncie, IN: Overland Models, 1980), 196.

121. Staff, *D-Day on the Western Pacific*, 113.

122. Drury, *Steam Locomotives*, 256.

123. Ibid., 200.

124. Marre, *Diesel Locomotives*, 278. The Rebel was the first application of an Alco built diesel engine to a streamlined train.

125. The GM&O was split between "north end" and "south end" for much of its existence. This may be surmised from the names of its two premier passenger trains.

126. For more on the Alton, see, Gene V. Glendinning, *The Chicago and Alton Railroad: The Only Way* (DeKalb: Northern Illinois University Press, 2002).

127. William D. Edson, "Diesel Locomotives of the Gulf Mobile and Ohio," *Railroad History* 158 (Spring, 1988): 146. Technically the first two units delivered in 1940 were specified as DL-105 on builders documents. Other than exterior cosmetic details the three units were essentially identical. For more information see Marre, *Diesel Locomotives*, 279–82.

128. The GM&O was also the home of the unique Ingalls shipbuilding locomotive. One of a proposed line of diesels, it was the only one ever produced by the Mississippi firm.

129. "GM&O–Alton 100 Per Cent Dieselized," *Railway Age* (December 24, 1949): 37. A large railroad was classified as one which had annual revenues of $50 million or more.

130. Ibid., 39.

131. Ibid., 37.

132. Lewis, *Handbook*, 108.

133. Despite the name, the Seaboard had nothing to do with air travel. Air line was an equivalent term to as the crow flies, signifying a straight line between two points.

134. Drury, *Steam Locomotives*, 350.

135. Warren L. Calloway and Paul K. Withers, *Seaboard Air Line Company Motive Power* (Halifax, PA: Withers Publishing, 1988), 175.

136. Ibid., 15.

137. Lewis, *Handbook*, 200.

138. Drury, *Steam Locomotives*, 349. Drury also states that a small 0–4–0 tank locomotive did operate on street trackage serving industries in Columbus, Georgia until 1959. However, this is clearly an exception that proves the rule.

139. The name of the train takes on added significance when one notes that the name of the president of the railroad was Champion McDowell Davis.

140. Warren L. Calloway, *Atlantic Coast Line, The Diesel Years* (Halifax, PA: Withers Publishing, 1993), 89.

141. Ibid., 15.

142. Ibid.

143. Drury, *Steam Locomotives*, 32

144. *Annual Report of the Southern Railway Company to the Interstate Commerce Commission for the year ended December 31, 1939.* Southern Railway Historical Society Collection, Southern Museum of Civil War and Locomotive History, Kennesaw, GA.

145. Ibid.

146. Drury, *Steam Locomotives*, 367–73. One example of a Southern 4–6–2 has been preserved in pristine condition at the Smithsonian in Washington, DC. It wears the Southern's unique green with gold lettering paint scheme.

147. *Revolutionary Diesel*, 106–107.

148. *Annual Report of the Southern Railway Company to the Interstate Commerce Commission for the year ended December 31, 1945.* Southern Railway Historical Society Collection, Southern Museum of Civil War and Locomotive History, Kennesaw, GA.

149. Lewis, *Handbook*, 205.

150. President's Fact Book, 12–13, Southern Railway Historical Society Collection, Southern Museum of Civil War and Locomotive History, Kennesaw, GA.

151. Drury, *Steam Locomotives*, 336.

152. Lewis, *Handbook*, 191.

153. Many of the modern steam locomotives were sold or leased to other railroads including the C&O.

154. Drury, *Steam Locomotives*, 230.

155. Charles B. Castner, Ronald Flanary, and Lee Gordon, *Louisville & Nashville Diesels* (Lynchburg, VA: TLC Publishing, 1998), 2.

156. Ibid., 4.

157. Ibid.

158. Drury, *Steam Locomotives*, 228.

159. Castner, Flanary and Gordon, *Louisville & Nashville Diesels*, 8–9. These results are from official reports in either the collection of the Louisville and Nashville Railroad Historical Society or the Louisville and Nashville collection at the University of Louisville.

160. Lewis, *Handbook*, 132.

161. Castner, Flanary, and Gordon, *Louisville & Nashville Diesels*, 11. Most of this remaining steam powered tonnage was coal from the coalfields, and most was hauled by the modern 2–8–4 types.

162. The L&N, SAL and ACL are today all part of CSX although many lines, especially of the former SAL have been abandoned or spun off into shortlines. The GM&O has been dismembered with many segments abandoned while others are operated by short lines, regional railroads and even parts of it by Union Pacific and Canadian National.

Chapter 4.   Dieselization Deferred

1. Technically, it should be called the New York Central System as it was composed of several railroads such as the West Shore, the Boston and Albany, the Cleveland, Cincinnati Chicago & St. Louis, and Peoria and Eastern. However, all were operated as part of the same system. The only exception was the Pittsburgh & Lake Erie which was controlled by the NYC but operated separately. Lewis, *Handbook*, 152.

2. New York Central System Annual Report, 1951, Hagley Museum and Library, Wilmington, DE.

3. William D. Middleton, *When the Steam Railroads Electrified* (Milwaukee, WI: Kalmbach Publishing, 1974), 37–52.

4. John F. Kirkland, *Dawn of the Diesel Age* (Glendale, CA: Interurban Press, 1983), 132. Ordered in December 1925, the locomotive first saw service in June 1928.

5. New York Central System Annual Report, 1929, Hagley.

6. Ibid., 1939, Hagley.

7. Drury, *Steam Locomotives*, 278.

8. Ibid., 279. The Hudson came to typify the passenger trains of the NYC. Streamlined versions debuted in the 1930s to haul such trains as the Empire State Express and the 20th Century Limited.

9. Ibid., 269–70. The customary name for the 4–8–2, Mountain, was not used on the New York Central. The railroad advertised itself as the "Water Level Route" and the name Mountain was seen as incompatible with this advertising slogan. Other steam locomotives bore names of other rivers that the New York Central paralleled or crossed.

10. Philip Atkins, *Dropping the Fire* (Clophill, Bedfordshire: Irwell Press, 1999), 16. Mr. Atkins was the librarian at the National Railway Museum in York, England.

11. Ibid., 17.

12. P. W. Kiefer, *A Practical Evaluation of Railroad Motive Power* (New York: Steam Locomotive Research Institute, Inc., 1947), 40. Kiefer was chief engineer, motive power and rolling stock, for the New York Central System and had helped design the Niagara.

13. Ibid., 48.

14. Ibid., 43.

15. Ibid., 38.

16. Atkins, *Dropping the Fire*, 16.

17. New York Central System Annual Report, 1946, Hagley.

18. Ibid., 1947.

19. Ibid.

20. Ibid., 1948, Hagley. The reader is reminded that small but substantial percentages of passenger and switching duties were performed by electric power.

21. Ibid., 14.

22. Ibid., 18.

23. Lewis, *Handbook*, 154. There were 139 electric locomotives in service.

24. For an extremely detailed roster of New York Central diesel locomotives, see William D. Edson with H. L. Vail and C. M. Smith, *New York Central System Diesel Locomotives* (Lynchburg, VA: TLC Publishing, 1995). Edson was chief mechanical engineer for the railroad from 1965 to 1968, while Smith also worked as a mechanical engineer for the railroad. The book contains lists, photos, and drawings, but little narrative.

25. The Pennsy, perhaps because of its size as well as the fact that its records have largely been saved, has received much more scholarly attention than most other railroads. Substantial record holdings are located at the Hagley Museum and Library in Delaware and the Pennsylvania State Archives in Harrisburg. This brief thumbnail sketch of the dieselization of the PRR is not intended to be a comprehensive study but merely to place the PRR in its respective position when compared with the rest of the North American railroad system. For an in depth look at the dieselization of the PRR, see Mark Mapes, "Losing Steam: The Decision Making Process in the Dieselization of the Pennsylvania Railroad," PhD. diss, University of Delaware, 2000.

26. Michael Bezilla, "Pennsylvania Railroad Motive Power Strategies, 1920–1950," *Railroad History* 164 (Spring 1991): 43.

27. The Pennsylvania Railroad Company Annual Report, 1929, Hagley.

28. Ibid.

29. Ibid., 1939.

30. Altoona also had a full size test plant where even the largest of locomotives could be tested under full load at great speed by running on huge rollers. It was one of only a few such test facilities in the country.

31. Drury, *Steam Locomotives*, 318.

32. Bezilla, "Pennsylvania Railroad Motive Power Strategies," 44.

33. The Pennsylvania Railroad Company Annual Report, 1929, Hagley. The other locomotives were mostly electric for operation into Pennsylvania Station in New York.

34. Ibid., 1929, Hagley.
35. Bezilla, "Pennsylvania Railroad Motive Power Strategies," 49.
36. Hirsimaki, *Black Gold–Black Diamonds*, 84. The wheel arrangement of this locomotive changed several times during design from 4–4–4–4 to 4–4–4–6 and finally to 6–4–4–6.
37. Mapes, "Losing Steam," 218–19.
38. Ibid., 220–2
39. Ibid., 173.
40. Ibid., 175.
41. Mapes, 225–27. The locomotive was never used on the South Wind but was instead put to use initially on the Red Arrow between Harrisburg and Detroit.
42. This unit was designed in response to the same antismoke legislation in New York that forced other roads to purchase diesel power. Due to unsatisfactory diesel engines from the Bessemer gas engine company the locomotive was a failure. The antismoke legislation goal was met with gasoline electric locomotives. Ibid., 184–87.
43. Ibid., 193.
44. Hirsimaki, *Black Gold–Black Diamonds* 82. This unit could open the mighty Pennsylvania to GM diesel power. The potential market was huge.
45. Ibid., 170.
46. Mapes, "Losing Steam," 201–2.
47. Ibid., 205.
48. Hirsimaki, *Black Gold–Black Diamonds*, 133–34. The massive locomotive was to contain two turbines, each generating 4,500 hp. A clear example of steam era thinking by concentrating as much power in one locomotive as possible.
49. Mapes, "Losing Steam," 238–40.
50. Ibid., 243–48, 252–58.
51. Ibid., 251. Mapes asserts that competition with other railroads was a primary factor for this initial order.
52. The Pennsylvania Railroad Company Annual Report, 1948, Hagley, 14.
53. Lewis, *Handbook*, 177.
54. The Pennsylvania Railroad Company Annual Report, 1952, Hagley.
55. The Pennsylvania Railroad Museum has several examples of historic PRR steam power but no steam locomotives more modern than the K4 Pacific. Fewer NYC steam locomotives are preserved but a few examples do reside in various museums including the famous 999 at the Chicago Museum of Science and Industry.
56. The reason for the nickname is unclear but it dates back to the late 1800s.
57. Herbert H. Harwood, *Invisible Giants: The Empires of Cleveland's Van Swearingen Brothers* (Bloomington: Indiana University Press, 2003), 43, 130–32.
58. Drury, *Steam Locomotives*, 282, 286. The last NKP 2–8–4 to be delivered in 1949 was also the last steam locomotive to be built by Lima Locomotive Works.
59. Kevin J. Holland, *Nickel Plate Road Diesel Locomotives* (Lynchburg, VA: TLC Publishing, 1998), 119. All data taken from official company documents.

60. Drury, *Steam Locomotives*, 286. The 4–6–4 types on the Nickel Plate were not advanced locomotives like other 4–6–4 types on railroads like the New York Central.

61. Holland, *Nickel Plate Road Diesel Locomotives*, 13. The fact that all main line passenger service could be dieselized by only eleven locomotives illustrates just how little passenger service the Nickel Plate provided.

62. John A. Rehnor, *The Nickel Plate Story* (Milwaukee, WI: Kalmbach Publications, 1965), 273.

63. Ibid., 277. Interestingly enough, in 1949 the NKP also tested a GE gas turbine locomotive. While impressed with its performance fuel costs were deemed too high.

64. Lewis, *Handbook*, 159.

65. Rehnor, *Nickel Plate Story*, 362.

66. Holland, *Nickel Plate Road Diesel Locomotives*, 20.

67. Rehnor, *Nickel Plate Story*, 376–77. The last steam run was in 1959. Because the NKP was late in dieselizing and because it ran in heavily populated territory with large fast steam locomotives it attracted a good deal of attention from railfans. Several of the 2–8–4 type locomotives have been preserved and some are occasionally operated on excursions.

68. The 4–12–2 was unique in several regards. It was a three cylinder locomotive, uncommon in North America as well as the only type with twelve drivers in service on the continent. Its long rigid wheelbase was a limitation on its operation. They were generally confined to long straight stretches of track in Wyoming, Kansas, and Nebraska. Mechanical forces did not care for the maintenance intensive machines. Klein, *Union Pacific*, 374.

69. *Annual Report, Union Pacific System, Year ended December 31, 1935.* Union Pacific Collection, Durham Western Heritage Museum, Omaha, NE. Hereafter abbreviated UP Collection.

70. Drury, *Steam Locomotives*, 404.

71. Lloyd E. Stagner, *Union Pacific Motive Power In Transition, 1936–1960* (David City, NE: South Platte Press, 1993), 12. Stagner, a well known author and historian of steam motive power, utilized primary source materials including letters and telegrams from the UP archives for his work. It stands as one of the best monograph studies of a particular railroad and dieselization.

72. Klein, *Union Pacific*, 388.

73. Letter, President's File, UP Collection. Quoted in Stagner, *Union Pacific Motive Power in Transition*, 10.

74. Many of these locomotives survive. Several Big Boys are enshrined in museums from Texas to Colorado to Steamtown in Pennsylvania. The UP also operates a Challenger and a 4–8–4 on special excursions. The 4–8–4, number 844 also has the distinction of never having been officially retired. The UP is currently alone among large railroads with its steam program.

75. Letter, President's File, August 2, 1945, UP Collection.

76. Ibid.

77. Union Pacific Railroad Company, Authority for Expenditure Number 11, March 4, 1940, ibid.

78. Letter, President's File, December 1, 1940, ibid.

79. "Union Pacific Obtains Five Diesels to aid S.L. in Curbing Smoke" *Salt Lake Telegram*, (August 20, 1940), ibid.

80. Letter, President's File, August 18, 1941, ibid.

81. Stagner, *Union Pacific Motive Power In Transition*, 46. Klein, *Union Pacific*.

82. Klein, *Union Pacific*, 443.

83. Union Pacific Railroad Company, Authority for Expenditure Number 6, January 12, 1947. UP collection. The order was split roughly 2/1 between EMD and Alco.

84. Stagner, *Union Pacific Motive Power In Transition*, 41. The main line from Omaha to Salt Lake was the least dieselized, while the Salt Lake to Los Angeles line was almost completely dieselized with less than 5 percent of passenger and freight mileage steam-hauled.

85. The standard history of the SP in the twentieth century is, Don L. Hofsommer, *The Southern Pacific, 1901–1985* (College Station: Texas A&M University Press, 1986).

86. Keilty, *Doodlebug Country*, 163–64.

87. Hofsommer, *Southern Pacific*, 134–35.

88. Garmany, *Southern Pacific Dieselization*, 55.

89. Ibid., 60–61.

90. Ibid., 87.

91. Technically, the train only went as far as Oakland, CA where passengers would board ferries for the ride across the bay.

92. Garmany, *Southern Pacific Dieselization*, 88. The train was advertised like a luxury ocean liner with a "sailing" every six days and as being new from "stem to stern" and the like.

93. Ibid., 110. Hofsommer, *Southern Pacific*, 136. One of these steam locomotives, the 4449, has been preserved by the city of Portland, Oregon and occasionally runs in excursion service.

94. Garmany, *Southern Pacific Dieselization*, 155. The streamliner units were jointly owned by all the operating railroads.

95. Ibid., 171. Also *Fifty-Eighth Annual Report of the Southern Pacific Company*, 1941, 59. California State Railroad Museum (CSRM) Collection, Sacramento, CA.

96. Drury, *Steam Locomotives*, 366.

97. The Sierra Nevada receives many feet of snow each winter and spring. To keep this heavy snow from interfering too much with operations, as well as to lessen the danger of avalanches, the railroad built many snowsheds, essentially long timber and later concrete buildings.

98. Drury, *Steam Locomotives*, 366. Hofsommer, *Southern Pacific*, 140.

99. Garmany, *Southern Pacific Dieselization*, 180.

100. Hofsommer, *Southern Pacific*, 192.

101. *Statistical Report of the Southern Pacific Company*, 1944, 59. CSRM Collection.

102. Garmany, *Southern Pacific Dieselization*, 189.

103. Ibid.

104. *Statistical Report of the Southern Pacific Company*, 1947, 59. CSRM Collection.

105. Ibid.

106. Hofsommer, *Southern Pacific*, 211.

107. "Benefits from Complete Dieselization of an Entire Division or Subdivision," *Railway Age* (June 25, 1949): 84–85.

108. *Southern Pacific Company Ten Year Motive Power Survey*, August 15, 1948, 11, CSRM Collection.

109. Ibid., Exhibit 1, 1.

110. Roseville is just west of Sacramento, while Sparks is just east of Reno.

111. Ibid., Exhibit 1, 19.

112. Ibid., Exhibit 1, 43.

113. Ibid., Exhibit 1, 14.

114. Ibid., Exhibit 2, 7–9.

115. *Statistical Report of the Southern Pacific Company, 1953*, 47, CSRM Collection.

116. *Survey of Motive Power*, May 24, 1954, 2, CSRM Collection.

117. Ibid., 4.

118. Ibid., 5.

119. *Southern Pacific Company Statistical Supplement to the 74th Annual Report, 1957*, 22, CSRM Collection.

120. Drury, *Steam Locomotives*, 357. Technically the last steam locomotive in regular operation on the SP system was on an isolated narrow gauge line in the California desert. The date for its last run was August 25, 1959. Because the line was narrow gauge and therefore isolated from the rest of the railroad system, this example is not included in the above analysis.

121. The steam operations of the N&W were immortalized in the photography of O. Winston Link in several books such as *Steam Steel and Stars* and *The Last Steam Railroad in America*.

122. Lewis, *Handbook*, 169.

123. Drury, *Steam Locomotives*, 308.

124. Ibid.

125. Ibid., 306. The last locomotive in this order, N&W number 244 was the last reciprocating steam locomotive built for common carrier service in the United States.

126. Atkins, *Dropping the Fire*, 25. Unlike business today, the railroad industry was dominated by presidents and other high ranking officials that had risen through the ranks and had much direct operating experience.

127. Keith L. Bryant, Jr., "Robert H. Smith," in *The Encyclopedia of American Business History and Biography: Railroads in the Age of Regulation*, ed. Keith L. Bryant, Jr. (New York: Facts on File, 1988), 404.

128. The lubritorium was not unlike a locomotive version of a "quick lube" for an automobile.

129. Drury, *Steam Locomotives*, 307.

130. For instance, EMD temporarily boosted the horsepower of the four unit diesel from 6,000 to 6,800. The N&W boosted the boiler pressure of the test locomotives from 300 to 315 pounds per square inch, added extra weight, and over bored cylinders by half inch. Atkins, *Dropping the Fire*, 24.

131. William E. Warden, *Norfolk & Western: Diesel's Last Conquest* (Lynchburg, VA: TLC Publishing, 1991), 3.

132. Atkins, *Dropping the Fire*, 25.

133. Warden, *Norfolk & Western*, 5.

134. Ibid. Saunders was accused of "lacking sentiment for steam" after the announcement. Saunders went on to infamy in the Penn Central merger and subsequent bankruptcy.

135. Atkins, *Dropping the Fire*, 25. President Smith also died in 1960.

136. Ibid, 41.

137. Drury, *Steam Locomotives*, 88.

138. Ibid., 83.

139. Philip Shuster, Eugene L. Huddleston, and Alvin Stauffer, *C&O Power* (Medina, OH: Alvin Staufer, 1965), 307.

140. Ibid., 299.

141. Charles V. Bias, "Walter J. Tuohy," in *The Encyclopedia of American Business History and Biography: Railroads in the Age of Regulation*, ed. Keith L. Bryant, Jr. (New York: Facts on File, 1988), 440.

142. Lewis, *Handbook*, 229.

143. Drury, *Steam Locomotives*, 419.

144. Lloyd D. Lewis, *Virginian Railway Locomotives* (Lynchburg, VA: TLC Publishing, 1993), 45.

145. Drury, *Steam Locomotives*, 418–19.

146. Lewis, *Virginian Railway Locomotives*, 54.

147. Ibid., 65. There was one exception to the pattern. A single, second hand, General Electric forty-four ton locomotive was purchased for switching industries in Suffolk, Virginia where a larger locomotive was not required.

148. George H. Drury, "Virginian Railway" in Middleton, Smerk, and Diehl, eds., *Encyclopedia of North American Railroads*, (Bloomington: Indiana University Press, 2007), 1084

149. The Illinois Central was assigned to the southern region by the ICC because the majority of its trackage was in that district. Lewis, *Handbook*, 112.

150. Ibid., 113.

151. Drury, *Steam Locomotives*, 207.

152. The Green Diamond was nicknamed the "Green Worm" and was widely regarded as the least aesthetically pleasing of all the streamlined trains of the 1930s.

153. Marre, *Diesel Locomotives*, 102.

154. Ibid., 161. Altogether there were three large transfer locomotives, two built by GE and one by EMC, purchased in 1936. All were for service in downtown Chicago transferring long trains to other rail yards.

155. Drury, *Steam Locomotives*, 204–205. Most rebuilding was performed at the expansive shops in Paducah, Kentucky.

156. Lewis, *Handbook*, 114.

157. Lloyd E. Stagner, *Illinois Central in Color* (Edison, NJ: Morning Sun Books, 1996), 104. Through passenger trains are generally trains that would be called Expresses or Limiteds. They travel from one major city to another and stop only at larger towns along the way. Local passenger services would stop at all stations and would generally travel less distance.

158. Ibid., 76.

159. Ibid.

160. Ibid.

161. The IC did much the same thing with its diesel fleet thirty years later. As the first generation of diesels (the GP-7 and 9 types) began to experience age related maintenance issues, the railroad opted to rebuild the locomotives at its Paducah shops. The result was almost new locomotives at a fraction of the price of new. Some of these rebuilds are still in service.

162. During most of the period under study (1920–56) class I railroads had annual operating revenue of $1 million or more. Most terminal and short lines were either class II or class III. From 1920 to 1956,

Class II railroads were designated as having revenues from $100,000 to $1 million with Class III railroads having revenues below $100,000. *Statistics of Railways in the United States,* Various.

163. "TRRA's Brooklyn Shops," *Terminal Railroad Association of St. Louis Historical and Technical Society* no. 17 (January, February, March, 1991), 6.

164. Ibid., 6, 15. The grades mentioned include the approaches to the Mississippi river bridges.

165. G. J. Michels, Jr., "Diesel Locomotives of the Terminal Railroad Association of St. Louis," *Terminal Railroad Association of St. Louis Historical and Technical Society* no. 51–52 (Summer/Autumn, 1999), 4. Manufacturers represented were EMC, Alco, and Baldwin.

166. Ibid., 5.

167. Ibid., 6.

168. EuDaly, *Missouri Pacific Diesel Power,* 130. In the late 1960s the A&S came under the control of the Missouri Pacific and Chicago & North Western Railroads, hence its inclusion in the above work.

169. Typical rail weights during the period of dieselization ranged from 90 pounds per yard up to over 150. Shortlines often had rail that weighed eighty, sixty, or even forty lbs/yd.

170. Shortlines, simply because of their size, often lack the extensive documentation that many larger roads have received. Most records are lost or scattered. Many shortlines were privately owned so there is little in the public records about them. An exception to this case is the Mississippi Central. The bulk of their records have been preserved at the University of Southern Mississippi in Hattiesburg.

171. Letter dated February 6, 1912, Mississippi Central collection, McCain Library and Archives, University Libraries, the University of Southern Mississippi. Collection hereafter abbreviated USM.

172. Motive Power Study for the Mississippi Central Railroad Company by Alco, August 1951, page 16, USM. In purchasing locomotives directly from a builder and not secondhand, the Mississippi Central was clearly among the more successful of shortlines.

173. Motive Power Study for the Mississippi Central Railroad Company by Alco, August 1951, 3, USM. Of interest is that the 14.1 percent figure was circled in red pencil.

174. Mississippi Central Railroad, The Application of Baldwin-Westinghouse Diesel Motive Power on the Mississippi Central Railway, January 1952, USM.

175. Application of General Motors Diesel Motive Power on the Mississippi Central Railroad, February 1952, 2, USM.

176. Memo, unlabled, July 13, 1953, Mississippi Central collection, USM.

177. Memo, File 1043, February 19, 1953, Mississippi Central Collection, USM.

178. Lewis, *Handbook,* 140. This technically placed the Mississippi Central in the class 1 category, but it would lose this status with the change in classification in 1956.

CHAPTER 5. ROUTES NOT TAKEN

1. Gas turbines were essentially jet engines optimized for shaft output. Steam turbines were in regular use in marine and stationary applications. Free-piston gasifiers were a cross between a conventional

piston engine diesel and a gas turbine. The engine was designed to produce hot, high pressure gas, not mechanical movement. For more on the proposed but never built nuclear powered locomotive, see Thornton Waite, "Dr. Borst's X-12: The Atomic Locomotive," *Railroad History* (Autumn 1996): 37–55.

2. George Woodman Hilton, *The Electric Interurban Railways in America* (Stanford, CA: Stanford University Press, 1964). See also William D. Middleton, *The Interurban Era* (Milwaukee: Kalmbach, 1961). In contemporary terms, most electric railroads would be classified as light rail systems. The rail as well as the vehicles operating on the rail are lighter in weight than regular railroads.

3. Drury, *Historical Guide to North American Railroads*, 246–47. Parts of the former Pacific Electric are now used for light rail commuter services in the LA region.

4. For more information on the IT, see Dale Jenkins, *The Illinois Terminal Railroad: The Road of Personalized Services* (Hart, MO: White River Productions, 2005).

5. William D. Middleton, *When the Steam Railroads Electrified*, 429.

6. Most of the data for the various electrification projects comes from William D. Middleton *When the Steam Roads Electrified* and his entry "Electrification" in the *Encyclopedia of North American Railroads*.

7. Middleton, *When the Steam Railroads Electrified* (Milwaukee, WI: Kalmbach Publishing, 1974), 428–35. The author vividly remembers trips into Chicago on 1920s vintage, green Illinois Central electric cars in the mid-1970s.

8. Mason Y. Cooper, *Norfolk & Western Electrics* (Forrest, VA: Norfolk & Western Historical Society, 2000).

9. Noel T. Holley, *The Milwaukee Electrics* (Edmond, WA: Hundman Publishing, 1999).

10. "The Electric Divisions of the Chicago Milwaukee & St. Paul Railway" General Electric Bulletin GEA-150A, November 1927, 43. Reprinted in *Electrification by GE*, Bulletin 116 of Central Electric Railfans' Association, Chicago, IL 1976.

11. Middleton, "Electrification," in *Encyclopedia of North American Railroads*, 419.

12. Middleton, *When the Steam Railroads Electrified*, 433. The N&W and Virginian merged in 1959, so technically the N&W operated electrics from 1915 to 1950 on its own line and then from 1959 to 1962 on the recently acquired ex-Virginian line.

13. The Milwaukee road would only last for another six years as a separate corporation. It went out of business and the former electrified lines were abandoned in 1980.

14. Michael Bezilla, *Electric Traction on the Pennsylvania Railroad, 1895–1968* (University Park: Penn State University Press, 1980), 161.

15. In Europe and Japan, electrification has been much more successful, precisely because of greater government involvement.

16. J. S. Newton and W.A. Brect, "A Geared Steam-Turbine Locomotive," *Railway Age* (February 17, 1945): 337–40. Drury, *Steam Locomotives*, 393–95.

17. Hirsimaki, *Black Gold–Black Diamonds*, 130–2.

18. Hagley, Chief of Motive Power Files.

19. Philip Shuster, Eugene L. Huddleston, and Alvin Staufer, *C&O Power* (Medina, OH: Alvin Staufer, 1965), 299.

20. Warden, *Norfolk & Western*, 11–12.

21. "Steam Locomotives" in *Encyclopedia of North American Railroads*, 1030.

22. Thomas R. Lee, *Turbines Westward* (Manhattan, KS: T. Lee Publications, 1975), 7–11.

23. Ibid., Horsepower on the "Big Blow" turbines was later raised to ten thousand.

24. Ibid., 32–34. The UP had online coal sources in Wyoming that this locomotive was designed to utilize.

25. Erik Hirsimaki, "Turbines, King Coal Battles the Diesel," in *Classic Trains* (Fall 2004): 24–35.

26. As more refineries invested in catalytic cracking technology in the 1950s, they were able to break down the heavy oil into lighter fuels such as diesel and gasoline.

27. Garmany, *Southern Pacific Dieselization*, 324–25.

28. Marre, *Diesel Locomotives*, 29, 329.

29. Garmany, *Southern Pacific Dieselization*, 326–28.

30. Adhesion is the friction between the wheel and the rail. The higher the factor, the greater pulling power a locomotive can exert before slipping.

31. P. V. Garin, "Diesel Hydraulic Locomotives" paper presented to West Coast meeting of Society of Automotive Engineers, San Francisco, CA, August 18, 1960, 22–23. SP Collection CSRM.

32. "Locomotives: A Study of Engineering and Performance Factors Influencing Their Design and Selection," August 6, 1962, SP Collection, CSRM.

33. Letter, President's File, April 28, 1959, SP Collection, CSRM.

34. Joseph A. Strapac, *Southern Pacific Historic Diesels, vol. 2* (Bellflower, CA: Shade Tree Books, 1993), 15.

35. Ibid.

36. Ibid., 29, 43.

37. Ibid., 37.

38. Krauss Maffei ML-4000 Operating Manual, http://gelwood.railfan.net/manual/km-gen.html (June 17, 2002).

39. Marre, *Diesel Locomotives*.

CHAPTER 6.   SHOVELING OIL

1. *Statistics of Railroads of Class I in the United States*, Association of American Railroads. Wages and Salaries only. Taxes, including payroll taxes, are counted separately.

2. Fireman was the official name for these employees. During the time period under study the operating employees of the railroads were almost entirely male. Therefore all references to gender reflect the spirit of the time and are essentially correct. While women were employed from the beginnings of railroading as office workers and telegraphers and during World War II as shop workers I have come across no evidence that women ever held the job of engineer or fireman in any numbers until the 1970s.

3. An engineer was quite different from an engineman, although both may have run locomotives. An engineman, also referred to as a hostler, could only move light locomotives (that is, locomotives not pulling a train) around an engine terminal or into and between shop

buildings while an engineer was responsible for running locomotives able to pull trains in yards and on the main line.

4. For further information into the lives of railroad workers in the nineteenth century see Walter Licht, *Working for the Railroad: The Organization of Work in the Nineteenth Century* (Princeton, NJ: Princeton University Press, 1983) and James H. Ducker, *Men of the Steel Rails: Workers on the Atchison, Topeka & Santa Fe Railroad, 1869–1900* (Lincoln: University of Nebraska Press, 1983)

5. *Wages and Labor Relations in the Railroad Industry, 1900–1941* (Executive Committee of the Bureau of Information of the Eastern Railways, 1942), 33–34.

6. The railroad wage structure was exceedingly complex. In addition to the above mentioned criteria, the fuel source of the locomotive, whether it was equipped with a stoker, and the geographic location of the railroad; East, West, or South, were all factors.

7. *Comparative Labor Standards in Transportation* (Washington, DC: Section of Research, Section of Labor Relations, Federal Coordinator of Transportation, March 1937), 133–34.

8. "Modern Machinery Increasing Unemployment," *Brotherhood of Locomotive Firemen and Enginemen's Magazine* 88 (February 1930): 103.

9. "Validity of Arkansas Full Crew Laws Again Sustained," *Brotherhood of Locomotive Firemen and Enginemen's Magazine* 88 (July 1930): 20.

10. *Locomotive Engineers Journal* 69 (May 1935): 371, and *Locomotive Engineers Journal* 70 (August 1936): 79–80.

11. *Locomotive Engineers Journal* 70 (December 1936): 899.

12. In fact, a major manufacturer of motorcars was the Brill Co. also a major manufacturer of trolleys and streetcars. Many motorcars were constructed more like streetcars than like regular, heavyweight railroad passenger coaches. See Debra Brill, *History of the J. G. Brill Company* (Bloomington: Indiana University Press, 2001).

13. "Texas Railroad Commission Issues Momentous Order Regarding Full Crew Law," *Brotherhood of Locomotive Firemen and Enginemen's Magazine* 88 (January 1930): 3. Hereafter abbreviated *BLE&FM.*

14. Ibid., 4.

15. "The Burlington's Obstinacy," *BLF&EM* 99 (September 1935): 133.

16. "The Burlington Settlement" *BLF&EM* 100 (January 1936): 9.

17. *BLF&EM* 100 (June 1936): 351.

18. There were some conspicuously absent railroads (including the Southern, Gulf Mobile and Northern, Mobile & Ohio, Louisville & Nashville, and the Atlantic Coast Line) all located in the south, but for all intents and purposes this was as close to a national agreement as could be achieved at the time. This agreement also led to a market for lightweight diesel locomotives that GE exploited with their forty-four ton (88,000 lbs) line of locomotives.

19. "Two Men for Diesel Road and Yard Engines," *BLF&EM* 102 (March 1937), 147.

20. *Revolutionary Diesel,* 7–8.

21. "Brotherhood Inaugurates Wage Movement" *BLF&EM* 110 (June 1941), 359.

22. This management position was also taken up by the locomotive builders. For instance they would refer to a 6,000 horsepower, four unit combination as one locomotive consisting of four units when it was for all intents and purposes four separate locomotives, all capable

of independent action, merely operating together and centrally controlled from the cab of the first unit. They also did not make space for crewmen to ride in the engine compartments.

23. Reed C. Richardson, *The Locomotive Engineer, 1863–1963* (Ann Arbor: Bureau of Industrial Relations, University of Michigan, 1963), 415.

24. John Patric with Frank J. Taylor, "'Featherbedding' Hampers the War Effort," *Readers Digest* (March 1943): 27. Reprinted from *Barron's*, February 8, 1943.

25. *Locomotive Enginemen's Magazine* (May 1943): 311.

26. Ibid., 312–16.

27. *Locomotive Enginemen's Magazine* (June 1943): 416.

28. Richard Saunders, Jr., *Merging Lines, American Railroads, 1900–1970*, (DeKalb: Northern Illinois University Press, 2001), 151.

29. "That's Railroading" *Time*, 9 August 1963.

30. Ibid.

31. Ann Schwarz-Miller and Wayne K. Talley, "Technology and Labor Relations: Railroads and Ports" *Journal of Labor Research*, vol. 32, no. 4 (Fall 2002): 516.

32. Statistics from AAR Annual Yearbook of Railroad Facts, various years quoted in, Stuart M. Rich, "Changing Railway Technology in the United States and its impact upon Railroad Employment since 1945," *Transportation Journal* vol. 25, no. 4 (Summer 1986): 57.

33. US Bureau of the Census, Census of Manufacturers, 1914, vol. 2 (Washington, DC., 1919) "Railroad Repair Shops," table 30. Some of the shops were for railroad car manufacture and repair and not exclusively for locomotives.

34. Jerry A. Pinkepank, "How the Diesel Changed Railroading," *Classic Trains*, Diesel Victory, special edition no. 4, (2006): 13–4.

35. Simon E. Herring, "Bellfontaine–Profile of a Railroad Town," *Trains*, vol. 23 (1963): 29. Quoted in, William Douglas Warren, "The Railroad Town: A Study of Urban Response to Changes in Technology, Operating Procedures and Demand for Railroad Service in the post World War II period" (PhD. diss., University of North Carolina at Chapel Hill, 1972), 12.

36. Figures from Association of American Railroads, Annual *Yearbook of Railroad Facts*, quoted in, Stuart M. Rich, "Changing Railway Technology in the United States and Its Impact Upon Railroad Employment Since 1945," *Transportation Journal* 25, no. 4 (Summer 1986): 57.

37. Ibid. Total railroad employment continued to fall. In 1984 employment was less than 350,000, or less than 24 percent of the 1946 level.

38. Warren, "Railroad Town." 38. The other major factor in the decline in railroad employment was the curtailment of large numbers of passenger services. Consolidation of trains together with dieselization and passenger train discontinuance accounted for probably 80 to 90 percent of job loss. Mergers and abandonment did not lead to significant job loss in the 1945–60 period.

39. For example, the Illinois Central had many shops from Chicago to New Orleans but all heavy overhaul work was performed at the large shops in Paducah, KY.

40. Data from US census, 1960.

41. Data from US census, quoted in Warren, "Railroad Town." Other information from Russell L. Crump, Stephen Priest, and Cinthia Priest, *Santa Fe Locomotive Facilities, vol. 1 The Gulf Lines* (Kansas City, MO: Paired Rail Railroad Publications, 2003).

42. Data from US census, quoted in Warren, "Railroad Town."

43. W. F. Cotrell, "Death by Dieselization: A Case Study in the Reaction to Technological Change," *American Sociological Review* (June 1951): 358.

44. Ibid., 360–61.

45. While these now classic and seemingly obvious symptoms of deindustrialization are well known, it must be remembered that the writer was writing in 1951, long before the term "Rust Belt" was coined.

46. Data from US census.

47. Cotrell, "Death by Dieselization," 365.

CHAPTER 7.   RED MARKERS

1. US Department of Energy, Energy Information Administration. Coal production would increase after 1960 to over one thousand million tons by 1990, almost exclusively for electric power generation. Much of this coal was hauled by railroads. Even fifty years after the end of steam, coal remains a vital and important part of freight traffic for all major North American railroads.

2. Amtrak and manufacturer Bombardier are currently working on a high-speed gas turbine passenger locomotive. Perhaps the gas turbine will again emerge as a source of railroad motive power.

Bibliography

Notes on Sources

HISTORIANS WORKING ON RAILROAD HISTORY have no shortage of sources available to them. Railroads themselves produced massive amounts of paper records, some of which are preserved at various locations. Today there are seven large railroads operating in North America; Canadian National, Canadian Pacific, CSX Transportation, Norfolk Southern, Union Pacific, Burlington Northern Santa Fe, and Kansas City Southern. During the period of dieselization there were over 125. Despite generating massive amounts of paper, most of the corporate records from those railroads were lost or are inaccessible. A few are preserved in locations such as the Hagley Museum and Library in Delaware, the Pennsylvania State Archives, Colorado Railroad Museum, Southern Museum of Civil War and Locomotive History, and at the California State Railroad Museum. Many of the corporate records of the principal components of the seven major railroads are still in company hands and are not available for research. A notable exception is the Union Pacific which has substantial archival holdings at the Union Pacific Museum in Council Bluffs, Iowa. Of those records available, many are not from the time period of dieselization. For example, CSX Transportation is made up of many earlier railroads including the Baltimore & Ohio and the Chesapeake & Ohio. The Baltimore & Ohio Railroad Museum in Baltimore has many of the records of the B&O but only up to 1927. Likewise, the Chesapeake & Ohio Historical Society in Clifton Forge, Virginia, has the corporate records for the C&O, but they end in 1947, just when things begin to get interesting as far as dieselization is concerned. Not all open and accessible archives were created equal. Many of the corporate collections contain legal, labor, and/or engineering documents but do not contain the memos, letters, and other personal correspondence of the president and board of directors that can be so illuminating of the behind the scenes decision making process.

The trade press, particularly *Railway Age*, was especially valuable as a source of contemporary news and information as well as some limited commentary. In addition to articles, advertisements and editorials also provide insight into the railroad industry and its concerns at mid century. Railroads,

319

being a highly regulated industry, generated reams of statistical data. This data, compiled by the Interstate Commerce Commission (ICC) as well as the railroad industry association, the Association of American Railroads (AAR), was especially valuable, particularly for the analysis of large, industry-wide trends. Individual railroad annual reports provide a wealth of financial and other data on specific railroads.

Beyond primary sources, there are many secondary sources on railroads, too many in fact for anyone to consult them all. The Railway and Locomotive Historical Society publishes the journal, *Railroad History* which is a great resource, especially for detailed roster information on steam and diesel locomotives. The National Railway Historical Society, or NRHS while it hasn't published a journal the quality of *Railroad History* for as long, has published some well researched and written articles in its various publications. Individual railroad historical society records and publications can be very helpful with details about specific locomotives or operations. While these works are not focused on the large scale portrait of the industry, they provide a much needed smaller scale view on specific topics. Most are firmly based in archival and oral history and are an important source. The excellent publications of the Anthracite Railroads Historical Society, TRRA Historical Society and Missouri Pacific Historical Society are examples of these sources. Like the railroad historical societies, popular railroad magazines like *Trains* and *Railroad* can provide useful information that can not be found elsewhere. While many articles are concerned with technical and operational details, a surprising number deal with various economic, social, and cultural aspects of railroading.

Railfans have produced a seemingly endless amount of books on various aspects of railroad industry and history. While many of these are primarily pictorial in nature, some are very useful as sources. Even pictorial works can illustrate key facilities or operations that can not be otherwise found. Often these railfan publications are the only readily available source for specific technical and operational data. However, the quality of these works is as varied as their topics. Some are firmly based on archival and first person research while others merely repeat information available in other publications, sometimes incorrectly. The railfan community has produced a wealth of magazine articles and books on aspects of dieselization, but most do not look at it from a critical historical perspective. There are a few railfan works that do stand out. For information on diesel production there are several excellent railfan sources. A basic handbook that documents types and numbers produced is Louis A. Marre, *Diesel Locomotives: The First 50 Years* (Waukesha, WI: Kalmbach Publishing, 1995). The best railfan history of the technical development of the diesel is J. Parker Lamb, *Evolution of the American Diesel Locomotive* (Bloomington: Indiana University Press, 2007). For more detailed information on specific railroads there are a few railfan works that are particularly well done. They include but are not limited to, John Bonds Garmany, *Southern Pacific Dieselization* (Edmonds, WA: Pacific Fast Mail, 1985), Robert E. Mohowski, *New York Ontario and Western in the Diesel Age* (Andover, NJ: Andover Junction Publications, 1994), and John B. McCall, *Santa Fe's Early Diesel Daze, 1935–1953* (Dallas: Kachina Press, 1980). There are others mentioned throughout the text. Many of the railfan publications such as locomotive news magazines, *Extra 2200 South* and *Diesel Era* contain vast amounts of useful data. Listings of locomotives, while providing little if any analysis, provide a wealth of data on the number, type, manufacturer, and service dates of all the locomotives owned by a particular railroad. There are many books that also include locomotive rosters, most often with photos and sometimes with other primary source material as well. Many are mentioned below and throughout the text. These railfan sources can provide information that is lacking from other sources, and, when put into context, can illuminate larger issues.

For general railroad history there are several well written scholarly works on specific railroads. The many excellent works of H. Roger Grant and Don Hofsommer for instance are a mandatory starting spot for any research into specific railroads. The best overall view of railroads in the twentieth century are the works of Richard Saunders, especially *Merging Lines* and *Main Lines*. There are other excellent railroad histories but many were written in the 1960s and have little on the time period of dieselization or the other challenges of highly regulated twentieth century railroading.

The scholarly work done specifically on dieselization is limited and mostly confined to economic studies that do not adequately address the multiplicity of influences on the dieselization process. Exceptions are noted below. John K. Brown in his book, *The Baldwin Locomotive Works, 1831–1915*, looks at the premier steam locomotive producer of the nineteenth century, Baldwin. Brown does briefly look at the decline of Baldwin and the rise of the Electro-Motive Division of General Motors (EMD), and more specifically how Baldwin's preoccupation with incremental improvements in steam locomotive technology blinded the company's management to the revolutionary aspects of the diesel.

The response of locomotive builders such as Baldwin, Alco, and the Electro-Motive Division of General Motors to dieselization was the subject of a dissertation and a later book by Albert Churella entitled, *Steam to Diesel*. Churella realized the distinctive nature of the diesel locomotive and its potential to reshape railroad operations, but the actual use of locomotives on the railroads themselves was not the emphasis of his work; instead he chose to focus on the business practices and corporate culture of the locomotive builders and their response to technological change. Regardless, it is essential reading for those interested in dieselization.

The most recent scholarly work on specifically on dieselization is a dissertation by Mark Mapes. In his work he examines in depth the dieselization of the Pennsylvania Railroad. He identifies many differing motives in the dieselization of the PRR including loyalty to the coal industry, early antismoke legislation, and competition with other railroads. These and other motives would appear in other railroads' decisions as well. However, as mentioned previously, the experiences of the large and powerful Pennsylvania railroad (PRR) can not be extrapolated to the entire railroad system.

I am certain that there are sources, particularly railfan sources, that I have not examined. The sheer volume prohibits detailed examination of all the sources on railroads from 1920 to 1960. However, the sources listed in the notes and below are wide and varied enough to give a accurate view of the complexities of dieselization on the railroads of the United States.

ARCHIVAL DOCUMENT COLLECTIONS

American Locomotive Company Papers, 1872–1969. Syracuse University Library, Syracuse, NY.

Atchison Topeka and Santa Fe Railroad Collection. California State Railroad Museum, Sacramento, CA.

Baldwin Locomotive Works Collection. DeGolyer Library, Southern Methodist University, Dallas, TX.

Brotherhood of Locomotive Firemen and Enginemen Records, 1890–1962. California State Railroad Museum, Sacramento, CA.

Denver and Rio Grande Western Railroad Collection. Colorado Railroad Museum, Golden, CO.

John "Jack" F. Weiffenbach Papers, 1936–56. California State Railroad Museum, Sacramento, CA.

Lehigh Valley Railroad Company Annual Reports: 1920 to 1969. Central of New Jersey Railroad Company Annual Reports: 1923 to 1955. Railroad Museum of Pennsylvania, Strasburg, PA.

Lehigh Valley Railroad Company Corporate Minutes: 1924 to 1955. Pennsylvania Historical and Museum Commission, Harrisburg, PA.

Mercantile Library collections, University of Missouri–St. Louis.

Mississippi Central Railroad Collection. McCain Library and Archives, University Libraries, The University of Southern Mississippi, Hattiesburg, MS.

Pennsylvania Railroad Collection. New York Central Railroad Annual Reports. Baltimore and Ohio Railroad Annual Reports. Hagley Museum and Library, Wilmington, DE.

Southern Pacific Railroad Collection. California State Railroad Museum, Sacramento, CA.

Southern Railway Collection. Southern Museum of Civil War and Locomotive History, Kennesaw, GA.

St. Louis–San Francisco Railroad Company collection. Missouri University of Science and Technology. Western Historical Manuscript Collection–Rolla, Rolla, MO.

Union Pacific Railroad Company Records Collection. Durham Western Heritage Museum, Omaha, NE.

UNPUBLISHED SOURCES

Candee, A. H. "Report on the Use of Diesel Electric Motive Power for Symbol Freight Train Services." Westinghouse Electric and Baldwin Locomotive Works, May 1948. Author's Collection.

Mack, James E. "Lehigh Valley Railroad Write-Ups." Historical Collection, Easton Public Library, Easton, PA, 1980.

Pohl, John Charles Jr. "A History of the Lehigh Valley Railroad In and About Easton Pennsylvania." Historical Collection, Easton Public Library, Easton, PA, 1952.

Sawyer, R. Tom. Manager Alco Products. "Motive Power–Past and Future." Speech given before Society of Automobile Engineers, Metropolitan Section, April 5, 1956.

MANUALS AND PAMPHLETS

Diesel: The Modern Power. Detroit: General Motors Corporation, 1936.

EMD F-3 Locomotive Operating Manual. La Grange, IL: General Motors Corporation, Electro-Motive Division, 1946.

EMD F-3 Locomotive Operating Manual. La Grange, IL: General Motors Corporation, Electro-Motive Division, 1948.

EMD Operating Manual, 600 and 1000 h.p. Switching Locomotives. La Grange, IL: General Motors Corporation, Electro-Motive Division, 1949.

General Motors Diesel Locomotives. Statement by C. R. Osborn, Vice President before Subcommittee on Antitrust and Monopoly of the U. S. Senate Committee on the Judiciary, December 9 1955. General Motors Corporation, Electro-Motive Division, 1955.

GP38-AC Operators Manual. La Grange, IL: General Motors Corporation, Electro-Motive Division, 1971.

Instructors Guide: On the Operation of Model F-2 Diesel Locomotives. La Grange, IL: General Motors Corporation, Electro-Motive Division, 1946.

Krauss Maffei ML-4000 Operating Manual. http://gelwood.railfan.net/manual/km-gen.html. July 17, 2000.

Operating Manual: 1500 h.p. Road Locomotive Units. Schenectady, NY: American Locomotive Co. General Electric Co., 1947.

Operating Manual: 2000 h.p. Road Locomotive Units. Schenectady, NY: American Locomotive Co. General Electric Co., 1948.

Operating Manual: 1600 h.p. Freight Passenger Locomotive. Schenectady, NY: American Locomotive Co. General Electric Co., 1950.

Operators Manual: Diesel-Electric Passenger Locomotive. Philadelphia: Baldwin Locomotive Works, 1946.

MAGAZINES

Locomotive Engineer's Journal. Brotherhood of Locomotive Engineers Union periodical. Cleveland, OH, 1930–1953.

Brotherhood of Locomotive Firemen's Magazine. Cleveland, OH, 1930–46.

Diesel Era

Diesel Power. New York, 1935–1955.

Extra 2200 South.

Railway Age. Philadelphia, 1920–1960.

Scientific American. May 1947.

Trains. Milwaukee, WI, 1945–2007.

REPORTS AND STATISTICAL SOURCES

Comparative Labor Standards in Transportation. Federal Coordinator of Transportation, 1937.

Federal Legislation, Etc. Affecting Railroad Employees. Brotherhood of Locomotive Firemen and Enginemen, 1940.

Historical Statistics of the United States, Colonial Times to 1970. US Census, 1976.

Jones, Harry E., ed. *Wages and Labor Relations in the Railroad Industry, 1900–1941.* Executive Committee of the Bureau of Information of the Eastern Railways, 1942.

Petroleum Facts and Figures, Centennial Edition. New York: American Petroleum Institute, 1959.

Railroads in This Century. Association of American Railroads, July 1947.

Railways of the United States, Their Plant, Facilities, and Operation. Washington, DC: Association of American Railroads, 1940.

A Review of Railroad Operations in 1960. Washington, DC: Association of American Railroads, Bureau of Railway Economics, 1961.

Statistics of Railways of Class I. Association of American Railroads, 1920–65.

Statistics of Railways in the United States. Interstate Commerce Commission, 1920–53.

Transportation in America. Association of American Railroads, 1947.

Wages and Labor Relations in the Railroad Industry, 1900–1941. Executive Committee of the Bureau of Information of the Eastern Railways, 1941.

Warren, John T., and Alexis P Bukovsky. *Study of Railroad Motive Power.* Washington DC: Interstate Commerce Commission, Bureau of Transport Economics and Statistics. File no. 66-A-11, statement no. 5025, May 1950.

Wartime Wages and Railroad Labor. Brotherhood of Railroad Trainmen, 1944.

PUBLISHED BOOKS AND ARTICLES

Aldag, Robert. "Steam Vs. Diesel Locomotives." *Railroad History* 167 (Autumn 1992): 148–57.

Archer, Eric H. *Streamlined Steam.* New York: Quadrant Press, 1972.

Archer, Robert F. *Lehigh Valley Railroad.* Berkeley, CA: Howell-North Books, 1977.

Armstrong, John H. *The Railroad: What It Is, What It Does.* 3d. ed. Omaha, NE: Simmons-Boardman Books, 1993.

Arnesen, Eric. *Brotherhoods of Color, Black Railroad Workers and the Struggle for Equality.* Cambridge, MA: Harvard University Press, 2001.

Atkins, Philip. *Dropping the Fire.* Clophill, Bedfordshire: Irwell Press, 1999.

Bezilla, Michael. *Electric Traction on the Pennsylvania Railroad, 1895–1968.* University Park: Pennsylvania State University Press, 1980.

———. "Pennsylvania Railroad Motive Power Strategies, 1920–1950," *Railroad History* 164 (Spring 1991).

———. "Steam Railroad Electrification in America, 1920–1950: The Unrealized Potential." *The Public Historian* 4, no. 1 (Winter 1982): 29–52.

Bijker, Wiebe E., Thomas P. Hughes, and Trevor Pinch, eds. *The Social Construction of Technological Systems.* Cambridge, MA: MIT Press, 1989

Bix, Amy Sue. *Inventing Ourselves Out of Jobs, America's Debate over Technological Unemployment, 1929–1981.* Baltimore: Johns Hopkins University Press, 2000.

Brill, Debra. *History of the J. G. Brill Company.* Bloomington: Indiana University Press, 2001.

Brown, John K. *The Baldwin Locomotive Works, 1831–1915.* Baltimore: Johns Hopkins University Press, 1995.

Bruce, Alfred W. *The Steam Locomotive in America.* New York: W. W. Norton & Co., 1952.

Bryant, Keith L. Jr., ed. *The Encyclopedia of American Business History and Biography: Railroads in the Age of Regulation.* New York: Facts on File, 1988.

Bush, Donald J. *The Streamlined Decade.* New York: George Braziller, 1975.

Calloway, Warren L. *Atlantic Coast Line: The Diesel Years*. Halifax, PA: Withers Publishing, 1993.

Calloway, Warren L., and Paul K. Withers. *Seaboard Air Line Company Motive Power*. Halifax, PA: Withers Publishing, 1988.

Castner, Charles B., Ronald Flanary, and Lee Gordon. *Louisville and Nashville Diesels*. Lynchburg, VA: TLC Publishing, 1998.

Cengel, Yunus A., and Michael A. Boles. *Thermodynamics: An Engineering Approach*. New York: McGraw-Hill, 1989.

Chandler, Alfred D. Jr. *The Visible Hand: The Managerial Revolution in American Business*. Cambridge, MA: Belknap Press, 1977.

Churella, Albert J. *From Steam to Diesel*. Princeton, NJ: Princeton University Press, 1998.

Coel, Margaret. "A Silver Streak." *American Heritage of Invention & Technology* (Fall 1986): 10–17.

Cooper, Mason Y. *Norfolk & Western Electrics*. Forrest, VA: Norfolk & Western Historical Society, 2000.

Constant, Edward. *The Origins of the Turbojet Revolution*. Baltimore: Johns Hopkins University Press, 1980.

Corbin, Bernard G., and William F. Kerka. *Steam Locomotives of the Burlington Route*. Red Oak, IA(?): Corbin-Kerka, 1960.

Cottrell, Fred. "Death By Dieselization: A Case Study in the Reaction to Technological Change." *American Sociological Review* 16 (June 1951): 358–65.

———. *Technological Change and Labor in the Railroad Industry*. Lexington, MA: Heath Lexington Books, 1970.

Crump, Russell L., Stephen Priest, and Cinthia Priest. *Santa Fe Locomotive Facilities. Vol. 1, The Gulf Lines*. Kansas City, MO: Paired Rail Railroad Publications, 2003.

Cummins, C. Lyle, Jr. *Diesel's Engine. Vol. 1, From Conception to 1918*. Wilsonville, OR: Carnot Press, 1993.

DeYoung, Larry. *Erie-Lackawanna in Color. Vol. 4: The Early Years*. Scotch Plains, NJ: Morning Sun Books, 1997.

Dolzall, Gary W., and Stephen F. *Diesels from Eddystone: The History of Baldwin Diesel Locomotives*. Milwaukee: Kalmbach, 1984.

Dover, Dan. "Lehigh Valley, Part I." *Extra 2200 South* 76 (July-September 1982): 22–29.

———. "Lehigh Valley, Part II." *Extra 2200 South* 77 (October-December 1982): 15–21.

Draney, John. *Diesel Locomotives: Electrical Equipment*. Chicago: American Technical Society, 1944.

———. *Diesel Locomotives: Mechanical Equipment*. Chicago: American Technical Society, 1945.

Droege, John A. *Freight Terminals and Trains*. 1925. reprint, Chattanooga, TN: National Model Railroad Association, 1998.

Drury, George H. *Guide to North American Steam Locomotives*. Waukesha, WI: Kalmbach, 1993.

———. *The Historical Guide to North American Railroads*. Waukesha, WI: Kalmbach, 1991.

Dubofsky, Melvyn, and Warren Van Tine. *John L. Lewis: A Biography.* Urbana: University of Illinois Press, 1986.

Ducker, James H. *Men of the Steel Rails.* Lincoln: University of Nebraska Press, 1983.

Duffy, Michael C. *Electric Railways, 1880–1990.* London, UK: The Institution of Electrical Engineers, 2003.

Edson, William D. "Diesel Locomotives of the Gulf Mobile and Ohio." *Railroad History* 158 (Spring 1988).

Edson, William D., with H. L. Vail, and C. M. Smith. *New York Central System Diesel Locomotives.* Lynchburg, VA: TLC Publishing, 1995.

Electrification by GE. General Electric, 1923, 1927, 1929. Reprinted as Bulletin 116 of Central Electric Railfans'Association, Chicago, 1976.

EuDaly, Kevin. *Missouri Pacific Diesel Power.* Kansas City, MO: Whiteriver Productions, 1994.

Farrington, S. Kip Jr. *Railroading the Modern Way.* New York: Coward-McCann, Inc., 1951.

Garmany, John Bonds. *Southern Pacific Dieselization.* Edmonds, WA: Pacific Fast Mail Publications, 1985.

Glendinning, Gene V. *The Chicago and Alton Railroad: The Only Way.* DeKalb: Northern Illinois University Press, 2002.

Gordon, Sarah H. *Passage to Union: How the Railroads Transformed American Life, 1829–1929.* Chicago: Ivan R. Dee, 1996.

Grant, H. Roger. *The Corn Belt Route: A History of the Chicago Great Western Railroad Company.* DeKalb: Northern Illinois University Press, 1984.

———. *Erie Lackawanna: Death of an American Railroad, 1938–1992.* Stanford, CA: Stanford University Press, 1994

———. *Follow the Flag: A History of the Wabash Railroad Company.* DeKalb: Northern Illinois University Press, 2004.

———. *The Northwestern: A History of the Chicago and North Western Railway System.* DeKalb, IL: Northern Illinois University Press, 1996.

———. *The Railroad: The Life Story of a Technology.* Westport, CT: Greenwood Press, 2005.

Harwood, Herbert H. *Invisible Giants: The Empires of Cleveland's Van Swearingen Brothers.* Bloomington: Indiana University Press, 2003.

Henry, Robert Selph. *This Fascinating Railroad Business* 3d. ed. Indianapolis, IN: Bobbs-Merrill Co., 1946.

Heywood, John B. *Internal Combustion Engine Fundamentals.* New York: McGraw-Hill, Inc., 1988.

Hilton, George Woodman. *The Electric Interurban Railways in America.* Stanford, CA: Stanford University Press, 1964.

Hirsimaki, Eric. *Black Gold—Black Diamonds: The Pennsylvania Railroad and Dieselization, Vol. 1.* North Olmstead, OH: Mileposts Publishing, 1997.

———. *Black Gold–Black Diamonds: The Pennsylvania Railroad and Dieselization. Vol. 2.* North Olmstead, OH: Mileposts Publishing, 2000.

———. *Lima.* Edmonds, WA: Hundman Publishing, 1986.

Hofsommer, Don L. *The Southern Pacific, 1901–1985.* College Station: Texas A & M University Press, 1986.

Holland, Kevin J. *Nickel Plate Road Diesel Locomotives.* Lynchburg, VA: TLC Publishing, 1998.

Holley, Noel T. *The Milwaukee Electrics.* Edmond, WA: Hundman Publishing, 1999.

Holton, James L. *The Reading Railroad: History of a Coal Age Empire, Vol. 2, The Twentieth Century.* Laurys Station, PA: Garrigues House, 1992.

Hoogenboom, Ari and Olive Hoogemboom. *A History of the ICC, From Panacea to Palliative.* New York: W. W. Norton & Co., 1976.

Horowitz, Morris A. "The Diesel Firemen Issue on the Railroads." *Industrial and Labor Relations Review* 13, no. 4 (July 1960): 550–58.

———. *Manpower Utilization in the Railroad Industry: An Analysis of Working Rules and Practices.* Boston: Bureau of Business and Economic Research, Northeastern University, 1960.

Hughes, Thomas P. *American Genesis.* New York: Penguin Books, 1989.

———. *Networks of Power: Electrification in Western Society.* Baltimore: Johns Hopkins University Press, 1983.

Jahn, Richard W. "Lehigh Valley Railroad Gas-Electrics," *Flags Diamonds and Statues* 6, no. 1 (1985): 4–37.

———. "An LV Roster Unique." *Flags Diamonds and Statues* 3 no. 2 (1980): 24–27.

———. "PA: Lehigh Valley Style." *Flags Diamonds and Statues* 7, no. 2 (1987): 4–18.

———. "The Buffalo Division." *Flags Diamonds and Statues* 11, no. 4 (1994): 4–43.

Jenkins, Dale. *The Illinois Terminal Railroad: The Road of Personalized Services.* Hart, MO: White River Productions, 2005.

Johnson, Ralph P. *The Steam Locomotive.* New York: Simmons-Boardman Publishing Corp., 1942.

Keilty, Edmund. *Doodlebug Country.* Glendale, CA: Interurban Press, 1982.

Kiefer, P. W. *A Practical Evaluation of Railroad Motive Power.* New York: Steam Locomotive Research Institute, Inc., 1947.

Kirkland, John F. *Dawn of the Diesel Age.* Glendale, CA: Interurban Press, 1983.

———. *The Diesel Builders: Fairbanks Morse and Lima Hamilton.* Glendale, CA: Interurban Press, 1985.

———. *The Diesel Builders. Vol. 2, American Locomotive Company and Montreal Locomotive Works .* Glendale, CA: Interurban Press, 1989.

———. *The Diesel Builders Vol. 3, Baldwin Locomotive Works.* Glendale, CA: Interurban Press, 1993.

Klein, Maury. "The Diesel Revolution." *American Heritage of Invention and Technology* (Winter 1991): 16–23.

———. "Replacement Technology: The Diesel as a Case Study." *Railroad History* 162 (Spring 1990): 109–20.

———. *Union Pacific: The Rebirth, 1894–1969.* New York: Doubleday, 1989.

Kolko, Gabriel. *Railroads and Regulation, 1877–1916*. New York: W. W. Norton and Co., 1965.

Kranefeld, James A. "The Number That Became a Name." *National Railway Bulletin* 58 no. 1 (1993): 5–12.

Kulp, Randolph L. ed. *Railroads in the Lehigh River Valley*. Allentown, PA: Lehigh Valley Chapter, National Railway Historical Society, 1979.

Lamb, J. Parker. *Evolution of the American Diesel Locomotive* . Bloomington: Indiana University Press, 2007.

———. *Perfecting the American Steam Locomotive*. Bloomington: Indiana University Press, 2003.

Lee, Thomas R. *Turbines Westward*. Manhattan, KS: T. Lee Publications, 1975.

Leslie, Stuart W. *Boss Kettering*. New York: Columbia University Press, 1983.

Lewis, Lloyd D. *Virginian Railway Locomotives*. Lynchburg, VA: TLC Publishing, 1993.

Lewis, Robert G. *Handbook of American Railroads*. New York: Simmons-Boardman, 1951.

Licht, Walter. *Working for the Railroad*. Princeton, NJ: Princeton University Press, 1983.

Lytle, Richard H. "The Introduction of Diesel Power in the United States, 1897–1912." *Business History Review* 42 (Summer 1968).

Marre, Louis A. *Diesel Locomotives: The First 50 Years*. Waukesha, WI: Kalmbach Publishing, 1995.

———. *Rock Island Diesel Locomotives, 1930–1980*. Cincinnati, OH: Railfax, 1982.

Marre, Louis A., and John Baskin Harper. *Frisco Diesel Power*. Glendale, CA: Interurban Press, 1984.

Martin, Albro. *Enterprise Denied, The Origin of the Decline of American Railroads, 1897–1917*. New York: Columbia University Press, 1971.

———. *Railroads Triumphant, The Growth, Rejection and Rebirth of a Vital American Force*. New York: Oxford University Press, 1992.

Marx, Thomas G. "Technological Change and the Theory of the Firm: The American Locomotive Industry, 1920–1955." *Business History Review* 50, no. 1 (Spring 1976): 1–24.

Matejka, Michael G., and Greg Koos. *Bloomington's C&A Shops: Our Lives Remembered*. Bloomington, IL: McLean County Historical Society, 1988.

McCall, John B. "Dieselisation of American Railroads: A Case Study." *Journal of Transport History* 6, no. 2 (September 1985): 1–17.

———. *Santa Fe's Early Diesel Daze, 1935–1953*. Dallas: Kachina Press, 1980.

Meikle, Jeffrey L. *Twentieth Century Limited: Industrial Design in America, 1925–1939*. Philadelphia: Temple University Press, 1979.

Michels, G. J. Jr. "Diesel Locomotives of the Terminal Railroad Association of St. Louis." *Terminal Railroad Association of St. Louis Historical and Technical Society* 51–52 (Summer/Autumn 1999).

Middleton, William D. *The Interurban Era*. Milwaukee: Kalmbach, 1961.

———. *When the Steam Railroads Electrified*. Milwaukee, WI: Kalmbach Publishing, 1974.

Middleton, Willaim D., George M. Smerk, and Roberta L. Diehl, eds. *Encyclopedia of North American Railroads*. Bloomington: Indiana University Press, 2007.

Miller, Edward L., and Norbert J. Shacklette. *My Brother: The IC Railroad and Southern Illinois, 1936–1942*. St. Louis, MO(?): Edward Miller and Norbert Shacklette, 2005.

Mohowski, Robert E. *New York Ontario and Western in the Diesel Age*. Andover, NJ: Andover Junction Publications, 1994.

Morgan, David P. *Diesels West: The Evolution of Power on the Burlington*. Milwaukee, WI: Kalmbach, 1963.

Morris, Stuart. "Stalled Professionalism: The Recruitment of Railway Officials in the United States, 1885–1940." *Business History Review* 47, no. 3 (Autumn, 1973).

Moul, Edward W. "Three Power Locomotives Delaware Lackawanna & Western Railroad Co." *Flags Diamonds and Statues* 8, no. 2 (1989): 13–19.

Nelson, James C. "Highway Development, the Railroads and National Transport Policy." *The American Economic Review* 41, no. 2, Papers and Proceedings of the Sixty-Third Annual Meeting of the American Economic Association (May 1951): 495–505.

———. *Railroad Transportation and Public Policy*. Washington, D.C.: The Brookings Institution, 1959.

Official Guide to the Railways and Steam Navigation Lines of the United States, Porto Rico Canada, Mexico and Cuba. New York: National Railway Publication Company, 1920–60.

Orenstein, Jeffrey. *United States Railroad Policy, Uncle Sam at the Throttle*. Chicago, IL: Nelson-Hall, 1990.

Our GM Scrapbook. Milwaukee, WI: Kalmbach, 1971.

Overton, Richard C. *Burlington Route: A History of the Burlington Lines*. New York: Alfred A Knopf, 1965.

Patric, John, with Frank J. Taylor. "Featherbedding Hampers the War Effort." *Readers Digest* (March 1943). 27. Reprinted from *Barron's* (February 8, 1943).

Pinkepank, Jerry A. "How the Diesel Changed Railroading." *Classic Trains*, Diesel Victory, Special Edition, no. 4, (2006).

———. *On Time*. Detroit, MI: General Motors Corporation, 1948.

Reck, Franklin M. *The Dilworth Story*. New York: McGraw Hill, 1954.

Rehnor, John A. *The Nickel Plate Story*. Milwaukee, WI: Kalmbach Publications, 1965.

Reutter, Mark. "The Lost Promise of the American Railroad." *Wilson Quarterly* (Winter 1994): 10–37.

The Revolutionary Diesel: EMC's FT. Halifax, PA: Diesel Era, 1994.

Rich, Stuart M. "Changing Railway Technology in the United States and Its Impact Upon Railroad Employment Since 1945." *Transportation Journal* 25, no. 4 (Summer 1986).

———. "Wisconsin's Railroads in the Postwar Era: Changes in Physical Plant and Industry Structure Between 1946 and 1990." *Journal of the West* (January 1992): 49–59.

Richardson, Reed C. *The Locomotive Engineer, 1863–1963*. Ann Arbor, MI: Bureau of Industrial Relations, University of Michigan, 1963.

Ripley, William Zebina. *Railroads Rates and Regulation* . New York: Longmans, Green and Co., 1912.

Rohal, Robert Ronald. "The Erie's 300-mile Division." *Trains* (June 2000): 52–53.

Rosbloom, Julius *Diesel Hand Book*. New York: Pioneer Publications, 1950.

Rose, Mark H., Bruce E. Seely, and Paul F. Barrett. *The Best Transportation System in the World; Railroads, Trucks, Airlines and American Public Policy in the Twentieth Century*. Columbus: Ohio State University Press, 2006.

Sagle, Lawrence W. *B&O Power, Steam Diesel and Electric Power of the Baltimore and Ohio Railroad, 1829–1964*. Medina, OH: Alvin F. Staufer, 1964.

———. *A Picture History of B&O Motive Power*. New York: Simmons-Boardman, 1952.

Saunders, Richard Jr. *Main Lines, Rebirth of North American Railroads, 1970–2002*. De Kalb: Northern Illinois University Press, 2003.

———. *Merging Lines: American Railroads, 1900–1970*. De Kalb: Northern Illinois University Press, 2001.

Schafer, Mike. *Vintage Diesel Locomotives*. Osceola, WI: Motorbooks, International, 1998.

Schneider, Paul D. *GM's Geeps, The General Purpose Diesels*. Waukesha, WI: Kalmbach, 2001.

Schwarz-Miller, Ann, and Wayne K. Talley, "Technology and Labor Relations: Railroads and Ports" *Journal of Labor Research*. Vol. 32, no. 4 (Fall 2002).

Shaw, Robert B. "A Brief History of the New York, Ontario & Western Railroad." *Railroad History* 175 (Autumn 1996).

Sheneman, J. F. *Sheneman's Pointers on Diesel Troubles*. Salisbury, NC: J. F. Sheneman, 1947.

Shuster, Philip, Eugene L. Huddleston, and Alvin Stauffer. *C&O Power*. Medina, OH: Alvin Staufer, 1965.

Smith, Vernon L. *One Man's Locomotives: Fifty Years Experience with Railway Motive Power*. Glendale, CA: Trans-Anglo Books, 1987.

Staff, Virgil. *D-Day on the Western Pacific: A Railroad's Decision to Dieselize*. Glendale, CA: Interurban Press, 1982.

Stagner, Lloyd E. *Illinois Central in Color*. Edison, NJ: Morning Sun Books, 1996.

———. *Missouri Pacific's Steam to Diesel Era, 1945–1955*. David City, NE: South Platte Press and Brueggenjohann/Reese, Inc., 2002.

———. *Union Pacific Motive Power In Transition, 1936–1960*. David City, NE: South Platte Press, 1993.

Stakem, Patrick H. and Patrick E. Stakem. *Western Maryland Diesel Locomotives*. Lynchburg, VA: TLC Publishing, 1997.

Staufer, Alvin F. *Steam Power of the New York Central System, Vol. 1, Modern Power, 1915–1955*. Medina, OH: Alvin F. Staufer, 1961.

Steckler, Carl. *Lehigh Valley Railroad Diesel Paint Schemes, 1925–1976*. Ithaca, NY: Hiker Publications, 1993.

Steinbrenner, Richard T. *The American Locomotive Company: A Centennial Remembrance.* Warren, NJ: On Track Publishers, 2003.

Stilgoe, John R. *Metropolitan Corridor, Railroads and the American Scene.* New Haven, CT: Yale University Press, 1983.

Stone, Richard D. *The Interstate Commerce Commission and the Railroad Industry: A History of Regulatory Policy.* New York: Praeger, 1991.

Stover, John F. *American Railroads* 2d. ed. Chicago: University of Chicago Press, 1997.

———. *History of the Baltimore and Ohio Railroad.* West Lafayette, IN: Purdue University Press, 1987.

Strapac, Joseph A. *Cotton Belt Locomotives.* Bloomington: Indiana University Press, 1977.

———. *Southern Pacific Historic Diesels: Vol. 2.* Bellflower, CA: Shade Tree Books, 1993.

———. *Western Pacific's Diesel Years.* Muncie, IN: Overland Models, 1980.

"TRRA's Brooklyn Shops." *Terminal Railroad Association of St. Louis Historical and Technical Society* 17 (January-February-March 1991).

Thomas, Donald E. *Diesel: Technology and Society in Industrial Germany.* Tuscaloosa: University of Alabama Press, 1987.

Usselman, Steven W. "Air Brakes for Freight Trains: Technological Innovation in the American Railroad Industry, 1869–1900." *Business History Review* 58 (Spring 1984): 30–50.

———. "Patents Purloined: Railroads, Inventors, and the Diffusion of Innovation in 19th Century America." *Technology and Culture* 32 (October 1991): 1047–75.

———. *Regulating Railroad Innovation: Business, Technology, and Politics in America, 1840–1920.* Cambridge: Cambridge University Press, 2002.

Wachhorst, Wyn. "An American Motif: The Steam Locomotive in the Collective Imagination." *Southwest Review* 72 no. 4 (Autumn 1987): 440–54.

Wallin, R. R. "Dick." *Gulf, Mobile & Ohio Color Pictorial.* La Mirada, CA: Four Ways West, 1996.

Warden, William E. *Norfolk and Western: Diesel's Last Conquest.* Lynchburg, VA: TLC Publishing, 1991.

Weitzman, David. *Superpower: The Making of a Steam Locomotive.* Boston: David R. Godine, 1987.

Westinghouse Electric Railway Transportation. Westinghouse, 1915, 1917, 1922, 1924, 1929, 1936. Reprinted as Bulletin 118 of Central Electric Railfans'Association, Chicago, IL 1979.

White, John H. *A History of the American Locomotive: Development, 1830–1880.* New York: Dover Publications Inc., 1968.

Williamson, Harold F., Ralph L. Andreano, Arnold R. Daum, and Gilbert C. Klose. *The American Petroleum Industry: The Age of Energy, 1899–1959.* Evanston, IL: Northwestern University Press, 1963.

Wilson, Jeff. *F Units: The Diesels that Did It.* Waukesha, WI: Kalmbach, 2000.

Withers, Paul K. *Diesels of the Chicago and North Western.* Halifax, PA: Withers Publishing, 1995.

Wolff, A. J. *Union Pacific's Turbine Era.* Halifax, PA: Withers Publishing, 2001.

Woodland, Dale W. *Reading Diesels, Vol. 1, The First Generation*. Laury's Station, PA: Garrigues House, 1991.

Yanosey, Robert J. *Lehigh Valley 2: In Color*. Edison, NJ: Morning Sun Books Inc., 1991.

Yochum, Gilbert, and G. Stephen Rhiel. "Employment and Changing Technology in the Postwar Railroad Industry." *Industrial Relations* 30, no. 1 (Winter 1991): 116–127.

Young, David M. *The Iron Horse and the Windy City: How Railroads Shaped Chicago*. DeKalb: Northern Illinois University Press, 2005.

Yungkurth, Chuck. *The Steam Era of the Lehigh Valley*. Andover, NJ: Andover Junction Publications, 1991.

Zenk, Robert J. "The Krauss-Maffei ML4000C'C' Diesel-Hydraulic Cab Units." *Mainline Modeler* (October 1984): 23–34.

———. "The Krauss-Maffei ML4000C'C' Diesel-Hydraulic Hood Units." *Mainline Modeler* (April 1985): 32–42.

DISSERTATIONS AND THESES

Bingham, Robert Charles. "The Diesel Locomotive: A Study in Innovation." PhD. diss., Northwestern University, 1962.

Churella, Albert John. "Corporate Response to Technological Change: Dieselization and the American Railway Locomotive Industry During the Twentieth Century." PhD. diss., Ohio State University, 1994.

Gzyrb, Gerard Jerome. "Death of a Craftsman: The Impact of Rationalization in the Railroad Industry on the Occupational Community and Occupational Culture of Operating Railroaders." PhD. diss., Washington University, 1977.

Hydell, Richard Paul. "A Study of Technological Diffusion: The Replacement of Steam by Diesel Locomotives in the United States." PhD. diss., Massachusetts Institute of Technology, 1977.

Mapes, Mark G. "Losing Steam: The Decision Making Process in the Dieselization of the Pennsylvania Railroad." PhD. diss., University of Delaware, 2000.

Marx, Thomas. "The Diesel-Electric Locomotive Industry: A Study in Market Failures." PhD. diss., University of Pennsylvania, 1973.

Morris, Cyril J. "Conversion of Railroads to Diesel Electric Power." MS thesis, Cornell, 1949.

Park, Donald K. "An Historical Analysis of Innovation and Activity: American Steam Locomotive Building, 1900 to 1952." PhD. diss., Columbia University, 1973.

Warren, William Douglas. "The Railroad Town: A Study of Urban Response to Changes in Technology, Operating Procedures and Demand for Railroad Service in the post World War II period." PhD. diss., University of North Carolina at Chapel Hill, 1972.

Index

Page numbers in *italics* indicate photograph.

TK 7881.15 .V58 1995

Vithayathil, Joseph.

Power electronics

DATE DUE

DEC 12 1995		
JUL 2 0 1998		
HL GZR		
7/5/04		

POWER ELECTRONICS
Principles and Applications

McGraw-Hill Series in Electrical and Computer Engineering

Senior Consulting Editor
Stephen W. Director, Carnegie Mellon University

Circuits and Systems
Communications and Signal Processing
Computer Engineering
Control Theory
Electromagnetics
Electronics and VLSI Circuits
Introductory
Power and Energy
Radar and Antennas

Previous Consulting Editors
Ronald N. Bracewell, Colin Cherry, James F. Gibbons, Willis W. Harman,
Hubert Heffner, Edward W. Herold, John G. Linvill, Simon Ramo,
Ronald A. Rohrer, Anthony E. Siegman, Charles Susskind, Frederick E.
Terman, John G. Truxal, Ernst Weber, and John R. Whinnery

Power and Energy

Senior Consulting Editor
Stephen W. Director, Carnegie Mellon University

Chapman: *Electric Machinery Fundamentals*
Elgerd: *Electric Energy Systems Theory*
Fitzgerald, Kingsley, and Umans: *Electric Machinery*
Gonen: *Electric Power Distribution System Engineering*
Grainger and Stevenson: *Power System Analysis*
Krause and Wasynczuk: *Electromechanical Motion Devices*
Nasar: *Electric Machines and Power Systems: Volume I, Electric Machines*
Stevenson: *Elements of Power System Analysis*
Vithayathil: *Power Electronics: Principles and Applications*

Also Available from McGraw-Hill

Schaum's Outline Series in Electronics & Electrical Engineering

Most outlines include basic theory, definitions and hundreds of example problems solved in step-by-step detail, and supplementary problems with answers.

Related titles on the current list include:

Analog & Digital Communications
Basic Circuit Analysis
Basic Electrical Engineering
Basic Electricity
Basic Mathematics for Electricity & Electronics
Digital Principles
Electric Circuits
Electric Machines & Electromechanics
Electric Power Systems
Electromagnetics
Electronic Circuits
Electronic Communication
Electronic Devices & Circuits
Electronics Technology
Feedback & Control Systems
Introduction to Digital Systems
Microprocessor Fundamentals
Signals & Systems

Schaum's Solved Problems Books

Each title in this series is a complete and expert source of solved problems with solutions worked out in step-by-step detail.

Related titles on the current list include:

3000 Solved Problems in Calculus
2500 Solved Problems in Differential Equations
3000 Solved Problems in Electric Circuits
2000 Solved Problems in Electromagnetics
2000 Solved Problems in Electronics
3000 Solved Problems in Linear Algebra
2000 Solved Problems in Numerical Analysis
3000 Solved Problems in Physics

Available at most college bookstores, or for a complete list of titles and prices, write to: Schaum Division
McGraw-Hill, Inc.
1221 Avenue of the Americas
New York, NY 10020